Very respectfully,
S. J. Quinn.

THE HISTORY *of the* CITY OF FREDERICKSBURG VIRGINIA

FROM
ITS SETTLEMENT
TO THE PRESENT TIME

Prepared and printed by authority of the
Common Council thereof,
under the direction of its Committee on Publication, consisting of the following Councilmen: H. B LANE, WM. E. BRADLEY and S. W. SOMERVILLE

S. J. Quinn, Historian

HERITAGE BOOKS
2011

HERITAGE BOOKS
AN IMPRINT OF HERITAGE BOOKS, INC.

Books, CDs, and more—Worldwide

For our listing of thousands of titles see our website
at
www.HeritageBooks.com

A Facsimile Reprint
Published 2011 by
HERITAGE BOOKS, INC.
Publishing Division
100 Railroad Ave. #104
Westminster, Maryland 21157

Copyright © 1908,
On all original matter herein,
by
H. B. Lane, Chairman of History Committee
for the City of Fredericksburg, Va.

— Publisher's Notice —
In reprints such as this, it is often not possible to remove blemishes from the original. We feel the contents of this book warrant its reissue despite these blemishes and hope you will agree and read it with pleasure.

International Standard Book Numbers
Paperbound: 978-1-55613-518-7
Clothbound: 978-0-7884-8887-0

Dedication

TO THE MEMORY OF THOSE WHO BRAVED THE DANGERS OF LAND AND WATER IN 1608, AND DISCOVERED THE SPOT UPON WHICH THE CITY OF FREDERICKSBURG, VIRGINIA, NOW STANDS, AND TO THOSE WHO WROUGHT SO HEROICALLY AND SUCCESSFULLY IN THE SETTLEMENT AND PROSPERITY OF THE SAID CITY TO THE PRESENT TIME, 1908, A PERIOD OF THREE HUNDRED YEARS, THESE PAGES ARE RESPECTFULLY AND AFFECTIONATELY DEDICATED BY THE PRESENT COMMON COUNCIL OF THE CITY OF FREDERICKSBURG

PREFACE

To Messrs. H. B. Lane, Wm. E. Bradley and Prof. S. W. Somerville, Committee on History of the Common Council:

GENTLEMEN—When I was requested by your predecessors to write a history of Fredericksburg, I regarded it as quite an honor, and in the discharge of the duty I have found great pleasure. Not that the material needed was ready at hand and the task was easy, but because I found so many of the best of our citizens eager to assist in getting the material together, that had been laid away for ages, and placing it at my disposal. Moreover, their kind words very much encouraged me, and I wish I could here record their names, but as it might not be proper, I take much pleasure in extending to them my grateful thanks.

The records concerning the town reach back only to the close of the Revolutionary war. If Major Lawrence Smith, who constructed the fort and governed the settlers by military law or "as a county court might do," ever kept any records of his acts, we have been unable to find them, and the same is true of the Trustees who had the managment of the town from the time it was "laid out by law," until it was chartered by the Legislature of Virginia. Therefore, much that is found in the following pages in reference to "the olden time," came from families who had preserved it in various forms for many generations.

In presenting this history it is not claimed that all is said about Fredericksburg that could have been said or that incidents have not been related as others have heard them, but it is believed that all important events have been referred to and incidents given as they have been related to us by those well informed and who were regarded as authority on such matters. Nor is there any claim made for originality. The book is intended to be a history of Fredericksburg, and "history is a narration of facts and events which may be given chronologically or topically," therefore we have written in the main what others have spoken and have disregarded chronology and even the arrangement of subjects. But it is believed that the arrangement herein is probably best adapted to impress the reader with the splendid history of the town and the magnificent achievements of her sons and those men of fame who sprang from her immediate vicinity.

It is believed this book will be welcomed by all citizens and their friends, whether those friends be former residents or descendants of such, or those veteran soldiers on either side of the late Civil Contest who performed such gallant deeds upon our hills and within our valleys. No soldier of either army—the Army of the Potomac or the Army of Northern Virginia—can ever forget Fredericksburg. It was in the four great battles fought in and around Fredericksburg that he won imperishable glory as an American soldier, that name which to-day is written on the highest pinnacle of military fame.

No living citizen, or the descendant of such noble sires, wheresoever dispersed, can ever forget the town or lineage from which he sprang. None such can ever fail to appreciate those citizens, who, in the most trying times, and under the most adverse circumstances, were conspicuous for their love and loyalty, suffering and sacrifice, daring and doing for home and country.

Let their deeds and sacrifices be preserved for imitation of future generations, which is one of the objects of this book.

Very respectfully,

S. J. QUINN.

LIST OF ILLUSTRATIONS.

	Facing Page
Baptist Church	132
Butterfield Monument	288
Capt. S. J. Quinn	*Frontispiece*
Catholic Church	272
Chancellorsville Tavern	82
Charity School	232
Christian Church	240
Church of God	304
City Hall	192
Com. M. F. Maury	320
Confederate Cemetery	122
Confederate Monument	264
Court House	22
Eagle Hotel	182
Entrance to Confederate Cemetery	222
Entrance to National Cemetery	256
Exchange Hotel	172
Federal Hill	32
Fire Department	232
First Mayor's Residence	182
Forsythe's Birthplace	102
Fredericksburg College	172
Fredericksburg from Marye's Heights	12
Fredericksburg from Stafford Heights	12
Free Bridge	22
Free Lance—Star Office	248
Hon. Montgomery Slaughter	72
Jackson Monument	202
Kenmore	212
Marye Mansion	328
Mary Washington House	32
Mary Washington Monument	52

List of Illustrations.

	Facing Page
Masonic Lodge	222
Meditation Rock	152
Mercer Monument	92
Methodist Church	162
M. W. M. Lodge	142
Old Planters' Hotel	296
Opera House	296
Postoffice	280
Power Dam	152
Presbyterian Church	162
Presbyterian Memorial Chapel	62
Public School	288
Remarkable Tombstone	264
R., F. & P. R. R. Bridge	312
Rising Sun Tavern	52
Section Stone Wall	112
Sentry Box	102
Shiloh Church, N. S.	304
Shiloh Church, O. S.	272
Stevens House	192
St. George's Church	62
Stone House	92
Sunken Road	82
Superintendent's Lodge	256
Trinity Church	240
Trustees' Office	112
Union House	212
View on Princess Anne St.	42
Wallace Library	142
Water Power Office	328
Wm. Paul's Gravestone	280

CONTENTS

Chapter I

Captain John Smith Explores the Rappahannock River—The Flight of Pocahontas—Major Lawrence Smith's Fort—Governor Spotswood's Miners at Germanna, - - 11

Chapter II

The Knights of the Golden Horse Shoe—Governor Spotswood's Expedition over the Blue Ridge Mountains, - 27

Chapter III

Fredericksburg Incorporated by the House of Burgesses—Col. Byrd Walks about Town—A Church Building Erected—Rev. Patrick Henry Rector—Augustine Washington a Town Trustee—Stock Fairs Inaugurated—Limits of the Town Extended, - - - - - - - - 37

Chapter IV

Encouraging Home Industries—Further Extension of the Town—Tobacco Inspectors Appointed—Modes of Punishing Criminals—Prosperity—Military Ardor—Under the United States Government—A New Order of Things, - 46

Chapter V

Lease of the Market-House Lots—The First Serious Fire—Fredericksburg an Important Center—An Act Concerning Elections—Half of the Town Destroyed by Fire—Fredericksburg an Important Postal Point—How the Mails were Carried—A Congressional Investigation—Amendatory Acts of 1821—The Great Fire of 1822—The Trade of the Town—Contagious Diseases—The Town in 1841—Acts of Extension, 1851, 1852, 1858, 1861, - 57

Chapter VI.

The War Clouds Gather—Fredericksburg in the Southern Confederacy—Troops Raised and Equipped—Town Surrendered to Federal Authorities—Citizens Arrested and Held as Hostages—Thrilling Evacuating Scenes—Citizens Flee from their Homes—Bombardment of the Town, 71

Chapter VII

The Great Battle—The Town Sacked by Soldiers—The Federals Recross the River—A Great Revival of Religion—The Battle of Chancellorsville—Gen. Sedgewick Captures the Town—The Wilderness Campaign—Many Noncombatant Citizens Arrested and Imprisoned—A Statement by the Council—The Citizens and Federal Soldiers Released, - - - - - - - - - - 90

Chapter VIII

The Armies Transferred to Richmond and Petersburg—Gen. Lee Surrenders his Army—Citizens Return Home—Action of the City Council—Fredericksburg Again Under the Old Flag—The Assassination of President Lincoln Denounced—Reconstruction Commenced—An Election Set Aside by the Military—All Civil Offices Set Aside and Strangers Appointed—The Financial Condition of the Town—The Town Again in the Hands of its Citizens—Splendid Financial Showing, - - - - - - - 107

Chapter IX

The Courts of Fredericksburg—The Freedman's Bureau—Court Orders and Incidents—First Night Watch Appointed—Ministers Qualify to Perform Marriage Ceremony—First Notary Public—Fixing the Value of Bank Notes—Prison Bounds for Debtors—Church Buildings, 123

Chapter X

Public Buildings—Court House—The Jail—Town Hall—Fire Department—School Buildings—Wallace Library—Normal School—Government Building, - - - - 136

CHAPTER XI

Ancient and Historical Buildings—Mary Washington Monument—General Mercer's Statute—Mary Washington's Will, - - - - - - - - - 148

CHAPTER XII

Hotels of the Town, old and new—Agricultural Fairs and Toll Bridges—Care of the Dependent Poor—City Water Works—City Gas Works—Electric Light—Telephone Company—Fire Department, - - - - - - - 164

CHAPTER XIII

Volunteer Militia—The Confederate Cemetery—The National Cemetery—The Confederate Veterans—The Sons of Confederate Veterans—The Schools, Private and Public, - 182

CHAPTER XIV

The Churches of Fredericksburg, - - - - - - 202

CHAPTER XV

Charitable and Benevolent Societies—Mary Washington Hospital—Newspapers and Periodicals—Political Excitement—Strong Resolutions Against the Administration—An Address Approving the President's Foreign Policy—The Names of Those who Signed the Address, - - - 217

CHAPTER XVI

Distinguished Men Buried in Fredericksburg—A Remarkable Grave Stone—Three Heroic Fredericksburgers, Wellford, Herndon, Willis—The Old Liberty Bell Passes Through Town—Great Demonstration in its Honor—What a Chinaman Thought of it, - - - - - - 235

CHAPTER XVII

Visits of Heroes—Gala Days—The Army of the Society of the Potomac Enters the Town, - - - - - - 251

CHAPTER XVIII

The Society of the Army of the Potomac Continued—Welcome Address—Laying a Corner Stone, - - - - - 263

CHAPTER XIX

Doctor Walker's Expedition—Bacon's Rebellion, so-called—The Fredericksburg Declaration—The Great Orator—Resolutions of Separation—The Virginia Bill of Rights, 280

CHAPTER XX

Declaration of Separation—The Declaration of Independence—Washington Commander-in-Chief of the Armies—John Paul Jones Raises the First Flag—First to Throw the Stars and Stripes to the Breeze—Fredericksburg Furnishes the Head of the Army and Navy—The Constitution of the United States, - - - - - - 292

CHAPTER XXI

The First Proclamation for Public Thanksgiving—Pennsylvania Whiskey Rebellion—John Marshall and the Supreme Court—Religious Liberty—The Monroe Doctrine—Seven Presidents—Clarke Saves the Great Northwest—The Vast Western Territory Explored—The Louisiana Purchase—The Florida Purchase—Texas Acquired—The War with Mexico and its Rich Results—The Oceans Sounded, Measured and Mapped—The Ladies' Memorial Association—The Mary Washington Monument—General Mercer's Statue, - - - - - - - 306

CHAPTER XXII

Fredericksburg at Present—The Health of the City—its Financial Solidity—Its Commercial Prosperity—Its Lines of Transportation—Its Water Power—Its Official Calendar—List of Mayors, - - - - - - - - 322
Official Calendar—September 1, 1908 - - - - - 333
Mayors of Fredericksburg in Their Chronological Order - - 336

HISTORY

OF THE

City of Fredericksburg, Virginia,

FROM ITS

Settlement to the Present Time

CHAPTER I

Capt. John Smith Explores the Rappahannock River—The Flight of Pocahontas—Maj. Smith's Fort—Gov. Spotswood's Miners at Germanna.

In what year the white man first set his foot upon the present site of Fredericksburg is not certainly known. The mind of man, of the present generation, does not run back to that time, and if the first white visitor to the place thought it of sufficient importance to make a note of it that note was not preserved; or, if it was, it is unknown to the present inhabitants of the town, unless that visitor was Captain John Smith.

It is stated that after John Smith was captured by the Indians, while on his trip exploring the Chickahominy, his captors marched him through the country, amid great rejoicing, visiting the Indian towns on the Pamunkey, Mattapony, Piankitank, Rappahannock and Potomac rivers, but it is not stated that he was taken as high up the Rappahannock as the falls. This trip through the country, however, while it was attended with hideous yells, cheers and all sorts of mournful noises by the excited throng, gave John Smith some idea of the rich and fertile valleys, the beautiful rivers that flowed from the mountains, and a desire to explore them if he should be fortunate enough to get back to the English settlement alive.

For soon after his release, in writing of the discoveries, having already explored the Chesapeake bay, he says:* "There is but one entrance by sea into this country, and that is at the mouth of a very goodly bay, the wideness whereof is near eighteen or twenty miles. The cape on the south is called Cape Henry, in honor of our most noble Prince. The show of the land there is a white hilly sand like unto the Downes, and along the shores great plenty of pines and firs. The north cape is called Cape Charles, in honor of the worthy Duke of York.

"Within is a country that may have the prerogative over the most pleasant places of Europe, Asia, Africa or America and for large and pleasant navigable rivers, heaven and earth never agreed better to frame a place for man's habitation, being of our constitutions, were it fully manured and inhabited by industrious people. Here are mountains, hills, plains, valleys, rivers and brooks, all running most pleasantly to a fair bay, compassed, but for the mouth, with fruitful and delightsome land. In the bay and rivers are many isles, both great and small, some woody, some plain, most of them low and not inhabited. This bay lies north and south, in which the water flows near two hundred miles and has a channel for one hundred and forty miles of depth betwixt seven and fifteen fathoms, holding in breadth, for the most part, ten or fifteen miles. From the head of the bay at the north, the land is mountainous, and so in a manner from thence by a southwest line. So that the more southward, the further off from the bay are those mountains, from which fall certain brooks, which after come to five principal navigable rivers. These run from the northwest into the southeast, and so into the west side of the bay, where the fall of every river is within twenty or fifteen miles one of another."

Early in the year of 1608, his life having been saved by Pocahontas, John Smith made a number of trips, exploring the rivers of this section of Virginia, entered the mouth of the Rappahannock and, but for an accident that befell him, might have continued his trip to the falls.

They found fish in abundance in all the streams and, "near the

---
* Description of Virginia by Smith, his spelling modernized.

View of Fredericksburg from Marye's Mansion, showing ground charged over by Federals in battle 1862. Confederate line at fence.
(See page 91)

View of Fredericksburg from Stafford Heights, where Federal guns were located in 1862, showing the old Scott bridge.
(See page 171)

mouth of the Rappahannock, Smith plunged his sword into a singular fish like a 'thornback,' with a long tail and from it a poisoned sting. In taking it off it drove the sting into his wrist, producing a torturing pain, and in a few hours the whole hand, arm and shoulder had swollen so fearfully that death seemed inevitable. He pointed out a place for his grave, and his men, with heavy hearts, prepared it. But Dr. Russell applied the probe and used an oil with such success that Smith was soon well and ate a part of the same fish for supper."*

Some writers contend that it was while on this trip that Smith came up the Rappahannock to the falls and had a battle with the Indians, but this is a mistake. This trip was commenced on the 20th of June, 1608, and it was directly after entering the mouth of the river that he saw so many fish in the clear stream and caught one on the point of his sword; for Russell, the physician, who accompanied him, says after Smith was thought to have been fatally poisoned, "having neither surgeon or surgery, but that preservative oil, we presently set sail for Jamestown. Passing the mouth of the Piankatank and Pamunkey rivers, the next day we safely arrived at Kecaughtan."† If Smith had been very far up the Rappahannock he could not have passed the mouth of these two rivers the next day.

The voyage that Smith made, during which he explored the Rappahannock river to the falls, was commenced on the 24th of July, more than a month after he entered the mouth of the river and was stung by the fish which turned him back. As this trip up the river is of great interest, being the first made by white men, it is here given in full as narrated by Anthony Bagnall, Powell and Todkill, Smith's companions, who wrote it down at the time. They say:

"In the discovery of this river, that some called Rappahannock, we were kindly entertained by the people of Moraughtacund. Here we encountered our old friend Mosco, a lusty savage of Wighconisco, upon the river Patawomeck [Potomac]. We supposed

* Howison's U. S. History, from Smith.
† Walter Russell, in Smith.

him some Frenchman's son because he had a thick, black, bushy, beard, and the savages seldom have any at all, of which he was not a little proud to see so many of his countrymen. Wood and water he would fetch us, guide us any whether; nay, cause divers of his countrymen help us tow against wind or tide from place to place till we came to Patawomeck.

"The next morning we went up the river, [Rappahannock] and our friend Mosco followed us along the shore, and at last desired to go with us in our boat. But, as we passed by Pisacack, Matchopeak and Mecuppom, three towns situated upon high white cliffs; the other side all a low plain marsh, and the river there but narrow, thirty or forty of the Rapahanocks had so accommodated themselves with branches, as we took them for little bushes growing among the sedge, till seeing their arrows strike the targets and drop in the river; whereat Mosco fell flat in the boat on his face, crying, the Rapahanocks, which presently we espide to be the bushes, which, at our first volley fell down in the sedge: when we were near half a mile from them, they showed themselves dancing and singing very merrily.

"The kings of Pessassack, Nandtaughtacund and Cultatawoman, used us kindly, and all their people neglected not anything to Mosco to bring us to them.

"Betwixt Secobeck and Massawteck is a small isle or two which cause the river to be broader than ordinary; there it pleased God to take one of our company called Master Fetherstone [Richard Fetherstone, Gent.], that all the time he had been in this country, had behaved himself honestly, valiantly and industriously; where in a little bay, called Fetherstone's bay, we buried him with a volly of shot: the rest, not withstanding their ill diet and bad lodging crowded in so small a barge, in so many dangers, never resting, but always tossed to and again, had all well recovered their healths.

"The next day we sailed so high as our boat would float; there setting up crosses and graving our names in the trees. Our sentinel saw an arrow fall by him, though we had ranged up and down more than an hour, in digging in the earth, looking of stones, herbs and springs, not seeing where a savage could well hide himself.

"Upon the alarm, by that we had recovered our arms there was about an hundred nimble Indians skipping from tree to tree, letting fly their arrows so fast as they could; the trees here served us as baricades as well as they. But Mosco did us more service than we expected; for having shot away his quiver of arrows he ran to the boat for more. The arrows of Mosco at the first made them pause upon the matter, thinking by his bruit and skipping, there were many savages. About half an hour this continued, then they all vanished as suddenly as they approached. Mosco followed them so far as he could see us, till they were out of sight. As we returned there lay a savage as dead, shot in the knee; but taking him up we found he had life: which Mosco seeing, never was dog more furious against a bear, than Mosco was to beat out his brains. So we had him to our boat where our Chirurgian [A. Bagnall], who went with us to cure our Captain's hurt of the stingray, so dressed this savage that within an hour after he looked somewhat cheerfully and did eat and speak. In the mean time we contented Mosco in helping him to gather up their arrows, which were an armful; whereof he gloried not a little.

"Then we desired Mosco to know what he was and what countries were beyond the mountains; the poor savage mildly answered, he and all with him were of Hassininga, where there are three kings more, like unto them, namely the King of Stegora, the King of Tauxsintania and the King of Shakahonea, that were come to Mohaskahod, which is only a hunting town, and the bounds betwixt the Kingdom of the Mannahocks and the Nandtaughtacunds, but hard by where we were.

"We demanded why they came in that manner to betray us, that came to them in peace and to seek their loves; he answered, they heard we were a people come from under the world, to take their world from them.

"We asked him how many worlds he did know; he replied, he knew no more but that which was under the sky that covered him, which were the Powhatans, with the Monacans and the Massawomeks that were higher up in the mountains.

"Then we asked him what was beyond the mountains, he answered the sun; but of anything else he knew nothing because the woods were not burnt. [A foot note says 'they cannot travel but where the woods are burnt.']

"These and many such questions were demanded concerning the Massawomecks, the Monacans, their own country and where were the kings of Stegora, Tauxsintania and the rest. The Monacans, he said, were their neighbors and friends, and did dwell as they in the hilly countries by small rivers, living upon roots and fruits, but chiefly by hunting. The Massawomeks did well upo a great water, and had many boats, and so many men that they made war with all the world. For their kings, they were gone every one a several way with their men on hunting. But those with him came thither a fishing till they saw us, notwithstanding they would be all together at night at Mahaskahod.

"For his relation we gave him many toys, with persuations to go with us: and he as earnestly desired us to stay the coming of those kings that for his good usage should be friends with us, for he was brother to Hassininga. But Mosco advised us presently to be gone, for they were all naught; yet we told him we would not till it was night. All things we made ready to entertain what came, and Mosco was as dilligent in triming his arrows.

"The night being come we all embarked, for the river was so narrow, had it been light the land on the one side was so high they might have done us exceeding much mischief. All this while the King of Hassininga was seeking the rest, and had consultation a good time what to do. But by their spies seeing we were gone, it was not long before we heard their arrows dropping on every side the boat; we caused our savages to call unto them, but such a yelling and hallowing they made that they heard nothing, but now and then [we shot off] a piece, aiming so near as we could where we heard the most voices. Moor than twelve miles they followed us in this manner; then the day appearing, we found ourselves in a broad bay out of danger of their shot, where we came to an anchor, and fell to breakfast. Not so much as speaking to them till the sun was risen.

"Being well refreshed, we untied our targets that covered us as a deck, and all showed ourselves with those shields on our arms, and swords in our hands, and also our prisoner Amoroleck. A long discourse there was betwixt his countrymen and him, how good we were, how well we used him, how we had a Patawomek with us [who] loved us as his life that would have slain him had we not preserved him, and that he should have his liberty would they be his friends; and to do us any hurt it was impossible.

"Upon this they all hung their bows and quivers upon the trees, and one came swiming aboard us with a bow tied on his head, and another with a quiver of arrows, which they delivered our Captain as a present: the Captain having used them so kindly as he could told them the other three Kings should do the like, and then the great King of our world should be their friend; whose men we were. It was no sooner demanded than performed, so upon a low moorish point of land we went to the shore, where those four Kings came and received Amoroleck: nothing they had but bows, arrows, tobacco-bags and pipes: when we desired, none refused to give us, wondering at everything we had, and heard we had done: Our pistols they took for pipes, which they much desired, but we did content them with other commodities. And so we left four or five hundred of our merry Mannahocks singing, dancing and making merry and set sale for Moraughtacund.

"In our returns we visited all our friends, that rejoiced much at our victory against the Mannahocks, who many times had wars also with them, but now they were friends; and desired we should be friends with the Rapahanocks. Our Captain told them, they had twice assaulted him that came only in love to do them good, and, therefore, now he would burn all their houses, destroy their corn, and forever hold them his enemies till they made him satisfaction. They desired to know what that should be. He told them they should present him the King's bow and arrows, and not offer to come armed where he was; that they should be friends with the Moraughtacunds, his friends, and give him their King's son in pledge to perform it; and then all King James and his men should be their friends. Upon this they presently sent to the Rapahanocks to meet him at the place where they first fought where would be the Kings of Nantantacund and Pissassac: which according to their promise were there so soon as we; where Rapahanock presented his bow and arrows, and confirmed all we desired, except his son, having no more but him he could not live without him, but instead of his son he would give him the three women Moraughtacund had stolen. This was accepted: and so in three or four canoes so many as could went with us to Moraughtacund, where Mosco made them such relations, and gave to his friends so many bows and arrows, that they no less loved him than admired us. The three women were brought our Captain, to each he gave a chain of beads: and then causing Moraughtacund, Mosco and Rapahanock stand before him, bid Rapahanock take her he loved best, and Moraughtacund choose next, and to Mosco he gave the third. Upon this away went their canoes over the water, to fetch their venison, and all the provision they could; and they that wanted boats swam over the river. The dark [darkness] commanded us then to rest.

"The next day there was of men, women and children, as we conjectured, six or seven hundred, dancing and singing; and not a bow nor arrow seen amongst them. Mosco changed his name to Uttasantasough, which we interpret stranger, for so they call us. All promising ever to be our friends and to plant corn purposely for us; and we to provide hatchets, beads and copper for them, we departed; giving them a volley of shot, and they us as loud shouts and cries as their strenghs could utter."

This account of Capt. Smith's exploration of the Rappahannock river, and the country bordering on the stream is highly interesting for three reasons. It shows beyond dispute, we think, that Capt. Smith and his little band were the first white men to tread the soil where is now located the city of Fredericksburg. It gives us a complete history of the voyage, so that we may become his travelling companions as he ascends the river, encounters the Indians, prospects for gold and other rich deposits in the earth about the falls; also as he descends the river and calls the Indian kings together, makes friends of them, settles differences between them and their tribes and sails out of the river loaded with provisions, carrying with him their promise that they will raise more for him in the future. It gives us the names of many of the tribes of Indians, on the Rappahannock, their kings, towns and other places, so that we may look at his map of Virginia and locate many of them. It informs us that Richard Fetherstone, who accompanied Smith, was taken sick and died while he was here and was buried in the vicinity of Fredericksburg, he being the first white man to find sepulture in this part of Virginia.

The locations of the following places, found on Smith's map of Virginia, and mentioned in this work, will be of interest to many, and especially to those who are familiar with the country. They seem to be located as follows: Secobeck was just west of the city's almshouse; Massauteck was located just back of Chatham; Fetherstone's bay is in Stafford, opposite the upper end of Hunter's Island; Accoqueck was near R. Innis Taylor's residence; Sockbeck was in the neighborhood of J. Bowie Gray's; Anasheroans were about Moss Neck; King Nandtaughtacund lived near Port Royal; King Cultatawoman was located in Stafford, just below Snowdon; King Pissassack was located in Westmoreland county, near Leedstown; King Tapahanock lived in the upper part of Lancaster county; Mahakahod was about the line of Stafford and Culpeper counties; Hassininga was about Indian Town in Orange county; Stegara was in the upper part of Orange, on the Rapid Ann river; and Tauxuntania was located near the foot of the Blue Ridge mountains.

The several towns at and near the falls of the river made it a general rendezvous of all tribes for this part of Virginia. It was a favorite place at which to meet for hunting, fishing and other sports, as was the case when Smith reached here. It is more than probable that the beautiful and fascinating Pocahontas, who saved the life of John Smith and who captivated the bold and fearless Rolfe, spent some time at this point, in her journeyings, resting here and feasting her youthful eyes upon the magnificent scenery of the Rappahannock falls, and engaging in the sports and pastimes of her distinguished father's subjects.

We are told* that in 1611 she was entrusted by her father, Pow-

---
* Howe's History of Virginia.

hatan, to Chief Japazaws, who carried her to his home on the Potomac river, where she lived some time in retirement—that is, away from the stirring scenes around Jamestown. It is not, therefore, unreasonable to suppose that much of the time she was with Japazaws was spent at this point, the favorite gathering place of all the tribes at the different seasons of the year.

Why Pocahontas left her home for the protection of Japazaws is not positively known. Howe thinks Powhatan was preparing for a great war with the new settlers and wanted to get his daughter away from danger and the exposure and discomfort that would result from such a conflict. Stith gives no reason, "except it was to withdraw herself from being a witness to the frequent butcheries of the English, whose folly and rashness, after Smith's departure, put it out of her power to save them."

In the year 1612 Capt. Argall took a trip up the Potomac in search of corn and other supplies for the English settlers, fell in with the old chief and purchased the young princess from him, the price agreed upon being a copper kettle, which was readily given. This prize Argall took to Jamestown, where he hoped to receive a considerable sum from Powhatan for her redemption, but the old King became very angry and refused to pay anything, but declared he preferred to fight for her. The young princess afterwards married Capt. John Rolfe.

At what time the first settlement was made at Fredericksburg is unknown, but it must have been at a very early date. It is more than likely that it was one of the many plantations that dotted the banks of our principal rivers in the early settlement of the country, for, in 1622, John Smith proposed to the London Company "to protect all their planters from the James to the Potomac"* which territory must have included one or more plantations on the Rappahannock river, because it lies immediately between the James and Potomac rivers and is the largest stream between those two rivers. And if there was a plantation on the Rappahannock it was, no doubt, in the neighborhood of Fredericksburg. John Smith had visited the place twelve years before and had found it "beautiful and invit-

---

* Howe's History.

ing" and an excellent place for a settlement, and possibly he recommended and procured the location of a plantation in this vicinity.

But, whether or not this supposition be true, we know that the Rappahannock falls some years afterwards became a point of considerable interest and steps were taken to fortify and defend it; and for that purpose a fort was ordered to be built here in 1676 to protect settlers from the incursions of the Indians, who continued troublesome, which was garrisoned by quite a number of men. "At a grand assemblie held at James cittie, between the 20th of September, 1674, and the 17th of March, 1675," it was ordered that "One hundred and eleven men out of Gloucester be garrisoned at one ffort or place of defence, at or near the ffalls of Rappahannock River, of which ffort Major Lawrence Smith to be Captain or Chiefe Commander," and that the fort be furnished with "ffour hundred and eighty pounds of powder and ffourteen hundred and fforty three pounds of Shott."*

This fort, it seems, was not constructed that year, but in 1679, Major Lawrence Smith, upon his own suggestion, was authorized to settle or "seate down at or near said fort by the last day of March, 1681," which we are informed he did, and to have in readiness, on all occasions at the beating of a drum, fifty able men, well armed, with sufficient ammunition, and two hundred more within the space of a mile along the river, prepared always to march twenty miles in any direction from the fort; and it was stipulated that should they be obliged to go more than twenty miles distance, they were to be paid for their time thus employed at the rate paid to other "soulders." He was also empowered "to execute Martiall discipline" among the fifty "souldiers so put in arms," both in times of war and peace, and with "two others of said privileged place," he was to hear and determine all cases, civil and criminal, that should arise in said limits, as a county court might do, and to make by-laws for the same. These military settlers were privileged from arrest for any debts except those due the King and those contracted among themselves, and were free from taxes and levies except from those laid within their own limits.

* Acts of House of Burgesses.

This fort was not named by the act authorizing its construction, and if any was given it after its completion, it does not appear in the histories or records at our disposal. It is quite likely it had some designation, if nothing more than the Rappahannock fort—Smith's fort on the Rapphannock—and it may have been known by one or the other until the place was laid out for a town and received its present name. Or it may have been known as "The Lease Land," the designation it had when it was incorporated forty-six years afterwards.

It has been sugggsted, and believed by some few to be true, that this fort was built at Germanna, about eighteen miles above the Rappahannock falls, but this claim cannot be maintained. It is known that all of these plantations and military stations were located on navigable rivers and were reached and communicated with mostly, if not exclusively, by sail vessels, and it is not reasonable to suppose that this fort was located eighteen miles above tidewater, where it could not be reached by such vessels. In addition to this objection, it may be added that the "gallant cavalier, Governor Spotswood, at the head of the chivalry of Virginia," never made his dash above the falls to the "blue ridge of mountains" until the year 1720* [1716 is the correct date], nearly fifty years after the construction of the fort at or near the falls.

Besides this, Governor Spotswood did not come to Virginia as Governor until the year 1710. After coming to this country he became possessed of lands on the Rappahannock, at the mouth of Massaponax run, and from there up the ridge, west of Fredericksburg, to the Rapidan river at Germanna. We do not know when he became possessed of these lands, but it is known that he built a wharf near the mouth of Massaponax run and opened the ridge road from there to Germanna, now called Mine Road, over which he hauled his iron ore for shipment. And so it was said, and it was true, that he could go from his wharf on the Rappahannock to Germanna on the Rapidan on his own lands without crossing a stream.

Germanna was settled in April, 1714, thirty-eight years after this fort was built and thirty-four years before Governor Spots-

---

* Howe's History of Virginia.

The Free Bridge over the Rappahannock River to Stafford Heights.
(See page 171)

The City Court House and Clerk's Office.
(See page 142)

wood came to Virginia. It was settled by twelve German families, who had been induced by Governor Spotswood to come over from Germany to develop the iron and silver mines he desired opened on his land, recently acquired by him, several miles above the falls. These were the first iron mines opened and operated in this new country, and being the first worker in iron gave him the honorable appellation of the "Tubal Cain of America."

It has been a tradition held by some that the Germans, who settled Germanna, came to this country as paupers, and when they landed at Tappahannock, where their vessel anchored, they were unable to pay their passage and were virtually sold to Governor Spotswood for a term of years, he to pay the passage money and furnish the land upon which they were to settle. It is further said that he induced them to settle on the river, above Fredericksburg, where they built small huts, called the place Germanna and opened the mines which proved so remunerative to the Governor.

Much of this statement, however, is denied by the descendants of these pioneers, who resent the charge of pauperism and show that these first settlers were men of education, were skilled miners, and that they came to this country under contract with Governor Spotswood, bringing with them letters of commendation from gentlemen of influence and official position.

From a paper prepared, and left to posterity, by Rev. James Kemper, a grandson of the emigrant, John Kemper,* we are able to cull some interesting facts connected with these people, who became neighbors and friends of the early settlers of Fredericksburg, and many of whose descendants are now among us.

These Germans "did not 'happen' to come to Virginia, but came upon the invitation of the Baron de Graffureid, who was a friend to Governor Spotswood, and for the express purpose of developing the iron ore deposits discovered by the latter upon his lands in the present county of Spotsylvania. These people came from the town of Müsen, which was then in the old province of Nassau Siegen, Westphalia, Germany. At Müsen there is an iron mine which has been worked since the early part of the fourteenth century, and is

---

* Furnished by Chas. E. Kemper, Esq.

operated to this day. They were skilled workers in iron and steel from the Müsen mines and built the old furnace in Spotsylvania county."

These pioneers remained at Germanna until about 1720, when, owing to some difference with Governor Spotswood, they removed to what is now Fauquier county, then Stafford, later Prince William, and in 1759 the portion they settled became Fauquier. They settled about nine miles south of Warrenton on a small stream called Licking Run and named the place Germantown—thus keeping up the German identity,— which is one mile north of Madison station on the Southern railroad.

Rev. James Kemper, in the paper referred to, says the first year they were in Germantown they "packed all of their provisions from Fredericksburg on their heads and raised their first crop with their hoes, in both of which the women bore a part." This shows that the village, afterwards called Fredericksburg, was the trading place of the country above the falls at that period.

The names of the twelve men who, with their families, settled Germanna, are John Kemper, John Huffman, Jacob Holtzclaw, Tillman Weaver, John Fishback, Harman Fishback, Harman Utterback, John Joseph Martin, Peter Hitt, Jacob Coons, ——— Wayman and ——— Hanback. The Rev. Henry Hagen was their minister.

These people were picked men for a special purpose, to do that which no one then in Virginia could do—manufacture iron. Their descendants are scattered all over this country and have filled high positions in the Army and Navy, as well as in State and Church. They did two things worthy of note: They laid the foundation of the German Reformed Church in the United States,* and also the iron and steel industry, which now requires billions of dollars to carry on successfully, and both of these were done at Germanna, in Spotsylvania county, Virginia.

It has also been contended that the fort, built near the falls of

---

* It is claimed by Rev. James Kemper that the German Reformed Church, organized at Germanna in 1714, was the first church of that denomination planted in this country.

the Rappahannock river, was constructed on the north side of the river and that the place where Falmouth now stands was the center of the military district.* This assertion is not substantiated by any record we have seen, and we are not prepared, in the absence of proof, to accept it.

There are two reasons which may be given which, we think, will show that the site of Falmouth would have been an improper and unsafe location for the fort, both of which would have suggested themselves to the constructors of the fort. One is, that the place is on the bend of the river and is surrounded by high hills, now known as Stafford Heights. From the crest of these hills the fort could have been attacked by the enemy and captured by any small force. And if it had not been captured the elevation would have given the Indians great advantage over the garrison, making their arrows very effective. To have placed the fort on either one of the high hills would have thrown the garrison too far from the river to protect their sail vessels, and in case they had been compelled to give up the fort they could not have reached their vessels in the river, which, in the past, had proved a safer refuge than the poorly constructed forts of that day.

The other reason is, that to have constructed the fort on the north side of the river would have placed the almost impassable Rappahannock between the garrison and their remote friends on the south side, from whom alone they could look for relief in case they had been besieged, or if they had been compelled to retreat.

For these reasons, if for no other, we are satisfied that the fort was not located on the north side of the river, but on the south side and in the vicinity of where Fredericksburg now stands.

But this author, in speaking of the fort, says "not one stone or brick of the fort is left on another, but the terraces on the long hill back of the riverside houses still bear traces of ancient work." But this does not prove the contention.

It should be remembered that forts were not constructed in those times of stones and bricks, nor even of earthen walls, as they have

---

* Mr. M. D. Conway, in Magazine of American History, Vol. 27, No. 3, page 186.

since been, but of wooden poles or logs, and very temporary at that. John Fontaine gives a minute description of the fort built by the Germans at Germanna in the year 1714, which will help us to understand what a fort was in those days.

"We walked about the town, which is palisaded with stakes stuck in the ground, and laid close the one to the other, and of substance to bear out a mussket-shot. There are but nine families, and they have nine houses, built all in a line; and before every house, about twenty feet distant from it, they have small sheds built for their hogs and hens, so that the hog-sties and houses make a street. The place that is poled in is a pentagon, very regularly laid out; and in the very center there is a block-house, made with five sides, which answer to the five sides of the great enclosure; there are loop holes through it, from which you may see all the inside of the enclosure. This was intended for a retreat for the people, in case they were not able to defend the palisadoes, if attacked by the Indians."*
Col. Byrd, in 1732, called this a fort.

---

* Memoirs of a Huguenot Family, page 268.

CHAPTER II

THE KNIGHTS OF THE GOLDEN HORSE SHOE.

Governor Spotswood and Others Start on an Expedition over the Blue Ridge Mountains—They Pass Through what is now Fredericksburg—They Join Others at Germanna, where they make Extensive Preparations—The Country Rough and the Woods Dense—Bears, Deer, Turkeys, Squirrels and Snakes Plentiful—The Summit of the Mountain Reached—The Sublime Scene—The Health of the King Drank and the Country Taken Possession of in His Name—The Shenandoah River, &c.

Two years after the settlement of Germanna Governor Spotswood visited the place, in company with gentlemen and others who were to accompany him in his famous expedition over the Blue Ridge mountains, which has been the theme of the writers of song and story, and upon which has recently been founded a secret benevolent order. So much has been written about this expedition, in this country and in Europe, into which so much romance has been woven, and yet so little is known about it by the general public, at the expense of length and tediousness to the reader of the narrative, we propose to give John Fontaine's* diary, written daily as they progressed on the journey, from the time he left Williamsburg with the Governor, until he returned to that city, that we may be thoroughly informed of all the particulars. The expedition was made in August and September, 1716, and the following is John Fontaine's diary:

Williamsburg, 20th August, 1716.—In the morning got my horses ready, and what baggage was necessary, and I waited on the

---

* John Fontaine was the son of Rev. James Fontaine, of France, a Huguenot who fled to England to avoid religious persecution, and thence settled in Scotland, where he ended his days. The name originally was *De la Fontaine*, but John's grandfather, "from motives of humility, cut off the *De la*, the indication of the nobility of the family." John came to this country in 1716, with his brother Peter, and at once became a friend and companion of Governor Spotswood's, while Peter became a minister of ability and was very popular. From these two brothers sprang the Fontaines of this country.

Governor who was in readiness for an expedition over the Appalachian mountains. We breakfasted and about ten got on horseback, and, at four came to the Brickhouse, upon York River, where we crossed the ferry and at six came to Mr. Austin Moore's house* on Mattapony River, in King William County; here we lay all night and were well entertained.

21st.—Fair weather. At ten we set out from Mr. Moore's, and crossed the river of Mattapony, and continued on the road, and were on horseback till nine of the clock at night, before we came to Mr. Robert Beverley's house where we were well entertained, and remained this night.

22nd.—At nine in the morning we set out from Mr. Beverley's. The Governor left his chaise here, and mounted his horse. The weather fair, we continued on our journey until we came to Mr. Woodford's where we lay, and were well entertained. This house lies on Rappahannock River ten miles below the falls.

23rd.—Here we remained all this day, and diverted ourselves and rested our horses.

24th.—In the morning, at seven, we mounted our horses and came to Austin Smith's house† about ten, where we dined, and remained till about one of the clock, when we set out, and about nine of the clock we came to the German-town, where we rested that night—bad beds and indifferent entertainment.

German-town, 25th.—After dinner we went to see the mines, but I could not observe that there was any good mine. The Germans pretend that it is a silver mine; we took some of the ore and endeavored to run it, but could get nothing out of it, and I am of opinion it will not come to anything, no, not as much as lead. Many of the gentlemen of the county are concerned in this work. We returned and to our hard beds.

26th.—At seven we got up, and several gentlemen of the country,

---

* Austain Moore lived at Chelsea, on the Mattaponi river. He was the Governor's son-in-law.—Maury's History of Virginia.

† Austin Smith lived in the village or settlement afterwards named Fredericksburg. He is supposed to have been a descendant of Lawrence Smith, who commanded the fort here in 1681. He no doubt has descendants here now bearing the name of Smith, while some are known by other names.

that were to meet the Governor at this place for the expedition, arrived here, as also two companies of Rangers, consisting each of six men, and an officer. Four Meherrin Indians also came.* In the morning I diverted myself with other gentlemen shooting at a mark. At twelve we dined, and after dinner we mounted our horses and crossed the Rappahannoc River that runs by this place, and went to find out some convenient place for our horses to feed in, and to view the land hereabouts. Our guide left us, and we went so far in the woods that we did not know the way back again; and so we hallowed and fired our guns. Half an hour after sunset the guide came to us. and we went to cross the river by a ford higher up. The descent to the river being steep, and the night dark, we were obliged to dismount and lead our horses down to the river side, which was very troublesome. The bank being very steep, the greatest part of our company went into the water to mount their horses, where they were up to the crotch in the water. After we had forded the river and came to the other side, where the bank was steep also, in going up, the horse of one of our company slipped and fell back into the river on the top of his rider, but he received no other damage than being heartily wet, which made sport for the rest. A hornet stung one of the gentlemen in the face which swelled prodigiously. About ten we came to the town, where we supped, and to bed.

27th.—We got our tents in order, and our horses shod. About twelve I was taken with a violent headache and pains in all my bones, so that I was obliged to lie down, and was very bad that day.

28th.—About one in the morning I was taken with a violent fever, which abated about six at night, and I began to take the bark, and had one ounce divided into eight doses, and took two of them by ten of the clock that night. The fever abated, but I had great pains in my head and bones.

29th.—In the morning we got all things in readiness, and about

---

* These Indians came from the Meherrin river, where Governor Spotswood owned a large body of land. He had opened a school there for the education and conversion of the Indian children, which made him quite popular with the Indians in that quarter. The Governor and Mr. Fontaine visited that part of the country a few weeks before they started on this expedition.

one we left the German-town to set out on our intended journey. At five in the afternoon, the Governor gave orders to encamp near a small river, three miles from Germanna, which we called Expedition Run, and here we lay all night. The first encampment was called Beverley Camp, in honor of one of the gentlemen of our party. We made great fires, and supped, and drank good punch. By ten of the clock I had taken all of my ounce of Jesuit's Bark, but my head was much out of order.

30th.—In the morning about seven of the clock, the trumpet sounded to awake all the company, and we got up. One Austin Smith, one of the gentlemen with us, having a fever, returned home. We had lain upon the ground under cover of our tents, and we found by the pains in our bones that we had not had good beds to lie upon. At nine in the morning, we sent our servants and baggage forward, and we remained, because two of the Governor's horses had strayed. At half past two we got the horses, at three we mounted, and at half an hour after four, we came up with our baggage at a small river, three miles on the way, which we called Mine River, because there was an appearance of a silver mine by it. We made about three miles more, and came to another small river, which is at the foot of a small mountain, so we encamped here and called it Mountain Run, and our camp we called Todd's Camp. We had good pasturage for our horses, and venison in abundance for ourselves which we roasted before the fire upon wooden forks, and so we went to bed in our tents. Made 6 miles this day.

31st.—At eight in the morning we set out from Mountain Run, and after going five miles we came upon the upper part of Rappahannoc River. One of the gentlemen and I, we kept on one side of the company about a mile, to have the better hunting. I saw a deer, and shot him from my horse, but the horse threw me a terrible fall and ran away; we ran after, and with a great deal of difficulty got him again; but we could not find the deer I had shot, and we lost ourselves, and it was two hours before we could come upon the track of our company. About five miles further we crossed the same river again, and two miles further we met with a large bear, which one of our company shot, and I got the skin. We killed several deer, and about two miles from the place where we killed the bear, we encamped upon Rappahannock River. From our encampment we could see the Appalachian Hills very plain. We made large fires, pitched our tents, and cut bows to lie upon, had good liquor, and at ten we went to sleep. We always kept a sentry at the Governor's door. We called this Smith's Camp. Made this day fourteen miles.

1st September.—At eight we mounted our horses, and made the first five miles of our way through a very pleasant plain, which lies where Rappahannock River forks. I saw there the largest timber, the finest and deepest mould, and the best grass that I ever did see.* We had some of our baggage put out of order, and our company dismounted, by hornets stinging the horses. This was some hindrance, and did a little damage, but afforded a great deal of diversion. We killed three bears this day, which exercised the horses as well as the men. We saw two foxes but did not pursue them; we killed several deer. About five of the clock, we came to a run of water at the foot of a hill, where we pitched our tents. We called the encampment Dr. Robinson's Camp, and the river Blind Run. We had good pasturage for our horses, and every one was cook for himself. We made our beds with bushes as before. On this day we made 13 miles.

2nd.—At nine we were all on horseback and after riding about five miles we crossed Rappahannoc river,† almost at the head, where it is very small. We had a rugged way; we passed over a great many small runs of water, some of which were deep, and others very miry. Several of our company were dismounted, some were down with their horses, others under their horses, and some thrown off. We saw a bear running down a tree, but it being Sunday we did not endeavor to kill anything. We encamped at five by a small river we called White Oak River,‡ and called our Camp Taylor's Camp.

3rd.—About eight we were on horseback, and about ten we came to a thicket, so tightly laced together, that we had a great deal of

---

* This must be at the junction of the Rapidan and Robinson rivers.

† This is the Rapidan river probably.

‡ It is likely that this was Conway river, a tributary of the Rapidan, and the line between Madison and Green counties.

trouble to get through; our baggage was injured, our clothes torn all to rags, and the saddles and holsters also torn. About five of the clock we encamped almost at the head of James River,* just below the great mountains. We called this camp Colonel Robertson's Camp. We made all this day but eight miles.

4th.—We had two of our men sick with the measles, and one of our horses poisoned with a rattlesnake. We took the heaviest of our baggage, our tired horses, and the sick men, and made as convenient a lodge for them as we could, and left people to guard them, and hunt for them. We had finished this work by twelve, and so we went out. The sides of the mountains were so full of vines and briers, that we were forced to clear most of the way before us. We crossed one of the small mountains this side of the Appalachian, and from the top of it we had a fine view of the plains below. We were obliged to walk up the most of the way, there being an abundance of loose stones on the side of the hill. I killed a large rattlesnake here, and the other people killed three more. We made about four miles and so came to the side of James River, where a man may jump over it, and there we pitched our tents. As the people were lighting the fire, there came out of a large log of wood a prodigious snake, which they killed; so this camp was called Rattlesnake Camp, but it was otherwise called Brook's Camp.

5th.—A fair day. At nine we were mounted; we were obliged to have axe-men to clear the way in some places. We followed the windings of James River, observing that it came from the very top of the mountains. We killed two rattlesnakes during our ascent. In some places it was very steep, in others it was so that we could ride up. About one of the clock we got to the top of the mountain; about four miles and a half, and we came to the very head spring of James River, where it runs no bigger than a man's arm, from under a large stone. We drank King George's health and all the Royal Family's at the very top of the Appalachian mountains. About a musket-shot from the spring is another, which rises and runs down on the other side; it goes westward, and we thought we

---

* This is unquestionably the north fork or north branch of the Rivanna river, a tributary of the James, which runs through Green county, its head waters coming from the sides of the Blue Ridge mountain.

"Mary Washington House," home of Mary, the Mother of Washington, and where she died in 1789; now the property of the A. P. of V. A.
(See page 157)

"Federal Hill," home of Thomas Reade Rootes, Gov. Brooke, etc.; now the residence of Mrs. H. Theodore Wight.
(See page 153)

could go down that way, but we met with such prodigious precipices, that we were obliged to return to the top again. We found some trees which had been formerly marked, I suppose, by the Northern Indians, and following these trees, we found a good, safe descent. Several of the company were for returning; but the Governor persuaded them to continue on. About five we were down on the other side, and continued our way for about seven miles further, until we came to a large river, by the side of which we encamped. We made this day fourteen miles. I, being somewhat more curious than the rest, went on a high rock on the top of the mountain, to see fine prospects, and I lost my gun. We saw, when we were over the mountains, the footing of elks and buffaloes, and their beds. We saw a vine which bore a sort of wild cucumber; and a shrub with a fruit like unto a currant. We eat very good wild grapes. We called this place Spotswood Camp, after our Governor.

6th.—We crossed the river, which we called Euphrates.* It is very deep; the main course of the water is North; it is fourscore yards wide in the narrowest part. We drank some healths on the other side, and returned; after which I went a swimming in it. We could not find any fordable place, except the one by which we crossed, and it was deep in several places. I got some grass hoppers and fished; and another and I, we caught a dish of fish, some perch, and a fish they called chub. The others went a hunting, and killed deer and turkeys. The Governor had graving irons, but could not grave anything, the stones were so hard, I graved my name on a tree by the river side; and the Governor buried a bottle with a paper enclosed, on which he writ that he took possession of this place in the name and for King George the First of England.* We had a

---

* This is the Shenandoah river, as no other river in the Valley answers to Mr. Fontaine's description, and which is a very important part of his narrative. The distance of the river from the mountains and the description of the streams crossed in reaching the mountains, enable us to determine with considerable accuracy the route the Governor and his party took as they crossed the Blue Ridge into the beautiful Shenandoah Valley, "the Granary of the World." A careful inspection of the map will show that they passed through the counties of Orange, Madison and the northern portion of Green over into Rockingham, where the Shenandoah river is about seventy-five or eighty yards wide and runs within a few miles of the Blue Ridge mountains.

good dinner, and after it we got the men together, and loaded all their arms, and we drank the King's health in Champagne, and fired a volley—the Princess's health in Burgundy, and fired a volley, and all the rest of the Royal Family in Claret, and a volley. We had several sorts of liquors, viz: Virginia red wine and white wine, Irish usquebaugh, brandy, shrub, two sorts of rum, champagne, canary, cherry, punch, water, cider, &c.

I sent two of the rangers to look for my gun, which I dropped in the mountains; they found it, and brought it to me at night, and I gave them a pistole for their trouble. We called the highest mountain Mount George, and the one we crossed over Mount Spotswood.

7th.—At seven in the morning we mounted our horses, and parted with the rangers, who were to go further on, and we returned homewards; we repassed the mountains, and at five in the afternoon we came to Hospital Camp, where we left our sick men, and heavy baggage and we found all things well and safe. We camped here, and called it Captain Clouder's Camp.

8th.—At nine we were all on horseback. We saw several bears and deer, and killed some wild turkeys. We encamped at the side of a run, and called the place Mason's Camp. We had good forage for our horses, and we lay as usual. Made twenty miles this day.

9th.—We set out at nine of the clock, and before twelve we saw several bears, and killed three. One of them attacked one of our

---

* Governor Spotswood, when he undertook the great discovery of the Passage over the Mountains, attended with a sufficient guard, and pioneers and gentlemen, with a sufficient stock of provision, with abundant fatigue passed these mountains and cut his Majesty's name in a rock upon the highest of them, naming it Mount George; and in complaisance the gentlemen from the Governor's name, called the mountain next in height Mount Alexander.

For this expedition they were obliged to provide a great quantity of horse shoes (things seldom used in the lower parts of the country, where there are few stones); upon which account the Governor, upon their return, presented each of his companions with a golden horse shoe, (some of which I have seen studded with valuable stones resembling the heads of nails,) with this inscription on one side: *Sic juvat transcendere montes,* and on the other is written the tremontane order.

This he instituted to encourage gentlemen to venture backwards, and make discoveries, and new settlements; any gentleman being entitled to wear this golden shoe that can prove his having drunk his Majesty's health upon Mount George.—Hugh Jones, 1724.

men that was riding after him, and narrowly missed him; he tore his things that he had behind him from off the horse, and would have destroyed him, had he not had immediate help from the other men and our dogs. Some of the dogs suffered severely in this engagement. At two we crossed one of the branches of the Rappahannock River, and at five we encamped on the side of the Rapid Ann, on a tract of land that Mr. Beverley hath design to take up. We made, this day, twenty-three miles, and called this Captain Smith's Camp. We eat part of one of the bears, which tasted very well, and would be good, and might pass for veal, if one did not know what it was. We were very merry, and diverted ourselves with our adventures.

10th.—At eight we were on horseback, and about ten, as we were going up a small hill, Mr. Beverley and his horse fell down, and they both rolled to the bottom; but there were no bones broken on either side. At twelve as we were crossing a run of water, Mr. Clouder fell in, so we called this place Clouder's Run. At one we arrived at a large spring, where we dined and drank a bowl of punch. We called this Fontaine's Spring. About two we got on horseback, and at four we reached Germanna. The Governor thanked the gentlemen for their assistance in the expedition. Mr. Mason left us here. I went at five to swim in the Rappahannoc River, and returned to the town.

11th.—After breakfast all our company left us, excepting Dr. Robinson and Mr. Clouder. We walked all about the town, and the Governor settled his business with the Germans here, and accommodated the minister and the people, and then to bed.

12th.—After breakfast went a fishing in the Rappahannock, and took seven fish, which we had for dinner; after which Mr. Robinson and I, we endeavored to melt some ore in the Smith's forge, but could get nothing out of it. Dr. Robinson's and Mr. Clouder's boys were taken violently ill with fever. Mr. Robinson and Mr. Clouder left us, and the boys remained behind.

13th.—About eight of the clock we mounted our horses, and went to the mine, where we took several pieces of ore; and at nine we set out from the mine, our servants having gone before; and about three we overtook them in the woods, and there the Governor and I dined. We mounted afterwards and continued on our road. I killed a black snake about five feet long. We arrived at Mr. Woodford's* on Rappahannoc River, about six, and remained there all night.

14th.—At seven we sent our horses and baggage before us; and at ten we mounted our horses; we killed another snake, four feet nine inches long. At twelve we came to the church, where we met with Mr. Buckner, and remained till two, to settle some county business; then we mounted our horses, and saw several wild turkeys on the road; and at seven we reached Mr. Beverley's house, which is on the head of the Mattapony River, where we were well entertained. My boy was taken with a violent fever, and very sick.

15th.—At seven my servant was some what better, and I sent him away with my horses, and about ten o'clock the Governor took his chaise, and I with him, and at twelve we came to a mill-dam, which we had great difficulty to get the chaise over. We got into it again, and continued on our way, and about five we arrived at Mr. Baylor's, where we remained all night.

16th.—My servant was so sick, that I was obliged to leave him, and the Governor's servants took care of my horses. At ten we sent the chaise over the Mattapony River, and it being Sunday, we went to church in King William County, where we heard a sermon from Mr. Monroe. After sermon we continued our journey until we came to Mr. West's plantation, where Colonel Basset waited for the Governor with his pinnace, and other boats for his servants. We arrived at his house by five of the clock, and were nobly entertained.

17th.—At ten we left Colonel Basset's, and at three we arrived at Williamsburg, where we dined together and went to my lodgings, and to bed, being well tired as well as my horses.

I reckon that from Williamsburg to the Euphrates River is in all 219 miles, so that our journey, going and coming, has been in all 438 miles.

---

* This Mr. Woodford is supposed to be the father or grandfather of General Wm. Woodford, of Revolutionary fame.

CHAPTER III

Fredericksburg Incorporated by Law—Col. Byrd Walks About Town—Church Erected—Patrick Henry Rector—Augustine Washington a Trustee—Fairs Inaugurated—Limits of the Town Extended, &c.

Although the site upon which Fredericksburg now stands was settled by white men, possibly in 1622, in the location of plantations by the London Company referred to by Capt. John Smith, and certainly in 1681 by the construction of Major Lawrence Smith's fort, yet the town was not incorporated for many years thereafter. That it was a trading station and a place of importance before its incorporation is admitted in the act of incorporation itself, besides earlier writers refer to it as such. If the inquiry should be made as to why the town was not incorporated earlier if it was a place of importance, it might be answered with the fact that prior to that time the authorities did not seem to think it was necessary, as neither Richmond, Petersburg, Norfolk nor Alexandria was incorporated for several years after Fredericksburg had a legal existence.

Fredericksburg was founded by law in 1727 and named for Frederick, Prince of Wales, son of George the Second, by which act the people of the town showed their attachment to the royal family of England. But this was not all; they emphasized that attachment by calling nearly every street in the original survey of the town after some member of the royal family or of some country to which English royalty was closely allied. Sophia street was named for the sister of George II; Caroline for his wife; Princess Anne for one of his daughters, and Prince Edward for his grandson. The cross streets were named, Princess Elizabeth for a daughter of George II; Frederick for his oldest son; William for his second son, and Amelia for a daughter. George was named for the King himself; Charlotte for the wife of George III; Hanover for the House of Hanover, and Prussia for the country of Prussia. This includes every street in the original survey except Charles and Wolfe. We do not know for whom these two streets were named, and we think the evidence is very clear that they were not laid out as streets at the time of the original survey.

The act of the House of Burgesses, establishing Fredericksburg, in which are preserved as near as possible the form, orthography, punctuation and capitalization, is as follows:

I. Whereas great Numbers of People have of late seated themselves and their Families upon and near the River *Rappahannock,* and the Branches thereof above the Falls, and great Quantities of Tobacco and other Commodities are every Year brought down to the upper Landings upon the said River to be shipped off and transported to other Parts of the Country and it is necessary that the poorer Part of the said Inhabitants should be supplied from thence with Goods and Merchandise in return for their Commodities, but for Want of some convenient Place, where Traders may cohabit and bring their Goods to, such Supplies are not to be had without great Disadvantages, and good Houses are greatly wanted on some navigable Part of said River, near the Falls for the Reception of safe keeping of such Commodities as are brought thither and for the Entertainment and Sustenance of those who repair thither from remote Places with Carriages drawn by Horses and Oxen; and forasmuch as the Inhabitants of the County of *Spotsylvania* have made humble Supplication to the General Assembly that a Town may be laid out in some convenient Place near the Falls of said River, for the cohabitation of such as are minded to reside there for the purposes aforesaid, whereby the peopling of that remote Part of the county will be encouraged, and Trade and Navigation may be increased:

II. BE *it enacted, by the Lieutenant Governor, Council, and Burgesses, of this present General Assembly, and it is hereby enacted, by the Authority of the same,* that within six Months after the passing of this Act fifty Acres of Land, Parcel of a Tract of Land belonging to *John Royston* and *Robert Buckner,* of the County of *Gloucester,* situate, lying and being upon the South Side of the River Rappahannock aforesaid in the County of *Spotsylvania* commonly called or known by the Name of the *Lease Land,* shall be surveyed and laid out, taking the whole Breadth of the Tract of Land upon the River, by the Surveyor of the said County of *Spotsylvania;* and the said fifty Acres of Land, so to be surveyed and laid out, shall be and is hereby vested in *John Robinson,* Esq; *Henry Willis, Augustin Smith, John Taliaferro, Harry Beverley, John Waller,* and *Jeremiah Clowder,* of the County of *Spotsylvania,* Gentlemen, and their Successors, in Trust, for the several purposes hereafter mentioned; and the said *John Robinson, Henry Willis, Augustin Smith, John Taliaferro, Harry Beverley, John Waller* and *Jeremiah Clowder,* are hereby constituted and appointed Directors and Trustees for designing, building, carrying on, and maintaining, a Town upon the said Land: And the said Directors and Trustees, or any four of them, shall have power to meet as often as they shall think necessary, and shall lay out the said fifty Acres in Lots and Streets, not exceeding Half an Acre of Ground in each Lot, and also to set apart such Portions of said Land for a Church and Church-Yard, a Market Place, and publick Key, and to appoint such Places upon the River for publick Landings, as they shall think most convenient, and, if the same shall be necessary, shall direct the making and erecting of Wharfs and Cranes at such publick Landings, for the publick Use. And when the said Town shall be so laid out the said Directors and Trustees shall have full Power and Authority to sell all the said Lots by publick Sale or Auction, from Time to Time, to the highest Bidder, so as no Person shall have more than Two Lots; and when such Lots shall be sold, any two of the said Trustees shall and may, upon Payment of the Purchase Money, by some sufficient Conveyance or Conveyances, Convey the Fee Simple, Estate of such Lot or Lots to the Purchaser or Purchasers: And he or they, or his or their Heirs and Assigns, respectively, shall and may for ever thereafter peaceably and quietly have, hold, possess, and enjoy, the same, freed and discharged of and from all Right, Title, Estate, Claim, Interest, and Demand whatsoever of the said *John Royster* and *Robert Buckner* and the Heirs and Assigns of them respectively, and of all Persons whatsoever claiming by, from, or under them or either of them.

III. PROVIDED *nevertheless,* that the said Directors and Trustees shall pay, or cause to be paid, unto the said *John Royston* and *Robert Buckner,* out of the Money to be raised by the Sale of the said Lots, as soon as the same shall be by them received, after the Rate of forty Shillings for every Acre of the said fifty Acres of Land, according to the Right which the said *John Royston* and *Robert Buckner* now respectively have to the same; and the said *John Royston* and *Robert Buckner* shall also have each of them two Lots, which shall be assigned to them by the said Directors and Trustees, and they shall respectively remain seized of such Lots of the same Estate whereof they were respectively seized in the said Land before the making of this Act.

IV. AND *be it further enacted, by the Authority aforesaid,* that after the said Lots shall be so laid out and disposed of, as aforesaid, the said Directors, or any four of them, shall have full Power and Authority to apply all the overplus Money which shall be raised by the Sale of the said Lots to such publick Use; for the common Benefit of the Inhabitants of the said Town, as to them shall seem best.

V. AND *be it further enacted, by the Authority aforesaid,* that the Grantee or Grantees of every such Lot or Lots, so to be conveyed and sold in the said Town, shall, within two Years next after the Date of the Conveyance for the same, erect, build, and finish, on each Lot so conveyed, one House, of Brick, Stone or Wood well framed, of the Dimensions of Twenty Feet square, and nine Feet Pitch at the least, or apportionably thereto, if such Grantee shall have two Lots contiguous; and the said Directors shall have full Power and Authority to establish such Rules and Orders, for the more regular placing the said Houses, as to them shall seem fit, from Time to Time. And if the Owner of any Lots shall fail to pursue and comply with the Directions herein prescribed, for the building and finishing one or more House or Houses thereon, then such Lots upon which such Houses shall not be so built and finished shall be revested in the said Trustees, and shall and may be sold and conveyed to any other Person or Persons whatsoever, in the Manner before directed, and shall revest, and be again sold, as often as the Owner or Owners shall fail to perform, obey, and fulfil, the Directions aforesaid; and if the Inhabitants of the said Town shall fail to obey and pursue the Rules and Orders of the said Directors, in repairing and amending the Streets, Landings, and publick Wharfs, they shall be liable to the same Penalties as are inflicted for not repairing the Highways of this Colony.

VI. AND for the continuing the Succession of the said Trustees and Directors, until the Governour of this Colony shall incorporate some other Persons by Letters Patents, under the Seal of this Colony, to be one Body Politick and Corporate, to whom the Government of the said Town shall be committed, *Be it further enacted*, that in Case of the Death of the said Directors, or of their Refusal to act, the surviving or other Directors, or the major Part of them, shall assemble, and are hereby Empowered, from Time to Time, by Instrument in Writing, under their respective Hands and Seals, to nominate some other Person or Persons, being an Inhabitant or Freeholder of the said Town, in the Place of him so dying or refusing; which new Director or Directors, so nominated and appointed, shall from thenceforth have the like Power and Authority, in all Things relating to the Matters herein contained, as if he or they had been expressly named and appointed in and by this Act, and every such Instrument and Nomination shall from Time to Time be recorded in the Books of the said Directors.

VII. AND whereas *William Livingston* is possessed of a Lease under the said *John Royston,* for certain Years to come, of Part of the said fifty Acres of Land, and hath erected buildings and made several Improvements thereon, which will be taken away when the said Town shall be laid out: For making Satisfaction for which,

VIII. BE it further enacted, that the two Lots to be assigned to the said *John Royston,* pursuant to this Act, shall include the Dwelling-House and Kitchen of the said *William Livingston,* and shall be held and enjoyed by him for the Residue of the said Term, and at the Expiration thereof shall revert unto, and be vested in, the said *John Royston,* as aforesaid; and, moreover, the said Trustees are hereby enjoined and required to pay unto the said *William Livingston* the Sum of twenty Pounds current Money out of the Monies arising by Sale of Lots, as a Consideration and Compensation for the said Lease.

IX. AND *be it further enacted,* that the Town aforesaid shall be called by the Name of *Fredericksburg.*

This act of incorporation which elevated the Lease Land into the town of Fredericksburg, was signed by William Gooch, Esq., Governor, and John Holliday, Speaker.

By the authority conferred upon the trustees of the town by the sixth section of the above act, the following paper was issued by the board of trustees, appointing Augustine Washington, the father of General George Washington, one of the trustees of the town. The original was presented to the town some years ago by one of the descendants of Augustine Washington, and is now preserved in the clerk's office:

"Whereas, at a meeting of the Trustees of the town of Fredericksburg, April 6th 1742, according to directions of act of ‗ ‗ ably, Intitled an Act for erecting a Town in both of the counties of Spotsylvania and King George, To Supply the number of Trustees in the Room of those Gentlemen deceased, we have Unanimously made Choise of, and Elected, Augustine Washington, Gent., to be one of the Trustees or Feoffees for the town of Fredericksburg, in Spotsylvania county to fill up and compleat our full number and for confirming of the same We have according to Directions of the Sd Act, set our hands and seals, this 20th day of April, 1742.

    John Taliaferro,   John Allen,
    John Waller,   Rob Jackson.
    Ira Thornton,

In the year 1732 the seat of justice, which had been located at Germanna, where Governor Spotswood had settled, and where he started and operated the first iron works in this country, heretofore mentioned, was removed to Fredericksburg as a more convenient place. That change did not continue long, for, in 1749, the law was again changed and the court was moved back to Germanna, where it was held for several years, and until it was located at

Princess Anne Street looking East.

Holidays, thence to the old Courthouse and finally to Spotsylvania Courthouse, where it was held until abolished by the new Constitution.

In 1732, five years after the town was established by law, Col. Byrd, then living on the James river, where Richmond now stands, made a visit to Fredericksburg. This visit was made at the time he made his trip to Germanna to see his old friend Governor Spotswood. While here Col. Byrd wrote a description of the new town to a friend as he saw it, as follows:

"Colonel Willis walked me about his new town of Fredericksburg. It is pleasantly situated on the south shore of the Rappahannock river, about a mile below the falls. Sloops may come and lie close to the wharf, within thirty yards of the public warehouse which is built in the figure of a cross. Just by the wharf is a quarry of white stone that is very soft in the ground, and hardens in the air, appearing to be as fair and fine grained as that of Portland. Besides that, there are several other quarries in the river bank, within the limits of the town, sufficient to build a large city. The only edifice of stone yet built is the prison, the walls of which are strong enough to hold Jack Sheppard, if he had been transported thither. Though this be a commodious and beautiful situation for a town, with the advantages of a navigable river, and wholesome air, yet the inhabitants are very few. Besides Colonel Willis, who is the top man of the place, there are only one merchant, a tailor, a smith, an ordinary-keeper, and a lady, Mrs. Livingston, who acts here in the double capacity of a doctress and a coffee-woman. It is said the courthouse and the church are going to be built here, and then both religion and justice will help to enlarge the place."

The church spoken of was built soon after Col. Byrd's visit. It was located on the lot where St. George's church building now stands. It was a wooden structure, about thirty by forty feet, to which two additions were made as the town increased in population. The first addition was made to the side of the church, which gave the building the shape of a capital T, and the second one was made a few years afterwards on the opposite side, giving the building the form of a cross.

The first rector of the new church was Rev. Patrick Henry, uncle of the great Virginia orator, Patrick Henry. Mr. Henry remained rector for a short time, and was followed, in 1734, by Rev. James Marye, of Goochland county, who was the great great grandfather of our late honored fellow citizen, Gov. John L. Marye. Mr. Marye had charge of two churches within the parish, one located on the Po river and the other at Fredericksburg. His salary for the first year for the entire parish was discharged with sixteen thousand pounds of "farm tobacco." St. George's church is noticed more at length under the head of churches.

CATTLE AND MERCHANDISE FAIRS.

In the year 1738 a law was passed by the House of Burgesses authorizing and directing that "fairs should be held in Fredericksburg twice a year for the sale of cattle, provisions, goods, wares, and all kinds of merchandise whatever." The act provided that all persons at such fairs, going to or from them, were privileged from arrest and execution during the fairs, and for two days before and two days after them, except for capital offences, breaches of the peace, or for any controversies, suits and quarrels that might arise during the time. These fairs were continued from time to time, by various acts and amendments, until 1769, when the right of holding them was made perpetual, they having proved a benefit to both town and county. We have no record as to when they ceased to be held and no citizen now living remembers to have attended one. They may have been changed into agricultural fairs, which are mentioned elsewhere.

ANOTHER SURVEY OF THE TOWN.

In March, 1739, the trustees of the town found it necessary to have another survey and plat of Fredericksburg made. This work was done by William Waller, Surveyor of Spotsylvania county. By this new survey it appears that the lots and buildings of the town had not only occupied the original fifty acres, but had also encroached upon the lands of Henry Willis and John Lewis; and, as this gave rise to controversies and threatened law suits, the Lieutenant-Governor, Council and Burgesses of the General Assembly passed an act in May, 1742, which was declared to be "for removing all doubts and controversies," and which declared that these lands, belonging to the estate of Henry Willis and John Lewis, should be held and taken to be part of Fredericksburg and vested in the trustees, and purchasers claiming under them; provided, that the trustees should pay to the executors of Henry Willis five pounds, and to John Lewis fifteen pounds. The area of the town, as ascertained by this survey, was not quite fifty-three acres.

The irregularity of the buildings having necessitated an enlargement of the original fifty acres, the style of buildings must have caused serious apprehensions of danger from fire, as we find that, in 1742, it was represented to the General Assembly that the people were often in great and imminent danger of having their houses and effects burned by reason of the many wooden chimneys in the town, and, therefore, it was made unlawful to build any wooden chimneys in the town thereafter, and unlawful, after the expiration of three years, to use any wooden chimney already built; and, in case the owners did not, within three years, pull down and destroy these wooden chimneys, the sheriff was authorized to do so, at the expense of the owners thereof.

CHAPTER IV

Encouraging Home Industries—Further Extension of the Town—Tobacco Inspectors—Modes of Punishment—Prosperity—Military Ardor—Under the United States.

In 1759 an act was passed by the General Assembly to encourage the "Arts and Manufactures in the Colony," but wine and silk making seemed to have predominated all others, wine having the decided preference as will readily be seen. In the act it was set forth that five hundred pounds should be paid as a premiun to the person who should, in any one year, within eight years from the date of its passage, make the best wine in quantity not less than ten hogsheads, and one hundred pounds should be paid to the person making the second best. It was provided that the money for these premiums should be raised by the annual subscriptions of public-spirited gentlemen who were willing to encourage the undertaking; and it was further provided that, if the subscriptions would justify it, a handsome premium should be given for silk making. It was also stipulated that if there was an "overplus of money," after the premiums on wine and silk making were provided for, it was to "be given for the encouragement of such other articles as should appear to the committee most advantageous to the colony." Among those who contributed the first year for this purpose, who were then, or had been, citizens of Fredericksburg, were the following gentlemen who subscribed two pounds each: Robert Carter, Pressley Thornton, George Washington, James Mercer, William Bernard, David Ker, Philip Rootes, Thomas Reade Rootes, Alexander Ross, John Champ.

FURTHER EXTENSION OF THE TOWN.

In 1763 an act was passed by the General Assembly extending the corporate limits of the town, but to what extent we do not know, as we have been unable to find the act or any of its provisions.

REGULATING TOBACCO INSPECTORS.

In 1764 the General Assembly passed an act for "Amending the Staple of Tobacco and for Preventing Frauds in his Majesty's Customs." It was a very lengthy bill, having seventy-seven sections, ten more than any other act ever before passed by that body, and severe penalties were prescribed for its violation. The bill was necessarily long and severe penalties were prescribed because it had reference to the raising, curing, packing and sale of tobacco, which was one of the principal products of Virginia, and the duties and responsibilities of tobacco inspectors and their proper management of tobacco warehouses. Besides tobacco being one of the important crops raised in the colony, if not the most important one, large quantities of it were shipped to the old country and sold for good prices. In addition to this, tobacco was used in the colony as a substitute for money, as all debts between private individuals, as well as those due the colony, were paid in tobacco. The bill provided for public warehouses, for the proper inspection of tobacco and for public inspectors, appointed by the Governor and his Council, not less than two at each warehouse, who, besides taking an oath of office, were placed under heavy bonds with security, the penalty being five hundred pounds sterling for the faithful performance of their duties. One of these public warehouses was located in Fredericksburg, and may have been the old stone house on Water street, just below the free bridge. The oath required to be taken by these public inspectors was as follows:

"You shall swear that you will diligently and carefully view and examine all tobacco brought to any public warehouse or warehouses where you are appointed to be inspector, and that not separately and apart from your fellow, but in his presence; and that you will not receive any tobacco that is not in your judgment sound, well conditioned, merchantable and clear of trash, nor receive, pass or stamp any tobacco, hogshead or cask of tobacco, prohibited by one act of Assembly, entitled an act for amending the sample of tobacco, and preventing frauds in his Majesty's customs; and that you will not change, alter or give out any tobacco, other than such hogsheads or casks for which the receipt to be taken was given; but that you will in all things well and faithfully discharge your duty in the office of inspector, according to the best of your skill and judgment and according to the directions of said act, without fear, favor, affection, malice or partiality. So help me God."

The receipts given by the inspectors of the public warehouse in Fredericksburg, according to the provisions of the act, were to pass and be current in the town and county of Spotsylvania for the payment of all quit-rents, county and town levies and for officers' fees. As this provision of law made them current for public dues, the public also adopted them as currency and they were used for the payment of all obligations. These receipts were protected by severe penalties against counterfeiting and forgery, and each one represented so many hundred pounds of tobacco deposited at the public warehouse.

MILITARY ARDOR OF THE TOWN.

Fredericksburg continued to grow in population and material prosperity, and also improve in the intelligence and public spirit of its inhabitants, until the year 1775, when the affairs between Great Britain and the American Colonies were verging to a crisis. Her leading citizens were among the very first in Virginia to adopt the principle that the American Colonies ought not only to be exempt from taxation by the Mother Country, but should be free and independent States. The battle of Lexington was fought on the 19th day of April, 1775, and on the 20th, the following day, Lord Dunmore secretly removed twenty barrels of gunpowder from the public magazine in Williamsburg to the Magdalen Man-of-war, which anchored off Yorktown. When the news of the battle of Lexington, and of the removal of the powder, reached Fredericksburg, great excitement prevailed. Over six hundred men armed themselves, from the town and surrounding country, assembled at the Courthouse in town and offered their services to George Washington, who was then in Williamsburg, to defend that city from Lord Dunmore's threatened attack, and the country from his tyranny.

After assembling they dispatched delegates to Richmond and

Williamsburg to ascertain the condition of affairs and to what point they should report for duty. In the meantime, those ardent patriots, George Washington, Peyton Randolph and Edmund Pendleton, transmitted their advice to the people of Fredericksburg, and especially those who had formed the military organization, to abstain for the present from hostilities until a congress, then called or soon to be called, should decide upon a general plan of resistance.

On the receipt of this advice, these patriots held a council, consisting of more than one hundred men, representing fourteen companies, who, by a majority of one vote, decided to disperse for the present They were burning with indignation at the murderous attack made upon their brethren of Lexington, Mass., by the armed soldiers of Great Britian, and the unlawful arrests, and retention as prisoners, of some of the leading citizens of Massachusetts by British military officers. And this feeling of indignation was intensified when they saw that this outrage was followed the next day by another perpetrated in their own colony and by their own Governor; and when he threatened to return from Yorktown, whither he had fled for safety, and attack Williamsburg with a man-of-war they were convinced that the enemies of the Patriots, the British and Tories, understood each other and were acting in concert. Yet, upon the advice of those whose lead they were willing to follow, and whose commands they were ready to obey, they agreed to disband for the present. Before dispersing, however, they drafted an address, which was tantamount to a declaration of independence, in which they firmly resolved to resist all attempts against their rights and privileges, from whatever quarter they might be assailed.

They went further than to just pass resolutions; they pledged themselves, solemnly and firmly one to the other, to be in readiness, at a moment's warning, to reassemble, and, by force of arms, to defend the laws, liberties and the rights of this or any sister colony, from unjust and wicked invasions. They then sent dispatches to patriots assembled in Caroline, Berkeley, Frederick and Dunmore counties, thanking them for their offer of service and acquainting them with the condition of public affairs and their determination to be ready at a moment's notice to respond to any call that might be made by the patriotic leaders, who were then holding a council in Williamsburg. The resolutions and pledges were read at the head of each company of patriots encamped at Fredericksburg, and unanimously approved and adopted. The address concluded with the impressive words, "God, save the liberties of America," which were a substitute for the oft-repeated words, "God, save the King."

These resolutions were passed twenty-one days before the celebrated Mecklenburg resolutions in North Carolina were, and more than a year before the Declaration of Independence by the American Congress, which showed the intense patriotic fervor of the people of Fredericksburg at that early period, many of whom bore a heroic part in the subsequent struggle of the Seven Years' war that followed. Among the number assembled with these lovers of liberty, and most prominent, were Gen. Geo. Weedon, who served on Gen. Washington's staff, commanded with distinction a division at the surrender of Yorktown, and afterwards for several terms served as mayor of the town; Gen. Hugh Mercer, who rose to the rank of Major-General and was killed at Princeton, New Jersey, on January 3, 1777, and Gen. Gustavus B. Wallace, who served gallantly through the war, attaining to the rank of Brigadier-General.

FREDERICKSBURG UNDER THE UNITED STATES.

The long tobacco act of the House of Burgesses was the last act passed by that body that affected the commercial interest of the town or the agricultural interest of the surrounding country that we have any knowledge of. The Revolutionary war soon followed and our independence and new government was the result. It is not considered necessary in this work to attempt to give the part Fredericksburg bore in that struggle—the generals she furnished to command the armies and navy of the country, the line officers and soldiers she sent forth to meet and repel the invader, the statesmen she gave to provide for the armies or to form the new government and to guide it to a successful, permanent and solid establishment. All of these things are told by the records and histories of the State and country more accurately and in a more pleasing style than we can narrate them. We therefore pass to the new order of things.

FREDERICKSBURG IN THE REPUBLIC.

The first act of the Legislature of Virginia in reference to Fredericksburg, after the establishment of the young republic, was to grant it a charter, which bill was passed in 1781. It provided for the town a Mayor, Recorder, Board of Aldermen and a Common Council, and required that all of them should be freeholders. They were made a body politic by the name and designation of Mayor and Commonalty of the town of Fredericksburg, and by that title were to have perpetual succession. The Mayor, Recorder and the four Aldermen were *ex-officio* Justices of the Peace, and had power to hold a court of hustings once a month, and to "hold pleas in all cases whatsoever originating within the limits" of the town and to "low water mark on the northwest side of the Rappahannock river and half a mile without and around the other limits of the said town." They were given the sole authority and power of "licensing tavern keepers and settling their rates," to appoint a sergeant with the powers of sheriffs, a "constable and other necessary officers of court and surveyors of the streets and highways." A surveyor of the streets was appointed at the first hustings court held by the Mayor and his fellow magistrates, but he was known as the "Geographer" of the town for more than half a century, and was often so entered upon the court records.

In civil cases the hustings court was not to have jurisdiction where the amount in controversy exceeded one thousand pounds of leaf tobacco, or its value in money, unless both parties to the suit were citizens of the town when the suit was instituted.

The corporate authorities were authorized to assess the inhabitants and all property within the actual bounds of the town for all the charges of repairing the streets, and other matters of municipal expense. They were empowered to erect workhouses, houses of correction, prisons and other public buildings, and to pass all necessary ordinances for the good government of the town. They were to have two market days in each week, and appoint a clerk of the market, "who shall have assize of bread, wine, wood and other things," and perform all the duties of Clerk of the Market. The market days were fixed by law on Wednesdays and Saturdays. It was also provided in the charter that if any person elected to an office failed or refused to serve, he was to be fined. The fines were regulated as follows: "For a Mayor-elect, fifty pounds; for the Recorder, forty pounds; for any Alderman, thirty pounds; for any Common Councilman, twenty-five pounds; for the City Sergeant, one hundred pounds; for the Constable, fifty pounds; for the Clerk of the Hustings Court and the Clerk of the Market, each fifty pounds; the Surveyor of Streets or Roads, each thirty pounds." These several fines were to be imposed by the hustings court, and "to be levied by execution against the goods and chattles of the offender."

The charter also provided that in case of "misconduct in the office of Mayor, Recorder, Aldermen or Common Councilmen, or either of them, the others, being seven at least, shall have power to remove the offenders," and in case the other officers were guilty of misconduct, the power appointing them was clothed with the authority of revoking the appointment. It was provided that if the office of Mayor should become vacant, the Recorder was to succeed to the office, the oldest Alderman was to become Recorder, and "so on according to priority."

It was further provided "that all the property, real and personal, now held and possessed by the trustees of the said town of Fredericksburg, in law or equity, or in trust, for the use and benefit of the inhabitants thereof, and particularly the charity donation of Archibald McPherson, deceased, now vested in the trustees of said town in trust, for the education of poor children, shall be and the same are hereby transferred and vested in the Mayor and Commonalty of said town, to and for the same uses, intents and purposes as the trustees of the town now hold the same."

At the session of the Legislature in 1782 the charter of the town was amended and the jurisdiction of the hustings court was extended one mile without and around the former limits of the town on the south side of the Rappahannock river, and made a court of record and as such was authorized to receive probate of wills and deeds and grant administrations in as full and ample manner as the county courts could or might do. But no will was to be admitted

"Rising Sun Tavern," kept by Gen. Geo. Weedon prior to 1775; now the property of the A. P. of V. A.
(See page 148)

Mary Washington Monument, erected by the Women of America; Wm. J. Crawford, architect.
(See page 157)

to proof and no administration was to be granted unless the parties were citizens and residents of the town at the time of their death, and no deeds for conveyance of land were to be admitted to record unless the lands conveyed lay within the limits of the corporation. The court was empowered and authorized to appoint a person skilled in the law to prosecute for the Commonwealth and pay him a reasonable salary for his services, and when the Attorney for the Commonwealth was appointed for the town, it was to be exempt from paying any part of the salary of the Attorney for the Commonwealth of Spotsylvania county.

RAPID GROWTH OF THE TOWN.

On the petition of sixty-four of the leading citizens of the town, property owners and tax payers, complaining that certain provisions and requirements of the original charter of the town, granted in 1727, had not been enforced by the Council and complied with by lot owners, the Common Council, in 1782, passed an order which resulted in great benefit to the town in the way of improving vacant lots, erecting buildings and furnishing permanent homes for artisans, mechanics and laboring men. In the memorial submitted to the Council, these property owners complained of "being frequently subjected to the payment of many heavy Taxes and charges for the general benefit and improvement of the said Town of which many proprietors of unimproved Lotts pay no part, although their property is thereby daily rendered more valuable; That the proprietors of said Lotts, although wealthy, will neither build on them, nor sell to those who would, unless for exorbitant prices, by means whereof Rents are high and many useful tradesmen are prevented from residing in the said Town, to remedy which your petitioners pray that you, as Guardians of the said Corporation, will take into your consideration an Act of Assembly, passed in the year of our Lord One thousand, seven hundred and twenty seven, entitled an Act for erecting a Town in each of the counties of Spotsylvania and King George* or so much of the

---

* The town referred to in the county of King George is the town of Falmouth, on the opposite side of the river, and a mile and a half above Fredericksburg. The act that made Fredericksburg a town also gave Falmouth a legal existence. At the time of the passage of the act that territory belonged to King George county, but now to Stafford county.

said Act as may relate to the said Town of Fredericksburg. A due execution of said Law, your petitioners Conceive, will be productive of many real and very essential advantages to the said corporation; by encouraging the peopling of it and increasing its Trade and Navigation. Your petitioners do not wish that any immediate advantage may be taken of failures or defaults already heretofore suffered, by noncompliance with the above mentioned Act, but that Public notice may be given to the proprietors of such unimproved Lotts that a strict execution of the above mentioned Act of Assembly will be observed with all such as shall, in future, fail to perform, fulfil and comply with the rules and directions therein set forth."

In consideration of the complaints of these citizens and the wise suggestions made in their communication, as well as the requirements of the act referred to, the Council ordered "that notice be given to the Proprietors of unimproved Lotts within this corporation, by advertisement in the Public News Papers, that they immediately pay up the Taxes due on said Lotts within this Town and that they be informed that they must build on their unimproved Lotts, agreeable to the Act of Assembly, passed in One thousand seven hundred and Twenty-seven, for establishing a Town in the County of Spotsylvania, otherwise the Lotts will be sold agreeble to the said Act."

In consequence of the enforcement of this order of the Common Council, both the taxable values, and the inhabitants of the town, increased rapidly. Instead of an empty treasury, as the town then had, and the necessity it found itself under of appealing to the public for subscriptions for money with which to repair and enlarge the church, to repair the market house, the courthouse and jail, so they could be used, the town soon had money for ordinary purposes, and also for repairing the public buildings, many of which had been used during the war by the soldiers of General Washington's army, leaving a good balance in the treasury, after the work was done. Nor was that all; in 1791, under the "Domestic Loan Act" of Congress, the town loaned to the general government $3,500. This loan was evidenced by four certificates, issued by the

History of Fredericksburg, Virginia 55

"Loan office" of the Government in Washington and are duly recorded in the record book of the Common Council.

METHODS OF PUNISHMENT.

It may be interesting to note that in the olden times there were other methods resorted to for punishing criminals besides fines, jails and penitentiaries, which are not used in this day and time. The Common Council, in 1785, passed a resolution ordering Sergeant John Richards to "erect immediately a whipping post, stocks and ducking stool." The whipping post was used mainly for the slaves who were guilty of small infractions of the law, but for aggravated offences, the penalty was "thirty-nine lashes on his bare back, well laid on," to which was added "burning in the left hand, in the presence of the court." The whipping post is said to have been used for habitual persistent absence from church, but it was very seldom used for that purpose, and never in Fredericksburg so far as we have discovered from the records.

The stocks were used to punish white persons for petty offences, such as vagrancy, trespassing and similar infractions of the law. The stocks consisted of a frame of timber, with holes in which the ankles and wrists of the offenders were confined. The stocks were erected in the public square and it is said the passers-by, and those who had gathered around them, through curiosity, would taunt and jeer at the criminals thus confined for punishment.

The ducking stool was used for punishing common scolds, refractory women and dishonest tradesmen, especially brewers and bakers. The ducking stool for Fredericksburg was erected on the bank of the Rappahannock river, at the foot of Wolfe street, near where the old Stafford bridge spanned the river. There are several of our old citizens now living who remember when it was in use, and when it was dispensed with, nearly seventy years ago. A "ducking" always brought together a large crowd, most of whom were rude and disorderly, and jeers at and ridicule of the party "ducked" would rend the air, while the sentence of the court was being carried out. It is said that some of the "scolding women," as they would emerge from the water would send forth volumes of abuse at the disorderly crowd, while the officer waited for the next bath, and this was kept up until the order of the court was fully executed. It seemed to be the wish of the authorities that the whole population would turn out and witness these different modes of punishment, with the hope that it would deter others from committing similar offences.

CHAPTER V

The Lease of the Market-House Lots—The First Serious Fire—Fredericksburg an Important Center—An Act Concerning Elections—Half of the Town Destroyed by Fire—Fredericksburg an Important Postal Point—How the Mails were Carried—A Congressional Investigation—Amendatory Act of 1821—The Great Fire of 1822—The Trade of the Town—Contagious Diseases—The Town in 1841—Acts of Extension, 1851, 1852, 1858, 1861, &c.

In the year 1789 an enactment was passed by the Legislature empowering the Mayor and Commonalty of the town of Fredericksburg to lease for three lives, or twenty-one years, such unimproved parts of the market-house lots as to them shall seem most proper, and apply the rents arising therefrom for the benefit of the corporation. In the same year an act was passed authorizing the Trustees of the Fredericksburg Academy to raise, by way of lottery, the sum of four thousand pounds to defray the expenses of erecting a building on the academy lands for the purpose of accommodating the professors and the rapidly increasing number of students. We could not learn the result of this latter scheme.

THE FIRST SERIOUS FIRE.

In 1799 the first serious fire the town ever had occurred. It took place in the night time and quite a number of houses were destroyed. By many persons it was supposed to have been the work of an incendiary, but others believed that it was caused by a "wooden chimney or a stove pipe, run through a window or through the side of a wooden house, without being properly protected." The Council decided to meet both views, and offered five hundred dollars for the arrest and conviction of the incendiary, and issued an emphatic condemnation against wooden chimneys and stove pipes projecting through windows or the sides of houses without having them "fire proof." This nuisance was thereby abated.

FREDERICKSBURG AN IMPORTANT CENTER.

As early as 1796 Fredericksburg was an important commercial center, and manufactories of various kinds were in operation. Iron works and mills and other industries were successfully prosecuted, and the trade of the town, in the general merchandise department, was in the hands of public-spirited, energetic merchants; and it would no doubt surprise the merchants of the present day to read the advertisements and note the extent and variety of stocks of goods kept here at that period. The growth and development of the trade was gradual and decided in all departments, the leading article being tobacco, which up to and during the War of 1812 and 1814, was increased heavily and necessitated the employment of vessels of great tonnage to carry it. And, though strange as it may appear to our present population, in those days of prosperity in manufactories, farms and workshops, and when nearly all merchandise and supplies reached our town in said vessels, large three-masted ships were moored at our wharves; and, until large cities sprang up along the coast, that diverted trade by reason of railroad transportation, our leading merchants carried on a direct trade with the West India Islands, as well as with many of the European countries. Our wharves then were a scene of busy activity and the river was crowded with vessels from all quarters of the country.

AN ACT CONCERNING ELECTIONS.

In 1806 an act of the Legislature was passed providing that on the next annual election day for members of the "Common Hall of the Town," which term was used to denote the Common Council, a Mayor and Recorder and eight persons should be elected by ballot to act as Justices of the Peace for the town, who should "continue in office during good behavior." Three of these justices were empowered to hold a hustings court, except in cases of the examination or trial of free persons or slaves charged with felonies, in which case five of the eight justices were necessary to constitute the court. This court had the same power and jurisdiction that the hustings court had under the act of 1781, but the members were ineligible for the Common Council and they had no power to lay a tax for the support of a night watch.

At this election the voters were also to elect by ballot twelve persons as members of the Common Council of the town, who were to continue in office for one year and until their successors should be elected and qualified. The powers of the Common Council should be the same as had been previously conferred upon the Mayor, Recorder, Aldermen and Common Council of the town "in Common Hall assembled." The Common Council, at their first meeting, were to elect one of their number to the office of Mayor and another to the office of Recorder. It was the duty of the Mayor to preside over the deliberations of the body, and, in his absence, the Recorder was to discharge that duty. The Mayor, or in his absence, the Recorder, or any two members of the Council, could call a meeting of the body, but it required seven members present to constitute a quorum. After the Council assembled in the first meeting after the election of the members, and elected the proper officers, the body then consisting of the Mayor, Recorder and the other ten members elected as common councilmen, constituted the "Common Hall" of the town, and all ordinances were adopted by that body.

HALF OF THE TOWN DESTROYED BY FIRE.

In the year 1807 Fredericksburg was visited by a terrible conflagration which destroyed nearly one-half of the town. It was in October of that year, when the town was almost depopulated, the citizens, old and young, having left their homes to attend and witness the horse racing just below town, on "Willis's Field" farm. The fire broke out in the dwelling house of Mr. Stannard, which was located on the lot where the residence of Mr. George W. Shepherd now stands, on the north corner of Princess Ann and Lewis streets. A high wind prevailed at the time, the house was inflammable, the weather very dry, and in a short time the fire swept down Main street, the flames leaping from house to house to Henderson's store, on the south corner of Main and Amelia streets; thence down both sides of Main to George street, destroying every building in its track except Henderson's corner, which alone escaped destruction. The Bank of Virginia, which stood on the spot where Shiloh Baptist church (old site) now stands, on Water street, although more than a quarter of a mile from where the fire originated, was the second house to take fire and was entirely consumed. Mr. Stannard, at whose residence the fire started, was lying a corpse in the house at the time of the fire, and his remains were rescued from the flames with great difficulty.

Preparations to rebuild the burnt district were at once commenced, and buildings of a more substantial character took the places of those destroyed and prosperity again smiled upon the town. Yet strange to say the square on the west side of Main street, from Lewis to Amelia, then in the business part of the town, and now in the residential part, although before the fire was lined with buildings, was without a building until some five years ago. A tool chest, saved from destruction in this fire, by the debris of the building falling upon it and covering it up, and which escaped the destruction wrought in town by the Federal soldiers in December, 1862, is now in the possession of Police Officer Charles A. Gore. It was the property of his grandfather, Jacob Gore, who had been working at Mr. Stannard's a few days before the fire occurred and left it there temporarily.

FREDERICKSBURG AN IMPORTANT POSTAL POINT.

Fredericksburg, as early as 1820, was a very important point for mail distribution, and the mail matter of not less than five States was assorted here and sent on to its destination. About the breaking out of the War of 1812 mail matter to Fredericksburg rapidly increased, and continued to increase, for several years, which necessitated a change in the method of transporting the mails from Washington, an increase of pay, and finally scandalous reports were put in circulation which resulted in a congressional investigation.

A paper on this investigation, prepared by Henry Castle, Esq., Auditor, from the records in the Postoffice department, and kindly furnished us, will prove interesting.

"The year 1820 had arrived; James Monroe was President and

Return J. Meiggs, Jr., of Ohio, was Postmaster General. There were then over three thousand post offices, and the revenues had increased to $1,000,000 per annum, a sum considerable in excess of the expenditures, a feature which seldom characterized the service after that date. It appears from the records that vague rumors of certain irregularities had been afloat throughout the country and in the 'public prints' for some time, and that they finally assumed such a tangible shape that a resolution was introduced into the United States Congress providing for an investigation of the charges.

"A committee of the House of Representatives, of which Hon. Elisha Phelps was chairman, proceeded in accordance with instructions of the House, in due form and great deliberation, to investigate the general conduct of the office under Postmaster General Meiggs, and especially the features which had been subjected to more immediate criticism. Mr. Meiggs's service, as Postmaster General, extended from March 17th 1814, to June 26th 1823, a period of more than nine years. The gravest of the charges made against his administration were substantially as follows:

"First. That he had introduced an irregular financial system which had led to serious losses of the public funds.

"Second. That he had illegally and improperly increased the compensation of certain contractors for carrying the mail.

"With slow formality and tedious reiteration of assurances of distinguished consideration, the solemn committee of the Honorable House of Representatives, and the Honorable Postmaster General, finally reached a point where questions were asked and answered and a tolerably clear understanding of what had really occurred may be gained. The statement of the Postmaster General, divested of all its superfluities and reduced to its simplest form, showed no dereliction in either case, but read at this late day gives an almost ludicrous insight into the diminutive transactions which then sufficed for this great, free and intelligent Republic.

"Postmaster General Meiggs's answer to the second charge was perhaps even more interestingly significant as a revelation of the day of small things. He admitted that he had increased the compensation of contractors for carrying the mails, but justified his action on the ground of an imperious necessity.

"The case as he explained it was this: His predecessor in office had about the year 1813, let a contract to certain parties for transporting mail from the Seat of Government at Washington to Fredericksburg, Virginia, a distance of seventy miles. This great mail route, which would now be termed a trunk line, carried substantially the mail for the five States of Virginia, Tennessee, North Carolina, South Carolina and Georgia. The contract provided that these mails should be carried by stage coach in summer and, as the roads were impassable in winter, they were to be carried on horseback.

"But," says the Postmaster General, "by the increased popular interest in the war of 1812, correspondence was greatly stimulated and the circulation of the public journals was enormously increased. Consequently, it was found impracticable to transport all this heavy mail for five States, on horseback from Washington to Fredericksburg; therefore contractors were authorized to place a sulky, or curricle service thereon and the remuneration was increased accordingly.

"This explanation was apparently satisfactory to the Honorable Committee as it certainly appears very reasonable on its face, and will appeal to man's inherent sense of justice, even in this exacting era. The final action of Congress is not contained in the records, but it was no doubt exculpatory since, as shown above, Postmaster General Meiggs, continued to discharge the duties in his high office for several years thereafter."

AMENDATORY ACT OF 1821.

Under the previous acts of the Legislature, extending the limits of the town and providing for laying out streets, and the amendments thereto, it was claimed that mistakes had occurred and irregularities had resulted therefrom. In order to correct these mistakes, and provide for the better government of the town, an amendatory act was passed by the Legislature in the year 1821. In that act the Common Council was authorized and empowered to

The St. George's Episcopal Church.
(See page 203)

The Presbyterian Memorial Chapel.
(See page 208)

elect the Mayor from their own number or from the body of the citizens, and in case he was elected from the Council, thus creating a vacancy in that body, it was to be filled by the Council. Under this act the Mayor was eligible to reëlection from year to year as long as the Council was pleased to elect him, was made custodian of the corporation seal, and was to keep an office in the town where he should transact the public business, and where the citizens could call upon him and present any grievance or complaint they might have to make.

When the hustings court was not in session the Mayor was to act as a Justice of the Peace and superintend and control the police and night watch. He was to qualify in ten days after his election, and was to preside at the sittings of the hustings court; and in his absence the Recorder, upon whom all the powers and authority of the Mayor were conferred, was authorized to perform his duties. The Common Council had to regulate and fix the salary of the Mayor, which could not be increased or diminished during his term of office. The same act extended the jurisdiction of the hustings court to high water mark on the Stafford side of the Rappahannock river, and exempted the citizens of the town from the assessment and payment of all taxes and levies to Spotsylvania county, to which they were subject under the former laws.

By the provisions of the act of 1821 the Common Council was authorized to assess and levy a tax on the inhabitants of, and property within, the town for the purpose of repairing and keeping in order the streets and alleys and for other purposes and charges as to them might seem right and proper, and for the improvement, convenience and well being of the town. They were authorized to provide a night watch for the protection of the town and for the "better execution of this duty the power and authority, now exercised by field officers of the militia concerning patrols, shall hereafter be vested in and exercised by the said Mayor, Recorder and Common Council over the militia of the said town," and the militia of the town were, by the same act, exempted from patrol duty beyond the city limits.

In order to correct defects in laying out streets under the former acts, by this act a Commission, consisting of John W. Green, John Mundell, George Cox, Silas Wood and David Briggs, was appointed to survey and locate the streets of the town according to existing laws and authentic ancient surveys. This Commission was to locate the streets by metes and bounds, making such alterations as its members might think expedient, with the consent of the proprietors of lots effected by such alterations, but not otherwise. It was also required to mark the boundaries of the streets by stones or otherwise, which were to be designated on the map of the town made by it. These Commissioners were to report their plan, with explanatory notes, to the Common Council, and if approved by that body it was to be taken as the authentic plan of the town.

But in making this survey of the streets it was especially provided that if a house should be found, in whole or in part, in the street, it was not to be considered a nuisance or an illegal obstruction of the street, but if such building should perish, or in any manner be destroyed, it was not to be rebuilt so as to encroach upon or obstruct the street.

THE GREAT FIRE OF 1822.

After the great conflagration of 1807, a regular and decided increase in population is noted with a marked improvement in local trade. So things progressed with no unusual or startling calamities to disturb the usual serenity of a prosperous town—not bustling, but active—until the year 1822, when the quiet was disturbed by another serious conflagration. It was not as disastrous as its predecessor was, but it was of such a character as to cause great loss of property, and to retard, to a very great extent, the general prosperity of the town. This fire originated at the corner of Main and George streets, where Mr. Thomas N. Brent's dry goods store now stands, and, curious enough, just where the great fire of 1807 was checked. It was then known as Wellford's corner, because Mr. C. C. Wellford, for a great many years, kept store there. From that corner the fire made its way down Main street totally destroying every building on that side of the street from there to Hanover street, which square was then known as the "Commercial Block," because of the large trade carried on there.

With the energy and enterprise so characteristic of the citizens of the town at that day, steps were at once taken to rebuild the burnt district. Soon the street was almost blocked up with building material, laborers were busily at work, clearing away the debris and preparing the foundations for the new buildings. Carpenters and brick masons were in great demand and large numbers flocked to the town from neighboring cities and villages. That part of the town was soon a busy scene and the music of the hammer, the saw and the trowel greeted the ear from early morning until late in the afternoon. And there were soon erected, with an occasional exception, the substantial block of brick buildings which now stand as monuments to the good judgment and excellent workmanship of that early day. The work of rebuilding was speedy and complete, and the character of the new buildings was an improvement upon the old ones they replaced. With the rebuilding of that portion of the town, and the resumption of business by the burnt-out merchants, came an unusual degree of prosperity, and for a long period the general peace and happiness of the people were undisturbed.

THE TRADE OF THE TOWN.

At this time the trade of the town was chiefly of a local character, except the products of the country extending even beyond the Blue Ridge mountains, as from the early years of the town, were brought to market in wagons, and it was no uncommon sight to see daily as many as fifty or sixty four and six-horse teams here at one time from that part of the country. The merchants were men of exalted character and fine business capacity, and the amount of business transacted was, considering the times and circumstances, simply enormous.

CONTAGIOUS DISEASES.

To the credit of the authorities of the town it can be truthfully said that, in all the past, they have been very watchful of and solicitous for the health of the people. At all times, upon reports, or even rumors, that contagious or infectious diseases were prevailing in contiguous communities, they were on the alert, taking every precaution to prevent their introduction here, and it may be said to their credit that such strict observance and enforcement of the laws of health, and temporary quarantines at the proper time, have prevented all kinds of epidemics in the past history of the town.

Before the first of the nineteenth century, in 1790, the people of the town were very much excited about the small pox. It was raging in Philadelphia as an epidemic, and the large trade carried on between the two places, altogether by water, made it necessary that numerous vessels should bear the merchandise. In order to prevent the small pox from reaching this place a strict quarantine was established at the mouth of Hazel Run, just below town, and a hospital was located at Sligo. Dr. Brooke and Dr. Ker, two skillful physicians of the town, agreed to attend the sick at the hospital without charge, whether sailors or citizens. The wise precaution taken in establishing the quarantine prevented any case from reaching the town, to the great relief of the citizens generally. In 1792 the same disease broke out in Baltimore and a quarantine was again established at Hazel Run and a hospital at Sligo. The citizens were greatly alarmed, fearing its introduction here either by land or water. The greatest precautions were taken by the health officers, who were nobly assisted by the town authorities, and the disease was kept out as it had been two years before, not a single case having made its appearance in the place.

In 1833, it is said by old citizens, a remarkable case of either fright or disease occurred in Fredericksburg, which proved fatal. In that year several parts of the United States were visited and scourged by the Asiatic cholera. The country generally was in great terror, and Fredericksburg came in for her share of excitement. In fact, she may have been more alarmed than other places which were as far removed from the seat of the scourge, because of a prediction that had previously been made, and which made its impression on many people. Rev. Lorenzo Dow, an able, but eccentric, itinerant Methodist minister, when on a visit to the town the year previous to the scourge, it was reported had predicted the appearance of cholera in Fredericksburg. Some people believed the disease would come because Mr. Dow had predicted it, and the excitement ran high, especially among those who believed the prophecy. A Mr. Shelton became dreadfully alarmed and whether from fright or from actually contracting the disease, died in the month of June and the cause of his death was pronounced sporadic or accidental cholera. His was the only case then, and to this day there has been no other, Fredericksburg having enjoyed singular and perfect immunity from epidemics of all kinds.

THE TOWN IN THE YEAR 1841.

In describing the town in 1841, an intelligent visitor says "Fredericksburg is regularly laid out and compactly built; many of its buildings are brick. The principal public buildings are a courthouse, clerk's office, a jail, a market-house, an orphan asylum, one Episcopal, one Presbyterian, one Methodist, one Baptist and one Reform Baptist church. The town also contains two banks and one male and one female seminary of the higher class. It is supplied with water from the river* by subterraneous pipes and is governed by a Mayor and Common Council. A canal, extending from the town to Fox's mill, a point on the Rappahannock, thirty-five miles above, has been commenced and partly completed.

"Fredericksburg enjoys considerable trade, chiefly in grain, flour, tobacco, maize, etc., and considerable quantities of gold are exported. Its exports have been computed at over four millions of dollars annually. The falls of the Rappahannock, in the vicinity, afford good water power. There were in 1840, by the United States statistics, seventy-three stores, with a capital of $376,961; two tanneries, paints, drugs, etc., with a capital of $37,000; one grist mill, two printing offices, four semi-weekly newspapers; capital in manufactures, $141,200; five academies, with 256 students, and seven schools, with 156 scholars. The population in 1830, whites, 1,797; slaves, 1,124; free blacks, 387—total, 3,308. The population in 1840 was 3,974."

But the commercial prosperity of the town even in 1840 was not equal to its advantages, but it steadily grew and prospered during the next decade. The completion of a canal, extending from the town to a point on the Rappahannock river, a distance of forty

---

* The water came from two springs—Poplar spring and Smith's spring.

miles, railroad facilities and river navigation by sail vessels and steamboats, greatly enlarged her commercial advantages and increased her export trade, and the beginning of the year 1850 found her enjoying a degree of material prosperity, presaging a glorious commercial future. Commencing the year 1850 under circumstances so encouraging, the next decade was expected to exceed in all departments of trade the preceding one.

The failure to build a railroad through the section of country from which the bulk of our trade was drawn, and the substitution therefor of a plank road, with the building of the Orange and Alexandria railroad, now the Western, and the advance of the Baltimore and Ohio railroad along the upper line of the Shenandoah Valley, greatly injured the trade of Fredericksburg by diverting from her a large amount of produce, which was formerly brought to town in wagons, and while in 1860 the population had somewhat increased, the general trade of the town was diminished.

THE CORPORATE LIMITS EXTENDED.

In the year 1851 the Legislature passed a bill extending the limits of the town, in accordance with a plan made by Commissioners appointed by the Common Council. That extension embraced the territory we now have within the corporate limits except a portion of the Water Power Company, the survey having been made by Mr. William Slaughter, City Surveyor, in 1850, and reported to the Council by Joseph Sanford, John Minor and John Pritchard, who were appointed a committee by the Council to "enquire into the expediency of extending the limits of the said town." After making a thorough examination, this committee reported back to the body that it was both expedient and desirable that the extension should be made, which report and recommendation were adopted. To carry out this action, the Council appointed Hugh S. Scott, Wm. S. Barton, John James Chew, Joseph Sanford and John Pritchard, and they were instructed and empowered as a Commission, under the provisions of the act of the Legislature, to locate and lay out such streets in the part of the town annexed by the provisions of the bill, as they might think proper, and report back to the Council, with a full plan of their work. But it was provided that none of the new streets reported upon were to be opened unless the Council should decide it necessary, and in that event, if the owners of the lots did not relinquish their claims to the town, damages were to be paid by the Council in such sums as should be ascertained by three disinterested freeholders of Spotsylvania county, who should be appointed by the county court of said county for that purpose. The Commission performed the duties assigned them by the Council, and laid out the new portion of the town into streets, giving a name to each, but many of them were never opened, as they were not needed, and remain closed to this day.

The same act made it unnecessary for either the Mayor or Recorder of the town to be present and preside over the hustings court, but made it lawful for any three Justices of the Corporation to hold the court, except, as in the former act, where parties were to be examined or tried for felonies it required that five Justices should be present and preside. In consequence of this provision the court would convene with five Justices when felony cases were to be considered, and after they were disposed of, two of them would be excused and the other three would continue the session until the business of the court was completed. These Justices were appointed by the Governor, on the recommendation of the hustings court, and were among the best citizens and most successful business men of the town, and what they lacked in a knowledge of the law, it is generally agreed they more than made up in good common sense and unyielding integrity.

In the following year, 1852, the Legislature passed another amendment to the charter of the town, extending its limits, but this amendment was only made necessary to correct an error in the section of the act of the year before, extending the corporate limits. The metes and bounds were left the same as prescribed in the act of 1851.

In 1858 an act was passed by the Legislature enabling the Council to sell real estate for delinquent taxes due the town. It authorized the authorities to sell all real estate within the corporation returned delinquent for the non-payment of taxes and interest, and to make such regulations for affecting the sale and collecting the taxes as they might deem expedient. In case the sale was not made and the taxes remained unpaid, the taxes became a lien on the property and ten per centum was charged thereon until they were paid. The act also provided that if the taxes due on real estate were paid by the tenant, who was not the owner of the property, the amount might be deducted from the rents of the same in settlement with the owner. In cases where the property was owned by non-residents, and was vacant or unimproved, and no levy could be made to satisfy the taxes, the town was authorized to take summary proceedings before any court in the State, on ten days' notice to the parties owning the delinquent property.

In 1861 another act was passed by the Legislature, extending the corporate limits of the town. This was done in order to bring certain property within the limits of the town for the purpose of city taxation, according to a previous agreement with the owners of the Fredericksburg Water Power. That agreement was that all mills and manufactories, using the water of that company for power, erected after the completion of the canal, should be liable for, and should pay, city taxes. The extension by this act is described as follows:

"Beginning at a point Sixty-seven feet North $64\frac{1}{2}$ degrees east from the northeast cornerstone of the present boundary of said town; and running thence to the Rappahannock river twelve hundred and fifty feet to a stone; thence south $58\frac{1}{2}$ degrees west, four hundred and sixty-six feet to a stone; thence south $13\frac{1}{2}$ degrees west, three hundred and seventy feet to a stone; thence south $35\frac{1}{2}$ degrees east, six hundred and eight feet to a stone; thence south $38\frac{3}{4}$ degrees, two hundred and eighty-five feet to a stone; thence south $25\frac{1}{4}$ degrees east, one hundred and forty-four feet to a stone in a line with the present corporation line; thence with said line north $64\frac{1}{2}$ degrees east six hundred and eighty feet to the point of beginning, and particularly set out and described in a survey and plat made by Carter M. Braxton, dated the 23rd day of January, 1861, and deposited in the clerk's office of the corporation court of said town."

CHAPTER VI

The War Clouds Gathering—Fredericksburg in the Confederacy—Troops Raised and Equipped—The Surrender of the Town to the Federal Authorities—Arrested and Held as Hostages—Citizens Flee from their Homes—The Bombardment of the Town, &c.

Nothwithstanding the fact that Fredericksburg had been growing for so many years, and the further fact that she had enjoyed the prosperity which is claimed for her, and of which we have written, the town had attained at this time only to the moderate proportions of a population of about five thousand inhabitants. But it was a delightful place, nevertheless, with a salubrious climate, good water, charming society, picturesque surroundings and cheapness of living, and had about it a quiet and chastened dignity of age and respectability, both attractive and impressive. Such was Fredericksburg when the storm-cloud of war burst upon her in 1861.

FREDERICKSBURG IN THE CONFEDERACY.

We shall not attempt in these pages to fully portray the scenes enacted in the town, or narrate the part played by Fredericksburg in that terrible war. A true portrayal and narration of them is beyond the power of the tongue of the finished orator, the pen of the most gifted writer or the brush of the most skilled artist. No one can know them save those who endured them and were a part and parcel of them, and even they are unable to describe them with all of their horrible, bloody and destructive realities. It would take a pen almost inspired to truthfully describe the fiery scenes, the devastation, the trials, the privations, the sufferings of body and mind and the heroism of the inhabitants, who were then in town, in the terrible ordeal through which they passed, and the fortitude with which they stood the test.

A great change was now about to take place. The quiet of the staid and sober town was about to be broken by the sound of the drum and the tramp of armed men. The activity of commerce had ceased, a spirit of patriotism prevailed; and this patriotism was not demonstrative only, it was deep and real, and was afterwards sealed by the best blood of the town.

TROOPS RAISED AND EQUIPPED.

There was never any doubt as to the part the citizens of Fredericksburg would take in the war. It is true the town was always conservative and loyal to the government; it had sent a Union man to the State Convention, which was to consider and pass upon the question of union or disunion; he had received almost a two-thirds vote of the qualified voters of the town, but all this was done with a strong hope that the political differences of the two great sections of the country—North and South—could and would be settled without a separation. When it was ascertained that such a settlement could not be had, and when that assurance was followed by a call on the States from President Lincoln for seventy-five thousand troops to coerce the seceded Southern States back into the Union and that Virginia was expected to furnish her quota of that number, the sentiment of the entire population changed, and the most ardent Union men, with few exceptions, became strong sympathizers of the Southern movement and were ready to take up arms in defence of the South. The Constitutional Convention, that up to that time was supposed to be against the adoption of the ordinance of secession, rapidly changed front, and when the ordinance was submitted to a vote it was passed by a large majority, the delegate from Fredericksburg, Hon. John L. Marye, Sr., voting for its adoption.

The two volunteer militia companies, which had been in existence in town for many years, became the nucleus around which was formed the Thirtieth Regiment of Virginia Volunteers. This regiment, commanded successively by Colonel Milton Cary, Colonel Archibald Harrison and Colonel Robert S. Chew, immediately entered upon active duty and performed good service throughout the war. The Fredericksburg artillery, under Captain Carter M. Braxton, was organized at the beginning of the war, and under its gallant commanders, Captain Carter M. Braxton, Captain Ed-

Hon. Montgomery Slaughter,
"The War Mayor" of Fredericksburg.
(See page 74)

ward Marye and Captain John G. Pollock, greatly distinguished itself.

It is claimed that this company fired the first shot at the battle of Fredericksburg and was honored with a like distinction at Gettysburg; and yet a greater honor awaited this heroic band than either of these or the two combined, which each member and his descendants will ever cherish with pride. Its members claim to have fired the last gun at Appomattox on the 9th of April, 1865, the day on which General Robert E. Lee surrendered the Army of Northern Virginia to General U. S. Grant, where and when the Star of the Southern Confederacy went down, never, never more to rise. All honor to such brave and heroic men! The following is a correct list of the members of the Fredericksburg artillery at the time of the surrender, furnished by a member of the company, most of whom are now living:

Captain John G. Pollock, Lieutenant A. W. Johnson, Lieutenant Clinton Southworth, Sergeant Henry G. Chesley, Sergeant L. T. Bunnell, Sergeant James Taylor, Sergeant Charles B. Fleet, Gunner M. C. Hall, Gunner Samuel H. Thorburn, Picket Sergeant J. L. Marye, Jr., H. P. Martin, Quarter Master Sergeant; Gunner J. R. Ferneyhough, Gunner P. V. D. Conway, Gunner W. F. Gordon, Gunner R. W. McGuire, Harrison Southworth, Guidon; Privates W. A. Anthony, John Scott Berry, John J. Berrey, Wm. E. Bradley, J. A. Bowler, Oscar Berry, James E. Berrey, Wm. Bowler, Robert C. Beale, J. H. Butzner, Henry Berry, C. B. Cason, L. P. Carter, Walter Carter, W. M. Chewning, J. S. Cannon, W. S. Chartters, Jacob Crowder, G. W. Clarke, J. H. Clarke, S. H. Crockford, A. P. Carneal, Charles Donahoe, James Donahoe, W. B. Dickinson, Elijah E. Fines, R. C. Fitzhugh, M. A. Ferneyhough, Duff Green (of Brooke), J. T. Goolrick, R. C. Grymes, J. R. Gouldman, Landon Gallahan, Henry Gallahan, John M. Garrett, James W. Hogans, George F. Harrison, George M. Harrison, John E. Harrison, Robert Haislip, Matthew Hudson, John S. Johnson, W. Stanfield Jones, J. Chester Jones, C. W. Jenkins, John T. Knight, David Corbin Ker, Hubbard M. Long, Charles Lyell, Alfred J. Marye, J. W. McWhirt, J. A. Marye, A. Stewart Marye, J. W.

Mitchell, Frank A. Maddox, Thomas E. Maddex, Charles W. Manley, John McKay, W. Nelson Marye, George Oakes, M. B. Pollock, George B. Pearson, Joseph S. Payne, Harvey W. Proctor, Anthony Patton, John T. Roberts, Henry Robinson, W. T. Robinson, John D. Smith,* R. B. Semple, Warner L. Sisson, Lawrence Sanford, Charles H. Scott, John Sullivan, Peter Sullivan, H. Cabell Tabb, A. Byrd Waller, H. H. Wallace, Arthur Wallace, George Willis.

Many of the young men at the first opportunity entered the various branches of the service—the cavalry, infantry, navy, marine, and other positions necessary and honorable—where they served their country well and faithfully, and in many cases with distinguished ability. So rapid were these enlistments, that in less than twelve months the town was almost stripped of her youths and arms-bearing men, and of her former population—those remaining at home were the older men, the women and a few colored people.

THE SURRENDER OF THE TOWN TO THE FEDERAL AUTHORITIES.

Gen. McDowell's Forces Arrive.

On the 19th of April, 1862, the town first fell into the hands of the Federal Army. On that day a meeting of the Common Council was held, and a committee, consisting of Mayor Slaughter, Wm. A. Little, Esq., Thomas B. Barton, Esq., Dr. J. Gordon Wallace, Rev. William F. Broaddus, D. D., and Gov. John L. Marye, Jr., three members on the part of the Common Council and three representing the citizens, was appointed to confer with the commanding officer of the United States forces, relative to the surrender of the town. They were instructed to inform him that inasmuch as the forces of the Confederate States had evacuated the town no resistance would be made to its occupation by the United States troops, and to ask such protection for persons and property as was consistent with the rules of civilized warfare. They were also instructed to inform the Commanding General "that the population of this town have been in the past, and are now, in conviction and senti-

---

* Died at Crystal Springs, Miss., March 1, 1900.

ment, loyal to the existing government of the State of Virginia and Confederate States.". This was an honest and frank statement, made by the Common Council of the threatened town to the Commanding General of the invading army, and there can be no doubt that this honest acknowledgment won the friendship and respect of the commandant of the post and saved much property from destruction and many of the inhabitants from indignities on the part of the garrison.

The United States forces took possession of the Stafford hills, which commanded the town, on the 19th day of April. The destruction of the bridges connecting the town with the Stafford shore delayed the actual presence of the troops in town for several days, and it was not until the morning of the 27th that General Marsena R. Patrick established his headquarters and took provost command of the town. Unlike many of the subordinate commanders Gen. Patrick was considered a generous man and a kind, humane officer, and many of the citizens who were at their homes, while he was here in command, unite in bearing testimony, that under his government military rule in Fredericksburg was kindly exercised and the people were not oppressed, and not a few of them conceived a sincere respect for his character, and to this day his acts of kindness and thoughtful consideration are gratefully referred to by them.

This state of things continued until after the disastrous result to General George B. McClellan's army in the Seven Days' battles around Richmond. After those engagements General McClellan was superseded in the command of the Army of the Potomac by General John Pope. General Pope was from the Western Army, and upon taking command of the army in Virginia issued a high-sounding, pompous order in which he belittled the valor of the Confederate soldiers of the west, asserting he had "only seen the backs of the enemy," and his purpose in coming to this army was to lead it to victory and success. In that order he declared that he did not want to hear such phrases as "taking strong positions and holding them," "lines of retreat" and "bases of supplies," which he was told was common in the army. He declared that the glory of the soldier was in pushing the enemy and studying the lines of his retreat, which he then proposed to do.

He announced his purpose to subsist the invading army by enforced supplies from his enemies, and, in order to prepare the world and give it some idea of his rapid movements and brilliant feats, issued orders from "headquarters in the saddle." This unique order, full as it was of boastings of what he had done and what he proposed to do, failed to frighten the Confederate commanders, as General Pope, no doubt, thought it would do. On the contrary, without loss of time they concentrated their forces, gave him battle and the Federal commander was ingloriously driven from the field, with great loss of men, arms and supplies. And so in less than sixty days from the time he took command of the army he was relieved by General McClellan, whom he superseded, having lost every engagement fought during the time. His advance through the counties of Fauquier and Culpeper to Fredericksburg, when he took command of the army, caused great consternation because of his unreasonable and cruel exactions. Many private citizens, who had never entered the Confederate service, were arrested upon their refusal to take the oath of allegiance to the United States government, and were ruthlessly dragged from their homes and confined in Northern prisons.

GEN. POPE TAKES POSSESSION OF THE TOWN—HELD AS HOSTAGES.

Finally the power of this pompous commander reached Fredericksburg, and many of her citizens shared the fate of the unfortunate citizens of Fauquier and Culpeper counties. By General Pope's order nineteen of our most prominent and highly esteemed citizens were arrested and sent to Washington, where they were incarcerated in Old Capitol prison. These men were arrested in retaliation for the arrest of two Union men by the Confederate authorities—Major Charles Williams, of Fredericksburg, and Mr. Wardwell, of Richmond—and confined in prison at Richmond. Major Williams was a native of Fredericksburg and died here several years after the war, and Mr. Wardwell, we are informed was a northern man and was appointed superintendent of the penitentiary when Virginia was made "Military District No. 1, with headquarters at Richmond."

These nineteen gentlemen were arrested in August, 1862, and confined in Old Capitol prison until the latter part of the following September, a period of about six weeks. It will be seen from the list of the names that they were the leading citizens of the town, exempt from military service by reason, either of age or official position, and were the natural guardians of the helpless women and children who were then in town. The list is as follows:* Rev. Wm. F. Broaddus, D. D., James McGuire, Charles C. Wellford, Thomas F. Knox, Beverley T. Gill, James H. Bradley, Thomas B. Barton, Benjamin Temple, Lewis Wrenn, Michael Ames, John Coakley, John H. Roberts, John J. Berrey, Dr. James Cooke, John F. Scott, Montgomery Slaughter, George H. C. Rowe, Wm. H. Norton, Abraham Cox.

The *Christian Banner*, then published in Fredericksburg by Rev. James W. Hunnicutt, of the Free Will Baptist denomination, himself a strong Union man, and who would not have written complimentary of these gentlemen beyond their respective merits, published the following short sketches of the "Fredericksburg prisoners":

Thomas B. Barton is the oldest lawyer at the Fredericksburg bar and Attorney for the Commonwealth. He was originally an Old Line Whig and a member of the congregation of the Episcopal church.

Thomas F. Knox was a large wheat speculator and flower manufacturer, an Old Line Whig and a prominent member of the Episcopal church.

Beverley T. Gill was, for a number of years, a large merchant tailor, but for several years past had retired into private life. Was an Old Line Whig and a prominent member of the Presbyterian church.

Charles C. Wellford was an extensive dry goods merchant, the oldest in town, than whom none stood higher. Was an Old Line Whig and an elder in the Presbyterian church.

---

* This list was obtained from a diary kept by John J. Berrey while in prison.

James McGuire was one of the oldest merchants in Fredericksburg, an Old Line Whig, a prominent member of the Presbyterian church and a most excellent man.

James H. Bradley was a grocery merchant, an Old Line Whig and a deacon in the Baptist church.

Rev. William F. Broaddus, D. D., was the pastor of the Baptist church in Fredericksburg and an Old Line Whig. He conducted a female school in addition to his pastoral work.*

Montgomery Slaughter, Mayor of Fredericksburg, was a large wheat speculator and flour manufacturer, was an Old Line Whig and a member of the Episcopal church.

George H. C. Rowe was a talented jurist, a Democrat and a Douglas elector during the late presidential election and a member of the Baptist church.

---

* Some amusing incidents are related of Dr. Broaddus while a prisoner worth relating in these pages. The Doctor was an educated, polished gentleman, and quite a humorist. When he was received into prison the keeper proceeded in his usual manner to ascertain his name, age and place of nativity. When asked his name he said it was William F. Broaddus. "What does the F stand for?" asked the keeper. The Doctor replied that he did not know. "Don't know?" demanded the keeper. "I will tell you the circumstances," said the Doctor, "and let you decide for yourself. My name was William Francis Ferguson. I did not like the two F's and asked my mother to let me drop one. She consented and I dropped one, but I never could tell whether I dropped the one that stood for Francis or the one that stood for Ferguson. Now, can you tell me which one I dropped?" The keeper saw he was beaten, and demanded, "What is your age?" "I was born in the year of one," replied the Doctor. "What! Do you mean to tell me you are 1861 years old," shouted the keeper. "Not at all," said the Doctor. "Well, then, explain yourself," demanded the keeper, showing some impatience. "I was born in the year one of this century," responded the Doctor. "Where were you born?" indignantly asked the keeper. "Now, you've got me again," answered the Doctor. "That's a question I have long wanted settled, and I'll state the case and perhaps you can help me settle it. My birthplace at the time of my birth was in Culpeper county. Changes in county lines afterwards placed it in Rappahannock county. Now, if I were to tell you I was born in Culpeper, and you should go down there to inquire, you would find the place in Rappahannock. If I were to tell you I was born in Rappahannock and you were to investigate you would find that when I was born the place was in Culpeper and there was no Rappahannock county at the time. Now, will you please tell me where I was born?" The keeper passed him without further questions.

It was the habit of Dr. Broaddus to preach on Sunday mornings to his fellow prisoners, and such others as would come to hear him while the prison chaplain would hold services in another part of the prison. It is related of the superintendent of the prison, that in making the announcements for preaching he would cry out: "All who wish to hear the gospel according to Abraham Lincoln come this way; those who wish to hear it according to Jeff. Davis go over there," pointing to Dr. Broaddus and his congregation.

History of Fredericksburg, Virginia 79

John Coakley was for many years a merchant, but for several years past had retired from business, and, at the time of his arrest, was Superintendent of the Fredericksburg Aquaduct Company. He was an Old Line Whig and a very prominent member of the Episcopal church.

Benjamin Temple was a wealthy farmer, an Old Line Whig and, we believe, a member of no church, but a most excellent man.

Dr. James Cooke was a druggist, owning the largest establishment, perhaps south of the Potomac river; was an Old Line Whig and a prominent member of the Episcopal church.

John F. Scott was proprietor of the large Fredericksburg foundry and carried on an extensive business up to the time the Union troops took possession of Fredericksburg, was an Old Line Whig and a prominent member of the Episcopal church.

John H. Roberts lived off his income, was an old Line Whig and, we believe, was a member of no church.

Michael Ames was a blacksmith, an Old Line Whig and a member of no church.

John J. Berrey, formerly engaged in a large produce business, but at the time of his arrest connected with a hardware store, was an Old Line Whig and a member of no church.

Abraham Cox was a tailor, a Breckinridge Democrat and a Southern Methodist.

William H. Norton was a house carpenter, an Old Line Whig and a member of the Baptist church.

Lewis Wrenn, no particular business, an Old Line Whig and a member of the Baptist church.

After these gentlemen had been in prison some four weeks they procured a parole and permission to send Dr. Broaddus to Richmond to effect the release of Major Williams and Mr. Wardwell, that he and his friends might be liberated and permitted to return to their homes. Armed with a parole and passports, Dr. Broaddus proceeded to Richmond, where he called upon Judge Beverley R. Wellford, Jr., formally of Fredericksburg, who went with him to see Mr. Randolph, Secretary of War. After hearing the case Mr. Randolph ordered the release of the two prisoners, and

Dr. Broaddus returned to Washington with great joy, supposing that he and his fellow prisoners would be at once set at liberty. But not so. The Federal authorities changed their requirements and demanded also the release of two gentlemen by the name of Turner, who resided in Fairfax county, and were then held in a Confederate prison.

It took nearly two weeks to effect the release of these Turners, and when it was done the certificate of release, signed by General Winder, the Commandant of the post at Richmond, was rejected by the Federal authorities as evidence of the release of the prisoners, and the personal presence of the Turners was demanded in Washington before the release of the Fredericksburg party. This took time, but it was finally accomplished, and the Fredericksburgers were permitted to leave their prison pen and again "breathe the air of freedom." They were sent down the Potomac river on a steamer to Marlborough Point, from which landing they walked to town to greet their families and friends. There was great rejoicing on their return, and the whole population turned out to meet them and give them a cordial welcome. Of that party of nineteen not one of them is living to-day. The "last one to cross the river" was Mr. Abraham Cox, who died December 28, 1898, eighty-six years of age.

But the unkindness of the military authorities and their harsh treatment of our citizens, by the order of General Pope, did not cease with the arrest and incarceration of the nineteen gentlemen above mentioned. Among other things, the Federal Provost Marshal of Fredericksburg was charged with too much leniency to the citizens and was removed; Col. Scriver was falsely charged with furnishing the destitute with food, and was ordered to stop it at once, if he had done so, and not to repeat it, and the stores and places of business were closed, it was said, to prevent the citizens from obtaining supplies. General Pope's plan seems to have been, as he declared, to subsist his army as much as possible on the country and to starve the old men and women into submission to his demands. In this, however, he was not sustained by the Washington authorities, and especially by President Lincoln.

This condition of things in Fredericksburg continued only for a short time. The campaign, inaugurated by General Pope, which resulted in the Second Battle of Manassas and so disastrously to the Federal army, was speedily followed by the advance of the Confederate army into Maryland, the capture of Harper's Ferry, with General Nelson A. Miles's whole force of eleven thousand prisoners and immense military supplies, by General Thomas J. (Stonewall) Jackson, aided by General Wm. Barksdale, on the Maryland Heights, and General John B. Floyd, on the Loudoun Heights, and the fierce and bloody, but undecided, struggle between General Lee and General McClellan at Sharpsburg.

In consequence of the results of these events the Federal authorities found it necessary to recall from the line of the Rappahannock, which they were unable to hold, the forces then occupying the same, and therefore on the 21st day of August, 1862, Fredericksburg was evacuated by the Federal forces, and thus for a brief time the town was relieved from the presence and rule of the enemy until the following November, when Gen. Burnside moved against the town.

EVACUATION SCENES.

The scenes incident to the evacuation of Fredericksburg are well remembered to the present day by those who were present and witnessed them. They are indelibly impressed upon their minds and can never be forgotten, and are often related with great interest. In describing this stirring event and the reoccupation of the town in the Fall of 1862, we use the eyes of citizens, who were present and witnessed the scenes described and the words of another, who wrote of them years afterwards.* Crowds at the corners of the streets indicated that some unusual excitement prevailed, and clouds of smoke rose from the encampments on the Stafford side of the river. Everything indicated an immediate departure. The guards were drawn up in line; the horses and wagons packed at headquarters; cavalry officers rode up and down, giving orders;

---

* The scenes of the evacuation of Fredericksburg are taken principally from "The Past, Present and Future of Fredericksburg, by Rev. Robert R. Howison, LL. D., who was aided in its preparation by diaries kept by those present at the time and the recitals of other eye witnesses, besides newspaper articles, the reports of Generals in both armies and our own knowledge, being present.

company after company of pickets were led into town from different ruads and joined the regiment at the City Hall; ambulances, with the sick, moved slowly through the streets; the provost marshal and his adjutant rode by, and, in a few minutes, the command was given to march, and the infantry and cavalry marched down to the bridges, each one moving by different streets. This march was quietly made. There was no music, no drum, no voice, but the command of the officers' forward, march!

The ladies, standing in groups along the streets, found it difficult to repress their exultation. Glad to be relieved of the presence of the enemy, and to be freed from the restraints of their power; glad to be once more within Southern lines, and to be brought into communication with their own dear people; but the great gladness was that the evacuation of Fredericksburg showed that the enemy had been defeated on the upper line and could no longer hold the line of the Rappahannock river. And this gave them strong hope that Virginia might yet be free from the armies of the invader.

Several severe explosions followed the blowing up of the two bridges, and, as the bright flames seized upon and leaped along the sides and floors of the bridges, the whole horizon was illuminated. The burning continued all night. A guard was at once organized by the citizens, for the protection of the town against any stragglers or unruly persons who might chance to be prowling about.

With the departure of the Federal troops came now the desire on the part of the citizens of town and country to meet and greet each other, and also a longing to welcome the appearance of the Confederates, a sight which had so long been denied them. In this, to their great delight, they were soon to realize their wish, for on the 2nd day of September about two hundred people came into town from the surrounding country, and general congratulations ensued. On the evening of that day a small force of Confederate cavalry rode into town and were received with shouts of joy. The ladies lined the streets, waving their hankerchiefs and loudly uttering their welcome.

On the morning of the 4th of September the soldiers in camp at Hazel Run were treated to breakfast by the ladies, and greatly en-

"Chancellorsville Tavern," Gen. Hooker's Headquarters during the battle there in 1863. Burnt during that battle, May 3rd.
(See page 95)

"The Sunken Road," along which the "stone wall" stood, forming breastworks for the Confederates in 1862 and 1863.
(See page 91)

joyed the hot rolls, beefsteak and hot coffee, after their long abstinence from such delicacies, and probably from rations of any sort. After a brief season of comparative quiet, disturbed only by the general interest felt in the operations of our armies, the condition of the country generally, and the liability to the reoccupation of the town at any time, Fredericksburg was again the subject and recipient of war's horrors in their most appalling form.

GENERAL BURNSIDE'S OCCUPATION OF FREDERICKSBURG.

The Preliminaries to the Great Battle.

On Sunday morning, the 10th of November, 1862, a company of Federal cavalry, commanded by Captain Ulric Dahlgren crossed the Rappahannock river, above Falmouth, and charged rapidly down Main street, with drawn sabres. A small force of Confederate cavalry (Colonel John Critcher's battalion), was quartered in town, who, recovering from the disorder into which they were thrown by the sudden and unexpected appearance of the enemy, quickly rallied, and, aided by citizens and Captain Simpson's company, of Colonel W. B. Ball's command, attacked the raiders, pursued and drove them across the river, inflicting upon them a slight loss in men and horses. The Federal army then began to move down from Fauquier, Culpeper and Prince William counties, through Stafford county, to occupy Fredericksburg.

To Colonel Wm. A. Ball, an experienced officer, who had greatly distinguished himself at the battle of Leesburg, and in other encounters, was entrusted by General Lee the duty of holding the town, and in retarding the approach of the enemy, if possible, with the promise of speedy reinforcements. The divisions of Gen. Lafayette McLaws and General Robert Ransom, of General Longstreet's corps, with General Wm. H. F. Lee's brigade of cavalry and a battery of artillery, were marched hurriedly to this point, and the whole of General Lee's army prepared to follow.

On Sunday, November 16th, Colonel Ball's scouts announced the approach of the enemy on three roads—the Warrenton, Stafford Courthouse and the Poplar. He telegraphed to General Gustavus W. Smith, in Richmond, for reinforcements. General Smith promptly sent him a battalion of four companies, under Major Finney, from the Forty-second Mississippi. With his small force, which scarcely exceeded five hundred men, the gallant Colonel proposed to engage the enemy, if he sought to cross the Rappahannock near Fredericksburg. Colonel Ball placed his infantry in the millrace and mill opposite Falmouth, stationed his cavalry in the upper part of Fredericksburg and planted Captain John W. Lewis's battery of four guns and eighty men on the plateau around the old Fitzgerald residence, at Little Falls, half a mile above the town.

At 10 o'clock on Monday, the 18th, the Southern scouts were driven across the river by the enemy's cavalry, and several hours thereafter a Federal corps, of twelve thousand strong, appeared on the Stafford Heights, opposite Fredericksburg, and planted their field-batteries, consisting of more than twenty guns. Capt. Lewis's men maintained their ground and replied to the rapid firing of the enemy. The distance was short—less than half a mile. The firing of the men was accurate, yet the Confederate fire was kept up, and the Federals, uncertain as to the force opposing them, made no attempt to cross the river.

Colonel Ball, with five hundred men, maintained his front, in the face of the twelve thousand Federals, encouraged by General Lee, who telegraphed him, "Hold your position if you can. Reinforcements are hurrying to you." On Tuesday, the 18th, the enemy's force was largely increased. General Burnside's whole force was pouring down to the Stafford hills. They were waiting for pontoon bridges, and did not cross the river.

Meanwhile Gen. Lee's army was rushing down the roads from Culpeper and Orange counties to occupy the crest of hills around Fredericksburg. Wednesday, at daybreak, General Fitzhugh Lee's cavalry arrived. The next morning General McLaws, with his own division and that of General Ransom's, was in position, and on the 20th the Commander-in-Chief was at hand to direct the movements of the remainder of General Longstreet's command and General Jackson's corps, which rapidly followed him.

On Tuesday, the 20th of November, by request of General Lee, Montgomery Slaughter, Mayor of Fredericksburg, accompanied by the Recorder, William A. Little, Esq., and by Mr. Douglas H. Gordon, a member of her Council, held an interview with the Confederate Commander-in-Chief. It was held at Snowden, the residence of the late John L. Stansbury, about a mile above town. On Friday, the 21st, General E. V. Sumner, of the Federal Army, sent over a flag of truce, with a written message to the Mayor and Common Council of Fredericksburg. General Patrick, the bearer of the message, was met by Colonel Wm. A. Ball at "French John's" wharf, at the foot of Hawke street. General Sumner's letter, to the town authorities was as follows:

"GENTLEMEN:— Under cover of the houses of your town, shots have been fired upon the troops of my command. Your mills and factories are furnishing provisions and material for clothing for armed bodies in rebellion against the Government of the United States. Your railroads and other means of transportation are removing supplies to the depots of such troops. This condition of things must terminate; and by direction of Major-General Burnside, commanding this army, I accordingly demand the surrender of the city into my hands, as the representative of the Government of the United States, at or before five o'clock this afternoon (5 o'clock P. M. to-day). Failing an affirmative reply to this demand by the time indicated, sixteen (16 hours) hours will be permitted to elapse for the removal from the city of women and children, the sick, wounded and aged; which period having elapsed, I shall proceed to shell the town.

"Upon obtaining possession of the town every necessary means will be taken to preserve order and secure the protective operation of the laws and policy of the United States Government."

Colonel Ball simply stated to General Patrick that before delivering the letter to the civil authorities it must be referred to his commanding military officer. But neither he nor the Mayor gave any intimation of the actual presence of General Lee, with a large part of his army, on the heights in rear of the town. General Patrick was obliged to remain in the log house from ten o'clock in the morning to seven in the afternoon, on the 21st. Meanwhile

Colonel Ball, through the proper channels forwarded the letter to General Lee. At twenty minutes before five o'clock in the afternoon the letter was received at his office by the Mayor, through General J. E. B. Stuart, who communicated in full General Lee's decision. With the aid of his advisers, Mayor Slaughter prepared a written reply, bearing date, "Mayor's Office, Fredericksburg, November 21st, 1862." This reply was to the effect that the communication of General Sumner had not reached the Mayor in time to furnish a reply by 5 o'clock P. M., as requested; that it had been sent to him after passing (by General Patrick's consent) through the hands of the commanding officer of the Confederate States forces near the town; that as to the shots complained of in the northern suburbs of the town, they were the acts of the Confederate military force holding the town; that the Mayor was authorized to say that the several subjects of complaint would not recur; that the Confederate troops would not occupy the town, and neither would they permit the Federal troops to do so. Mayor Slaughter, attended by Dr. Wm. S. Scott and Samuel S. Howison, Esq., repaired to the place of meeting, and, at about seven o'clock in the evening, delivered the reply to General Patrick.

In view of the threatened shelling of the town, General Lee advised the inhabitants to remove from it as rapidly as possible. The bombardment was not opened the next morning, but it became apparent that the enemy would cross, and the town would be exposed, not only to their fire, but to the most terrible desolations of war. The humane and considerate Chief of the Confederate army urged the women and children to leave the town, and furnished wagons, ambulances and every facility in his power for their aid.

THE INHABITANTS LEAVE THEIR HOMES.

Then followed a scene, illustrating both the horrors of war and the virtues to which it sometimes gives birth. The people of Fredericksburg, almost *en masse,* left their homes rather than yield to the enemy. Trains of cars departed, full of refugees. Upon the last the enemy opened a fire of shells; they afterwards explained that it was a mistake. Wagons and vehicles of every kind left the town filled with women and little children, with the few articles of apparel and necessity that could be removed. Many were seen on foot along the roads leading into the country. Winter had commenced, and snow had fallen. Many were compelled to take refuge in cabins, barns and tents, scattered through the woods and fields. They were dependent for food on the exertions of their friends and the humane efforts of the Southern army.

A few families remained in Fredericksburg, determined to brave the horrors of war as long as possible. The hardships and privations, incurred by these people, who surrendered their homes and property to destruction rather than remain with them and fall into the hands of the enemies of their country, excited the sympathy and won the admiration of the South. A movement to aid them commenced in Richmond. A committee of relief and treasurer was appointed, and funds were liberally contributed throughout the South, and the soldiers in the field, of their small rations and pay, contributed generously, both in food and money. The contributions of the people and army continued until more than ninety thousand dollars had been received and disbursed by the committee in Richmond and nearly an equal, if not greater, sum was distributed by Mayor Slaughter.

A number of skirmishes of an unimportant character were soon followed by the grand movement of the enemy. On the night of December the 10th the armies prepared for action. Two hundred and fifty thousand armed men, like crouched lions ready to spring upon their adversary, were ready for the bloody conflict. It was the most restless, anxious night ever passed by the citizens of Fredericksburg. It was the night of terror! The dread of to-morrow hung like a pall over the devoted city, and everybody was hurriedly preparing for the awful destruction that was at hand and could not be averted. The threatened bombardment had long been delayed, and many citizens had returned from their flight. From one end of the town to the other, all during that sleepless night, could be seen in nearly every home dim lights, where busy hands with heavy hearts were preparing for the flight at the sound of the first gun. What to attempt to carry, and what to leave to be destroyed by the enemy, was the perplexing question, and so in the anxiety of the refugees to take with them sufficient food, clothing and bedding to prevent suffering from cold and hunger, they overtaxed their strength and had to abandon many things on the roadside.

THE BOMBARDMENT OF THE TOWN.

Having received his pontoon bridges, General Burnside prepared to throw his grand army across the river. At two o'clock on the morning of Thursday, December the 11th, his troops were put in motion and two signal guns from the Confederate side, at five o'clock,* sounded a note of warning to the people and the army. General Burnside commenced throwing three pontoon bridges across the Rappahannock river. One was to span the river at French John's wharf, at the foot of Hawke street, one at Scott's Ferry, at the lower end of Water street, and one at Deep Run, about two and a half miles below town. General Wm. Barksdale's brigade, consisting of the Thirteenth, Seventeenth, Eighteenth and Twenty-first Mississippi regiments, held the town.

"General Barksdale kept his men quiet and concealed until the bridges were so far advanced that the working parties were in easy range, when he opened fire with such effect that the bridges were abandoned at once. Nine separate and desperate attempts were made to complete the bridges under fire of their sharpshooters and guns on the opposite bank, but every attempt being attended with such severe loss from the Confederates, posted in rifle-pits, in the cellars of the houses along the banks, and behind whatever offered concealment, that the enemy abandoned their attempts and opened a terrific fire from their numerous batteries concentrated along the hills just above the river. The fire was so severe that the men could not use their rifles, and, the different places occupied by them becoming untenable, the troops were withdrawn from the river bank back to Caroline street at 4:30 P. M. The enemy then crossed in boats, and, completing their bridges, passed over in force and advanced into the town. The Seventeenth Mississippi

---

* See General Lafayette McLaws's report of the battle.

and ten sharpshooters from Colonel J. W. Carter's regiment (the 13th) and three companies of the Eighteenth regiment, Lieutenant Colonel Luse, under Lieutenant William Ratliff, were all the troops that were actually engaged in defending the crossings in front of the city."*

The other regiments and parts of regiments were held in reserve, and were not brought into action until the enemy had crossed the river. At the first dawn of light on the morning of December the 11th the Federal artillery commenced its work of destruction. From the heights above the town of Falmouth, north of Fredericksburg, to the Washington farm below, on every available place artillery was stationed, bearing upon the town. About one hundred and seventy-five of the grim monsters, ready to "belch forth death and destruction," were placed in position the day before, well manned, and only waiting for the signal to send forth their deadly messengers of shot and shell.

At the hour appointed the signal was given, and the thunder of artillery, the lightning from bursting shells in the air, the crashing of solid shot through the houses, the roar of musketry on both sides of the river, the shrieks of frightened women and children, the bustle and confusion that followed, may be imagined, but can never be described. From early morning until four o'clock in the afternoon, with only half an hour's cessation between one and two o'clock, this deluge of shot and shell was poured upon the streets and houses of the town. The few inhabitants who remained in the town fled to their cellars and sought to save their lives from the storm which was beating their homes to pieces. Many houses were burned with all or most of their contents, the result of hot shot, it was claimed, thrown from the enemy's guns on the Lacy farm, just opposite the town. Among the houses that were burned were the residence of Mr. Reuben T. Thom, in which was located the post-office; the Bank of Virginia, where the Operahouse now stands, and several other private residences on Main street. And yet the worst was still to come.

---

* Extract from Gen Lafayette McLaws's official report of the battle of Fredericksburg, made to General James Longstreet—War of Rebellion, Series 1, Vol. 21, page 578.

CHAPTER VII

The great battle—The town sacked by soldiers—A wonderful display of humanity—The Federals recross the river—A great revival of religion—The battle of Chancellorsville—The Wilderness campaign—Citizens arrested—A statement by the Council—The citizens and Federal soldiers release, &c.

To those who had a proper idea of the sacrifices made, the sufferings endured and the privations experienced by the inhabitants of Fredericksburg, up to this period, whether that idea was formed from observation, from reading the narratives or from their rehearsals by those who experienced them, it might appear that their cup of sorrow was full even to overflowing, and from further troubles and trials they might be exempted. But not so. Probably the worst was yet to come; but they firmly believed that the same patriotic devotion to the cause they had espoused, and the same fidelity to principle which enabled them to "bear the spoiling of their goods" with composure in the past, would sustain them in any additional trials and sacrifices they might have to endure in the future. Patriotic, self sacrificing and confiding in the right, they were prepared for the worst, and the worst came.

On taking possession of Fredericksburg the Federal soldiers abandoned themselves to pillage and destruction. They entered the stores and dwellings, forcing their way where force was necessary, rifling them of all that they wanted of their contents and destroying those things that they could not remove. China and glassware were broken up and scattered promiscuously; silverware was carried away, books and family pictures were mutilated and destroyed; furniture was cut up or broken up and converted into fire-wood, beds, bedclothing and wearing apparel were destroyed or carried off, and the residences were left despoiled of their contents. In the three days they occupied the town they made the destruction complete. But it is a gratification, even to those who suffered by this occupation, to know that the commanders were not to blame for the sacking of the town. It was the work, so it is asserted, of stragglers and camp followers—the most detestable and destructive scabs of an army.

On Friday, the 12th of December, the Union army was drawn up in line of battle, prepared to advance. Not less than sixty thousand men were on the south bank of the river, with more than a hundred pieces of artillery. Near the mouth of Deep Run there were probably as many more ready for the final charge. The Confederate army was confronting them in a line extending from Fall Hill to Hamilton's Crossing, between six and seven miles in length. At one o'clock the heavy batteries on each side opened, and for an hour kept up a brilliant duel of shell and round shot. On the morning of Saturday, the 13th of December, a dense fog hung over the river and the adjoining fields. Under its cover the Federal army advanced. By eight o'clock it was in position and the dreadful conflict began.

Line after line of battle advanced on the Confederate position, at the stone wall at the foot of Marye's Heights, to be repulsed with great slaughter. This was kept up without cessation, charge after charge, as rapidly as they could reform the men, from eight o'clock in the morning until four o'clock in the afternoon, when one desperate charge, with troops *en masse,* was made all along the line in front of the stone wall, accompanied by the most terrific fire of artillery. In this last and grandest effort, the men, marching to death and destruction through an open field, got within twenty-five yards of the stone wall, notwithstanding the deadly aim of the Confederate infantry behind it and the destructive fire of the artillery on the heights above, so skillfully arranged by General E. P. Alexander.

It was a sublime spectacle, and the gallantry of both officers and men won the admiration of the commanders on both sides, Lieutenant-General Longstreet, on the Confederate side, declaring that such gallant conduct deserved success. But success was not to be theirs. The gallant charges of the Federals were met with that undaunted coolness and courage so characteristic of the Confederate soldier, and a disastrous Federal defeat was the result. The fighting was the most desperate that had been witnessed up to that time, and the Union loss was very great, being nearly fifty per cent. of the numbers engaged. The battle-field was covered with the dead, wounded and dying, and it is related by those behind the stone wall that all during the night the most piteous groans and cries, for water of the wounded could be heard, but no relief could be afforded, although the Confederates deeply sympathized with them.* Thus ended the battle of Fredericksburg, fought, it is claimed, against the judgment and advice of every corps commander in the army who refused to renew the attack next day, although it was the desire of Gen. Burnside to do so.

THE FEDERALS RECROSS THE RIVER.

On Monday night, December the 15th, General Burnside withdrew his army across the river and removed his pontoons. The citizens returned to their houses, to find them stripped of everything that was left in them. What could not be carried away was broken up and destroyed. Private residences, orphan asylums, church buildings and lodges of benevolent and charitable institutions, all fared alike. Not only were the residences of the refugees deprived of everything left in them, but the returning citizens were without money and food. They were in a destitute condition, and, between the two great armies, with no prospect of relief, unless it

---

* It is said that just south of the Stevens house, about a hundred yards in front of the Confederate line, lay a wounded Union soldier on the night of the 13th. His supply of water gave out. Just before daylight he began to call for water. The cry was incessant. Both lines could hear him, but no one seemed willing to venture to his relief. As the day dawned he seemed to cry louder— water, water, water; but none came. Among those who heard him, and whose heart was touched with pity, was a Confederate youth, yet in his teens. He determined to answer the call or die in the attempt; and so informed Gen. Kershaw, his commander, who tried to dissuade him from it. But his purpose was fixed, and it is said that just as "the sun was gilding the blue arch above with his golden beams," this youth took his canteen, filled with water, jumped over the stone wall, and, with form bending low, carried it to the sufferer. Just as the deed was accomplished a yell of approval went up from both Confederate and Union lines, such as was never heard before, and which was repeated time and again. The boy soldier did not have to bend his form in returning to his post. He went back a hero, and a good Samaritan, proclaimed such by both armies, and he has since been immortalized in verse. That youth was Richard Kirkland, of Co. E. 2nd S. C. Vol. He has a memorial stone in the Church of the Prince of Peace at Gettysburg, and the inscription: A hero of benevolence; at the risk of his life he gave his enemy drink at Fredericksburg. He was killed at Chickamauga.

Gen. Hugh Mercer's Monument on Washington avenue.
(See page 162)

Old Stone House near Free Bridge. Supposed to have been a tobacco warehouse before the Revolutionary War.
(See page 47)

came from friends in the way of a contribution. It was at this critical period that the appeal, made but a few days before, brought to them relief in the way of money and supplies. The contributions in money amounted to $164,169.45, and the provisions were ample to relieve the present needs. Thus the wants of the destitute of the town were supplied and untold suffering prevented.

A GREAT REVIVAL OF RELIGION.

From the first of January to the second day of June, 1862, General Barksdale's brigade, that had guarded the banks of the river from the arrival of the Confederate army at this point to the great battle of the 13th of December, was quartered in town for picket and provost guard duty. About the first of April, 1863, one of the most remarkable and successful religious revivals took place here that was known to that generation. The dangers and hardships of war were to yield for a time for the comforts of religion. The services were commenced in the Presbyterian church by Rev. Wm. B. Owens, Dr. J. A. Hackett, Rev. E. McDaniel and Rev. W. T. West, chaplains in the brigade, aided by Rev. John L. Pettigrew, then a private soldier in Company A, Thirteenth Mississippi regiment, but afterwards appointed to a chaplaincy in a North Carolina regiment. Mr. Owens, a Methodist minister, had charge of the services, and for some reason the meetings were transferred from the Presbyterian church to the Southern Methodist church, then standing on the corner of Charles and George streets, where Mr. P. V. D. Conway's residence now stands.

The interest in the meetings deepened, their influence spread to the adjoining camps,* and the congregations became so large that they could not find standing room in the building. To accommodate these rapidly-increasing crowds, Rev. A. M. Randolph, then rector, tendered the use of St. George's church, which was gladly accepted, and the services were conducted there until the close of the meeting, in the latter part of May. Before the close, this revival attracted the attention of the leading ministers of nearly all denominations, many of whom came to the assistance of Mr. Owens

---

* See Christ in the Camp, by Rev. J. Wm. Jones, D. D.

and his co-workers. Among those who were at times present, preached and rendered valuable assistance, were Rev. J. C. Stiles, D. D., Rev. Wm. J. Hoge, D. D., Rev. James D. Coulling, Rev. James A. Duncan, D. D., Rev. J. Lansing Burrows, D. D., Rev. Alfred E. Dickinson, D. D., and Rev. W. H. Carroll. During the meeting more than five hundred soldiers, most of whom belonged to Barksdale's brigade, were converted and united with churches of the various Christian denominations.

Of this wonderful religious awakening, Rev. Dr. Wm. J. Hoge wrote to the *Southern Presbyterian* as follows: "We found our soldiers at Fredericksburg all alive with animation. A rich blessing had been poured upon the labors of Brother Owens, Methodist chaplain in Barksdale's brigade. The Rev. Dr. Burrows, of the Baptist church, Richmond, had just arrived, expecting to labor with him some days. As I was to stay but one night, Dr. Burrows insisted on my preaching. So we had a Presbyterian sermon, introduced by Baptist services, under the direction of a Methodist chaplain, in an Episcopal church! Was not that a beautiful solution of the vexed problem of Christian union?"

Mr. Owens, who worked so faithfully in the great meeting at Fredericksburg, endeared himself to all who had the pleasure of attending the services. On his return to his Mississippi home, at the close of the war, he at once entered upon his work as a travelling minister, and was drowned while attempting to cross a swollen stream on horseback, endeavoring to reach one of his preaching stations.

GENERAL JOHN SEDGWICK TAKES THE TOWN.

Chancellorsville campaign.

In the Spring of 1863, as soon as the roads began to dry off, the armies were put in readiness to move, preparatory to another great battle. General Joseph Hooker, known as "Fighting Joe Hooker," had succeded General Ambrose E. Burnside in the command of the Army of the Potomac, which he claimed was the finest army on the planet. His desire was to reach Richmond, which his predecessors, General McDowell, General McClellan, General Pope and General

Burnside, had failed to do. Accordingly, about the last of April, detaching General John Sedgwick, with twenty-two thousand men, to threaten General Lee's rear at Fredericksburg, he crossed his army at the several fords of the Rappahannock river above town and concentrated it at Chancellorsville. His plan seems to have been to turn General Lee's right flank with the forces under General Sedgwick, double back his left flank with the corps under General Howard, and then, with the forces of General Crouch and General Meade, make a bold and desperate dash against the center, crush it and capture the entire army of his adversary. This accomplished, Richmond would be an easy prey.

But while General Hooker was moving to execute his plans, General Lee had the Army of Northern Virginia in motion, and when General Hooker reached Chancellorsville he found to his great astonishment, the Confederate army in his front and prepared to dispute his advance. Skirmishers were thrown out by both armies and soon the engagement of May the 2nd and 3rd commenced. On the morning of the 2nd General Stonewall Jackson commenced his famous flank movement that has been the study and wonder of military men of this and other countries, which resulted in a great disaster to the Federal army and a great calamity to the Southern cause. General Hooker was badly defeated and driven in haste from the field, but General Jackson lay mortally wounded. Of that attack and result we use in substance the language of General Lee in his official report of the Battle of Chancellorsville.* After a long and fatiguing march, General Jackson's leading division, under General Rodes, reached old turnpike, about three miles in the rear of Chancellorsville, at four in the afternoon. As the different divisions arrived they were formed at right angles with the road— Rodes in front, Trible's division, under Brigadier-General R. E. Colston, in the second, and General A. P. Hill's in the third line.

At six o'clock the advance was ordered. The enemy were taken by surprise and fled after a brief resistance. General Rodes's men pushed forward with great vigor and enthusiasm, followed closely by the second and third lines. Position after position was carried,

---

* See War of the Rebellion, Series 1, Vol. 25, Part 1, page 798.

the guns captured, and every effort of the enemy to rally defeated by the impetuous rush of our troops. In the ardor of pursuit through the thick and tangled woods, the first and second lines at last became mingled and moved on together as one. The enemy made a stand at a line of breastworks across the road at the house of Melzi Chancellor, but the troops of Rodes and Colston dashed over the entrenchments together and the flight and pursuit were resumed and continued until our advance was arrested by the abatis in front of the line of works near the central position at Chancellorsville.

It was now dark, and General Jackson ordered the third line, under General Hill, to advance to the front and relieve the troops of Rodes and Colston, who were completely blended, and in such disorder, from their rapid advance through intricate woods and over broken ground, that it was necessary to reform them. As General Hill's men moved forward, General Jackson, with his staff and escort, returning from the extreme front, met his skirmishers advancing, and in the obscurity of the night were taken for the enemy and fired upon. Captain J. K. Boswell, chief engineer of the corps and several others were killed and a number wounded. General Jackson himself received a severe injury and was borne from the field. He was taken to the Chandler house, at Guiney's station, in Caroline county, where, notwithstanding everything possible was done for him that loving hearts could do or medical skill could suggest, he died on the 9th of May. Amid the sorrow and tears of the Southern people he was laid to rest at his home in Lexington, Virginia.

General Jubal A. Early had been left at Fredericksburg to watch General Sedgwick, and had been instructed, in the event of the enemy withdrawing from his front and moving up the river, to join the main body of the army. This order was repeated on the 2nd, but by some mistake General Early was directed to move unconditionally. Leaving Hays's brigade and one regiment of Barksdale's at Fredericksburg, he moved with the rest of his command towards Chancellorsville. As soon as his withdrawal was perceived the enemy began to advance, and General Early returned to his original position.

The line to be defended by Barksdale's brigade extended from the Rappahannock, above Fredericksburg, to the rear of Howison's house, a distance of more than two miles. The artillery was posted along the heights in rear of the town.

Before dawn on the morning of the 3rd General Barksdale reported to General Early that the enemy had occupied Fredericksburg in large force and had bridged the Rappahannock river. Hays's brigade was sent to his support, and placed on his extreme left, with the exception of one regiment, stationed on the right of his line behind the Howison house. Seven companies of the Twenty-first Mississippi regiment were posted by General Barksdale between the Marye house and the Plank road, the Eighteenth and the three other companies of the Twenty-first occupied the Telegraph road, behind the stone wall, at the foot of Marye's Hill, the two remaining regiments of the brigade being farther to the right on the hills near Howison's house. The enemy made a demonstration against the extreme right, which was easily repulsed by General Early. Soon afterward a column moved from Fredericksburg along the river bank as if to gain the heights on the extreme left, which commanded those immediately in rear of the town. This attempt was foiled by General Hays and the arrival of General Wilcox from Banks's Ford, who deployed a few skirmishers on the hill near Dr. Taylor's house and opened on the enemy with a section of artillery. Very soon the enemy advanced in large force against Marye's Heights and the hills to the right and left. Two assaults were gallantly repulsed by Barksdale's men and the artillery. After the second, a flag of truce, it was claimed, was sent from the town to obtain permission to provide for the wounded, which was granted.

At the end of the truce three heavy lines advanced and renewed the attack. They were bravely repulsed on the right and left, but the small force at the foot of Marye's Hill, overpowered by more than ten times their numbers, was captured after a heroic resistance, and the Heights carried. Eight pieces of artillery were taken on Marye's and the adjacent heights. The remainder of Barksdale's brigade, together with that of General Hays, and the artillery on the right, retired down the Telegraph road. The success of the enemy enabled him to threaten Gen. Lee's communications by moving down the telegraph road, or gain his rear at Chancellorsville by the Plank road. He at first advanced on the Telegraph road, but was checked by General Early, who had halted the brigades of Barksdale and Hays with the artillery, about two miles from Marye's Hill, and reënforced them with three regiments of General John B. Gordon's brigade. The enemy then began to advance up the Plank road, his progress being gallantly disputed by the brigade of General Cadmus M. Wilcox, who had moved from Banks's Ford as rapidly as possible to the assistance of General Barksdale, but arrived too late to take part in the action. General Wilcox fell back slowly until he reached Salem church, on the Plank road, about four miles from Fredericksburg.

Information of the state of affairs in our rear having reached Chancellorsville, General McLaws, with his three brigades and one of General Anderson's, was ordered to reinforce General Wilcox. He arrived at Salem church early in the afternoon, where he found General Wilcox in line of battle, with a large force of the enemy—consisting, as was reported, of one army corps and part of another, under Major-General Sedgwick—in his front. The brigades of General Kershaw and General Wofford were placed on the right of General Wilcox and those of Semmes and Mahone on the left. The enemy's artillery played vigorously upon our position for some time, when his infantry advanced in three strong lines, the attack being directed mainly against General Wilcox, but partially involving the brigades on his left.

The assault was met with the utmost firmness, and after a fierce struggle the first line was repulsed with great slaughter. The second then came forward, but immediately broke under the close and deadly fire which it encountered, and the whole mass fled in confusion to the rear. They were pursued by the brigades of General Wilcox and General Semmes, in the direction of Banks's Ford, where the enemy crossed to the Stafford side of the river.

The next morning General Early advanced along the Telegraph road and recaptured Marye's Heights and the adjacent hills without difficulty. General Barksdale's brigade entered the town, to find the enemy gone, with the exception of some stragglers who had secreted themselves in cellars and elsewhere about town. These were captured and sent to the rear, and the brigade took up its former quarters in the town, where it remained until the first of June.

After some four weeks of rest and reorganization the army was again put in motion, the object of Gen. Lee being the invasion of Pennsylvania. After the removal of the army Fredericksburg was left practically without any armed troops, and soon relapsed into her usual quiet, so characteristic of the place. This condition of things existed until the return of the army from its invasion in the Fall, when the town was occasionally visited by scouting cavalry from the Confederate army, the main body of the troops camping west of Fredericksburg.

GEN. GRANT'S ARMY IN POSSESSION.

The Wilderness Campaign.

With the opening of the Spring of 1864, was inaugurated the most active and bloody campaign of the war in Virginia. This battle embraces those of Mine Run, the Wilderness, Todd's Tavern, the Po, the Ny and those around Spotsylvania Courthouse, in which both armies, the Confederate, under General Robert E. Lee, and the Federal, under General Ulysses S. Grant, lost heavily. Many thousands of the wounded Federals were sent in ambulances and wagons to Fredericksburg, where hospitals were established, under the charge of United States surgeons. Every house in the town that was at all available was converted into a hospital. Residences, stores, churches and lodge rooms were all occupied by the wounded and the surgeons were kept busy day and night. As fast as the wounded could be moved they were sent north, and others were brought from the battle-fields. This was kept up from the time the battles commenced, on the 4th of May, until they closed, on the 20th of May, the first batch reaching town with their authorized attendants on the 9th of May.

On Sunday, the 8th, a small body of Federal troops, numbering about sixty, most of them slightly wounded, came into town. They were armed, and the citizens demanded their surrender as prisoners of war. This demand was acceded to and they were delivered over to the Confederate military authorities at the nearest post. from which they were sent to Richmond. This action of the citizens was regarded by the Federal authorities as a violation of law, and the arrest of an equal number of citizens was ordered by the Federals, that they might be held as hostages until these Union soldiers were released and returned.

This order caused great consternation in town. No one could foretell the fate of those arrested and the worst for them was feared. Many of the male citizens sought hiding places, but quite a number made no effort to escape or elude the officers, as they did not consider they had done any wrong—certainly no intentional wrong— and they were willing to abide the consequences until an impartial investigation was made, when they believed they would be exonerated from any crime. In the execution of this order, sixty-two citizens were arrested and carried to Washington, ten of whom were there liberated and the remaining fifty-two were sent to Fort Delaware. Afterwards five other citizens were arrested and sent to the same prison.

The families of these citizens were almost frantic at being thus deprived of their protectors, while the town was overrun by Federal soldiers, many of them stragglers, without any one to restrain them, and others brought here from the Wilderness and other battle-fields, wounded and dying, their groans and shrieks filling the air. No one can imagine the distressing scenes enacted in town about this time who did not witness them, or form any conception of the terrible ordeal through which these helpless families passed save those who shared their privations and sufferings.

The town had been the scene of a bombardment unparalleled; two fearful battles had been fought here, with their accompanying destruction of property and consumption of food and family supplies; the town had been in possession of both armies at different times; therefore these families were destitute of food and the comforts of life, and now comes the order for the arrest and imprisonment of those whom God had given them to protect and provide for them. Notwithstanding the intense excitement of the people of the town, and the sufferings and entreaties of the bereaved ones, it was thought prudent to defer public action until further developments, in the hope that the prisoners would be released and allowed to return to their homes.

Having impatiently awaited the release of the prisoners, and their hopes not being realized, on the 31st of May a meeting of the Common Council was called, and upon assembling the Mayor informed the body that the object of the meeting was to take some steps for the relief of those citizens who had been arrested and who were then suffering in prison at Fort Delaware. A paper was submitted by Mr. Wm. A. Little, which was unanimously adopted, looking to their release. As the paper contains the views of the citizens of Fredericksburg, with reference to the arrest of the Federal soldiers, and also the names of the citizens arrested, it is here copied in full, as follows:

FREDERICKSBURG, VA., May 31st, 1864.

To the Honorable James A. Seddon,
　　Secretary of War of the Confederate States,
　　　　Richmond, Virginia.

At a meeting of the Mayor and Common Council of Fredericksburg, Virginia, held this 31st of May, 1864, a committee of two citizens, to wit: Montgomery Slaughter and John F. Scott, were appointed to repair to Richmond and present to you the following statement and application.

Statement.

On Sunday, the 8th instant, a number of slightly-wounded and straggling Federal soldiers, who entered the town, many of them with arms in their hands, and with the capacity and intention, we feared, of doing mischief in the way of pillage and injury to our people, who were unprotected by any military force, were arrested by order of our municipal authorities and forwarded to the nearest military post as prisoners of war, under the guard of citizens. These prisoners amounted to about sixty men, of whom but few are said to have been slightly wounded. In retaliation of this act, the provost marshal, under orders from the Secretary of War at Washington, arrested on the 20th instant some sixty of our citizens and forwarded them to Washington, to be held as hostages for said prisoners. Ten of the citizens were afterwards released in Washington, and have returned to their homes, leaving some fifty-one citizens still in confinement, who have been sent to the military prison at Fort Delaware.

In behalf of these unfortunate people, who are thus made to suffer so seriously, and for their suffering families who are thus left without their natural protectors, and many of them without their means of support, we appeal to you to take such steps as may be proper and in accordance with military regulations to return the said prisoners to the Federal authorities and thus secure the release of our citizens. Surely the matter of a few prisoners cannot be allowed to interfere with the humane and generous work of restoring to these desolated homes, and these mourning women and children, the only source of comfort which the fate of war has left them in this war-ravaged and desolated town, the presence of those loved ones who are separated from them and imprisoned at Fort Delaware. The following is a list of the citizens arrested and carried to Washington as aforesaid:

James H. Bradley, Thomas F. Knox, James McGuire, Councellor Cole, Michael Ames, John G. Hurkamp, John J. Chew, George H. Peyton, Wm. H. Thomas, John D. Elder, who were released at Washington.

F. B. Chewning, R. B. Rennolds, James B. Marye, George Aler, Charles Mander,* Benjamin F. Currell, John L. Knight, Wm. C. Smith, Joseph W. Sener, E. W. Stephens, Charles Cash, Charles B. Waite, Charles G. Waite, Jr., George W. Wroten,* Thomas Newton, Robert H. Alexander, Robert Smith, Lucien Love, George F. Sacrey, Henry M. Towles, Landon J. Huffman, Lewis Moore, John T. Evans, Walter Bradshaw, Samuel D. Curtis, Lewis Wrenn, Wm. White, John Solan, George W. Eve, James Mazeen, Abraham Cox,

---
* Still living.

Birthplace of Hon. John Forsythe, the brilliant Georgia Statesman.
(See page 154)

The "Sentry Box," the home of Gen. Hugh Mercer; now the residence of O. D. Foster, Esq.
(See page 150)

Wm. Brannan, James A. Turner, A. E. Samuel, Tandy Williams, Robert S. Parker, Christopher Reintz, Thomas F. Coleman, Patrick McDonnell, Charles Williams, Wm. Cox, Walter M. Mills, Thomas S. Thornton, John Joyce,* John Miner, Richard Hudson, Wm. B. Webb, Alexander Armstrong, Wm. Wiltshire, Gabriel Johnston, George Mullin, William Burke.

The following citizens were arrested subsequently and are still held by the Federal authorities: Wm. Lange, Thomas Manuell, Joseph Hall, Wm. W. Jones, Wyatt Johnson.

The committee appointed by the Council proceeded to Richmond and laid the matter before the Secretary of War, and, on their return home, reported to the Council in writing. This report was filed, but was not entered upon the records of the Council, and, from indications as shown by subsequent entries in the Council proceedings, the committee appointed Mr. George H. C. Rowe to visit Washington, interview the Federal authorities and ascertain what could be done. Some of the members of the Council claimed that this action of the committee was without authority, as the appointment should have been made by the Council itself and not by the committee of the Council. This claim was, no doubt, well founded, and the action of the committee may have been a stretch of its authority, but their great anxiety to have these gentlemen released from prison and have them restored to their families and friends, was a sufficient explanation and apology, if such had been needed, for their action, independent of the Council. And furthermore, the propriety of, and authority for, this action of the committee may be explained, if not justified, by the fact that one of the committeemen was the Mayor and executive officer of the town and the other one was a leading member of the Common Council.

But be that as it may, Mr. Rowe proceeded to Washington, and on his return, on the 20th of June, made a report of his visit to the Council, stating that he was well received by the Federal authorities

---

*An amusing incident is told of Mr. Joyce when he was arrested. He is a native of Ireland, as every one will readily perceive when he hears him speak. When arrested he was asked in a brusque tone by the officer—"Where are you from?" He replied instantly: "Be Jasus, oim a Virginnyan, and niver denoi the place of moi netivity."

and was assured by the Secretary of War that the exchange could be effected. Mr. Rowe further stated that the proposition made by the Secretary of War was that the Federal prisoners should be released and placed in his care, and he be permitted to take them through their lines with the assurance that the citizen prisoners would be turned over to him. Mr. Rowe concluded his report as follows:*

"This proposition, it seems to me, obviates all difficulties of misconstruction, and I will undertake the delivery and receipt of the prisoners at Alexandria. It is proper to state that in 1862, I undertook and executed, a similar Commission of exchange of citizens Captured, with success, and thorough satisfaction to our Government,† and I am sure with its assent and coöperation as proposed, I will now reap a similar result."

Upon the reception of this report by the Council Mayor Slaughter and Mr. Rowe were appointed a commission to visit Richmond and secure the release of the Federal prisoners, and, when so released, the commission was authorized to do what might be necessary to effect the final exchange. On their arrival in Richmond they called on the Confederate authorities and stated the terms of agreement, and through their solicitation the following order was issued by Colonel Robert Ould, the Confederate commissioner of exchange of prisoners:

"RICHMOND, VA., June 23rd, 1864.

Brigadier General M. M. Gardner—SIR: I will thank you to deliver to M. Slaughter, Mayor of Fredericksburg, fifty-six Federal Soldiers (privates) who are to be exchanged for an equal number of our people, captured in Fredericksburg. I will thank you also to furnish M. Slaughter the necessary guard, &c., for their transportation to Fredericksburg. Please send two or three surgeons with the party.

Resp'y yr Obt. Sert.,

R. OULD, Agt."

---

* See Council proceedings, June 20, 1864.
† That record not found. Mr. Rowe must have assisted Rev. Wm. F. Broaddus, D. D., in the release of the nineteen citizen prisoners.

The issuance of this order, with the previous assurance of the Federal authorities, encouraged and rejoiced the hearts of all interested parties. The mourning changed to rejoicing, and nothing now remained to complete the joy but the presence of the loved ones, who yet lingered in prison. An order was at once issued by the Common Council authorizing Mr. Slaughter and Mr. Rowe to procure all the necessary transportation and make proper arrangements for the exchange and effect the release of the imprisoned citizens as speedily as possible. From the final report, made on the subject, it appears that the whole matter of making the exchange of prisoners was turned over to Mr. Rowe. On his return from Washington he reported the transactions in full to the Council, on the 8th of July, in the following words:*

"I have the honor to report that I reached the military lines of the United States in safety with the fifty-six prisoners of war and four civil officers of the so-called State of West Virginia, committed to my charge by the corporation authorities, to be exchanged for the captive citizens of Fredericksburg. After some difficulty in obtaining personal access to the authorities at Washington, and several days' discussion there, I succeeded in closing a negotiation that the Federal prisoners delivered by me should be released from their paroles simultaneously with the delivery of fifty-three captive citizens of Fredericksburg, and seven Confederate prisoners of war, on board of a flag of truce steamer, with transportation to Split Rock, on the Potomac river.

"In execution of this obligation the Federal authorities delivered to me, on board the Steamer Weycomoke, whence they were landed at Split Rock on yesterday, forty-nine citizens and two prisoners of war, according to the roll which accompanies this report, marked A.† The four citizens and five prisoners of war still due, I have solid assurances will be forwarded by the same route at an early day."

At the conclusion of Mr. Rowe's report, on motion made by Mr. John James Young, the Council unanimously adopted the following resolution:

"That the thanks of this body be tendered to Mr. Rowe for the

---

* From Council proceedings of July 8, 1864.
† Not found in the Council proceedings.

energetic and efficient manner in which he has effected the exchange of Federal prisoners for our captive citizens."

Having been set at liberty at Split Rock, on the banks of the Potomac river, the march to Fredericksburg was soon commenced. Some few of the party, and especially the sick, were fortunate enough to have carriages sent for them, some got seats in wagons, but a large majority of them made the journey on foot, and were delighted at the privilege of doing so. The distance is about twelve miles. It is unnecessary to attempt (for we could not if we did) to describe the scene upon the arrival of these unfortunate ones to their homes and families. It is sufficient to say they reached home in safety amidst the shouts of welcome and the rejoicing of the inhabitants of the town, the returned prisoners joining in the refrain, bearing testimony to the truth of Payne's declaration, "There's no place like home."

The small batch of wounded and straggling Federal soldiers, who were arrested by the citizens on the 8th of May, was followed next day and the succeeding days, until there were in the different improvised hospitals in town about fifteen thousand sick and wounded soldiers. They were attended by a large body of surgeons and assistants of every kind, including nurses. The native population of the town at this time was small, and consisted entirely of women, children and elderly men. Even the colored population had become very much reduced.

The sudden increase of the population by the advent of this large number of sick and wounded soldiers, and their numerous attendants, caused great suffering and distress, and during this occupation by the wounded, the suffering, disease and sorrow endured by the people of Fredericksburg were greater than any that had previously visited them. But notwithstanding this, and notwithstanding the harsh and cruel treatment they received at the hands of General Pope and his subordinates, truth demands the record and admission that these scenes of horror were greatly mitigated by many acts of courtesy and considerate aid on the part of the Federal officers stationed here, which even now are kindly remembered and spoken of by many of our citizens who were participants in the scenes referred to above.

CHAPTER VIII

The Armies Transferred to Richmond and Petersburg—Gen. Lee's surrender—Citizens Return Home—Action of the Council—Fredericksburg Again Under the Old Flag—The Assassination of President Lincoln Denounced and Deplored—Reconstruction Commenced—An Election Set Aside—The Iron-Clad Oath—All Offices Vacated and Strangers Appointed—The Financial Condition of the Town—The Town Again in the Hands of its Citizens—Splendid Financial Showing, &c.

At the conclusion of the battles around Spotsylvania, during which time Fredericksburg was the base of supplies for the Federal army, the two armies moved south and the scenes of war were transferred from Fredericksburg to Richmond and Petersburg. From the time the main armies moved south to the close of the war Fredericksburg was first in the Federal lines and then in the Confederate lines. After the base of supplies for the Union army was moved from Fredericksburg to City Point about the only troops that visited the town were scouting or raiding parties, and be it said to their credit very little damage to property was done by them. Communication was kept up all the time with Richmond and the citizens were not without hope that the Federal army would be driven back and the scenes of war transferred to other parts. But these hopes were delusive. General Grant was constantly receiving reinforcements, until he had over 200,000 men, by which he was enabled to extend his lines, while General Lee's small army, not exceeding 45,000 men, was becoming smaller and his lines of battle thinner by reason of casualties, resulting from daily engagements with the enemy. In consequence of this he was unable to hold his long lines against the vigorous attacks of General Grant.

About the first of April General Lee suffered several reverses on his extreme right, which resulted in turning his right flank on the 2nd of April. On the morning of the 3rd he commenced the evacuation of Richmond, abandoned his entire line in front of Petersburg and retreated in the direction of Danville. The overwhelming numbers of Grant against him made his retreat very difficult and enabled the Federals to harass him on every side. When General Lee reached Burkeville he found the Federals between him and Danville, his objective point, and it became necessary for him to change the direction of his column. There was but one way open for him and that was the road to Lynchburg. But this road was soon closed. At the battle of Sailors' Creek, near Farmville, on the 6th of April, the Confederates lost over six thousand men and several general officers. From the result of this engagement it was plainly seen that the end had come. By fighting in the day and marching at night General Lee reached Appomattox Courthouse on the 9th, with what few soldiers he had left, broken down from hunger and marching, his horses jaded and unable to do their work, and his artillery and wagon trains were falling an easy prey to the pursuing army. Although the men's courage never failed them, in the condition in which Gen. Lee found himself, there was nothing to do but to surrender. General Grant had already communicated with him and demanded his surrender, upon the ground that he could not longer resist, but he had not felt a willingness to yield until the morning of the 9th.

On that eventful morning General Lee opened communication with General Grant and invited a conference, to discuss the terms of surrender. They met, it is said, under an apple tree and adjourned to the residence of Mr. Wilmer McLane,* where the terms were agreed upon, written out and signed. It was from this building that General Lee mounted old Traveller,† to return to his lines to announce the sad news to the remaining remnant of his once

---

* Mr. McLane's residence was in the midst of the first battle between the two great armies, and, strange to say, it was in the midst of the last and that the terms of surrender were written and signed in his residence. When the war broke out Mr. McLane was living in Prince William county, and at the first battle of Manassas his residence was in the thickest of the fight. He afterwards moved to Appomattox county to get out of the reach of the war. During the last engagement of the two armies his residence was between the lines, and when General Lee and General Grant met they asked for a room in the house, which was furnished them, and there the terms of surrender were written and signed.

† Traveller was General Lee's war horse. Every soldier in the army knew him. At the death of this faithful old horse, that had carried General Lee through the war, he was turned over to the taxidermist, who prepared and mounted him. He is now at the Soldiers' Home in Richmond, looking as natural and life-like as when he bore the Confederate Chieftain into battle, or when he moved in General Lee's funeral procession, fully equipped for the march, but without his accustomed rider.

magnificent army. General Hooker declared the army of the Potomac, prior to his move to Chancellorsville, "the grandest army on the planet," but more than one of the Federal generals of high rank, who served in the Army of the Potomac, have since the war declared "that for sacrifice, suffering and for fighting qualities the world could not surpass the Army of Northern Virginia."

The terms of the surrender were liberal, even generous, and bore testimony to the affectionate consideration General Lee had for his men and the magnanimity of General Grant to those who had surrendered their arms. It was agreed that the officers were to give their individual paroles not to take up arms against the Government of the United States until properly exchanged, and each company or regimental commander was to sign a similar parole for their men. The arms, artillery and public property were to be stacked and packed and turned over to a United States officer. The officers and men were allowed to take their side arms, private horses and baggage and return to their homes unmolested and so remain as long as they observed their paroles. In addition to this, at the suggestion of General Lee, General Grant furnished the Confederate army with rations, which they had been without for several days. It is said that when it became known by the advanced lines of the Federal troops and those of the Confederate army that the terms of surrender had been signed and peace was at hand, their long pent-up feelings gave way in the loudest tumult of rejoicing.

There was no demand made by General Grant for the surrender of General Lee's sword, and there was no offer of the surrender of his sword on the part of General Lee. The officers were to retain their side arms which included the sword. "The number of men paroled was about twenty-six thousand, of whom not more than nine thousand had arms in their hands. About sixteen thousand small arms were surrendered, one hundred and fifty cannon, seventy-one colors, eleven hundred wagons and caissons and four thousand horses and mules. The Confederate troops, immediately upon receiving their paroles, separated and returned to their homes."*

---

* Blue and Gray.

The scene of separation of soldiers and commanders, who had served nearly four years together, and who were linked together by the strongest bonds of comradeship, not to say of genuine affection, was the saddest and most trying that had ever occurred in the past history of the army. Farewells, amid tears and audible sobbing of the brave, rough soldiers, were exchanged and they parted, never to meet as soldiers, in arms again! Before leaving for home, however, and as the last act of the closing drama, and the last act of General Lee as the Commander of the Army of Northern Virginia, the day following the surrender he issued a farewell address.[*] The address was printed on slips of paper and distributed to the soldiers, who felt unwilling to leave for their homes until they received the parting blessing and loving benediction of their idolized commander.

FREDERICKSBURG AGAIN UNDER THE STARS AND STRIPES.

The first news of General Lee's surrender received at Fredericksburg came from soldiers returning to their desolated homes, and with the sad tidings came also the feeling that the fate of the Confederacy was sealed. The population of Fredericksburg at this time had been increased by the presence of strangers and adven-

---

[*] GENERAL LEE'S FAREWELL ADDRESS.

Headquarters Army Northern Virginia,

Appomattox Courthouse, April 10, 1865.

GENERAL ORDERS, No. 9.—After four years of arduous service, marked by unsurpassed courage and fortitude, the Army of Northern Virginia has been compelled to yield to overwhelming numbers.

I need not tell the brave survivors of so many hard fought battlefields, who have remained steadfast to the last, that I have consented to this result from no distrust of them, but feeling that valor and devotion could accomplish nothing to compensate for the loss that must have attended a continuation of the contest, I determined to avoid the useless sacrifice of those whose past services have endeared them to their countrymen.

By the terms of agreement, officers and men can return to their homes and remain until exchanged. You will take with you the satisfaction that proceeds from the consciousness of duty faithfully performed, and I earnestly pray that a merciful God will extend to you his blessing and protection. With an unceasing admiration of your constancy and devotion to your country, and a grateful remembrance of your kind and generous consideration of myself, I bid you all an affectionate farewell.

R. E. LEE; *General.*

turers. The trade of the town was conducted, to a considerable extent, by those who were not permanent residents of the town, and there was but little population, business or general appearance to remind one of the Fredericksburg of other days.

But what a change in other respects had come over the town as to its character and condition! For four years it had been a part of the Southern Confederacy, and its devotion to the Southern cause had been demonstrated time and again by its sacrifices, sufferings for and contributions to that cause. Now the collapse of the Confederacy had come and the town was again a part of the United States and subject to its laws. The question was what shall be done to place the town in its proper position, and who shall take that action? That was the question.

After a conference of the leading citizens of the town it was decided that the Council was the only body that could represent the people, and that it should be convened to take such steps as might be suggested by the proper authorities. This step was deferred, however, until the 27th of April, when it was known the Confederate government had ceased to exist, on which day the Council was convened, the following members being present: M. Slaughter, Mayor; Wm. A. Little, Recorder; Charles Herndon, George Gravatt, Joseph W. Sener, Horace B. Hall, Wm. H. Cunningham, Charles S. Scott, Beverley T. Gill, John G. Hurkamp, James McGuire, John J. Young, Thomas F. Knox, Councilmen. The following paper was submitted and unanimously adopted:

"Whereas, this community finds itself, after four years of disturbing war, all of whose evils and sacrifices they have been called upon to endure, subject to the laws of the United States, and under the control of its authority;

And whereas, they are satisfied that the war is at an end, and that their interests and duty alike require that they should recognize the situation and submit to said authority and laws, and, as quiet and orderly citizens, acknowledge the powers that be, and endeavor to preserve that character of a law abiding and peaceable community, which it has been their purpose to maintain;

And whereas further, it is deemed proper that this community should, through their constituted representatives, give expression at this time to those views and communicate the same to the United States authorities, therefore resolved—

1. That M. Slaughter, Esq., Mayor, be, and he is, hereby appointed a Commissioner to proceed to Richmond and present a copy of these proceedings through General M. R. Patrick to said authority.

2. Trusting that as the community and State is in no way responsible for the causes which led to the revolution and have already suffered so seriously during its progress, a magnanimous government will be satisfied with the restoration of its authority, and adopt towards us the policy of leniency and reconciliation which will tend with the people of Virginia to restore friendly relations, soften the asperities and heal the wounds of the past, and enable us to resume our former position as peaceful and prosperous citizens of Virginia and the United States.

Resolved, That the crime of assassination, which has so recently deprived the United States of its President,* has, in all ages and countries, received the unqualified detestation of all honorable and civilized communities, and that the perpetrator of this crime deserves the utmost punishment of the law and the condemnation of all upright men."†

This action of the Council was Fredericksburg's declaration of her allegiance to the United States, and made her a part of the Union, so far as that action could make her. She had passed through the fiery furnace of suffering and sacrifice since Virginia had withdrawn from the Union, but she hesitated to take any action by which her loyalty and devotion to the Confederate States could be questioned, and declined to take any steps transferring her allegiance to the Union until she knew that the Confederate government had disbanded and ceased to exist.

Fredericksburg had suffered as no other town in the South had suffered and had sacrificed her all, yet instead of complaining she

---

* The assassination of Abraham Lincoln, President of the United States, by J. Wilkes Booth on April 14, 1865.

† See Council proceedings, April 27, 1865.

Marye's Heights and section of old Stone Wall. These heights were crowded with artillery in the battle of December 13, 1862.
(See page 91.)

Office of "Trustees of the Town from 1727 to 1781; constructed into a residence.
(See page 153.)

showed herself grand in her sufferings and glorious in her sacrifices. There clustered around her hallowed memories, grand historic events, individual achievements, that, with her war record, imparted to her a beauty and nobility of character that made her sublime even in her desolation.

As time progressed population increased. The old citizens who had refugeed returned to their homes; young and middle-aged men, who had faithfully served their country in the army, exchanged their weapons of war for the implements of peace, and business began to assume its legitimate channels and the old town was well nigh restored to its wonted activity and prosperity. The census of 1870, very imperfectly taken, gave Fredericksburg at that time a population of about four thousand inhabitants.

RECONSTRUCTION COMMENCED.
Virginia Military District No. 1

The period in Virginia known as Reconstruction, extending from the cessation of hostilities, in 1865, to the first day of July, 1870, when the officers, elected under the new constitution, assumed their places and performed their duties, free of military restraint, was one of deep humiliation to the people of Virginia, and especially to the citizens of Fredericksburg. Just after the close of the war Virginia appears to have been neither a State nor a territory, but was declared to be Military District No. 1, and United States army officers were placed in authority over her affairs, civil as well as military. It is true that soon after the order proclaiming Virginia a military district a provisional governor was appointed by the authorities, but he was dominated by the military in his administration of affairs of State, and was powerless, it appears, to do anything in his office as Governor not sanctioned and approved by the commanding military officer.

While the town was in the hands of the civil authorities—the Mayor and Common Council, elected at the last election held before the close of the war—it was only nominally so. They were powerless to do anything unless it met the approval of the military authority. This was plainly shown by a communication received from Brigader-General T. M. Harris, commanding, on the first day of August, 1865, addressed to the Mayor. In that communication General Harris said:

"The sanitary condition of your town will, of course, claim the first and earnest attention of your Council. I am desirous of co-operating, so far as I am able, in this matter and desire the co-operation of the city authorities in return. It will be indispensable to have labor, which cannot be procured without money. I would, therefore, suggest that you take into consideration the propriety of levying a small per capita and also property tax for this purpose."

Of course, under the condition of things, a suggestion from the General commanding was virtually an order, and it was so understood. Accordingly, on the 8th of August, the Common Council was convened by the Mayor, when General Harris's communication was laid before it, considered and the following tax levied:

"On all real and personal property, fifty cents on the one hundred dollars value; on moneys, solvent bonds and securities, except the bonds of the corporation, forty cents on the one hundred dollars value; on all capital invested or used in any manufacturing business or investment, used or employed in any trade or business, twenty-five cents on every one hundred dollars; on the moneys and personal property of joint-stock companies, forty cents on every one hundred dollars; on every white and colored male above twenty-one years of age, two dollars." The same tax was levied for 1867.

AN ELECTION SET ASIDE.

The municipal government that found itself in possession of the town at the close of the war continued without any election, or any attempt to hold an election, until the Spring of 1867. At that time it seemed to be the opinion and desire of the Mayor and Common Council that an election should be held and that a full corps of officers for the town should be chosen. The only law under which the Council could act and order an election was the charter which was in force prior to the war and which prescribed that elections for Mayor and Common Council should be held on the third Monday in March of each year.

In accordance with this provision of the charter the Council ordered an election to be held on the 18th of March, 1867, for the election of a Mayor and Common Council, but the question of the qualification of voters having arisen, and the Council being unable to decide who were entitled to vote under the new order of things, referred the question to General John M. Scofield, who was then in command of Military District, No. 1.

General Scofield suspended the election "until the necessary preparations can be made to fully and fairly carry out the provisions of the act of Congress of March 3rd, 1867, concerning the elective franchise and the qualification of officers." On receipt of this order of suspension the Council passed the following resolution:

"That in pursuance of said order, the election heretofore advertised to be held on Monday, the 18th instant, for Mayor and Common Councilmen, be and it is hereby suspended until further orders. And whereas, further, under General Orders No. 1, issued from the same headquarters, all officers under the existing provisional government of Virginia are continued in office for the present, this Council, in accordance with said orders, do hereby resolve that the persons at present, discharging the duties required by the charter of this corporation, be and they are hereby continued in their respective offices until further orders." And there was a peculiar significance in the word orders!

THE IRON-CLAD OATH.

In April, 1867, the famous order was issued from "Headquarters, Military District, No. 1, of the State of Virginia," requiring every officer in the Commonwealth, State, municipal and county, to take the oath adopted by Congress in 1862, commonly called the test oath, and which was known through the South after the close of the war as the Iron-clad oath. This order affected every officer in the State, from the Governor down to the smallest officer, and it created quite a sensation. The oath was as follows:

"I, ———, of the county of ——— and State of ———, do solemnly swear that I have never voluntarily borne arms against the United States since I have been a citizen thereof; that I have voluntarily given no aid, countenance, counsel or encouragement to persons engaged in hostility thereto; that I have neither sought nor accepted, nor attempted to exercise the functions of any office whatsoever under any authority or pretended authority in hostility to the United States; that I have yielded no voluntary support to any authority, pretended authority or constitution within the United States inimical thereto. So help me God!"

Fredericksburg had no officer serving at that time who could take such an oath. Some of the officers had, at some time during the war, been active participants on the Confederate side, and those who were too far advanced in age to enter the army had sympathized with the Confederate cause and had otherwise aided it, therefore every officer, from Mayor down to policeman, was removed and their places supplied, in some few instances, by residents who took the required oath, but in most instances the appointees were strangers and citizens of Northern States, who had floated down South in search of some office at the hands of the military commander.

The venerable and efficient clerk of the courts, Mr. John James Chew, who had held the office for forty years, was removed and an inexperienced and inefficient stranger was installed in his place and given the keeping and custody of our court papers and records. Many of the appointees of the Common Council were men of that class, and were therefore unable to conduct the affairs of the town, provide a revenue to meet the running expenses and pay the interest on the city bonds.

The Military Council was placed in possession of the city government in 1867, and conducted public affairs on the revenues brought in by the tax bill levied by their predecessors by permission of the commanding general. In the latter part of 1867 the creditors of the town were demanding their money, and no money was in the treasury. They threatened suits to enforce payment of their dues, and in order to meet these obligations, on the 23rd of May, 1868, the Military Council passed a tax bill levying a tax of one dollar and a quarter on the one hundred dollars value of all real and personal property, and on all males over twenty-one years of age a capitation tax of three dollars, but the Commissioner of Revenue never made up his tax books and the tax was never collected. This state of things continued through the year 1869; therefore, when the Common Council of the people's own choosing took charge of the city government on the first of July, 1870, under the provisions of the new State constitution, they found municipal affairs in a wretched condition.

THE NEW CHARTER FOR THE CITY.

The new charter for the town, granted under the new State constitution, was passed by the Legislature and approved by the Governor on the 23rd of March, 1871. It differed very much from the charter under which the town was governed before the war, both as to new offices provided for and the term of officers. The officers to be elected by the people were one Mayor, who should hold his office for two years; twelve Councilmen, who should hold for one year; but this was subsequently changed so that six Councilmen should be elected from each ward—the town having been divided into two wards—and they were to hold office for two years; one City Sergeant for a term of two years; one Commissioner of the Revenue for two years, which has since been changed to four years, and one City Treasurer for three years. Any person who was a qualified voter was eligible to any one of the offices named above, and when they were elected and qualified they were to "have the powers, perform the duties and be subject to the liabilities and responsibilities prescribed by the general laws" of the State.

They were not to enter upon their respective duties until they qualified before some person authorized to administer oaths, and, in addition to the oath of fidelity and the anti-duelling oath, each one had also to swear "that I recognize and accept the civil and political equality of all men before the law." This was another reminder to us that the "negroes were free," and was "intended as the lash to compel Southern courts to administer to them justice and to election officers to accord them all the privileges at the polls they were allowed."

The Mayor was to preside at the meetings of the Council, give the casting vote on questions before that body in case of a tie and act as a justice of the peace in civil and criminal matters arising in the corporation. He was to have control of the police of the town and appoint special police officers when he deemed it necessary; and, in addition to these duties, he was empowered to try all offences and controversies arising under the ordinances of the town, to impose fines and collect the same, saving to the parties the right of appeal when the matter in controversy exceeded the sum of ten dollars.

The Council was authorized to establish and regulate markets, to alter or improve streets, alleys, sidewalks and bridges, and keep the same in order; to provide for the lighting of streets, against accidents by fire; to establish fire companies, purchase engines, and to provide wells or cisterns for supplying water. It was authorized to prevent and punish, by reasonable fines, the practice of discharging fire-arms and running horses in the town; to license and regulate shows and other exhibitions, and tax them in such manner as may be expedient and lawful; to lay off public grounds and provide for and take care of public buildings, grounds and cemeteries; to conduct and distribute water into and through the town; to adopt rules for its own government and the transaction of its business. It was also to define the powers, prescribe the duties and fix the term of service and compensation of its own appointees, necessary for conducting the affairs of the town, not otherwise provided; to fix the salary of the Mayor and all other officers, but no compensation was to be allowed to any member of the Council unless he should act as clerk of the body. The Council was to make all such by-laws and regulations as it might deem necessary, consistent with the constitution and laws of the State, for the good government of the town, and to enforce the same by reasonable fines and penalties, not exceeding for any one offence the sum of ten dollars.

The Council was authorized to provide a revenue for the town and appropriate the same, and for that purpose it was made the duty of the Commissioner of the Revenue to make an annual assessment of taxable persons and property within the town, such as should be taxable under the revenue laws of the State, including dogs and other animals running at large.

This was the release of the liberty-loving people of Fredericksburg from military bondage and misrule, signed, sealed and delivered, for which they rejoiced as did the captive Israelite of old as he again returned from bondage to his beloved native land.

CITIZENS AGAIN IN CONTROL.

The Ante Bellum Debt of the Town.

Prior to the war the Council, by direction of the people, given through the ballot, had made large appropriations to public improvements, with a view of building up the town by retaining the trade of the surrounding country, which was threatened by other cities, and by drawing trade from other sections of the country that found markets elsewhere. From these improvements the hopes of the town were not realized. Some of them remained in an unfinished condition, while others had been rendered worthless by new lines of railroad that had diverted their business and rendered them worthless; yet, the debt owed by the town, by reason of these appropriations and other expenditures, amounted to $244,521.48.* All this debt was hanging over the desolated town and not a dollar's worth of property to show for it.

In addition to this loss no provision had been made by former Councils to meet the interest on these bonds for the past four or five years, and suits had been brought and judgments obtained to enforce payment and other suits were threatened. Under judgments and executions obtained against the corporation, all property belonging to the town, available, was sold at public auction by the officer of the law. Even the chairs in the council chamber, in which the members of the Council sat to conduct the public business of the town, were sold by the constable at public outcry under execution. The members of the Council attended this sale and each

---

* This amount was ascertained by Mr. St. George R. Fitzhugh, after a thorough examination of the indebtedness of the town at the close of the war, about 1895, which was published in the town papers and also in circulars and distributed.

one purchased his chair, and thereafter the members furnished their own seats at the council board, while they legislated for the public good, without fee or reward, other than the consciousness of duty nobly done.

The Common Council that took charge of municipal affairs in 1870 had many grave and difficult questions to meet and determine. Debts had accumulated against the city, while the taxable values had greatly diminished by the destruction of property during the war and the emancipation of the slaves. A large portion of the inhabitants had recently returned home—the women and children from refugeeing and the men from the army—almost penniless, to find their homes in ruins or badly damaged and despoiled of what had been left in them. Nearly everybody had to commence life anew.

The Council, therefore, had to provide for these debts, and, at the same time, not place a burden upon an impoverished people, in the form of taxation that they could not bear. It was a trying ordeal, but the members were equal to the emergency. That Council was composed of Walker Peyton Conway, J. Gordon Wallace, Hugh S. Doggett, George W. Eve, Patrick McCracken, Wm. C. Morrison, Joseph W. Sener, John T. Knight, John H. Myer, George Gravatt, Thomas Harrison and John James Young.

The finance committee of that Council, which was expected to provide for the finances and bring before the Council, for its consideration and adoption, such measures as would meet the emergency and not oppress the tax-payers, consisted of W. P. Conway, J. Gordon Wallace and Hugh S. Doggett. With great diligence they applied themselves to their task. A tax bill was formulated and brought before the Council levying a tax, which was adopted, and in a short time money was raised, the debts were paid in installments until all creditors were paid or satisfactory arrangements made with them.

In 1876 the old bonds of the city were funded, by mutual agreement of the Council and the bond holders, at sixty-six and two-third cents on the dollar, the new bonds to bear seven per cent. interest and run thirty years. This was a wise arrangement of the

Council, notwithstanding there was considerable opposition to it, the opponents of the measure claiming that the rate of interest of the new bonds should not exceed six per cent., although money was then bringing from ten to twelve per cent., and sometimes more than twelve. The amount of bonds issued under this funding act amounted to $125,000.

By this arrangement of funding one-third of the principal of the bonds was eliminated, the threatened suits for past-due interest were averted, and it put the Council in a position to provide for the interest as it should fall due, take care of the floating debt, and at the same time reduce the rate of taxation, which the tax-payer hailed with delight. Thus the delinquencies of the former years were met and provided for, the rate of taxation was not oppressive, and the town, being under the control of its own citizens, untrammelled by military authority, rapidly moved forward, public confidence in its ability to meet its obligations was restored and thus municipal affairs were placed in a satisfactory condition. The credit of the city is as good at present as any city of the State, and no bonds have been funded or sold in the last twelve years at a greater rate of interest than four per cent., or at any figure below their face value.

PRESENT INDEBTEDNESS, INCLUDING ANTE AND POST BELLUM BONDS.

The bonded indebtedness of the city, and the improvements for which said bonds were issued is a matter that concerns every citizen, and for their information are here given as of 1908:

Five per cent. water bonds, issued July 1, 1895, due January 1, 1909, coupons payable January and July 1st .... $ 30,000

Four per cent. gas bonds, issued January 2, 1900, coupons due July and January 2nd, bonds due January 2, 1920........... 25,000

Four per cent. bridge bonds, issued July 2, 1900, coupons due January and July 2nd, bonds due July 2, 1920............... 25,000

Four per cent. electric light bonds, issued January 1, 1901, coupons due July and January 1st, bonds due January 1, 1931... 12,000

Four per cent, sewer bonds, issued April 1, 1901, coupons due October and April 1st, bonds due April 1, 1931.............. 18,000

Four per cent. street improvement bonds, issued April 1, 1901, coupons due October and April 1st, bonds due April 1, 1931.... 20,000

Four per cent. water and gas bonds, issued April 1, 1905, coupons due October and April 1st, bonds due April 1, 1931..... 20,000
Four per cent. gas and water bonds, issued September 1, 1905, coupons due September 1st, $5,000 to be paid each year till paid, $5,000 already paid................................... 20,000
Four per cent. bonds funding the old 7 per cent. bonds, issued May 1, 1906, coupons due May and November, bonds due May 1, 1936... 119,400
Three bonds of $5,000, due National Bank of Fredericksburg and payable $5,000 on November 1, 1908, and yearly thereafter, bearing 4 per cent. interest............................... 15,000
Making the total bonded debt of the town $304,400

Many of these public improvements were constructed by the authority of the freeholders of the town, by a majority vote cast at special elections appointed and held for that purpose; others were constructed by action of the City Council under authority granted them by the new constitution enlarging the powers and duties of city councils, and appeared to have the sanction of a large majority of the tax-payers of the town.

Confederate Cemetery at Fredericksburg. The pyramid of stones marks the battle-field at Hamilton's Crossing, between Jackson and Meade.
(See page 185)

CHAPTER IX

The Courts of Fredericksburg—The Freedman's Bureau—Court Orders and Incidents—First Night Watch—Ministers Qualify to Perform Marriage Ceremony—First Notary Public—Fixing the Value of Bank Notes—Prison Bounds for Debtors—Public Buildings, &c.

If every one in this Christian land was a Christian, and was governed by the rule laid down and inculcated by the Christ, "whatsoever ye would that men should do to you, do ye even so to them," there would have been but little, if any, use for courts in this country. But all people are not Christians, and all Christians are not governed by that golden rule, therefore courts were necessary to punish crime, settle disputes, protect the weak against the strong, secure the widow and orphan in their rights, enforce provision for the indigent poor, and perform other functions for the benefit of society and the well-being of the country.

What courts Fredericksburg had before the Revolutionary war is unknown, as no record seems to have been left of them. In all probability the successors of Major Lawrence Smith were also authorized to execute martial law and hear and determine all questions, as a county court might do, until the town was chartered in 1727 and placed in the hands of trustees. These trustees had certain powers conferred upon them by act of the House of Burgesses, and they were to keep records of their proceedings, but these records cannot now be found and quite likely have long ago been destroyed.

It may have been possible that the Colonial Governors appointed magistrates to hear and determine causes within certain limits and to punish petty offences, while causes beyond those limits and felonies were heard and determined by the court sitting at Williamsburg. Of this, however, we are left to conjecture, as no records are at our command. But if this had been the manner of dispensing justice prior to 1781, it furnished a pattern for the

Virginia Legislature for many years thereafter with respect to the town, as is referred to elsewhere.

The first court established in Fredericksburg, that we now have any records of, was by an act of the General Assembly of Virginia, passed during the session of 1781. At that session Fredericksburg was regularly incorporated and given a Common Council and a hustings court, but the court did not organize until April 15, 1782. At its organization the following justices were present: Charles Mortimer, Wm. McWilliams, James Somerville, Charles Dick, Samuel Roddy and John Julien, "the same being Mayor, Recorder and Aldermen of the town," elected to their respective offices on the 18th day of March, 1782, in the order above named.

This continued as the only court of the town until 1788, when nineteen district courts were established in the State by the General Assembly, one of which was located at Fredericksburg. These courts were presided over by two judges of the General Court, located at Richmond, the number of judges of that court having been, by the same act, increased from five to ten judges.

This district court was regarded as a very important court, and was attended by some of the ablest lawyers in Virginia and adjoining States. Edmund Randolph, after he was Governor and twice a Cabinet Minister,* and also James Monroe, a citizen of this place, after he was Minister to England, France and Spain, were attorneys before and practised in this court. While attending a session of this court, on the 3rd day of May, 1798, Governor Randolph published the following card in the *Virginia Herald:*

"My business in the Court of Appeals and High Court of Chancery render it impossible for me to attend *constantly* the district court holden at this place. I have, therefore, come hither, during the present term, with a hope of finishing almost every cause in which I was employed; and have refused all fees, which have been offered to me in any suits, which I may not try before I leave the town. I am apprehensive, however, that I shall not succeed in concluding everything; and I have accordingly, made the following

---
* Attorney-General and Secretary of the Treasury in Washington's Cabinet.

arrangement: To some of my clients I have personally returned the fees; to all others, where the business has not been absolutely finished, or any step remains to be taken, except to move for the opinion of the court, the fee will be returned on application to John Chew, Esq., clerk of the court, who has been so obliging as to accept from me a list of all my suits, still depending, of the money received, and of their situation. Although the fees are to be returned yet I have obtained the favor of Colonel Monroe,* Colonel John Minor and Francis Brooke, Esq.,† to attend to these suits, agreeably to the memorandum which I have given each of them, with every paper and information in my power. In two of the cases, which are of peculiar importance, I shall attend myself at a future day; and in all instances, will cheerfully assist with my advice. If required, I will be ready to attend the trial of any particular suits, now or hereafter depending in this court whensoever the business of the Court of Appeals and High Court of Chancery will permit."

This court continued in existence for about twenty years, when, by an act of the General Assembly of 1808-9, it was abolished, and a "Circuit Court or a Superior Court of Law," was established in its stead. This new court was presided over by one of the judges of the General Court, the number of judges of that court, it appears, having been increased from ten to fifteen, to correspond with the number of circuits established in the State. These courts have continued to the present time, with slight changes at different periods as to their powers and territory, and are presided over by circuit judges.

In the year 1852 the State was divided into ten districts and a court was established for each district, known as the District Court of Appeals. The court for the Fourth district was located at Fredericksburg, and was held up-stairs in the north wing of the present courthouse. This court consisted of the judges of the circuit courts constituting the district and the judge of the Court of Appeals, elected from this section of the State, as president. It

---
* President James Monroe.
† Afterwards one of the Judges of the Supreme Court.

was provided that no judge should sit in any appeal case sent up from his circuit. This court continued until the adoption of what was known as the Underwood Constitution, which failed to make provision for district courts.

Prior to 1870 the corporation or hustings court was held by three or more justices of the peace, but when the State constitution of that year was adopted it raised that court to a higher dignity, its powers and jurisdiction were enlarged, and a judge prescribed "who shall be learned in the law." Since the establishment of this court it has had five judges to preside over it—John M. Herndon, John T. Goolrick, Montgomery Slaughter, A. Wellington Wallace, and Alvin T. Embrey. The new State constitution abolished all county courts and provided four annual terms of the circuit court, which were regarded ample for all purposes. In this change in the present constitution Fredericksburg lost her session of the circuit court and also her hustings court, but authority was conferred upon the City Council to continue the hustings court if it judged it necessary, the Legislature to elect the judge, whose term of office was to be ten years, and the Council was to pay his salary. In accordance with this authority the Council decided to continue the court, and Judge John T. Goolrick was elected by the General Assembly to preside over it.

The police court, established by the State constitution of 1870, is held by the Mayor of the town, and in his absence by the Recorder, or in his absence by any justice of the peace who may be designated by the Mayor for that purpose. This court has jurisdiction of misdemeanors and of civil cases, where the amount involved is less than one hundred dollars, with the right of appeal to the corporation court when the amount in controversy is ten dollars or more. After the first of January, 1909, by provision of State law, this court will be conducted by a police justice.

CIRCUIT COURT.

The new State constitution increased the number of circuits, when the county courts were abolished, to twenty-nine, and also increased the terms of the court to four annually, in order to enable the judges to do what the circuit courts previously did and most of the work formerly allotted to the old county courts. In order to do this the duties of the circuit clerks were greatly enlarged, that they might do much of the business heretofore transacted by the county courts. Fredericksburg is in the fifteenth circuit, but no session of the court is held within her borders. The circuit consists of five counties—King George, Stafford, Spotsylvania, Caroline and Hanover. Our circuit judge is the Hon. John E. Mason, who resides most of the time in Fredericksburg.

CHANGE IN CITY AFFAIRS.

The same constitution that changed the circuit courts and abolished the county courts made many changes also with government of cities and towns. In Fredericksburg, divided into two wards as it had been for some years, the six Councilmen from each ward were elected at the same time to serve two years, the Mayor being the presiding officer of the body. In these changes each ward is to elect three Councilmen every two years, who are to serve a term of four years, and the presiding officer is to be elected from the body of the Council. The present president is William E. Bradley, Esq., the first one having been Col. E. D. Cole.

THE FREEDMAN'S BUREAU.

The Freedman's Bureau was established in Fredericksburg in 1865. It was an unique judicial tribunal, and found its way in our midst by reason of the disjointed condition of the country at that time. It was brought into being by congressional enactment, to be operated alone in the Southern States that had formed the Southern Confederacy, which government had then ceased to exist. The geographical divisions in the South were no longer States, as heretofore stated, but military districts, designated by numbers, and it was the opinion of the Federal authorities, it seems, that in the chaotic condition of society and the impotency of our courts, or from some other cause, the colored people, who had just been emancipated from slavery, would not be justly dealt with by their former owners, hence the necessity of this civil-military tribunal.

These Freedman's bureaus were composed of three judges—one

an army officer and two citizens. In the organization of the bureau in Fredericksburg two of the judges were appointed by the commander of the military district and the third one was elected by the Common Council. Being thus formed it was supposed that all parties brought before the court would receive justice. It had original jurisdiction over misdemeanors, controversies involving labor and the observance of contracts, and appellate jurisdiction from the decisions of magistrates and police justices, where the rights of colored people and United States soldiers were involved.

The first court of this kind organized in Fredericksburg was composed of Major James Johnson, a United States army officer, Major Charles Williams, an ardent Union man, and James B. Sener, who was unanimously elected by the Common Council "a commissioner on the part of the citizens of the town in the Freedman's bureau, about to be organized."*

Many absurd and amusing stories were put in circulation about this court, and the colored people were variously impressed with its functions and purposes, as well as of its powers and jurisdiction. Persons who followed the Union army to town, and who professed great friendship for the colored people and secured their confidence, told them that one purpose of the Freedman's Bureau was to adjust financial matters between ex-slaves and their former owners and to remunerate them for labor performed while they were in slavery. The money for this purpose was to be made from the property of those who owned the slaves and who received the benefit of their services.

The most of the colored people believed these, as they did the other absurd stores,† and it was agreed that a test case should be made in Fredericksburg, and if it was decided in favor of the ex-slave that all the other ex-slaves should bring similar suits for their

---

* Council proceedings, 1867.

†Some of the colored people were told by wags that the object of the bureau was to furnish a bureau to every colored family that had none, as it was composed of bureaus. Believing this to be true, some colored women are said to have driven their wagons from Caroline county to town and applied to Major Johnson for their bureau, and could not conceal their disgust when they were informed that "It was a jestis bureau they had in Fredericksburg and not a furniture bureau."

ante-bellum services. The papers were prepared in such a case by one of the so-called lawyers, who made their appearance in our midst in those troublous times, one of our colored men being the plaintiff, but it was soon ascertained that such a suit would be "laughed out of court," and therefore the matter was dropped and nothing more was heard from it. It is said that after this the bureau was not popular even with the colored people.

COURT ORDERS AND INCIDENTS.

There are many orders made and incidents that happened in the old courts that will be of interest to-day, if for no other reason than for their age and the fact that they are not practised in our present courts. Among the first things that claimed the attention of the hustings court, after its organization and appointment of the officers of the court, was to fix the rates of charges for the tavern-keepers. This it did on the 20th day of May, 1782, entering the following schedule:

"Good West India rum, one pound per gallon; bread, ten shillings; whiskey, six; strong beer, four; good West India rum toddy, ten shillings; brandy toddy, seven shillings and six pence; rum punch, fifteen shillings; brandy punch, twelve; rum grog, six; brandy grog, five. Diet: one meal, one shilling and six pence; lodging, one shilling and three pence; "stablidge" and hay, two shillings; oats and corn, nine pence per gallon."

Nearly half a century passed before another order in reference to tavern rates was made, or recorded if made. It is presumed that the schedule of rates made in 1782 was in force until the 10th day of May, 1838, or was renewed from time to time, with slight changes. On the 10th of May, 1838, another list of prices was adopted by the court, and entered as follows, dollars and cents being substituted for pounds and shillings:

Breakfast, 50 cents; dinner 50; supper, 50; lodging, 25; grain per gallon, $12\frac{1}{2}$ "stablage" and hay per night, 25; Madeira wine, per quart, 1.00; champagne, per quart, 1.50; other wine per quart, 50; rench brandy, $12\frac{1}{2}$ per gill; rum, $12\frac{1}{2}$; gin, $12\frac{1}{2}$; whiskey, $12\frac{1}{2}$; corn per gallon, 25.

Another order was made by the court on the first day of March, 1784, when it "proceeded to settle the allowances to the officers of the corporation." That order gave to the officers their salaries as follows: Mr. John Minor, Jr., attorney for the Commonwealth, 2000 pounds of tobacco; Henry Armistead, clerk, 1200 pounds; John Legg, sergeant, 1200 pounds; Henry Armistead, for attending all courts of inquiry, 400 pounds; sergeant for same, 570 pounds, and Wm. Jenkins, "gaoler," 364 pounds. For several years the salaries of the corporation officers were paid in the same manner and in the same currency.

On the 2nd of August, 1784, it was "ordered that the clerk certify that this court do recommend Robert Brooke* as a person of probity, honesty and good demeanor." This recommendation, it is understood, was necessary in order for Mr. Brooke to obtain a license from the General Court to practise law; and on the 7th of February, 1785, Robert Brooke and Bushrod Washington† were admitted as practising lawyers before the court.

Henry Armistead, the first clerk of the court, died about the first of August, 1787, and on the 6th of August John Chew, Jr., was appointed clerk to fill the vacancy. By that appointment we have this remarkable record, that from the appointment of John Chew, Jr., on the 6th of August, 1787, to the death of Colonel Robert S. Chew, on the 17th of August, 1886, the clerkship of the hustings court was in the Chew family, except the short time it was held by W. C. Strait under military appointment. It went from father to son for the fourth generation, covering a period of ninety-nine years and eleven days. These generations served as follows: John Chew, Jr., from 1787 to 1806; Robert S. Chew, from 1806 to 1826; John James Chew, from 1826 to 1867, and Robert S. Chew, from 1870 to 1886.

On the 27th of February, 1789, we are told that "James Mercer, Esq., Chief Justice of the General Court this day in open court took the oath of a Judge to the District Court, pursuant to an act of the

---

* Governor of Virginia in 1794-96, and afterwards Attorney-General of the State.

† Appointed a Justice of the Supreme Court of the United States by President Washington.

General Assembly entitled an act establishing district courts, and for regulating the General Court, which is ordered to be certified accordingly." From this entry we learn that James Mercer,* a Fredericksburg lawyer, was not only the chief justice of the General Court, which was held in Richmond, but the judge of the first district court held in Fredericksburg. This district court was the first court held in the town having jurisdiction over higher crimes than misdemeanors. Before the institution of this court all white persons charged with felonies were sent to Richmond for trial by the General Court.

From the records of the hustings court it appears that the "Gentlemen Justices" for many years after the introduction of United States money entered up fines and judgments in pounds, shillings and pence. The clerk used dollars and cents in entering up costs as early as 1795, but the court did not adopt the American count until about July, 1797. It is also noticeable that the clerk in nearly all entries placed the dollar mark after the figures, instead of in front of them, according to the present custom.

The first intimation that the town needed a watch or police, in addition to the town sergeant, is given in an order of the court, entered April 25, 1801, when it was "ordered that the sergeant of this corporation do (within the time limited for the collection of the other taxes in this corporation) collect of the housekeepers, within the jurisdiction of this court, two per cent. on the amount of their rents, agreeable to the assessed value thereof, and that he pay the same to the chamberlain to be appropriated to paying a watch to be kept in said corporation, the same being this day levied for that purpose."

On March 27, 1802, the grand jury of the corporation presented "as a nuisance the numerous obstructions in the streets, particularly in St. George street lot, burying the dead in George and Princess Ann streets; also the irregular burying in the ground west of and adjoining Prince Edward street." The most of the obstructions complained of were on Hanover street, west of Princess Ann,

---

* Wrote Mary Washington's will and was one of the witnesses to her signature.

and on George street, from Main to the river. The burying ground adjoining Prince Edward street about twenty-five years ago was converted into Hurkamp park.

The court had been in existence more than twenty-two years before any record is found where a minister of the gospel, of any denomination, qualified to perform the rites of matrimony. It may have been that the law did not require such qualification prior to 1804, and was enacted that year. At any rate, the first one to appear before the court was on the 24th day of December, 1804. On that day "Benj. Essex, having produced to the court credentials of his ordination and of his being in regular communion with the Methodist Society, and having taken the oath of fidelity to the Commonwealth and entered into bond with security according to law, a testimonial is granted him to celebrate the rites of matrimony according to the forms and customs of the said Methodist church." Similar orders were entered by the court for ministers of other denominations as they applied to the court. From the record we find they applied as follows: Samuel Wilson, of the Presbyterian church, September 22, 1806; Samuel Low, of the Episcopal church, September 8, 1808, and Wm. James, of the Baptist church, June 13, 1811. So it is found that as early as 1811 any one could be married in Fredericksburg, according to the customs of the Methodist, Presbyterian, Episcopalian and Baptist churches.

On the 24th of December, 1805, John T. Lomax and Carter L. Stevenson qualified to practise law in the hustings court. They were two leading citizens of the town and served the public long and faithfully. John T. Lomax afterwards was made judge of the circuit court and one of the judges of the district court. He was also the author of several law books. Mr. Stevenson was thirty-five years Commonwealth's attorney in the town, holding the office a longer period than any other attorney, before or since his day.

The first notary public to qualify in the hustings court was John Metcalfe. He was appointed by Governor James Barbour, and on the 12th day of November, 1812, came into court and produced his commission as a notary public, "whereupon the said John Metcalfe took the oath of fidelity to the Commonwealth, and that he

The Baptist Church.
(See page 209)

will without favor or partiality, honestly, intelligently and faithfully discharge the duties of a notary public."

REGULATING THE CURRENCY.

In the early part of the nineteenth century "paper money" superseded tobacco and tobacco warehouse receipts as currency, and therefore much of it was issued. The notes of the denomination of one dollar, and more, were generally designated as bills, while those below one dollar were called "shin plasters." At first these notes were issued by States, cities and banks, but in a few years incorporated companies, and sometimes individuals, issued them. These notes were not always taken at their face value, especially when they were found any distance from their place of issue.

This being the case, it was difficult for the people to distinguish between the good and the doubtful, or to fix the proper rate of discount. Therefore the courts took the matter in hand. The question was considered and passed upon, for the first time in our courts, on the 14th of March, 1816, the subject being the difference between the paper currency of Virginia and the bank notes of other places, which were found in circulation in Fredericksburg. Having properly investigated and reached a conclusion, the court declared and entered on record, as follows:

"It appears to the satisfaction of the court that the chartered bank notes of the District of Columbia, State of North Carolina, and cities of Philadelphia and Baltimore, are current in this town, and it is the opinion of the court that the chartered bank notes of the District of Columbia, when compared with the chartered bank notes of Virginia, are at a depreciation of six per cent.; that the said notes of the cities of Philadelphia and Baltimore are at a depreciation of five per cent. and that the said notes of the State of North Carolina are of equal value with the said notes of Virginia."

A similar declaration was made by the court each year for several years thereafter.

On the 10th day of November, 1831, the will of Thomas Seddon*

---

* Mr. Thomas Seddon was the father of Hon. James A. Seddon, Confederate Secretary of War, and lived in the residence now owned and occupied by Mr. George W. Shepherd.

was admitted to probate. Philip Alexander, John Moncure and Arthur A. Morson were appointed and qualified as executors and entered into bond, without security, the deceased requesting that none be required, in the sum of $240,000, it being the largest bond ever before required by the court. Appraisers were appointed by the court to appraise his property in the town of Fredericksburg and the counties of Spotsylvania, Stafford, Prince William, Culpeper, Fauquier, Shenandoah and Page, and they were ordered to make returns to this court.

The court entered the following certificate on its records on the 12th day of January, 1832: "The court orders it to be certified that it was proved to their satisfaction by the evidence of Francis S. Scott, a witness sworn in court, that Major Robert Forsythe, of the Revolutionary army, had two children, one of whom, Robert, died under age and unmarried, and the other son, John, is now alive, being the Senator in Congress from Georgia."

THE POOR DEBTOR'S PRISON BOUNDS.

In the olden times, when some claim that the people were more honest and just and the laws more righteous than they are now, a person who failed or refused to pay his debts could, by proper process, be placed in "prison bounds," and kept there until he exhibited to the court a schedule of his property, made under oath. If he had nothing more in the opinion of the court, than a reasonable allowance under the law, the court could discharge him as a poor debtor from custody. For more than fifty years the prison bounds was the square on which the jail is located. The poor debtor was allowed the full width of the streets around the square, but was not allowed to enter a building on the opposite side. Many distinguished men, it is said, have been confined to this central point in the town because they were unable at the time to meet their obligations.

In 1840 the court extended the liberty of the poor debtor by enlarging the prison bounds to four squares, probably because the law had relaxed its hold upon him. He could roam anywhere on those four squares and in the streets bounding them, but he could not go beyond the limits without being in contempt and becoming liable to additional punishment by the court. This order of extension was made on the 11th of June, 1840, and recorded as follows:

"The court doth fix the prison bounds as follows, to-wit: Beginning at the intersection of Caroline and William streets, thence up William to Charles street, thence down Charles street to Hanover street thence down Hanover street to Caroline street, thence up Caroline street to William street, including the footways on each side."

And now having escaped the prison bounds we will visit the public buildings of the town and take a peep at them.

CHAPTER X

The Public Buildings—The Jail—Courthouse—Town Hall—Firehouse—School Buildings—Wallace Library—Normal School —Government Building, &c.

As it was found necessary to have courts to punish crimes, to settle disputes and to enforce law and order in the Commonwealth for the good of society, it was also found necessary to have buildings in which to hold the courts, to keep their records, and a place to confine criminals until they were tried by the courts, and then to punish them after conviction for their crimes. Therefore, the act that gave Fredericksburg a name and a place among the towns of the country, also gave it the authority, and enjoined it as a duty, to erect a courthouse and a jail, which was soon done; and it is almost certain that whatever court Fredericksburg had from 1727, when it was first incorporated, to 1781, when it was chartered by the Legislature of Virginia, was held in that courthouse and that the criminals were kept and punished in that jail.

When the hustings court was organized its sessions were held in the "coffee-house," but as soon as preparations could be made it was held in the old town hall, or market-house, on Main street, which appears to have had rooms sufficient for all public uses, as it was a favorite resort for the "lovers of balls and parties and other public gatherings."

The first thing, however, that claimed the attention of the court was the repairing of the "courthouse and common gaol, where criminals could be placed and safely kept and in due time brought before the court." The first jail erected for the town seems to have been built partly with brick, and, from a false notion of economy, was entirely too small, was uncomfortable and not fit to keep prisoners in. This was so patent that the matter was, at various times, and for several years, brought to the attention of the court. Various grand juries, upon examination, had reported that it was not a suitable place in which to confine prisoners.

In 1803 a grand jury brought in an indictment against the jail as a nuisance, and charged that a colored criminal, who had been confined therein, had contracted a disease of which he afterwards died. This colored man was arrested, charged with entering a house in the night time and stealing goods therefrom, which was a capital offence. He was tried by the hustings court, after considerable delay, and sentenced to be hung, but was recommended to the mercy of the Governor, who pardoned him.

It was while the colored man was awaiting a trial, and afterwards the action of the Governor, that it was claimed he contracted a disease, of which he died soon after his liberation. Upon this report of the grand jury the court ordered the small, brick jail torn down and a new one of stone to be erected in its place. This new building was completed in 1805, when Wm. Taylor was appointed by the court and ordered to "sell the brick and other materials of the old jail in this corporation on a credit of sixty days and make return to this court."

This jail stood on Princess Ann street, just north of the present clerk's office, and, long before it was torn down and removed, was "an eye-sore to the public," and especially to those who lived in that locality. In 1851, when it was decided to build a new courthouse, it was also decided to move the jail. This was a joint action of the court and Common Council, and it met with serious opposition by many of the tax-payers, on the ground that it was a waste of public money, the present jail being all that was needed.

But the order was given, and the jail was torn down and rebuilt in rear of the courthouse, the public scales, which stood on the spot, to be "moved to some more convenient place." The most of the stone in the old jail was placed in the new one, but a portion of it was taken for the foundation of the fence, which, until some six years ago, enclosed the courthouse yard and sustained the wall on George street and in Jail alley. The present granite alignment of the courthouse lot is a great improvement on the old iron fence.

THE COURTHOUSE.

The first courthouse the town had was built on a part of the ground occupied by the present building and stood several feet back from the street. It was a small, brick structure and very uncomfortable. It is supposed to have been the second courthouse built for the town, the first having been built soon after the town was laid out. As early as 1820 the courts complained of the building they had to occupy and declared that it was unsuitable for court purposes. Various requests and complaints were made and orders issued to the Common Council by the court, looking to the erection of a new and commodious building, but the Council appeared to take no action in the matter, except to lay on the table all communications from the court on the subject.

It appears that the town and county were joint owners in the jail and courthouse, they being public property and the town then being a part of the county, and possibly contributed some way to their erection. This may account to some extent for the tardiness of the Council in taking action, but whether it does or not, the court was not satisfied and did not attempt to conceal its displeasure.

Finding its requests and orders disregarded, the court issued an order declaring that the Council must build a new courthouse or provide a better place for holding court, but even this did not appear to hurry the Council, which moved along in its own quiet way. This controversy went on for several years, the court requesting, ordering, even threatening, without avail. It finally reached a point where it seems to have exhausted its patience and determined to assert its authority.

On the 14th of June, 1849, the court being composed of Mayor Semple and Justices Wm. H. White and Peter Goolrick, the following order was made and entered on the record book:

"It is ordered, that Thomas B. Barton, John L. Marye, Robert B. Semple, Wm. C. Beale and John J. Chew, who are hereby appointed a committee for that purpose, do examine and report to this court, some plan for the enlargement and repairs or rebuilding of the courthouse for this corporation, for the convenient administration of justice; and the said committee are also requested to examine and report whether any other public building, belonging to this corporation, can be so changed as to answer the above purpose, and to inquire and report the probable cost of such plan or plans as they may approve and report upon, and it is ordered that the justices for this corporation be summoned to attend here at the next court to consider and decide upon said report."

While this order and the appointment of the committee, with its instructions, created considerable comment, it did not seem to excite the Council or precipitate any action favorable to the proposed building. At the next court eight justices were present in answer to the summons issued at the last session of the court. Those present were R. B. Semple, Robert Dickey, Beverly R. Wellford, Wm. C. Beale, Wm. H. White, Peter Goolrick, Wm. Slaughter and Wm. Warren.

The report of the committee appointed at the previous court, was made, and the court declared "that in obedience to the act of the General Assembly, which requires that courts for the corporations within this Commonwealth should cause to be erected one good and convenient courthouse, that it is necessary and proper to build a courthouse for this corporation," and the report of the committee "having been returned to court, and therewith an order from the county court of Spotsylvania, releasing to this court all title and interest the said county has to the jail and courthouse, within this corporation, and the said lots on which they stand, being considered by this court, it is approved and confirmed."

The court then appointed a commission, consisting of Mayor Semple, Beverly R. Wellford, Wm. H. White, Thomas B. Barton and John L. Marye, who were instructed to contract with some responsible party to erect a good and substantial courthouse on lots 42 and 44, or either of them, according to the plan submitted to the court, or that plan modified, if it was found necessary, the cost not to exceed four thousand dollars. The commission was to report from time to time to the court.

This action looked as if the court intended to exhaust its powers or have a new courthouse, but a few days' mixing with the people seems to have raised a doubt in the minds of the members of the court as to the wisdom of their action. At any rate, when the August term came the full corps of magistrates was present. "A petition, and counter petition of the citizens of Fredericksburg, in relation to the action of the court upon the subject of rebuilding the courthouse, were severally presented, when, on a motion made to rescind the order for building the courthouse and laying a levy therefor, the vote stood as follows:

For rescinding, Robert B. Semple, Peter Goolrick, Wm. C. Beale, Robert Dicky, 4. Against rescinding, Beverley R. Welford, Wm. H. White, Wm. Slaughter, Wm. Warren, 4. The court being divided on the question of repealing or enforcing its own order, the subject was dropped so far as any action of the court was concerned, and was not again brought up for several months.

At the April term, in 1850, however, the court respectfully requested the Council to appoint a day to have an election, that the voters might express their wishes as to whether or not a levy should be made for the purpose of building a courthouse. This paper, although it placed the court before the Council in the attitude of an humble suppliant, was read before the Council and laid on the table, as all former papers from that source had been.

This seems to have ended the efforts of the court to secure a new courthouse or the repairing of the old, either by entreaties, threats or by the power given it under the acts of the General Assembly. Thus things continued for one year, although the question was warmly discussed by the citizens, who were very much divided on the subject. An election was to be held the following March, and the court, finding itself defeated in all former efforts, transferred the question to the people in their selections for members of the Council. This was a wise move for the friends of the measure. The election was held and a Council in favor of building a new courthouse was elected. The eyes of the public were now turned from the hustings court to the Common Council which had just been elected. The contest was not long delayed.

The election for Councilmen was held on the third Monday in March, 1851, and at the meeting, held on the first day of April, Messrs. Thomas B. Barton, John James Chew, J. Minor, Wm. Allen and Beverly R. Wellford were appointed a committee by the Council to consider the subject of the location and erection of a new courthouse and report thereon all matters connected with the cost, style and site of said building.

The next meeting of the Council was held on the 26th of April. It was one of unusual importance, because the committee on the new courthouse was to report, and every member except two was in his seat, and the chamber was crowded to its full capacity by citizens, who felt a special interest in the subject. The committee was in favor of erecting a new courthouse, and therefore reported to the Council plans and specifications for the building, drawn by J. B. Benwick, Jr., of Baltimore, giving the style and the probable cost at $14.000.

The committee recommended the site of the old courthouse, the removal of the jail to the back of the new building and the removal of the clerk's office and engine houses. The report was adopted and the committee was instructed to contract for the erection of the building inside of the estimated cost. This looked as if the Council meant business, and for the next three weeks the question was warmly discussed, and the opponents of the measure undertook to prevent the great waste of money, as they termed it, by petition and other influences. The Council met on the 21st of May to receive the report of the committee, appointed to contract for the building, and every member was present. The interest was intense and the opposition determined.

The committee made its report and the clerk of the Council made this record: "A contract with Wm. M. Baggett, for building a new courthouse, jail, &c., for the sum of $13,850, together with drawings and specifications of said buildings made by James Benwick, architect, and to be taken as part of said contract, and a bond executed by said Baggett, J. Metcalfe, J. S. Caldwell, and George Aler, in the sum of ten thousand dollars, for the faithful performance of said contract, by said Baggett, were submitted to the Council by T. B. Barton, chairman of the committee appointed for that purpose, for their approval or rejection.

"Whereupon, and before any action was had thereon, Mr. J. M. Whittemore, asked and obtained leave to be heard by the Council in support of a petition, signed by one hundred and seventy-two of the voters of the corporation, remonstrating against the extravagant scheme of pulling down the jail and other buildings on the courthouse lot, and praying the appointment of a committee of their own board,* to contract for the erection of a spacious and comfortable courthouse at a cost not exceeding six thousand dollars. Said petition was accordingly presented by Mr. Whittemore, and, being read, was, on motion, laid on the table.

"On motion, said contract was then approved and confirmed by the following vote to-wit: Ayes: F. Slaughter, Joseph Sanford, J. Minor, D. H. Gordon, J. Pritchard, L. J. Huffman, B. S. Herndon, Thomas F. Knox, Charles C. Wellford and John J. Berrey, 10. Nays: Hugh Scott and Wm. Allen, 2. And it was ordered that the Mayor, as evidence of said approval and confirmation, do sign an endorsement to that effect on said contract, and cause the corporation seal to be affixed thereto, and that said contract together with the drawings and specifications, be then delivered to the clerk of the hustings court for safe keeping," &c.

After this action was completed the Council appointed Messrs. Thomas B. Barton, John James Chew, J. Minor, Wm. Allen and Beverly R. Wellford a committee to superintend the entire work and see that it was done according to the plans and specifications. And so a question that had vexed the people of the town for more than thirty years, and had caused considerable friction between the hustings court and the Common Council, was settled and the town was to have a new courthouse.

The building was completed in 1852, when the courts and clerks were removed to spacious and comfortable quarters, and have remained there to the present day. The south wing on the lower floor has been used for fire engines until the companies were disbanded prior to the war; but, for several years in the past, they have been used for the public schools of the city, while the large room on the second floor is used for an armory. The vault, for the records and papers of all the courts of the past and present, as well as of those of the Common Council, is ample for the purpose and absolutely fire-proof. The building is one of the handsomest in the State and always attracts the attention of strangers.

---

* Thomas B. Barton, John James Chew and Beverly R. Wellford, of the committee, were not members of the Council, but appointed from the body of the citizens.

"The Lodge" at Mary Washington Monument. Constructed of Virginia Granite for Superintendent of Monument and Grounds.
(See page 160)

The "Wallace Library," now near its completion. The building and library a donation by the late Capt. C. Wistar Wallace.
(See page 145)

The old courthouse, that was torn down to make room for the new one, was provided with a bell for calling the people together. It was used to call public meetings, to notify the people of the assembling of the courts, and, until another bell was provided for the purpose, to sound the alarms for fires. This bell now hangs in the belfry of the present courthouse. It was presented to the town by Silas Wood in 1828 and has been on duty more than three-quarters of a century. Mr. Wood married a Fredericksburg lady, and it is reported that he was a believer in the adage that a fair exchange (rather an exchange for the fair) was not robbery; therefore, as he had taken one bell (belle) from Fredericksburg he ought to give it another in exchange. The bell has this inscription on it: "Revere, Boston. Presented to the Corporation of Fredericksburg by Silas Wood, A. D. 1828."

MARKET-HOUSE, OR TOWN HALL.

The first market-house, or town hall, Fredericksburg had, of which we have any account, either by record or tradition, was located on the west side of Main street, just below the present "Market alley." It was constructed mainly of brick, and had several rooms in it that were used for the courts, the Common Council, balls, sociables, public meetings and lodge rooms. The Common Council held its sessions in that building, when it organized at the "coffee-house," which no doubt was one of the rooms in the market-house, after the rooms were properly fitted up, and continued there from 1781 until the building was taken down in 1813.

At what period the market-house was built we do not know, but it was certainly prior to 1752, as we have record evidence of its existence at that time, and also evidence that it needed repairs, which shows that it had been standing for some years. During the Revolutionary war colonial troops used a portion of the building for barracks, and it was in this house that the great peace ball was given in 1783, which was attended by General Washington and his mother. In the year 1813 this old building was taken down and the present market-house erected.

While this information was obtained from Benj. Peyton, a very old colored man, who died some twenty-five years ago, who assisted in taking down the old and erecting the new building, the truth of it is borne out by the records. He was a youth at the time, learning the trade of brick mason, and was employed on both buildings. The present market-house is a substantial, two-story brick building, with market lot in the rear, market stalls in the basement and work shops for the city water and gas works. It has two wings, which have been at different times used for school rooms and printing offices, but are now used, the south wing for the Council Chamber and the north wing for the commissioner of revenue and city tax collector. The second floor is used by the Washington Guards as a reading room. In 1824 the building was brilliantly illuminated and beautifully decorated for a grand ball and reception in honor of Gen. Lafayette, who was then visiting this country, and passed through Fredericksburg, where he remained for several days.

THE FIRE-HOUSE.

The substantial brick house for the Fire Department, just south of the courthouse, was erected in 1890. It is two stories high, with a belfry on the front part of the building. The first floor is used for the reels, the hook and ladder truck and other fire apparatus. The belfry, or tower, is so constructed that in addition to its holding the fire bell, the fire hose can be suspended in it for drying after a fire.

SCHOOL BUILDINGS.

At present we have but two school buildings, one at the corner of Main and Lewis streets, known as the Union House, and the other at the corner of Princess Ann and Wolfe streets. The historical Union House, used by the white pupils, was built in the first part of the last century by a Mr. Ross for a residence and is quite substantial, being constructed of brick and spacious, and is three stories high, with a basement. Mr. Ross was a Frenchman, and royally entertained Gen. Lafayette and his retinue when he visited Fredericksburg in 1824. Seven grades occupy this building, while three grades are provided for elsewhere. The school authorities, in the discharge of their duties, have repeatedly called attention of the City Council to the fact that this building was inadequate for the rapidly increasing school population; that it was constructed for a residence and not for school purposes, the rooms being too small for the large number of pupils that had to be crowded in them.

A year ago conditions were investigated by the School Committee of the City Council (Prof. S. W. Somerville, chairman), which resulted in a movement of said committee to provide a suitable building for the schools. Soon plans and specifications were drawn and laid before the Council which were fully considered and finally adopted, and the committee was instructed to advertise for bids, let the contract and have the building completed as soon as possible. Work is now progressing on the building, which is to be quite a commodious one, with twelve rooms, with all the modern improvements as to heating, fire protection, &c. The contract price (Mr. E. G. Heflin, contractor, and Mr. Frank P. Stearns, inspector,) is $37,700, and the building is to be completed by February 1, 1909.

The only objection that any one could offer against these changes (and no one is likely to offer it) is the demolition of the venerable landmark, so long known as the Union House and the headquarters of Gen. Lafayette when he visited the town for the last time.

The school building at the corner of Princess Ann and Wolfe streets, a two-story, brick structure, with four spacious rooms, was constructed for, and is occupied by, the colored schools. For years after its construction it was found to be large enough to accommodate all the grades of that school, but when a grammar department was added this building was found to be fully occupied and the high grade had to be provided for elsewhere.

THE WALLACE LIBRARY.

By his will Capt. C. Wistar Wallace, a valuable citizen of the town, who was born and raised in Fredericksburg, and who died May 20, 1907, left to the town, under certain conditions, $15,000 for a public library, which was to bear his name. The conditions were that the city was to adopt legal papers binding itself to establish said library, within three years of the donor's death, as a permanent institution of the city and properly maintain the same; that the city was not to expend more than $5,000 of the legacy for the purchase of a suitable lot and the erection thereon of a suitable library building, and the balance of the legacy was to be expended for the purchase of books for the library. These books are to be purchased by a board not to exceed five members, to be chosen from time to time by the President of the University of Virginia, Washington and Lee, Richmond College and Randolph Macon College. In order to make these conditions binding upon the city, it was provided that necessary legislation should be procured by the General Assembly of Virginia as might be necessary to authorize and enable the city to comply with all of the conditions of the bequest.

The whole matter having been laid before the City Council and explained by the city attorney, Mr. St. Geo. R. Fitzhugh, and discussed, that body adopted the following:

*Be it resolved, that the city of Fredericksburg, Va., decides to establish and maintain a public library to be known as the "Wallace Library," and hereby accepts the said bequest of $15,000 upon the conditions and according to the terms of said bequest, and hereby binds itself to carry out the same.

Under the provisions of the Code of Virginia the duty of appointing the board of directors of this library devolved upon Major Thomas P. Wallace, Mayor of the town, the Council concurring. The following letter, therefore, was communicated to the Council by the Mayor:

"I herewith transmit, in pursuance to the resolution of your honorable body, passed at your meeting on the 18th day of July, 1907, the following named citizens, who shall constitute the board of directors contemplated by your resolutions: St. Geo. R. Fitzhugh, S. J. Quinn, A. T. Embrey, Rev. J. W. Roseboro, D. D., James S. Knox, E. D. Cole, A. P. Rowe, B. P. Willis and James T. Lowery.

* Council proceedings, July 18, 1907.

The board of directors organized by the election of Mr. St. Geo. R. Fitzhugh, president, and S. J. Quinn, clerk.

The Council and the General Assembly united in permitting the library building to be constructed on the courthouse lot, and the board of directors authorized the construction of the building to be proceeded with at once. It is a two-story house, with basement, and is now nearing completion. It is constructed under the direction of Mr. Wm. E. Bradley, chairman of the Public Property Committee, Mr. Geo W. Wroten, contractor, and Mr. A. M. Garner, inspector.

THE NORMAL SCHOOL BUILDING.

In addition to these public buildings the General Assembly has appropriated $25,000 and will supplement that with $25,000 additional to construct in or near the town a female normal school. The board of directors of this institution are now endeavoring to select a site for this school, and will likely succeed in the near future. The buildings will be commenced next Spring and pushed to completion.

The United States Government has also appropriated money for the erection of a very commodious brick building on the corner of Princess Ann and Hanover streets. This site has already been purchased by the government and will soon be in condition for the brick masons and carpenters. The work, however, has been delayed for an additional appropriation, in order to enable them to construct such a building as was contemplated by the architect of the postoffice department. When the building is completed it is to be occupied by the postoffice.

Having inspected the public buildings of the town, and discussed those now in course of erection and those which soon will be, we will now visit the private historical buildings and take a view of the monument erected by the ladies of the country to Mary, the mother of the illustrious Washington, and the handsome statue of Gen. Hugh Mercer, recently erected by the United States Government, who stands upon his pedestal, sword in hand, ready to strike for Liberty and Independence, for Truth and Victory. They both stand on Washington avenue.

CHAPTER XI

Ancient and Historical Buildings—Mary Washington Monument—Gen. Mercer's Statue—Mary Washington's Will, &c.

In stating that Fredericksburg has more ancient reminiscent and historical buildings than any other town of its size in this country, we do not fear successful contradiction. Fredericksburg is one of the oldest towns in the State and has from its settlement been the center of refinement and culture. Here the young men of this section of Virginia were taught and imbibed those principles of liberty and justice that made them leaders in the movement against oppression, which resulted in our constitutional rights and religious liberty. Here they were equipped for all the duties of life in whatever station they might be placed. Here was the home and birthplace of men who commanded armies, controlled navies, swayed statesmen, electrified assemblies, and many of those homes and birth-houses are still standing, and it will appear but natural if they shall be pointed out and written about by the inhabitants of Fredericksburg with patriotic pride. Notwithstanding the quaint architecture of many of them, and the ravages of time upon them, they are dear to us and are regarded as heirlooms of the town which have witnessed the advent and exit of many generations.

Among the oldest houses now in Fredericksburg are the residence of the late William A. Little, the Mary Washington House and the Rising Sun Hotel. It is impossible to give the order of seniority of these buildings, because we have no way of ascertaining when they were built. Mr. Little, several years ago, so renewed and extended his residence and adorned it as to almost destroy its ancient identity. This old mansion has recently passed to Mr. John C. Melville.

The Rising Sun Hotel, located on the west side of Main street, just above Fauquier, is one of the oldest buildings now standing. It is of the old style of architecture of wooden buildings that prevailed in the first settlement of the country, which, notwithstanding its hoary age and frequent necessary repairs, has never been changed. In the first of the eighteenth century, and even before the Revolutionary war, it was one of the leading hotels of the town, and was the stopping place of many of the Southern senators, representatives and other dignitaries as they journey to and from Washington city.

It is claimed that the eccentric John Randolph, of Roanoke, has more than once addressed the people of the town from the steps of this building. General George Weedon, long years before he entered the Colonial Army for American Independence, kept hotel in this house. Just prior to that war it became the property of General Gustavus B. Wallace, a Revolutionary patriot, and it has remained in the Wallace family until the death of Capt. C. Wistar Wallace, a public spirited citizen, a little over one year ago. At his death, May 20, 1907, it became the property of the Society for the Preservation of the Antiquities of Virginia, by the provisions of his will. The Fredericksburg branch of the society has charge of the building, a one and a half story wooden structure, and now has it in good condition and open for the inspection of those who would like to live for a short time in the far distant past, when Mrs. Livingston was the "doctress and coffee-woman" of the town. That society has renovated the building and it is now in good repair. It has not been kept as a hotel since the Civil war.

The handsome residence erected by Mr. Stannard, on the lot now occupied by Mr. George W. Shepherd, was destroyed by fire in the great conflagration that occurred here in 1807, which is mentioned elsewhere. The fire originated in that house and had made considerable headway before it was discovered. In the year 1815 the large, brick residence now standing on that lot was erected by Mr. Robert Mackay, a merchant of the town and Mayor for two years, from 1817 to 1819. It is said that the cost of erecting that building, and beautifying the grounds, was thirty thousand dollars, and it so embarassed Mr. Mackay that he never recovered from it.

For a number of years this place was the residence and home of Thomas Seddon, a wealthy gentleman, who died there in 1831. As is said elsewhere herein, he was the father of James A. Seddon, secretary of War of the Confederate States, who, it is claimed by some persons, was born there, although his biographers say, and it is substantiated by his relatives, that he was born in Falmouth, in Stafford county. It is not disputed, however, that Secretary Seddon spent his boyhood days in that building, having moved there when he was quite young, but his birthplace is beyond doubt as his biographers and relatives state it, as he was born the same year this residence was built, and Mr. Mackay occupied it for some years before Mr. Seddon moved there.

The old, one and a half story frame house, which stands on the east side of Princess Ann street, between Prussia and Wolfe streets, just below Shiloh Baptist church (new site), was at one time owned by James Monroe. He was elected to a seat in the Legislature, and the law required that members of the General Assembly should be owners of real estate. In order to make him eligible his uncle gave him a pocket deed to this house and lot. This was the first civil office, except that of Common Councilman of Fredericksburg, Mr. Monroe ever held. The house at the time stood on a lot in the upper part of the town and was without the wings it has at present. Mr. Monroe's boarding place was located on the same lot on which now stands the handsome residence of Mrs. James H. Bradley. His law office was in the row of low, brick buildings, formerly known as the "City Lunch," on Charles street, in rear of Colonel E. D. Cole's store.

The "Sentry Box," at the lower end of Main street, was the residence of General George Weedon, of Revolutionary fame, and was afterwards owned and occupied by Colonel Hugh Mercer, a son of General Hugh Mercer, who was killed at the battle of Princeton, and a nephew of General Weedon, to whom it was devised by General Weedon. We are unable to state when this house was erected or who built it. It is doubtless one of the oldest buildings in town. It is a large two-story frame house, with a wide hall through the center and overlooks the Rappahannock river. It has been known as the "Sentry Box" as far back as the mind of our oldest inhabitant goes, and the past generations knew it by that name. Tradition has brought the name down to us and we need not stretch our imaginations as to the "why it was so called." From the upper story of the southeast end of this stately building is a beautiful and unobstructed view of the river for some distance, and there sentinels were placed at various times during the Revolutionary war, to watch and give the alarm of the approach of the enemy. It was thus used for three wars to much advantage to the side with which Fredericksburg was in sympathy—the Revolution, as above mentioned, the war of 1812 and the Civil war, or the War between the States. Another thing that gives the "Sentry Box" additional historical interest is the claim that has been made, which may need verification, that in this house has been received and entertained every President of the United States from George Washington to James Buchanan. The property is now owned and occupied by Mr. O. D. Foster, a veteran of the Confederate army.

The splendid two-story brick residence, owned and occupied by Gen. Daniel D. Wheeler, of the United States army, on the east side of lower Main street, was built by Roger Dixon, a gentleman of means, who owned most of the land in the lower end of the town about 1764. A few years after its construction Mr. Dixon died, and most, if not all of his property, was purchased by Dr. Charles Mortimer. Dr. Mortimer was one of Mary Washington's physicians, and tradition has it that the last visit she made was to her much-loved physician; that upon her return home she was taken down with cancer and after that never left her home.

Of one of the many delightful dinings and balls at this splendid mansion, so frequent in that day with the "well to do folks" of Virginia, Mrs. Roger A. Prior, in "the Mother of Washington and Her Times" says, "Little Maria Mortimer, aged sixteen, was at the Fredericksburg ball. Her father, Dr. Charles Mortimer, issued invitations at the ball for a great dinner to the distinguished strangers the next day but one, and his wife (Sarah Griffin Fauntleroy), being too ill to preside, that honor fell to the daughter of the house. The house, an immense pile of English brick, (?) still stands on the lower edge of the town, facing Main street, with a garden sloping to the river, where Dr. Mortimer's own tobacco ships used to run up to discharge their return English cargoes, by a channel long since disused and filled up. * * * The table, as little

Maria described it in after years, groaned with every delicacy of land and water, served in massive pewter dishes, polished until they shone again. The chief sat beside the master of the house at the long table, although at his own house, his place was always at the side of the table among his guests. Little Maria, 'with her hair cruped high,' was taken in by the Marquis Lafayette, or Count d'Estaing, or Count Rochambeau—they were all present—and the little lady's heart was in her mouth, she said, although she danced with every one of them at the ball—nay, with Bettie Lewis's uncle George himself!"

Dr. Mortimer was the first Mayor of Fredericksburg. His remains are buried near the center of Hurkamp Park, which was for nearly a century a public burying ground. As has been said, he was Mary Washington's physician, but not the only one at her late illness, for it is quite certain that Dr. Elisha Hall, who was the grandfather of Dr. Horace B. Hall, and who lived on the lot now occupied by Dr. J. E. Tompkin's residence, was also one of her physicians in her last days. This is shown beyond a doubt by a letter, still preserved from Dr. Benjamin Rush, of Philadelphia, to Dr. Elisha Hall, his cousin, written July 6, 1789, a short time before Mrs. Washington's death. Dr. Hall had written to him for his experience and advice for cancer treatment and received the following:

"The respectable age and character of your venerable patient lead me to regret that it is not in my power to suggest a remedy for the cure of the disorder you have described in her breast. I know nothing of the root you mention, found in Carolina and Georgia, but, from a variety of inquiries and experiments, I am disposed to believe that there does not exist in the vegetable kingdom an antidote to cancers. All the *supposed vegetable* remedies I have heard of are compounds of some mineral caustics. The arsenic is the most powerful of any of them. It is the basis of Dr. Martin's powder. I have used it in many cases with success, but have failed in some. From your account of Mrs. Washington's breast I am afraid no great good can be expected from the use of it. Perhaps it may cleanse it, and thereby retard its spreading.

The Dam of the Water Power Co., the Canal emerging from left corner furnishes power for town.
(See page 329)

"Meditation Rock," Mary Washington's favorite retreat for reading, prayer and meditation.
(See page 157)

You may try it diluted in water. Continue the application of opium and camphor, and wash it frequently with a decoction of red clover. Give anodynes, when necessary, and support the system with bark and wine. Under this treatment she may live comfortably many years, and finally die of old age."

The house on the south corner of Prince Edward and Fauquier streets, purchased in 1898 by Mrs. Bernice Hart, tradition says, was for over one hundred years the clerk's office, and the court records of the trustees of the town were kept there. There may have been a court held in that small place under the Colonial charter of the town, but not a criminal court since that time, as the records show to the contrary. The records of courts held here before the War of the Revolution—if any were held here—and the record of proceedings of the trustees cannot be found at present. The house was a small, one and a half story frame building, similar in architecture to the old part of the Mary Washington House. The additions made to it in recent years have completely destroyed its original form and architecture and have given it a modern appearance. No one, of course, knows when it was built, but, judging from its style and the material of which it was constructed, it must take its place with the oldest of our ancient buildings. .

"Federal Hill," on Hanover street, owned and occupied by Mrs. H. Theodore Wight, was, in the latter part of the eighteenth and early part of the nineteenth centuries, the home of Thomas Reade Rootes, who was one of the most distinguished lawyers of his day. His third daughter was Sarah Robinson, who married Colonel John A. Cobb, of North Carolina, a son of Howell Cobb, of Virginia. Soon after his marriage Colonel Cobb settled in Georgia, where were born those two distinguished lawyers and soldiers, Howell and Thomas Reade Rootes Cobb. The latter was killed in front of the Stevens House, at the foot of Marye's Heights, on the 13th of December, 1862, it is claimed, by a shell, which was said to have been thrown from a gun stationed at Federal Hill, where his mother was born and married. A recent writer in a Northern journal, however, claims that General Cobb was killed by a shell thrown from the Stafford side of the river. But both accounts differ from the report of General Kershaw, who took command of the line when General Cobb was wounded. In his report of the battle he says General Cobb was killed by a sharp-shooter stationed in one of the houses to his left on Hanover street.* As General Kershaw was on the ground a few minutes after General Cobb was wounded, and saw and talked with him after he was wounded, his version is more than likely the correct one. No one knows when or by whom Federal Hill was built. At one time the property belonged to a gentleman by the name of Lovell, who moved to Fauquier county, and it may be he erected the residence.

The old, one and a half story frame building on the corner of Prince Edward and Fauquier streets, now owned and occupied by Mrs. Mary Knox Moncure, takes its place among the oldest buildings of the town. It was the birth-place and home of John Forsythe, who made such a brilliant record as a Statesman from Georgia, to which State he moved while a young man. His father was Robert Forsythe, a major in the Revolutionary war, who died in Fredericksburg early in the nineteenth century.

This house was also said to have been the home of John Dawson, an old bachelor, who represented this district in Congress from 1797 to 1814. His success at the ballot-box was due as much, perhaps, if not more, to his declaring himself a friend to the poor man (a hobby much ridden these days by politicians) than to any other one thing. He is said to have created quite a sensation in the courthouse in Fredericksburg during one of his heated campaigns, which gained him many votes. Political feeling ran high, the people were much stirred up, the canvas was exciting and the result doubtful. A public meeting had been extensively advertised to take place at the courthouse, and the building was early filled to its capacity to hear a joint discussion between the Congressional candidates. Mr. Dawson, a few minutes late, reached the courthouse, and, finding his way blocked by the dense crowd, shouted at the top of his voice from the door—"Make way, gentlemen, for the poor man's friend!" All eyes were at once turned to the speaker, and,

---

* See War of the Rebellion, Series 1, Vol. 21, page 590.

seeing it was John Dawson, the candidate, the crowd parted and he was escorted through to the stand, amid thundering applause. It is needless to say he was reëlected to Congress.

The old, frame building on the south corner of Main and Amelia streets, one and a half stories high, for many years of the first of the nineteenth century was occupied by a Mr. Henderson as a store, and was known for more than a century as Henderson's corner. It is a very old building and prior to the Revolutionary war, while political feeling was almost at fever heat, those who opposed resistance to the Mother Country congregated at this corner and discussed the "state of the country." This gave it the name of "Tory Corner," by which it was known for many years afterwards. This was the only building left in the track of the great fire of 1807, and has not been used as a storehouse for more than half a century.

The venerable brick mansion, known as "Kenmore," facing Washington avenue, and the residence of Clarance Randolph Howard, Esq., was built by Colonel Fielding Lewis, a man of great wealth, and who owned a large body of land west of the town. The bricks of which the house was built, tradition had it, came from England, but that is hardly possible, as elegant bricks were manufactured in this country at that time—in the seventeen forties—and the best of clay is found in that locality, where signs of a brick-yard can now be found. The interior stucco work of this colonial mansion is probably equal in workmanship to the best in this country, and is said to have been done by expert Englishmen. It has stood for a century and a half without repairs, so far as is known, until some fifteen years ago, when Mr. Wm. Key Howard gave it some slight touches, which compare favorably with the old work. Col. Lewis, for his second wife, selected Miss Bettie Washington, sister of Gen. George Washington, and to this beautiful mansion she was taken as a bride, and lived there until a few years before her death. Col. Lewis was an officer in the Patriot army and commanded a division at the Siege of Yorktown, where Cornwallis surrendered and where the Seven Years' war ended. He was an ardent patriot, and during the Revolutionary war, at one time, superintended the manufacture of arms, shells and shot on the north side of the Rappahannock river, just above Falmouth. The ruins of the old forge are still to be seen there, and also the old prison barracks, where some German prisoners were kept during that struggle. The garrison was commanded by Colonel Enever. Colonel Lewis was also a magistrate in the town after the war, a member of the City Council and represented the county in the Legislature.

He died in December, 1781, and, it is said, is buried under the front steps of St. George's Episcopal church. His wife, Bettie, survived him sixteen years. In the latter part of her life she went to Culpeper county and lived with one of her children, where she died and was buried. Colonal Fielding Lewis was the father of Captain Robert Lewis, who was one of President Washington's private secretaries, and Mayor of Fredericksburg from 1821 to the day of his death, February 11, 1829. Captain Lewis delivered the address of welcome to General Lafayette on his visit to the town in 1824.

Mary, the mother of Washington, must have lived in Fredericksburg the most of her widowhood, which was about forty-six years. Some time after her husband's death, on the opposite side of the Rappahannock river, she moved into the town, where she brought up her illustrious son George to manhood. The dwelling she occupied during that time is now standing on the west corner of Charles and Lewis streets. Until some fifteen years ago this old residence was owned and occupied by private individuals, but just prior to the World's Fair in Chicago a party from that city was negotiating for it, with a view of transferring it to Chicago. While a difference of five hundred dollars in the price was under consideration some ladies of Fredericksburg, who opposed its being disturbed, communicated the condition of things to the Society for the Preservation of Virginia Antiquities, at Richmond, who at once purchased the property at four thousand and five hundred dollars. The Society had the buildings put in good repairs and the purchase is considered a valuable addition to the possessions of the Society.

It is a plain, substantial, old fashioned one and a half story dwelling, of the prevailing order of architecture of that period, and though it has been thoroughly overhauled and repaired, the distinctive features of architecture and general appearance have been faithfully preserved. Mrs. Mary Washington died in the front room of this building in 1789, and was buried on a spot which she had selected for her grave there, on a part of the Kenmore tract, which belonged to the estate of Colonel Fielding Lewis, her son-in-law.

THE MARY WASHINGTON MONUMENT.

Within a few steps of the place where Mary, the mother of Washington, was buried is a ledge of rocks and a beautiful grove of original oak trees, much larger then in area than at present, to which she used often to resort for private reading, meditation and prayer. The grave was marked by a small, marble slab, appropriately inscribed. About forty-five years after her death a stately marble monument, designed to mark her grave and perpetuate her memory, was partly constructed by the private munificence of Mr. Silas Burrows, a wealthy merchant of New York.

The corner-stone of this proposed monument was laid on the 7th of May, 1833, with an imposing military and civic display, by Fredericksburg Lodge, No. 4, Ancient, Free and Accepted Masons, President Andrew Jackson, Past Grand Master of Masons in Tennessee, being present and participating. This monument, because of the failure of Mr. Burrows in business, remained in a half completed condition for nearly sixty years and was greatly mutilated by time and relic hunters.

An appeal for a Congressional appropriation to restore and complete the structure by the United States Government, made by a bill, introduced in the Forty-third Congress by Hon. James B. Sener, then representing this Congressional district, was unsuccessful, notwithstanding his patriotic efforts were seconded by a strong appeal of the Mayor and Common Council of Fredericksburg and unanimously recommended by a Congressional committee, who visited the place, of which Hon. Horace Manard, of Tennessee, afterward Post-Master General, was chairman. A similar effort was made some years thereafter by Hon. George T. Garrison, representing this district in Congress with the same result.

Upon the failure of the efforts of these two members of Congress, aided by the city authorities, to secure the completion of the monument by the government, came the women's opportunity. They were deeply interested in the subject, and cherished an honest pride in having the monument completed to perpetuate the memory and virtues of the greatest of American women.

In 1889, the centennial year of the death of this venerated lady, an association was formed by the devoted and patriotic ladies of Fredericksburg, with Mrs. James P. Smith as their leader, who resolved to spare no time or effort to raise the necessary money to complete the structure, and thus save the grave of this sainted woman from oblivion. A systematic correspondence and appeals were commenced, and in a short time, mainly, if not altogether, through the influence of the Fredericksburg association, a national association was formed in Washington, with Mrs. Chief-Justice Waite as president. These two associations coöperating, other strong appeals were sent out to the patriotic women of the United States, soliciting contributions, and soon money began to flow into the treasury of the association, until a sufficient sum was raised to complete the work.

A sufficient amount of money being in hand this perplexing question arose—should the old monument be renovated and completed, or should it be set aside and a new one constructed? This gave rise to considerable controversy, because there was quite a division of sentiment, and serious results were feared by members of both associations. This difficulty was met, however, by an order to have the unfinished monument examined by an expert, who, upon a thorough investigation, reported that it was so broken and mutilated that it could not be repaired, and so plans for a new monument were ordered. The plan submitted by Mr. Wm. J. Crawford, of Buffalo, New York, was adopted by the ladies and to him was intrusted the work of erecting the monument on the site of the unfinished structure, under which the remains of this venerable and venerated woman reposed. The monument is a square base, with a solid granite shaft fifty-one and a half feet high—total height, fifty-five feet—with the words "Mary, the Mother of Washington," in raised letters, cut on the base. The material of the old monument was broken up and placed in the foundation of the new one, except such of the fluted columns as remained unbroken, which were donated to different institutions. One of them was given to Fredericksburg Lodge of Masons, of this place, by Mr. Crawford, the architect, which is now in the lodge room.

In due time the monument was finished to the satisfaction of both the Fredericksburg and Washington associations, which was accepted, and the 10th of May, 1894, was designated as the time for its dedication. The Fredericksburg Masonic Lodge, which had laid the corner-stone of the old monument, was invited to conduct the ceremonies of dedicating the new, but it gracefully turned that honor over to the Grand Lodge of Virginia, which performed the work in good style, escorted and assisted by Lodges No. 4 and No. 22 of Alexandria.

The day for the dedication of the monument dawned beautiful and clear and found everything in readiness for the grand event. Besides the National Association being largely represented from Washington, headed by Mrs. Waite, there were President Grover Cleveland, with most of his cabinet and their wives; Vice-President A. E. Stevenson and lady, Chief-Justice Fuller, Justice Harlan, Senators and Representatives, Governor Charles T. O'Ferrall and Staff, the volunteer militia from different portions of the State, the Grand Lodge of Masons of Virginia, with Fredericksburg Lodge, No. 4, and Alexandria-Washington Lodge, No. 22, and distinguished men and Masons from different parts of the country.

The streets of the town were thronged with thousands of people from far and near, eager and anxious to witness the ceremonies. Never before was such a vast number of people seen in Fredericksburg, except at the great battle in December, 1862. The dedicatory services were conducted by the Grand Lodge of Masons of Virginia, Major Mann Page, Jr., Grand Master,* which were solemn and impressive. Addresses, appropriate to the occasion, were made by Mayor A. P. Rowe, Governor Charles T. O'Ferrall, President Grover Cleveland and Mr. Blair Lee, who were followed by Senator John W. Daniel, the orator of the occasion.

Fredericksburg Lodge, No. 4, gave a grand banquet at the opera house in the afternoon to the Masonic fraternity and several hundred invited guests, which was presided over by Judge James B. Sener. On that interesting occasion addresses were made by several distinguished guests, including President Cleveland, Vice-President Stevenson, Justice Harlan and others. The Marine band was present and furnished music of the highest order for both the dedication and banquet. Since the monument was finished the associations have erected a comfortable granite building on the grounds for a residence and office for the custodian of the monument and the grounds, and Mrs. John T. Goolrick, a descendant of George Mason, occupies that position.

MARY WASHINGTON'S WILL.

The last will and testament of Mary Washington has for many years attracted general interest, and numerous visitors call at the courthouse to inspect and feast their eyes upon the original document. So precious does the court regard this relic that an order was made for its preservation, and it is now is a case and receives the special attention and care of Mr. A. B. Yates, the polite and accommodating clerk of the court. The will is in these words:

"In the name of God, amen. I, Mary Washington, of Fredericksburg, in the county of Spotsylvania, being in good health, but calling to mind the uncertainty of this life and willing to dispose

---

* In his excitement, Grand Master Page dedicated the monument to Mary, the mother of our illustrious brother, George H. Washington. A brother remarked to another, "I didn't know there was an H in Washington's name. What does it stand for?" As quick as thought the shrewd Essex lawyer responded, "Hatchet—George Hatchet!" The fun that incident excited is not over with yet.

of what remains of my earthly estate, do make and publish this my last will, recommending my soul into the hands of my Creator, hoping for a remission of all my sins through the merits and mediation of Jesus Christ, the Saviour of mankind. I dispose of all my worldly estate as follows:

Imprimis. I give to my son General George Washington all my lands on Accokeek Run, in the county of Stafford, and also my negro boy, George, to him and his heirs forever; also my best bed, bedstead, and Virginia cloth curtains (the same that stands in my best room), my quilted blue-and-white quilt and my best dressing glass.

Item. I give and devise to my son, Charles Washington my negro man, Tom, to him and his assigns forever.

Item. I give and devise to my daughter, Betty Lewis, my phæton and my bay horse.

Item. I give and devise to my daughter-in-law, Hannah Washington, my purple cloth cloak lined with shay.

Item. I give and bequeath to my grand son, Corbin Washington my negro wench, old Bet, my riding chair, and two black horses, to him and his assigns forever.

Item. I give and bequeath to my grand son, Fielding Lewis, my negro man, Frederick, to him and his assigns forever; also eight silver table spoons, half of my crockery ware, and the blue-and-white tea china, with book-case, oval table, one bed, bedstead, one pair sheets, one pair blankets and white cotton counterpane, two table cloths, six red leather chairs, half my pewter, and one half of my iron kitchen furniture.

Item. I give and devise to my grand son, Lawrence Lewis, my negro wench, Lydia, to him and his assigns forever.

Item. I give and bequeath to my grand daughter, Betty Carter, my negro woman, little Bet, and her future increase, to her and her assigns forever; also my largest looking glass, my walnut writing desk with drawers, a square dining table, one bed, bedstead, bolster, one pillow, one blanket and pair of sheets, white Virginia cloth counterpane and purple curtains, my red-and-white tea china, tea spoons and the other half of my pewter, crockery-ware, and the remainder of my iron kitchen furniture.

Item. I give to my grand son, George Washington, my next best dressing glass, one bed, bedstead, bolster, one pillow, one pair sheets, one blanket and counterpane.

Item. I devise all my wearing apparel to be equally divided between my grand daughters, Betty Carter, Fanny Ball and Milly Washington; but should my daughter, Betty Lewis, fancy any one, two or three articles, she is to have them before a division thereof.

Lastly. I nominate and appoint my said son, General George Washington, executor of this my will, and as I owe few or no debts, I desire my executor to give no security nor to appraise my estate, but desire the same may be allotted to my devisees with as little trouble and delay as may be, desiring their acceptance thereof as all the token I now have to give them of my love for them.

In witness whereof, I have hereunto set my hand and seal this 20th day of May, 1788.

MARY WASHINGTON.

Witness *John Ferneyhough.*

Signed, sealed and published in our presence, and signed by us in the presence of the said Mary Washington, and at her desire.

J. MERCER,
JOSEPH WALKER."

The will was written by Judge James Mercer, first President of the Court of Appeals, or "Chief-Justice of the General Court."

THE MERCER MONUMENT.

In the year 1906 the government of the United States erected a monument to General Hugh Mercer, who was mortally wounded at Princeton, N. J., while gallantly leading his men in a charge against the British in 1777. He lived one week in great suffering, when he died and was buried near where he fell, but afterwards removed to Philadelphia, Pa., where he now sleeps. Gen. Mercer was born in Scotland, studied medicine at Aberdeen and graduated with high honors. After graduating he soon rose to distinction as

The Presbyterian Church.
(See page 207)

The Methodist Church.
(See page 211)

a surgeon and physician and did much service in the army. He was at the battle of Culloden Moor, Scotland, where his party was badly defeated, and those not taken prisoners fled to other countries to save their lives. Gen. Mercer came to this country and settled in Pennsylvania. He was with Gen. Braddock, who was killed at Fort Duquesne, and, being thrown with Gen. Washington, became attached to him and came to Fredericksburg "to be near him," landing here in 1763. He practised medicine and established a drug store at the corner of Main and Amelia streets.* Gen. Mercer married Isabella Wallace and lived at the "Sentry Box" with Geo. Weedon, who married his wife's sister, until the beginning of the Revolutionary War. Soon after his death Congress appropriated $5,000 for the erection of a monument in this place to his memory, but the matter was overlooked and the gratitude of the government for his services was not exhibited to the extent of a memorial until the year 1906, one hundred and twenty-nine years after his death. In 1905 a bill was passed by Congress appropriating $25,000 to erect a monument to perpetuate the memory of the grand hero—two-thirds of the interest of the amount appropriated in 1777—and he now appears in heroic size, on his pedestal, on Washington avenue, in the attitude of a patriot, drawn sword in hand, ready to strike for Home and Country—Liberty and Independence.

We naturally uncover our heads while we "behold this friend of Washington—this heroic defender of America!"

---

* One tradition is that this drug store was at the corner of Princess Ann and Amelia streets, where Mr. John Stansbury Wallace lives; but another tradition locates it at the corner of Main and Amelia, most likely adjoining the corner house. This tradition is strengthened by finding, some time ago, while repairing the house, many old papers and other things that must have come from a drug store, and no other such store was ever known at that place.

CHAPTER XII

Hotels of the Town, old and new—Agricultural Fairs—Ferries and Toll Bridges—Care of the Dependent Poor—City Water Works—City Gas Works—Electric Light—Telephone Company—Fire Department, &c.

Fredericksburg, from the time it was first chartered, found itself on the main line of travel from North to South and *vice versa*. For this reason it was the main point for stopping, if the traveller could reach it even by journeying a few hours after dark. As the postoffice department came into existence and the mail matter increased, the pony had to give way for the small vehicle, and the small vehicle for a larger one, and the larger one for the stage, and the one stage for two, three, four and five, for Fredericksburg was a great mail distributing office, and the travel to and fro, stopping in the town, became immense. This necessitated the construction and opening of inns, and so the town became famous for its many elegant hotels. This continued until broken up by the rapid transit of steamboats and railroads, where the travellers found floating palaces and moving cafés. They look not for the hotel in small towns—they have their dining cars of eatables and drinkables. But let us not forget the village hotel, our former friend "where we slaked our thirst, ate to the full," and where we lost ourselves in "balmy sleep, nature's kind restorer."

The old time hotels, which have passed out of the memory of the present generation, will no doubt prove one of the most interesting chapters of this historical sketch of the town. The ground upon which many of them stood is now bare or occupied by other buildings, and the names of many of their keepers have been lost to the town. A short reference to some of these public resorts will probably refresh the minds of the citizens of what was at one time one of the principal features of the town, and will introduce to the younger generation the names of these hotels and their keepers, so intimately associated with the "good old times." For most of these references we are indebted to the memory and pen of Mr. Wm. F. Farish, who died at Lanhams, Md., a few years since. He was born here eighty-four years ago and spent his boyhood days in the town.

Near the present opera house, on Main street, was a hotel and oyster house, kept by Mr. Thomas Curtis. This place was headquarters for the politicians, and it was there the merits and demerits of candidates were discussed and their success or defeat was determined upon. It was what would be called to-day the Tammany Hall of Fredericksburg. The beginning of the war was the end of this hotel, as it was destroyed during the shelling of the town in December, 1862.

The Rappahannock House was located on the east side of Main street, about half way between George and Hanover streets. It was kept by Thomas Goodwin. The name of this house was afterwards changed to the Shakespeare, and was conducted by a Mr. Parker. It was burned down soon after the close of the Civil war and store houses were built on the ground it occupied.

The Farmers' Hotel was situated on the west corner of Main and Hanover streets, and extended up Hanover street to Jail alley, then known as Hay Scales alley. A part of this building is still standing on the corner of Hanover street and Jail Alley and is now owned and occupied by Mr. M. E. Ferrell, who has changed it into a residence. The main part of the building, on the corner of Main and Hanover streets, was burnt many years ago. In its stead a large, brick structure has recently been erected, called the Enterprise Building, the lower part of which is used for store and postoffice and the upper floors for a public hall, sleeping apartments and offices. This Farmers' Hotel was regarded as the leading hotel of the town in its day, and was headquarters for both stage lines—Extra Billy (afterwards Governor and Confederate

General) Smith's* and Colonel Porter's. It was kept at different times by James Young, Wm. E. Bowen, Bowen and Ramsay, Turner H. Ramsay, Charles E. Tackett, Peter Goolrick and Daniel Bradford.

The Exchange Hotel, so well known and in operation to-day, on the south corner of Main and Hanover streets, was built in 1837 by Wm. D. Green. The brick work of this building, which was destroyed by fire in 1850, is said to have been the handsomest in the State. The front walls were of pressed brick, oil finished and were of a beautiful red. The first building had three stories and a hall for theatrical purposes, with an entrance on Hanover street. This hall was known as "Green's Assembly," and very fine companies occupied it, many of them for several nights in succession. The present three-story building was commenced soon after the first one was burnt, but was not fully completed until after the late Civil war. The Exchange was first opened by Mrs. Wm. D. Green and was succeeded by Mrs. Fenton Brooke Smith. Since the Civil war it has been conducted respectively by W. T. Freaner, Captain George Henry Peyton, Cadmus B. Luck, Cotton and Hills, H. B. Tuttle, John Ultz and W. L. Laughlin, who is the present landlord.

Just above the Exchange Hotel, on Hanover street, was the Eagle Hotel. It has recently been refitted for families and room-renters and is known as the "Eagle Flats." The Eagle was very

---

* General Smith got his name Extra Billy while in the stage business, long before he was either General or Governor Smith. It is reported to have happened in this way: At certain seasons of the year, before the days of railroads, travel was very heavy and far beyond the capacity of the regular stages on the road, which was the only means of travel over land at that time. When this occurred Billy Smith, as he was called, would put on an extra stage, and if the travel still increased he would put on another, and so on, until sometimes he would have on the road four or five stages, where one usually did the work. On this account, and because of his unsurpassed politeness, he became popular with travellers. On this occasion a traveller was anxious to get to Washington, and could get no seat in the stage. In hustling around he found two or three others who were anxious to go, but, like himself, could not get accommodations on any part of the stage, and the agent declared it impossible to provide for them. The impatient and anxious traveller cried out "Where is Extra Billy?" Extra Billy was sent for, an extra stage was provided and the travellers went on their way rejoicing, but "Extra Billy" remained with Mr. Smith, following him to his grave.

popular in its day and was a favorite stopping place for the farmers. It had a very good patronage also from passengers on the two stage lines. No hotel has been kept there for many years. In its day it was conducted by James Newby, James Cunningham, Jesse Pullen, Wm. P. Quisenberry and Wm. H. Murphy.

The Alhambra, on Main street, just below the Exchange Hotel, was first kept by James Timberlake, who was succeeded by Samuel Stone, and he by Charles F. Barlosius. After the death of Mr. Barlosius, several years ago, the house was repaired and remodelled by Capt. Thomas P. Wallace and leased to John W. Allison, Jr., who conducted it some time as the Alsonia. Some years ago it was purchased by Mr. Michael Long, who conducted it until his death. It is now a restaurant.

On the south corner of Main and Charlotte streets stood the Indian Queen Hotel. This was a fine, old building, erected probably in colonial times for a hotel, with a porch the entire length of the building, with colonnade. It was the favorite stopping place for members of Congress and other travellers going to and from Washington.* The first proprietor of the Indian Queen, in the memory of our oldest inhabitant, was Jacob Herndon. He was succeeded by James Young, John Gray, Robert Blackburn and Mr. Rawlings. The last to occupy it was a Mr. Whiting, and during his occupancy, in May 1832, the building was destroyed by fire and was never rebuilt. The lot to this large building extended to Princess Ann street, and the stage yard and stables were located where the Southern Foundry now stands. It was in this building that the statute of religious liberty was considered, adopted and written, and it is a matter of great regret that the house was destroyed. The committee that produced this wonderful document, which is given elsewhere, was composed of Thomas Jefferson,

---

* It is said on one occasion John Randolph, of Roanoke, stopped here. It was soon known, and the Democrats congregated to entertain him. They prepared a bowl of punch in an adjoining room, and when it was ready Mr. Randolph was invited to meet the gentlemen and join them in something to drink. In a gruff voice, he replied to the committee that waited on him, "I don't drink with strangers, and if I can't rest here one night without being disturbed by a mob, I will drive to the Sycamores. The Sycamores was a hotel twelve miles from town on the Bowling Green road. It was said he was not again disturbed.

George Wythe, Archibald Cary, George Mason and Ludwell Lee.

On the south corner of Main and Frederick streets stood Traveller's Rest, a tavern of considerable notoriety and popularity, kept by Jesse Pullen. It was headquarters for all circuses and manageries, and was frequented by large numbers of laboring men after their day's toil was over. Here were talked politics and the general topics of the day by the ward politicians, and where they laid schemes to carry elections. The house was destroyed some years before the Civil war and the lot remained vacant for nearly sixty years.

The Western Hotel was located at the corner of Commerce and Charles streets, where Mr. Robert T. Knox and Brother keep store. It was a frame building, and the business was conducted first by Thomas Procter, then by Walker Lucas, who was succeeded by Mr. Joseph Sanford. Mr. Sanford, some years before the war, tore the old frame building down and erected the present three and a half story brick structure and changed its name to the Planters' Hotel. During the Civil war it was conducted by Mr. Councellor Cole, and a short time after the war by a Mr. Mitzell. Since then it has not been kept as a hotel.*

Liberty Hotel was located on Liberty street, then outside of the corporate limits, but now a part of the town. For many years it was kept by Boswell Alsop and was headquarters for the sporting men of the town. General Sam Houston, after his return from frontier life, spent much of his time at this hotel, and quite a number of the leading men of the South, on their journeys to and from Washington, made it their stopping place. It is an old-fashioned frame house, one story and a half high, of the same style of architecture as the Mary Washington house, and shows that both of them were built about the same time.

---

* At the corner of Commerce and Charles streets, in front of this hotel, is a stone block about two and a half feet high and some two feet in diameter. It was placed there many years before the Civil war, it is said, for the sale and annual hire of slaves. The slave to be sold was required to stand on this block in the presence of the gathered traders, when he or she was "cried out" by the auctioneer to the highest bidder. Those slaves who were publicly hired out for the year also took their stand on this block and were hired out at the highest price bid. There is probably no relic in Fredericksburg that calls back more vividly the days of slavery than does this stone block.

History of Fredericksburg, Virginia 169

AGRICULTURAL FAIRS.

We have no means of ascertaining where the fairs previously referred to were held or how long they were continued under the act of 1769, or any similar act that might have been passed by the Legislature after Virginia became a State. In the first of the nineteenth century an agricultural fair was held on the Kenmore farm, near the Kenmore building. The gate leading to the grounds was on Lewis street, where it intersects with Winchester street. The stock was exhibited on the fair grounds and the ladies' department was kept on the upper floor of the present city hall.

At one time Mr. Samuel Gordon, then proprietor of Kenmore, was president of the association, who was succeeded by Hon. James M. Garnett, of Essex county. It was the custom of this association to have an address by the president on the first night of the exhibition on agriculture and stock raising, which was one of the main features of the fair, and drew together a large number of farmers and others to hear it.

A silver cup, awarded to Mr. Jacob Gore for the best wheat fan exhibited at one of these fairs, is now in possession of Police Officer Charles A. Gore, a grandson of Mr. Jacob Gore. It is in a good state of preservation, the inscription on it being "Presented by the Fredericksburg Agricultural Society, 1823." On the left of the inscription is a wheat fan, beautifully engraved, near which is the letter J, which stands for Jacob, and on the right is another fan, near which is the letter G, standing for Gore. We do not know when these annual fairs ceased.

About the year 1850, possibly a little earlier, fair grounds were laid out on Green House Hill, covering most of that part of the town where Prof. A. B. Bowering now lives. A Mr. White, of Caroline county, was the first president, Mr. W. N. Wellford succeeding him to that office. The first steam engine for threshing wheat ever seen in this country was exhibited at one of these fairs by the Hope Foundry, of this place, then operated by Messrs. Scott and Herndon. It was constructed by Mr. Benjamin Bowering, foreman of the works. A committee of farmers was appointed to examine it and report upon its merits. After witnessing its work the committee condemned it, because "it would burn all the wheat up." Fairs were held on these grounds about three years.

A year or so after the Green House Hill fair grounds were closed, the grounds on which Major W. S. Embrey now lives and those in front of him for some distance east of Spotswood street were purchased and converted into fair grounds. Very successful fairs were held there until the commencement of the Civil war, when they were closed. The last fair held on these grounds was in 1860, only a few months before hostilities actually commenced. At one time Major J. Horace Lacy was president of this society and Major J. Harrison Kelly was secretary.

After the closing of the fair grounds, in 1860, Fredericksburg had no other fair for twenty-five years. In 1887 steps were taken by the citizens of the town to inaugurate annual fairs. A charter for a society was obtained, stock was subscribed for and the Amaret farm, on the Fall Hill road west of the town and bordering on the Rappahannock river, was purchased and converted into excellent fair grounds. The society inaugurating these fairs is known as the Rappahannock Valley Agricultural and Mechanical Society, and its annual fairs have been a great success. The presidents of the society from its organization have been Hon. A. P. Rowe, of Fredericksburg; Charles Pierson, Esq., of Caroline county; Hon. S. Wellford Corbin, of King George county; Mr. Oliver Eastburn, of Spotsylvania county; Frank W. Smith, of Spotsylvania county; Captain Terence McCracken, of Fredericksburg; Colonel E. Dorsey Cole, of Fredericksburg; Capt. M. B. Rowe, of Spotsylvania; Chas. H. Hurkamp, of Stafford; Henry Dannehl, of Fredericksburg, and Thomas F. Morrison, of Spotsylvania.

FERRIES AND TOLL BRIDGES.

The first ferry across the Rappahannock river, provided by law, was an act of the House of Burgesses passed in 1748. This act provided for a ferry from the Fredericksburg warehouse, where the tobacco was deposited and inspected by public, bonded inspectors, to the land of Anthony Strother, on the Stafford side of the river. The charge for a horse, which seems to have been the only one regulated by law, was fixed at three pence. In the year 1796 a petition was presented to the General Assembly of Virginia for leave to build a toll-bridge across the Rappahannock river from the lower line of the land of William Fitzhugh, of Chatham. The Legislature granted the request and Mr. Fitzhugh built the bridge, which was kept open for the public travel as a toll-bridge until 1889.

This bridge has been destroyed several times, some times by floods and at other times by fire, and has been rebuilt, but the dates of its destruction have passed from the minds of our oldest citizens. The only dates that can be given, with anything like accuracy, are, that in 1820 it was destroyed by a great flood, in 1861 by fire, in accordance with military orders, and in 1889 by another great flood. In 1890 the city purchased the site and constructed the present iron bridge, which is about one thousand feet long. On its completion it was opened to free travel and has been continued such to the present time. It was at first a toll-bridge and owned by private parties for nearly a century, and yet so far as we can discover there have been but three owners up to the time it was purchased by the city. These three were William Fitzhugh, Esq., Judge John Coulter and Charles S. Scott.

Near the beginning of the nineteenth century a covered bridge spanned the river at the foot of Wolfe street, landing on the farm on the opposite side of the Rappahannock. The farm was then owned by a Mr. Thompson. No one knows when this bridge was built or to whom it belonged. It was known as the Stafford bridge, as the one above it was known as the Chatham bridge, until it was purchased by Mr. Scott, after which it was known as Scott's bridge. The two bridges were destroyed in the flood of 1820 and the Stafford bridge was never rebuilt.

CARE OF THE DEPENDENT POOR.

The first move made by the Common Council, or any other town organization, to provide for the dependent poor of the town was on the 25th of January, 1805, when the hustings court appointed five commissioners—Elisha Thatcher, James Smock, Wm. Benson,

Benjamin Botts and Wm. Taylor—to "enquire into the probable and comparative expense of erecting or renting a poor and work house for the reception of the poor of the corporation, and ascertain the probable salary of a steward for such poor and work house and the annual expense of supporting the same."

These commissioners were empowered to receive propositions from persons desiring to rent suitable houses for the purpose, and to ascertain who would be willing to act as steward and report at the next session of the court. The report was submitted at the March term of the court and was approved and filed; when another commission was appointed, with Dr. George French as chairman, to "rent a house for a term of one or more years," at a cost not exceeding fifty pounds, and John F. Gaullier was appointed steward of the poor and work house.

The steward was to be "allowed a salary at the rate of one hundred and fifty dollars per annum, with two rooms and so much provisions as may be necessary for himself and family," which should not exceed three in number. He was to be at his post at all times to receive the poor into the poor and work house, to "treat them with tenderness and humanity, but at the same time to make them work." For the better government of the institution five inspectors were appointed by the court, consisting of George French, from the lower end of the town to Wolfe street; James Brown, from Wolfe to Hanover street; James Smock, from Hanover to William street; Stephen Winchester, from William to Lewis street, and Wm. Taylor, from Lewis street to the upper end of town. From the record it appears that John Minor was appointed inspector for the town at large.

The inspectors were instructed to place all the poor in the poor and work house and to "advertise a request to the inhabitants to assist no poor person residing in town, lest imposition and idleness be encouraged." This manner of providing for the poor seems to have been continued to the beginning of the Civil war, and, in addition to looking after the steward and the inmates of the poor and work house, the inspectors (more frequently recorded overseers of the poor), were to bind out all orphans who had no one to look after and provide for them.

The Exchange Hotel.
(See page 166)

The Fredericksburg College.
(See page 198)

It is not stated in what part of the town the first poor house was located, but for many years before the Civil war it was located on the Lang property, near Gunnery spring, and afterwards the poor were quartered in a brick house near the western limit of Princess Elizabeth street, which was rented for the purpose and which is now owned by the Richmond, Fredericksburg and Potomac Railroad Company.

After the war, for about eighteen years, the poor were maintained at the private houses, with such families as would agree to take them. In some instances the town paid rent for the houses for the families who would take one of the poor, and in others a stipulated amount per month for their maintenance. This manner of providing for the poor caused much complaint, both from the city and its dependents. The city authorities charged that the cost per capita was entirely too much, running annually in the aggregate from two to three thousand dollars, and the poor complained that they were neglected in both food and clothing.

But the overseer of the poor (the number having been reduced from five to one under the city ordinances) aided and assisted by a committee of three from the Common Council, could do no better with the facilities at his disposal, and while the subject continued to be discussed the Council had been slow in making any change. This inaction, however, was not because the citizens did not favor providing better methods for taking care of the poor, because the public favored it, and the necessity was recognized, but because no member felt willing to take the lead in such a movement.

In the Fall of 1882 a case of small pox broke out in town, and, strange as it may appear, it caused the erection of the present almshouse. The small pox case occurred near the corner of Princess Ann and Frederick streets. The citizens in that part of the town became greatly alarmed and a stampede was threatened. An extra session of the Common Council was called in haste, to make arrangements for the removal of the patient (a colored man) to some isolated place. The Council met and discussed the matter, but it was found that there was no place to which he could be moved. The town owned no land where a temporary hospital could be erected, and land owners declined to rent to the city, for spreading a tent or for erecting a temporary hospital.

In this condition of things the economy of having an almshouse, in which to keep the poor, entered very largely into the discussion, and the result was the farm and residence of Mr. Frank Beckwith, on the hill about half a mile west of the town, was purchased for seventeen hundred dollars. The small pox patient, to the great delight of the citizens in the lower end of town, was at once sent to that place and the excitement subsided.

The following year the residence on the farm was greatly enlarged and a commodious department for the colored poor was built, under the direction of the Committee on Poor of the Common Council, consisting of Messrs. S. J. Quinn, E. D. Cole and M. B. Rowe, and the dependent poor of the town were sent to "Mount Nebo," which was the name given to the place, because of its commanding position and the splendid view of the town and surrounding country from that point.

Since the poor have been kept at the almshouse they are better provided for and are better satisfied, besides they are more comfortable than under the former system, and the expense of maintaining them has been reduced fully one-half. Mr. Albert Hooton, who was overseer of the poor of the town prior to the erection of the almshouse, was the first superintendent of the institution. Mr. Hooton died on the 23rd of November, 1897, and Mr. John Wesley Ball was elected to the vacancy and is now serving. Mr. A. Mason Garner is chairman of the committee of the Council having the almshouse in charge, and while it is conducted on economical principles, the poor are well provided for, in both food and clothing.

WATER WORKS.

For more than one hundred years after the charter by the House of Burgesses the town was without water works of any description. About the year 1832 a private company constructed the Poplar Springs Water Works, which distributed through the principal streets of the town the elegant water from Poplar springs, located on the Plank road, half a mile west of the city. About ten years afterwards the Smith spring was added, which increased the supply. But notwithstanding the addition of the Smith spring the supply was very inadequate; yet for more than half a century these springs, together with street pumps, furnished the only supply the town had. The works were constructed by a Northern contractor, whose name is not remembered, and are yet operated. Since the Civil war these works were under the superintendency of Captain Joseph W. Sener, until his death, in 1889, since which time Mr. Robert Lee Stoffregen has been superintendent.

The inadequacy of the water supply for domestic and manufacturing purposes, and the great necessity for fire protection, were subjects for the consideration of the Common Council for many years, without definite action. On several occasions committees were instructed to have surveys and estimates made for a system of water works, which were done and recommendations had been made by some of the committees that works should be constructed, but the Council in each case had failed to act upon them. As a case of small pox contributed to the erection of a long-needed almshouse, so a fire, that threatened the town with destruction, showing the authorities how helpless they were when confronted by flames, contributed to the construction of water works.

The fire occurred in rear of George E. Chancellor's store in 1883, at the corner of Charles and Commerce streets, now conducted by M. S. Chancellor, and while it was confined to the premises and did but little damage, it threatened to be a serious conflagration. There was no fire department in town and no water to supply an engine, if one was sent from Richmond. This aroused the authorities and the people generally, whose property was constantly threatened with destruction, and at the next meeting of the Council a plan was adopted for "an abundant supply of water for all purposes, including fire protection," which was submitted to a vote of the citizens for their approval or disapproval.

The plan submitted was adopted at the ballot-box by a large majority, and a special committee of the Council was appointed to carry out the will of the people, thus expressed, and construct the works, consisting of Messrs. S. J. Quinn, James S. Knox, Charles

E. Hunter, Terence McCracken and Wm. E. Bradley. After arranging the necessary preliminaries the committee contracted with Colonel Wm. W. Taylor, of Philadelphia, who constructed the works and turned them over to the committee in the latter part of February, 1885, at a cost of twenty-five thousand dollars, Mr. Benjamin Bowering having been appointed by the committee to superintend the laying of pipe, setting of the pump, etc.

The introduction of water into the buildings, the extension of water mains, the changing of the old for newly-patented fire hydrants, and the erection of additional fire hydrants since the works have been in possession of the town, together with additional pumps and steam engine and boiler, have increased the cost of the works to about fifty thousand dollars. At present there are about eighteeen miles of pipe, ranging in size from eight inches to one inch, and seventy-two fire hydrants. These hydrants are so located that they protect from fire all the property of the town.

The reservoir pressure is from fifty to fifty-six pounds to the square inch, according to draught, which is sufficient to throw streams of water over any of our ordinary buildings. The pressure, by the use of the pump, can be raised to one hundred pounds to the square inch.

The water is taken from the Rappahannock river, which is known to furnish the softest and purest of water, the analysis showing that it is free from any foreign substance, and the reservoirs are so well arranged that the citizens are seldom served with water that is the least discolored. The works are under the control of a committee of the Common Council and a superintendent. Since their construction they have been under the superintendency of Captain S. J. Quinn, and they are in good condition and a paying investment to the city, at a comparative small cost to the consumers. The present water committee consists of Josiah P. Rowe, H. B. Lane and A. M. Garner.

THE OLD GAS WORKS.

The old gas works of the town were constructed by a private company in 1843-44, at a cost, it is said, of about forty thousand dollars. The works have changed hands several times since their completion, it being a private company, and most of the stock holders residents of Philadelphia. In consequence of the wear and tear of the works, and the erection of an electric plant in town some twelve years ago, which secured the contract for lighting the streets, the stock of the gas company depreciated very much in value, and an effort was made on the part of the town to purchase the works.

For this purpose a special committee was appointed by the Common Council, consisting of Messrs. Wm. I. King, M. G. Willis, James S. Knox, Wm. E. Bradley and John T. Knight. They entered into negotiations with the officers of the company and finally purchased the works at a cost of twenty thousand dollars. Since their purchase the works have been placed in good repair and the mains have been extended in many parts of the town where they did not before run. There were about nine miles of pipe, but it was claimed by many who had examined the works that the plant was too small to supply the town, and there was much complaint of "no gas" on the part of the consumers, but it was then fashionable to complain against the city even if you were getting what you wanted, and so the matter went on until the "spirit of improvement" struck the town and estimates for a new gas plant were ordered, and before many months passed it was decided that the old works must be abandoned and a new plant constructed on a new site. And so the work of construction commenced and went forward with great rapidity. After the new plant was completed, and had been in running order for some time, the superintendent was asked for an article on the works for this volume, and he remarked that during the latter part of the year 1904 it became obvious that the old gas plant, which had been supplying the city with gas for fifty years, had gone beyond repair, and that for the sake of economy it would be necessary to erect a new plant. With this end in view a plot of ground was selected near the railroad depot and alongside the right-of-way of the railroad, and here the new works were built. Mr. Frederic Egner, an eminent gas engineer, was selected to draw the plans and engineer the construction.

Early in May, 1905, ground was broken and work progressed rapidly, and on the 25th of November the first gas was made in the new plant, and by the 28th everything was working smoothly and the old plant was abandoned. The plant is what is known as a coal gas works, using soft coal for manufacturing the gas. The manufacturing end of the plant consists of two benches of inclined retorts, four to the bench, with half depths regenerative furnaces, and has a manufacturing capacity of 100,000 cubic feet of gas each day of twenty-four hours.

Our plant is one of the most modern in the country, and no small plant now built surpasses it. Mr. Wm. Fitzpatrick, who had faithfully served the city as superintendent of the old plant for many years, retired upon the completion of the new plant and Mr. B. F. Bullock was made superintendent. Gas is $1.00 per thousand, and Mr. John C. Melville is chairman of the committee.

THE ELECTRIC LIGHT PLANT.

Fredericksburg was rather tardy in obtaining an electric light plant for street lighting, either through a private company or by city purchase. While the propriety of constructing a plant by the town was under consideration by the citizens, and often before the Council, application was made by a private company to erect one and the privilege was at once granted. In 1887 a plant of the Thompson-Houston system was erected by a Mr. NcNett. Soon after its construction Mr. McNett formed a company, many of whose members were citizens of the town. It has been purchased by others and is now the Rappahannock Light Co., with some changes. It has furnished the town with arc lights for the streets and many of the buildings with incandescent lights. The dynamo and power house were first located at Knox's mill, above town, but afterwards removed above the Bridge Water mills, where they are at present.

THE CITY'S ELECTRIC LIGHT PLANT.

The town authorities, concluding that our streets could be lighted better and at less cost if they had a plant of their own, arranged and purchased an outfit of machinery, wired the town and now have some seventy-five lights running. Those who opposed the city owning its own light before the plant was constructed have now changed their minds, not only as to the constancy and brilliancy of the light, but also of the cost of lighting the streets. The plant is located between the silk and woolen mills and is in charge of the Light Committee, Mr. Wm. Key Howard, superintendent.

TELEPHONE COMPANY.

In 1895 the Occoquan Woodbridge Telephone Company was organized in Fredericksburg by a Mr. Abner, of Occoquan, and a telephone line was erected. At first the undertaking did not appear to be popular and the company received very little encouragement. After the construction of the line the company, beginning with a small number of subscribers, grew rapidly in public favor and were soon enjoying a liberal patronage.

In 1897 all the property, rights and franchises were purchased by a few of our enterprising citizens, who organized and changed the name of the company to the Rappahannock, Fredericksburg and Piedmont Telephone Company; but subsequently the Bell Company extended their line through Fredericksburg to the South and the local company sold out to the Bell. The service, at first defective, was placed in splendid condition, and the service now equals that of the most favored towns and cities. Since the construction of the Bell line the town has become the center of many private country lines, which place the citizens in communication with all contiguous communities as well as with the cities of the country. The present manager of the local office is W. T. Jones.

FIRE DEPARTMENT.

More than a hundred years ago Fredericksburg had an organized fire department, and from reports, which, however, were seldom made, was sufficient in extinguishing fires. In the early part of the eighteenth century, when the town was built up mostly of wooden houses, with wooden chimneys, and the water was scarce and inaccessible, several fires occurred that spread over considerable territory and did great damage, but even in those instances, although the winds were high, the department did much to retard the progress of the fires and finally got them under control.

The first fire company organized in town was known as the Vigilant. It was organized in 1788 and the names of its members were certified to the hustings court and filed with the court papers, but their names were not placed on the record. How long this company remained in existence is not known, but in 1814 the Hope Company was organized, which was soon followed by the formation of the Union. It is not known who commanded these companies when they were first organized, but we are told that long before the middle of the century the Hope was commanded by Charles C. Wellford and afterwards by John Pritchard, and the Union, about the same time, was commanded by Albert G. Lucas, who was succeeded by John M. Whittemore.

These fire companies had suction and force engines and got water from the river, street pumps, and sometimes from the canal west of the town, after it was constructed, using the source most convenient, and did effective work. It is said the rivalry between these organizations was very great, the excitement in times of fires was intense, and often disputes would arise between the members as to which company did the most effective work, which often resulted in blows. When they were in their prime fires were frequent. Scarcely a week passed that a fire did not occur, and often two or three would take place inside of a week. Then there was a grand rush to see which company could get the first stream of water on the fire.

The frequent fires soon led to the suspicion that some of the firemen originated and were responsible for many of them, and, strange to say, the disbandment of the companies was encouraged by the property owners of the town, as a means of preventing fires and saving property. They were disbanded before the Civil war, and since that time, until the year 1885, the town was without a fire department, and was without any means of contending with the flames, save the feeble efforts of citizens in what was styled "the bucket brigade." This name was applied to the large number of citizens, who, in times of fire, carried water in buckets to extinguish it, and used "wet blankets" to prevent the flames from spreading to adjoining buildings.

In 1885, after the completion of the present city water works, a new fire department was organized, with thirty-three members, with Captain Terence McCracken as chief. This organization is very efficient, and has on several occasions saved the town from sweeping conflagrations. The department is now under the command of John H. Robinson, as chief, and consists of twenty-two members, all of whom render faithful and efficient service without compensation.

CHAPTER XIII

Volunteer Militia—The Confederate Cemetery—The National Cemetery—The Confederate Veterans—The Sons of Confederate Veterans—The Schools, Private and Public, &c.

In times of peace and quiet, in free America and even in conservative Virginia, it is necessary that cities should have some military organization that can be called upon to protect the citizens in their persons, rights and property in case of any emergency that might arise. It is true that such cases seldom occur in Virginia, but if they should, it is necessary to have some organized force, under the laws of the State, to meet and put them down. This being true, Fredericksburg has, in all periods of her history, encouraged and financially assisted volunteer militia companies.

And it can be truthfully stated that, in all the past of the town, the young men have shown a special fondness for military organizations, and, so far as we can gather from records and tradition, Fredericksburg has been well protected in this direction. It is very doubtful if at any time since Major Lawrence Smith seated himself "down at or neare" the falls of the Rappahannock river and manned a fort with one hundred and eleven men, Fredericksburg had not a military organization, either active or dormant, that she could easily call into service in case of need. It is quite certain she has been well represented in every war since the settlement of the country, in which her sons have played conspicuous parts and have been commended for their gallantry and brilliant achievements.

One of the first companies remembered from tradition was commanded by a Capt. Blackford, and is said to have been armed with wooden guns. This company was among the guard of honor to Gen. Lafayette when he was here in 1824. It met the General and his suite at the old Wilderness tavern, escorted him to Fredericksburg, and, when he left, accompanied him as far as Aquia Creek, on the Potomac river. It did not last long as an organization.

The first company remembered by the oldest inhabitants, which

The Home of Dr. Charles Mortimer, first Mayor. To her physician here was the last visit made by Mary Washington. Residence now of Gen. D. D. Wheeler.
(See page 151)

The Eagle Hotel, now the Eagle Flats.
(See page 166)

lasted any length of time, was the Fredericksburg Guards, which was organized many years before the Civil war. It is not known exactly when it was formed or who was its first commander, but it is remembered that at different periods it was commanded by Captains Wm. A. Jackson, Wm. M. Blackford, Robert Smith, John Pritchard and John S. Porter, the order in which they served being in doubt.

A company, known as the Mercer Rifles, was also organized and commanded by Capt. D. Lee Powell some years before the war, but in a year or so it was disbanded in consequence of the commander changing his residence to Richmond.

In the early part of 1859 the Washington Guards was organized, with Capt. Joseph W. Sener as commander. It was well equipped and elegantly uniformed and drilled. When John Brown and his party were captured at Harper's Ferry in the Fall of 1859 by Colonel, afterwards Gen. Robert E. Lee, and turned over to the State authorities, this company was ordered to Charlestown, by Governor Wise, to guard the prisoners, and remained there in that capacity until the last of the party was executed, when they were ordered home.

In the same year, 1859, the Fredericksburg Grays was organized, with Captain Wm. S. Barton as commander. It is said this company was called into existence because of the excited condition of the country and a determination on the part of the young men of the town to be ready for any emergency. On the return of the Washington Guards from Charlestown they were met at the railroad depot by the Grays, who extended them a warm welcome home, escorted them to the Shakespeare House, where a grand banquet was given them, which was followed by speeches and a good time.

These two companies, before the war and preparatory thereto, were formed into a battalion, of which Captain Barton was made major, Robert S. Chew becoming captain of the Grays. Many pleasant excursions and picnics were given by this battalion, which are well remembered by many, now living, who were participants and enjoyed them. But many of those who took part in those pleasant scenes have since then passed to the Great Beyond, and those now with us show the marks of Time upon them and are patiently waiting for the last call that shall transfer them to the great army above. The battalion had a drum corps, consisting of eleven drums, which was presided over by Mr. Pipenbrick, of Falmouth, who was appointed drum major.

A boy company, known as the Coleman Guards, commanded by Captain W. F. Gordon, was also organized just prior to the war. In 1860 great excitement was caused on the arrival of Robinson's circus here, the charge having been made that some of the employees or attaches had murdered a man by the name of Boulware at Port Royal the day before. Warrants were sworn out for the arrest of the supposed parties, and the three companies, with the civil authorities, arrested the entire circus and had the suspected parties before the Mayor. A two days' investigation disclosed no probable guilt and the circus was discharged from custody.

Another military company was organized in the town in 1861, known as the Gordon Rifles, with Captain Robert H. Alexander as its commander. These three companies, at the outbreak of the war, were placed in the Thirtieth Virginia regiment of infantry, that did such noble service during the Civil war. The Washington Guards, which became Company A, was commanded by Capt. Joseph W. Sener. He was succeeded by Capt. George H. Peyton and Captain John K. Anderson. The Fredericksburg Grays became Company B and was commanded by Capt. Robert S. Chew, and, on his promotion to Colonel, by Capt. H. S. Doggett. Capt. Doggett was on detached duty the most of his official term as captain and the company was commanded by Lieutenant James S. Knox in his absence, who was promoted to captain, but his commission never reached him. The Gordon Rifles became Company C and was commanded by Captain Robert H. Alexander and afterwards by Captain C. Wistar Wallace.

After the war the Fredericksburg Grays was reorganized, with Samuel S. Brooke, now of Roanoke, as captain. He was succeeded in command by Captain Maurice B. Rowe, and he by the following commanders in the order named: Captain Terence McCracken, Captain Robert B. Berrey, Captain George A. Walker and Captain Frank H. Revere.

When war was declared between the United States and Spain, and volunteers were called for by the government, the Washington Guards, which had been reorganized by Captain Maurice B. Rowe, promptly responded and was mustered into the United States service as Company K of the Third Virginia regiment of infantry. It went into camp at Richmond, Virginia, and was soon transferred to Camp Alger, named in honor of the then Secretary of War, near Washington city. Before these troops were ordered to the scene of action peace was declared and they were ordered back to Richmond and mustered out of service, having been in the service of the United States seven months. The company then returned to Fredericksburg.

The Guards numbered one hundred and twelve men on the rolls, was a splendid body of patriotic young men and reflected credit upon the town. Soon after being discharged from the United States army the company was reorganized, reëntered the service of the State and now numbers sixty-two men, under the command of Captain Thomas M. Larkin. They have often been called upon to discharge important and delicate service, and have responded with alacrity.

In 1883 a colored volunteer company was organized in town, called the Garfield Light Infantry Blues. It was organized by Benjamin Scott, of Richmond, who was its first captain. Captain Scott soon returned to his home in Richmond and was succeeded in command by Captain Lucien G. Gilmer. This organization continued in existence several years, but was finally disbanded, having fallen below the minimum number required by law.

THE CONFEDERATE CEMETERY.

Soon after the citizens of Fredericksburg returned to their desolated homes at the close of the Civil war, and had gotten their dwellings in a condition to be occupied, the thoughts of the patriotic ladies were at once turned to the Confederate soldiers who had fallen and were buried in Fredericksburg and on the several adjacent battle-fields. They were anxious that the remains of these brave men should be gathered up and interred in some place where their dust would be preserved and the names of the known saved from oblivion.

As a result of a consultation, and a call published in the newspapers of Fredericksburg, the ladies of the town met in the basement of the Presbyterian church on the 10th day of May, 1865, one month after the surrender of Gen. Lee, and organized the Ladies' Memorial Association of Fredericksburg, elected officers, appointed a board of directors, an executive committee and an advisory board. This was the first ladies' memorial association chartered in the South and among the first to decorate the soldiers' graves with flowers.

The best methods for accomplishing the patriotic work of the association were discussed and adopted at this early date. The plan was to raise as much money in town and in Virginia as possible and then issue an appeal to be sent all through the Southern States for funds, because every Southern State was represented on the battle-fields in and around the town by their heroic dead. These appeals were sent out as soon as they could be gotten ready and had the desired effect. Funds soon began to flow into the treasury and a suitable site was selected, west of and adjoining the city cemetery, which was purchased, and the work of gathering up the dead commenced. The number gotten from the different battle-fields and buried in the ground purchased by the association numbered about fifteen hundred. The circular sent out had, in addition to the organization of the association and the list of officers in full, an appeal, which was as follows:

"To all true hearted women and men, who would rescue from oblivion the memory of the brave, who died in defence of home and country, we present this appeal: The stern pressure of military necessity made it impossible, properly, to care for the remains of the gallant dead who fell on the bloody fields of Fredericksburg, Wilderness, Chancellorsville, Spotsylvania Courthouse and in scores of skirmishes which, in a war less terrible, would have been reckoned as battles.

"Our Association proposes to preserve a record, and, as far as possible, mark the spot where every Confederate soldier is buried in this vicinity, whether he fell on these memorable fields or otherwise died in the service. To the bereaved throughout our suffering South we pledge ourselves to spare no exertion to accomplish this work.

"In a land stripped of enclosures and forests, desolated and impoverished as ours, we cannot, without aid, guard these graves from exposure and possible desecration; we can only cover them with our native soil. And, with pious care, garland them with the wild flowers from the fields. But, with the generous aid and cordial coöperation of those who have suffered less, but who feel as deeply as we do on this subject, we confidently hope to accomplish far more—to purchase and adorn a cemetery, to remove thither the sacred dust scattered all over this region, and to erect some enduring tribute to the memory of our gallant dead.

"Shall that noble army of martyrs, who, for years of toil and suffering, bore, in triumph, the 'Conquered Banner' from Chattanooga to Gettysburg, sleep on the fields of their fame unnoticed and unknown? Shall their names pass from the knowledge of the living to be treasured only in the mind of Him 'to whom the memory of the just is precious?'

"What spot so appropriate for the last resting place of these heroes, as some commanding eminence overlooking the memorable plain of Fredericksburg? And what nobler work for the hearts and hands of Southern women, than upon its summit to rear a monument to the unrecorded Confederate dead, which, through all time shall testify to the gratitude of the people for whom they so gloriously died? As no State, and scarcely a town or county throughout the limits of the late Confederacy, is unrepresented on these battle-fields, may we not hope that the coöperation required in order to accomplish our holy work will be as universal?

"An act of the Legislature of Virginia will be obtained, incorporating our Association, so that the property may be held perpetually dedicated to its sacred uses. We solicit such contributions as the appreciative sympathy of friends in all parts of our country, and of the world, will extend us. As soon as sufficient means are obtained our Association will proceed to purchase and improve grounds appropriate for a cemetery, and remove thither the remains of the honored dead.

"Our Association, although its organization is but recent, has been enabled to rescue from oblivion the names and places of burial of many of the noble dead, who fell upon the fields of Fredericksburg, Chancellorsville, the Wilderness, and all the objects of the Association will be pressed as rapidly forward as the requisite means are procured. All auxiliary societies, which may be formed, are requested to correspond with our Association; and, should they desire their contributions to be specially appropriated to the graves of any individuals, or of any particular State or section, the trust will be sacredly discharged.

Mrs. John H. Wallace, President.
Miss Ann J. Carter,
Corresponding Secretary.

President—Mrs. John H. Wallace.

Vice-Presidents—Mrs. J. H. Lacy, Mrs. Jane Ficklin, Mrs. James W. Ford, Mrs. A. F. T. Fitzhugh, Mrs. Fannie S. White.

Board of Directors—Miss Mary G. Browne, Miss S. Freaner, Mrs. W. K. Howard,* Mrs. S. J. Jarvis, Mrs. E. A. Fitzgerald, Mrs. L. J. Huffman, Mrs. J. H. Bradley, Mrs. Magruder Maury, Mrs. Joseph Alsop, Mrs. Monroe Kelly, Miss Ellen P. Chew, Miss Lizzie Braxton.

Treasurer—Dr. F. P. Wellford.

Recording Secretaries—Miss L. G. Wellford, Mrs. Lucy Herndon.*

Corresponding Secretary—Miss Ann J. Carter.

Assistant Secretaries—Miss V. S. Knox,* Miss Mary Thom, Miss Bettie L. Scott,* Miss Lizzie Alsop, Miss N. S. Wellford, Miss Mary G. Browne, Mrs. L. T. Kearsley, Miss Helen G. Beale, Miss Nannie Taylor, Miss Virginia Goolrick, Miss S. Freaner, Miss Lizzie Braxton.

Executive Committee—Major J. H. Kelly, Thomas F. Knox, George Aler, J. W. Slaughter, Edwin Carter, Joseph W. Sener, Dr. L. B. Rose.

---

* Yet living.

Advisory Committee—Gen. D. H. Maury, Gen. Daniel Ruggles, Gen. C. L. Stevenson, Col. R. S. Chew, Col. C. M. Braxton, Col. W. W. Fontaine, Major George Freaner, Major Chas. S. Green,* Capt. C. T. Goolrick, Capt. W. R. Mason,* Rev. M. Maury, Rev. T. W. Gilmer, Rev. Patrick Donelan, Rev. W. H. Williams, Rev. F. C. Tebbs, Mayor M. Slaughter, Judge R. C. L. Moncure,† A. A. Little, J. H. Kelly, Judge R. H. Coleman, John L. Marye, Jr., John E. Tackett, D. H. Gordon, W. P. Conway, J. L. Stansbury, Ab. P. Rowe, James B. Sener, W. K. Howard."

In response to the appeal of the Association, liberal contributions were received from all the Southern States, with which the ground was purchased, the present cemetery laid out and the remains of all the Confederate dead, who were killed and buried throughout this community, gathered together, transferred to the cemetery and the graves marked with cedar posts. These posts were removed a few years afterwards and marble headstones took their places. The next work of the Association was to raise money for a monument to be placed in the center of the cemetery, and, as in their other patriotic work, the appeal was not in vain. The necessary amount was raised and the monument was erected and dedicated. Mr. Leyburn, of Lexington, Va., contractor; Mr. Cassell, of Baltimore, architect. The stone used is gray granite and was taken from the farm of Mrs. Mary Downman, in Spotsylvania county. The monument contains inscriptions as follows:

On the east side—S. Carolina, Virginia, N. Carolina.
On the north side—Missouri, Kentucky, Tennessee, Arkansas.
On the west side—Louisana, Mississippi, Texas.
On the south side—Georgia, Florida, Alabama.

The monument stands on a mound about five feet high, and is five feet and six inches high without the statue. With the statue it is twenty feet in height. On the west side, cut in the granite, are muskets; on the south side, a castle with battlements; on the north

---

* Yet living.

†One of the Judges of the Court of Appeals of Virginia for fourteen years before the war, and president of said court for twelve years after the war.

side, sabres; on the east side, cannon and the inscription "To the Confederate Dead." On each corner of the monument is a column of red granite, with gray granite plynth and base. The cornerstone was laid on the 4th of June, 1874, by Fredericksburg Lodge, No. 4, A. F. & A. M., Grand Master Wm. H. Lambert presiding, and was completed and unveiled on Memorial Day, June 9, 1884. The statue of a Confederate soldier, at dress parade, which crowns the apex, is of bronze, and was manufactured by the Monumental Bridge Company, of Bridgeport, Conn. It was ordered through Mr. George T. Downing and placed in position by him.

THE NATIONAL CEMETERY.

The National Cemetery, in which were gathered and interred the Union soldiers who died in camp and were killed in the various battles in and around Fredericksburg, was commenced in 1865, soon after the close of the war. It is located on Willis's Hill, about half a mile south of the town. It is on the range of hills known in the war histories and correspondents as Marye's Heights, which overlooks the beautiful valley of the Rappahannock and affords a fine view of Fredericksburg and the surrounding country. It afforded a splendid location for the Confederate artillery at both battles of Fredericksburg, which did such fearful execution as the Union troops were advancing on General Lee's position.

The remains of the Union soldiers were taken from their temporary graves and conveyed to the cemetery by a "burial corps," consisting of a large detail of Frederal soldiers and a few veterans employed by the superintendent. The work was continued for three or four years, and it was thought that all the dead had been cared for, but even now remains of soldiers are sometimes found in different places and turned over to the superintendent for interment. The Fredericksburg cemetery is not the largest in area in the United States, but it has a larger number of interments in it than any other in the country. Up to the present time the interments number 15,294, of these 2,496 are known and their names, regiments and State are registered in a book in the superintendent's office, and 12,798 are unknown. The superintendent of the cemetery is Major M. M. Jefferys, and under his management it is kept in good condition.

The superintendent has a "lodge" or residence near the cemetery gate, constructed of stone. It is made of the stone taken from the historical stone wall, behind which the Confederates were stationed when they successfully resisted the many gallant charges of General Hancock's men on the 13th of December, 1862. Several years ago the government constructed a Macadamized road from the railroad depot to the cemetery, making it a pleasant drive to that "city of the dead," and it is visited by numbers of persons, both citizens and strangers. In 1901 Gen. Daniel Butterfield erected a beautiful monument in the cemetery to the valor of the Fifth Army Corps, which he commanded, at a cost of $11,000.

MAURY CAMP OF CONFEDERATE VETERANS.

The Confederate veterans of Fredericksburg and surrounding country organized themselves into a camp in 1883. It was one of the first camps of the kind organized in the State and had quite a large membership. It was called Maury Camp in honor of General Dabney Herndon Maury, a native of Fredericksburg, who rose to the rank of major-general in the Confederate army, and distinguished himself as a skillful commander as well as for conspicuous gallantry on many fields of battle during the Civil war.

Maury Camp flourished for several years, having at one time in the neighborhood of one hundred and fifty members. At first it was independent and separate from any other camp, but upon the organization of R. E. Lee Camp, of Richmond, which obtained a charter from the General Assembly of Virginia, thereby giving it authority over other camps, Maury Camp obtained a charter from that organization, and holds its authority under that charter at present.

For some cause in late years the camp has not been prosperous; on the contrary, it has merely maintained its organization. Many of the members withdrew their membership or allowed their names to be dropped from the rolls, while those who still retain their membership, with a few exceptions, exhibit but little interest in the affairs of the camp. Notwithstanding its decline, however, it has done much good in the past in assisting needy Confederate veterans, besides they have relieved the necessities of the widows and orphans of veterans, and have decently buried their old comrades who have died in destitution. The camp has had for commanders at different periods Colonel Robert S. Chew, Judge John T. Goolrick, Capt. Daniel M. Lee, Thomas F. Proctor, Geo. Shepherd and Capt. S. J. Quinn. At present Prof. A. B. Bowering is the commander and the camp seems to be taking on new life.

SONS OF CONFEDERATE VETERANS.

The organization of Maury Camp of Confederate Veterans was followed in a few years by the organization of the Sons of Confederate Veterans. This camp came into existence on the 10th day of May, 1890. It was organized, mainly, if not entirely, through the efforts of Mr. James A. Turner, who was its first commander, and, by annual reëlections, without opposition, he was continued until he retired and Mr. Wm. H. Hurkamp was elected and is commander at this time.

This camp of the Sons of Confederate Veterans was named in honor of Colonel Robert S. Chew, who was, at the close of the war, Colonel of the Thirtieth Virginia regiment of infantry, a native of Fredericksburg and was honored and beloved by all who knew him. The camp has done a noble work in the way of looking after the comfort and supplying the needs of the destitute Confederate veterans, who are rapidly passing "over the river to rest under the shade of the trees," and providing for them a decent Christian burial when they shall have "answered the last roll call."

As an organization the R. S. Chew Camp has attended nearly all the reunions of Confederate veterans in the State, and has taken as much interest in them as if they had been veterans instead of the sons of veterans. In all of these visitations the camp, by the discipline and military bearing of its members, soon won for itself a position in the front rank of Sons of Confederate Veterans in the South. About thirty of its members volunteered in the United States army in the War with Spain, some of whom are

"Stevens House," on "Sunken Road"; the Confederate line of battle, 1862 and 1863, in front of fence. Gen. Thos. R. R. Cobb killed where gate swings to right.
(See page 91)

City Hall, in which are Mayor's Office, Council Chamber, etc., and where a ball was given in honor of Gen. Lafayette on his visit here in 1824.
(See page 144)

now in the regular army, holding important commissions. The camp has flourished from its organization, and has now nearly one hundred members on its rolls, who are earnest in their work and faithful to the memories of their fathers.

THE SCHOOLS OF FREDERICKSBURG.

Fredericksburg, from its earliest days, possessed educational advantages, greatly in advance of many larger towns of the colonies. Soon after its establishment by the House of Burgesses, schools of a high order were established here by the best of educators and it is highly probable that the leading men of the State—those who conducted public affairs in colonial times, and who were the first to oppose and resist British tyranny and who inaugurated and conducted the movement for separation and independence—were educated in those schools. And it can be safely said that from that time to the present Fredericksburg has not been without schools that would be creditable to any town.

In 1796 a lottery scheme—which was a popular method of raising money in those days for such purposes—was chartered by the Legislature of the State for the purpose of raising money to erect a school building on what was known as the "old poor-house grounds," at present the property of Alexander Lang's estate near Gunnery Spring. Whether or not this scheme was successful is not known, but it is a fact that a male academy was established by some French refugees, gentlemen of education and refinement, who, having lost their fortunes, adopted teaching as a means of support. Many distinguished Statesmen and jurists, in after years, were educated at this school, among them was Judge John Tayloe Lomax, who, in his old age, when president of the Young Men's Christian Association of Fredericksburg, referred to his connection with this school by contrasting the teaching of the school of French philosophy of that day with the instruction of Christian teachers of a later period, showing the advantages of the latter.

In a letter from Dr. John Brockenburg to Rev. Philip Slaughter, D. D., in 1846, about another matter, he said: "I had been entered as a student at the Fredericksburg Academy, then (1790) in high repute, under the Rev. Mr. Ryan, an eminent classical scholar and a graduate of Trinity College, Dublin." Dr. Brockenburg finished his education in this school, preparatory to entering a medical college in Edinburg, and speaks highly of it.*

It is also claimed that Washington, Madison, Monroe, and others who made their mark as soldiers, statesmen, and in the various professions, were educated in the schools of Fredericksburg.

The establishment of a female college at "Federal Hill," in the year 1789, and which was kept up by different teachers for half a century or more, was an important event in the history of the town, and, in connection with the male academy, gave to Fredericksburg great distinction as an educational center.

On the 27th of September, 1795, a fund was created by the sale of lands, which were devised for the purpose by Mr. Archibald McPherson, which fund was held in trust by the Mayor and Common Council of the town for the time being, and afterwards, by an act of the Legislature, by six trustees, annually appointed for the benefit of the Charity School of Fredericksburg. These trustees organized into a board, the first president being Major Benjamin Day, who continued as such to the day of his death. The school was kept in the brick building on the north side of Hanover street, just below the Masonic hall, now used by Miss Willie F. Schooler for her Hanover school. The funds derived by the sale of some of the McPherson property were afterwards supplemented by a legacy from Mr. Thomas Colson in 1805.

In the back part of the room in which this male charity school was kept are to be found three tablets of marble let into the brick wall, in good preservation, with these inscriptions:

"In memory of Mr. Archibald McPherson. He bequeathed his property to the trustees of this town for the education of the poor. By an act of the Legislature the funds were transferred to this institution as best fulfilling the testator's charitable design. Died A. D. 1754; age 49."

"In memory of Thomas Colson, Esq., who, by his last will and

---
* Slaughter's Bristol Parish. Va., 2nd edition.

testament, contributed largely to the permanent funds of this school. His benevolence claims the gratitude of the poor, and the respect of all. Died A. D. 1805."

"In memory of Major Benjamin Day, one of the founders of this institution and its first president. This office he filled for twenty-six years with zeal and fidelity. As an humble tribute to his philanthropic services this simple monument is erected. Died A. D. 1821; age 69."

On Major Day's tombstone, in the burial ground of Fredericksburg Masonic Lodge, in reference to this school, is found these words: "The Male Charity School of Fredericksburg is chiefly indebted to him for its origin in 1795, and for its prosperity to his unremitted attention in the principal management of its concerns, over which he presided until the time of his death."

These tablets and tombstones furnish a history of this school that can be had nowhere else, and their transcription here will, it is hoped, enshrine the memories of these charitable men for their munificence to the poor of the town in the hearts of the present generation and indelibly impress upon their minds the solemn, but oft unheeded, words of the Master, "ye have the poor with you always, and whensoever ye will ye may do them good." Mr. George W. Rothrock conducted this male school as teacher for many years, but upon his death, before the Civil war, it was closed and has never been resumed.

A reference to other schools of Fredericksburg, some contemporary with the Male Charity School and the Federal Hill Female College, and others of a later date, will no doubt be of interest to the numerous descendants of those who were educated in them, and will recall to many of our older citizens pleasant memories of their youthful days, as well as the labor over "tare and tret, which made them mad and sweat."

Among these was the excellent female school taught by Rev. Samuel Wilson, in which many of the most accomplished ladies in Fredericksburg received their early education. Mr. Wilson was succeeded by Miss Mary Ralls, who was assisted by Mr. Herard, whom she afterwards married.* Mr. Herard was a Frenchman, and although he could not speak English, taught writing and French in the school. Here commenced the education of a large number of girls and boys, who were afterwards well known in the social circle and business pursuits of Fredericksburg and of many other parts of the country, and some of them are to-day honored citizens of the town.

The school kept by Mr. John Goolrick, in the small, brick building on the lower end of Main street, now occupied by Mr. W. Snowden Hitt, was famous in its day, and in that school were educated some of our substantial business men and accomplished women. He was assisted in his school by his son, George, who was an accomplished teacher and cultured gentleman. George Goolrick succeeded his father in the conduct of the school and continued it for many years.

Mr. Thomas H. Hanson, who came to Fredericksburg from Georgetown, D. C., was principal of the Fredericksburg Male Academy. He was a fine classical scholar and his school enjoyed a wide-spread reputation as a classical school. He taught in the north wing of the City Hall, and for several years on Prince Edward street, above Amelia, in a brick building, where the residences of Misses Hay and Misses Wissner now stand. The building was torn down several years ago, when residences were built. Some few of his pupils are now living. One died a short time ago, at a ripe old age, with the honorary LL. D. attached to his name.

Rev. George W. McPhail conducted a school for some years on the west side of Main street, just above Commerce. The house was a large, frame building, with a store on the ground floor and school-room above. It was destroyed at the shelling of the town in December, 1862. Mr. McPhail's first school-room was located on George street west of the Presbyterian church, but, it being too small to accommodate his pupils, he moved to Main street.

---

* It is related by the "old folks" that when the ceremony closed the minister looked at the groom and said "kiss your bride." The groom, not understanding English and imagining it was some figure in the dance, innocently took the bride by the hands and merrily waltzed up and down the aisle to the amusement of the audience, but to the great mortification of the bride.

Messrs. Powell and Morrison, for many years, conducted a school for girls in Citizens' Hall, which stood on Princess Ann street where the Catholic parsonage now stands. It was known as the Fredericksburg Institute, and was one of the best schools of that day. It was moved to Richmond and is now conducted by members of Mr. Powell's family.

Professor Richard Sterling conducted a school for boys in the old Colonnade building on Princess Ann street, opposite the courthouse, long before the war. He was succeeded by Mr. J. J. Halsey. The building was partially destroyed by fire during the Civil war, and finally, in 1880, was removed to give place to the Presbyterian Memorial chapel.

For a number of years a school for girls was conducted by Mrs. John P. Little, first at her residence, on Princess Ann street, and then for some time at Federal Hill and at the Union House. which is now used for the public schools. She was assisted in her school by an accomplished French teacher by the name of Guillet.

More than half a century ago Misses Ann and Mary Drinnan conducted a flourishing school for girls on Charles street, above Lewis, where the Misses Goodwin now live, and Mrs. Mary Hackley conducted a large boarding school over the store now occupied by Mr. Thomas N. Brent. For several years before the war Rev. Wm. F. Broaddus, D. D., taught a school for young ladies in the basement of the Baptist church. These schools were all of a high order and fully sustained the reputation of Fredericksburg as a town possessing the most enlarged educational advantages. Besides the schools above referred to, schools for boys were taught by Richard Stern, Mr. Hudson, Mr. Jamison, Stephen A. Boardman, James G. Read, Edward Henry, Mr. Tchudi, Buckner & Henry, Buckner & Temple, Chas. E. Tackett, Thomas Moncure, H. W. Rhinehart, Mrs. Judith Anstice, Mrs. A. L. Magrath, Maria Woodruff, Miss Willie Schooler and others.

After the war Judge Richard H. Coleman taught a high school for boys at Kenmore, and Colonel W. Winston Fontaine taught a high school for girls on the south corner of Main and Frederick streets, and Professor Volley M. Johnson conducted a similar school at the Union House. When Judge Coleman moved his school to Guiney's in Caroline county, Messrs. Cuthbert Buckner and Charles W. Temple opened a school of the same grade. They were succeeded by Messrs. Cuthbert Buckner and Wm. Caruthers, and they by Messrs. Charles E. Tackett, James W. Ford and Wm. B. Marye, who added a military feature to the school, which made it quite popular. These schools were located on Prince Edward street in a one-story brick house, known as the Academy, where the Misses Hay have recently erected a modern residence.

After Colonel Fontaine moved South a high school for young ladies was opened by Mr. Wm. Caruthers in the Presbyterian Asylum, known now as Smithsonia, assisted by his sisters, Mrs. Davis and Miss Caruthers. He was succeeded by Mrs. Wm. A. Campbell and daughter, two excellent teachers, but the school did not appear to prosper and was finally closed. In addition to these schools of high grade there were many excellent primary schools for girls and boys, which succeeded well until the public free schools were opened, which became popular because of their graded system and the thoroughness of their instruction. Since then most of the private schools have been abandoned, yet some few are yet conducted and are doing well.

THE ASSEMBLY'S HOME AND SCHOOL.

The Assembly's Home and School was founded by Rev. A. P. Saunders, D. D., then pastor of the Presbyterian church in Fredericksburg, in 1893. It was incorporated by an act of the Virginia Legislature December 16, 1893. It consisted originally of a home designed for the maintenance and education of the orphans of deceased Presbyterian ministers and missionaries, and also of a college. The latter was intended as a place for the education of these orphans and also for the youth of other denominations.

The General Assembly of the Presbyterian church, each year, commended the institution to the confidence of the churches within its bounds, and by their contributions the Home was maintained. The college for some time was supported partly by contributions from the churches, but more largely by the pay students attending the school from home and abroad.

In the year 1897 the General Assembly of the church separated the college from the Home and ordered the sale of the college and all the property belonging to it. The city of Fredericksburg recognizing the value of such an institution in its midst, had subscribed ten thousand dollars of bonds, the interest on which was to pay for ten annual scholarships in the college, the scholars being selected from the highest grade of the public schools of the town.

This arrangement continued until 1898, when the college and property were sold and the ten thousand dollars of bonds were returned to the city authorities and cancelled. The property was purchased by Rev. F. P. Ramsay, who conducted the college for two years, the city continuing its patronage of ten scholarships, paying the tuition in money.

In the year 1900 Mr. Ramsay sold the college and property to Rev. John W. Rosebro, who had just become pastor of the Presbyterian church in Fredericksburg. He is a gentleman of rare ability, and, with his corps of able assistants, is making the college worthy of the confidence and support of the public. A bright and prosperous future is predicted for the institution under the management of this scholarly gentleman.

The Assembly Home is still in operation, supported by the denomination, and holds a strong place in the affections of the Presbyterian church. It is now under the management of Professor Samuel W. Somerville.

THE PUBLIC SCHOOLS.

The public schools were established in Fredericksburg, under what is known as the Underwood Constitution, in 1870. For several years they were not well patronized, principally from the fact that the system was not popular with the people. When the system was first put in operation in town the schools were kept at private houses, because the city had no public school houses and was then unable to build them, and as the appropriations for school purposes were small the sessions were held only for five or six months in the year. The teachers, in a majority of cases, were selected more because of their need of the salary than because of their ability and fitness to teach.

In the year 1876 the schools were graded, and the funds received from the city and State were largely supplemented from the Peabody fund, which enabled the school board to adopt a ten months' session. By this arrangement the efficiency of the schools was greatly promoted; they grew in public favor, the citizens patronized them, and soon they became so large and popular the town was compelled to provide larger buildings for the accommodation of the pupils. To accommodate this large increase of attendance a commodious two-story brick building was erected on the north corner of Princess Ann and Wolfe streets for the colored schools, sufficiently large to accommodate four schools, and the Union House, a three-story brick building on the north corner of Main and Lewis streets, was purchased for the white schools and converted into a building capable of accommodating six schools.

In addition to the schools held at the Union House there are two schools for the first primary grades, one held in the forenoon and the other in the afternoon, under one teacher, and were kept in the south wing of the courthouse until two years ago, when they were moved to the Union House and other grades removed to the courthouse. The grammar grade of the colored schools is taught at Samaritan Hall, on Douglas street. These schools have an efficient corps of teachers and the instruction is as thorough as is found in any of the schools of the State.

There are ten grades in the white schools—seven in the primary department and three in the grammar department. There are six grades in the colored schools—five in the primary department and one in the grammar department. The town is divided into two school districts, the Upper and the Lower, George street being the dividing line. There are three trustees from each school district, the six members constituting the school board of the town.

There have been four superintendents of schools since the inauguration of the free school system in 1870, who have served in the following order: Mr. John Howison, General Daniel Ruggles, Mr. Edgar M. Crutchfield and Mr. Benjamin P. Willis. All of these gentlemen have passed away except Mr. Willis, who is now serving as superintendent. The school board has had but four presidents since its organization, thirty-eight years ago, who served in the following order: John James Young, Captain Joseph W. Sener, Wm. H. Cunningham and Andrew B. Bowering. Only one is now living—A. B. Bowering, who is serving at present.

CHAPTER XIV

The Churches of Fredericksburg.

If the morals and correct lives of the people of a town are to be judged by the number of churches within its borders, giving due consideration to the number of inhabitants, the people of Fredericksburg would be rated with the best. One of the first things that received the attention of the founders of the town, under the charter granted by the House of Burgesses in 1727, was the building of a house of worship and its dedication to the service of the Almighty, and since that time Fredericksburg has been blessed with regular divine services. And as the inhabitants of the town increased in numbers, and the little building became too small to accommodate all who would wish to attend upon the House of the Lord, the authorities were not too much engrossed with money-making and money-getting to enlarge the church and provide for the spiritual comfort and necessities of the increasing population. So the church building was enlarged time and again as the growth of the town demanded it.

Up to the first of the nineteenth century the only denomination holding regular services in town was the Episcopalians, as that was the only denomination that had a house of worship, but in the early part of that century other denominations organized churches in town, built houses of worship and have continued to occupy them to the present. Since then Fredericksburg has not been without a sufficient number of churches for the accommodation of her entire church-going population. There are at present eleven church buildings in town—seven for the whites and four for the colored people. The seating capacity of the white church buildings is about three thousand and that of the colored churches about one thousand five hundred, making the total seating capacity of the churches of Fredericksburg about four thousand five hundred, being ample accommodation for the church-going population, both white and colored.

Jackson Monument. Erected where he was mortally wounded May 2, 1863.
(See page 96)

ST. GEORGE'S EPISCOPAL CHURCH.

The history of the Episcopal church in Fredericksburg is of peculiar interest to the people of the town because of its antiquity and because of its intimate connection with the history and affairs of the town. In the year 1732, seven years after the town was laid out and named, the first church building was erected in Fredericksburg.* It was in St. George's parish, which embraced the whole of Spotsylvania county, which then contained all the territory west, as far as it was or might be settled by the whites. A church building had previously been erected in the county, on the Po river, for the accommodation of the people of the county. This church is said to have been located on the Catharpin road, on the top of the hill west of Mine run, on the south side of the road, where the Yellow church was afterwards built by the Baptists and which was destroyed some years ago. This stream is not the Po, but one of its tributaries and may then have been called the Po.

The first pastor the Fredericksburg church had after the completion of its building was Rev. Patrick Henry, uncle of the great orator and statesman of that name. He served the church for two years, and in 1735 was succeeded by Rev. James Marye,† of Goochland county, who died as rector of the church in 1769, having served it faithfully for thirty-four years. Rev. James Marye was succeeded in the rectorship by his son, Rev. James Marye, Jr., who was rector for eleven years. From 1780, when the second James Marye closed his labors, to 1813 the church had many rectors, but their stay was of short duration.

In the year 1787 the Common Council, through a committee of its members, repaired and enlarged the church building by adding another wing, (one having been previously constructed, mentioned elsewhere,) which made the building a cross in shape. The cost for this work amounted to four hundred and six pounds, a part of which was raised by the committee by an appeal to the private citizens for donations, because of the depleted condition of the city treasury. In the same year the Council prepared and adopted a

---
* Some authorities give 1735 as the date of the erection of this church.
† Great grandfather of Governor John L. Marye.

petition to the Legislature of Virginia, praying for a division of St. George's parish and for vesting "the property of the old church and the new burying ground in Fredericksburg in the corporation of said town."

Mr. James Monroe,* who was a member of the Council and a vestryman of St. George's church, (who was afterwards a member of the Legislature, a Representative in Congress, a United States Senator, twice Governor of Virginia, twice Minister to France, twice Minister to England, Minister to Spain, Secretary of State, Secretary of War, two terms President of the United States, Presiding Justice of Loudoun county and Visitor of the University of Virginia,) was appointed chairman of the committee to present the petition and secure the desired action of the Legislature. If any report was ever made by Mr. Monroe, neither it nor any reference to it can be found. It is quite likely that the law separating church and State, which was passed that year, made it unnecessary.

As has been stated, that after the death of the younger Marye, for more than thirty years the pastorates of the church were short and unsatisfactory. The cause for this state of things has not been recorded and conjecture is needless. In 1813 Edward C. McGuire, of Winchester, Virginia, came to the church as lay reader, being highly recommended by Rev. Wm. Meade (who afterwards became bishop of the diocese) as a young man of character and piety. Mr. McGuire was soon ordained and became rector of the church, serving it with great acceptance and success to the day of his death, in 1858, a period of forty-five years.†

Mr. McGuire was greatly beloved by all classes of persons, his ministerial labors were signally blessed, and the number of communicants was largely increased. From the death of Mr. McGuire

---

* It has been claimed, and it is probably true, that James Monroe held more important public positions in his life than any other one man, either before or since his day.

† A memorial tablet erected in St. George's church has this inscription: "Rev. Edward McGuire, D. D., born in Winchester, Va., July 26, 1783, died Oct. 8, 1858. During forty-five years the faithful, beloved and highly blessed pastor of St. George's church, Fredericksburg. Amiable in character, prudent in action, wise in counsel, evangelical in doctrine, experimental in preaching, he was a pastor of great influence and success, highly esteemed for his sound judgment and consistent conduct during a long and useful life."

to the present the church has had several rectors, who did good work and who greatly endeared themselves to the congregation and people of the town. These pastors served in the following order: Rev. A. M. Randolph, D. D., now bishop of the Southern Diocese of Virginia; Rev. Magruder Maury, Rev. Edward C. Murdaugh, Rev. Robert J. McBryde, Rev. J. K. Mason, Rev. Wm. M. Clarke, Rev. Wm. D. Smith and Rev. Dr. Robert J. McBryde, a second time, who is the present rector. During a portion of the time that Dr. Murdaugh was rector he had as his assistant Rev. Arthur S. Johns, a son of the late Bishop Johns. St. George's church has a flourishing Sunday school, of which Dr. M. C. Hall was superintendent for thirty-eight years, his duties closing at his death. This long service as an officer of St. George's church has been exceeded only by one rector, Rev. Edward C. McGuire, and one vestryman and senior warden, Reuben T. Thom, Esq.*

There have been three buildings erected on the ground where the present house of worship stands. The first one was built in 1732, and was an oblong, frame building. As the inhabitants of the town increased an addition was built on one side, and in 1787 another addition was constructed, rendered necessary by a further increase of the population and larger congregations. By the year 1814 the old building seems to have become so old and dilapidated that a new house was thought necessary, and therefore the old one, which had stood for over three-quarters of a century, was torn down and a new one was erected in its stead. An aged citizen, some forty years ago, describing this first building, said: "It was cruciform in shape, with steeple and bell, capable of holding large congregations. In each projection of the cross there was a small gallery; one contained the organ, the others two pews each. It was a frame building, painted yellow. The pulpit was at one of the angles of the cross, highly elevated, with reading desk, and clerk's desk in front below. A clerk, in his desk, generally responded to the minister in the service, while the people were silent."†

---

* A memorial slab erected in St. George's church gives this remarkable record: "Reuben T. Thom, born 1782, died 1868. He was for 52 years a vestryman, and for 45 years senior warden of St. George's church. A father in Israel he was respected and beloved by three generations."

† From a communication in an old copy of the *Fredericksburg News*, furnished by Dr. Horace B. Hall.

The second house was made of brick, but, like the former one, was not large enough to hold the growing congregation. The work was commenced in 1814, the corner stone having been laid that year, with imposing ceremonies. It was completed in the following year, and was reported to the Council in 1816 by Bishop Moore, who stated to that body that he had consecrated a handsome, brick edifice in Fredericksburg and confirmed sixty persons.

In the short space of thirty-three years it was found that this new, brick house was too small, and so, in 1849, it was removed and the present brick building was erected, which is one of the handsomest church edifices in the State, outside of the large cities. While this house was in the course of erection the church worshipped in the old Methodist church, just back of the park, which was destroyed by fire about 1852. The new church was consecrated and occupied in the Fall of 1849. A few years after its completion it was very much damaged by fire, but it was at once repaired and restored to its former beauty.

TRINITY EPISCOPAL CHURCH.

Trinity Episcopal church, composed of members who withdrew from St. George's church, and organized with Rev. Dr. E. C. Murdaugh as rector, worshipped for some time in the courthouse, and afterwards in the Hanover-street Methodist church, which had not been used for religious services since the Civil war.* With commendable zeal this new congregation went to work, puchased a lot on the south corner of Prince Edward and Hanover streets and erected a handsome house of worship, which in due time was consecrated to the service of the Lord. The change for the purposes for which this ground was used was indeed radical; it was from theatrical to church purposes. It is said that after the Revolutionary war this lot had on it a large frame house, which was at

---

* In the occupancy of this building we have this coincidence: When the members of St. George's church were building their present house, in 1849, they occupied the Methodist church, back of the park, which had been vacated for the new house on Hanover street. More than thirty years afterwards, when Trinity Episcopal church was organized, they occupied the Methodist church on Hanover street, the Methodists having moved to their new house on George street.

History of Fredericksburg, Virginia

first intended for an extensive stable, but was converted into a hall for theatrical purposes. Theatrical companies visiting town would sometimes remain for a week exhibiting every night to large audiences of the elite of the town.

The first rector of Trinity church was Dr. Edward C. Murdaugh, who was succeeded by Rev. J. Green Shackelford, Rev. John S. Gibson, Rev. J. S. Gray, Rev. Edwin Green, Rev. W. L. Reaney and Dr. H. H. Barber, who is now serving the church. Some few years ago the congregation erected a beautiful and commodious rectory near the church building, which adds much to the comfort and convenience of the pastor.

THE PRESBYTERIAN CHURCH.

The Presbyterian church in Fredericksburg was constituted in the early part of the nineteenth century. In the year 1806 Rev. Samuel B. Wilson,* a young minister of that denomination, came to town. At that time there were but two Presbyterians in the place. As St. George's church, which had the only house of worship in town, was without a pastor, Mr. Wilson was invited to preach in that church. This invitation was gladly accepted, and for some time he preached in St. George's church, large congregations attending the services. In a few years Mr. Wilson succeeded in getting together a sufficient number of Presbyterians to organize a church, and a house of worship was erected in 1810 on the lot where the asylum (at present known as Smithsonia) now stands on Amelia street.

This house was occupied until the present brick building on George street was erected, which was in 1833, and was dedicated on the 26th of July of that year. The old church on Amelia street stood back several yards from the sidewalk and was approached through a gate, near which the bell was suspended on a cross-beam erected on two uprights. In the gallery of the church, where the choir was seated, a large brass ball was arranged on the

---

* In the Presbyterian church a marble tablet is erected with this inscription: "Samuel B. Wilson, first pastor; born March 17, 1783; died Aug. 1, 1869. They that be wise shall shine as the firmament, and they that turn many to righteousness as the stars forever and ever."

principle of a metronome, which marked the time for the singers. Some years after the house on George street was built a comfortable manse was erected on the same street, near the church, for the pastor.

In 1880 the "Memorial Chapel" was erected just in rear of the present church building, fronting on Princess Ann street and neatly fitted out by Mr. Seth B. French, a Fredericksburg man, then residing in New York city, as a memorial to his daughter Margaretta, who died just as she was entering into womanhood; upon the death of his wife, a few years afterwards, who was the daughter of Judge John M. Herndon, he placed a very beautiful and costly window in the east end of the building as a memorial of her. This house is built of granite, quarried on the old Landram farm, two miles west of Fredericksburg, and is of a superior quality. The Presbyterian house of worship, like other houses of worship in town, was dismantled during the Wilderness campaign in 1864 and used by the Federal authorities as a hospital. After the war the Presbyterians had no bell and their church had been sacked by Federal soldiers.

In connection with this condition of things an amusing incident occurred, which was related to us by the perpetrator of the joke, and which is too good to be lost. Just after the war, when the different church buildings had been repaired and fitted up for occupation by the respective congregations, Mr. James McGuire, a prominent member of the Presbyterian church, met Mr. Reuben T. Thom, senior warden of St. George's church, on the corner of the street near the Presbyterian church, St. George's being on the diagonal corner. They engaged in conversation, during which Mr. McGuire appeared to be very much troubled because all the other churches had bells to call their congregations together while the Presbyterians had none. Mr. Thom, kind hearted as he was, sympathized with them very much and undertook to console Mr. McGuire. Seeing Mr. Thom was very much concerned, and casting his eyes up towards St. George's bell, just across the street, his countenance brightening up as if a new idea had struck him, queried: "Well, Mr. Thom, won't you let the Presbyterians come to church by St. George's bell?" Mr. Thom, being anxious to accommodate the Presbyterians, but feeling that he was not authorized to decide the matter, replied: "Eh, eh, I have no objection myself, Jimmie, but, but I will lay the matter before the vestry, and will inform you of its action!"

Mr. Wilson served the church as pastor until 1841, when he resigned to accept a professorship in the Union Theological Seminary, then at Hampden-Sidney, in Prince Edward county, Virginia. He was succeeded by Rev. George W. McPhail, D. D., and Rev. A. A. Hodge, D. D. Rev. B. T. Lacy supplied the pulpit for some time prior to the Civil war, but was never the regular pastor of the church. The church has had the following pastors since the war: Rev. Thomas W. Gilmer,* Rev. James P. Smith, D. D., Rev. A. P. Saunders, D. D., Rev. Benjamin W. Mebane, D. D., Rev. John W. Rosebro, D. D., and Rev. J. H. Henderlite, who is now serving the church. Governor John L. Marye was a ruling elder of this church for more than forty-seven years, giving faithful and efficient service.

THE BAPTIST CHURCH.

The Baptists came into notice as early as the year 1768,. when John Waller, Lewis Craig and James Chiles, three zealous Baptist ministers, were seized by the sheriff of Spotsylvania county, carried before three magistrates in the yard of the church building, on the charge of "preaching the gospel contrary to law." They were ordered to jail in Fredericksburg, and, while in jail, preached through the iron gratings of the windows and door to large crowds, who assembled to see and hear them.† It is said as they marched through the streets of the town to jail, in the custody of the officers of the law, followed by a large, noisy crowd jeering at them, they sang that old hymn by Watts, to the tune of Wyndham:

> "Broad is the road that leads to death.
> And thousands walk together there;
> But wisdom shows a narrow way,
> With here and there a traveller."

---

* On a memorial tablet erected in the church is this inscription: "Thomas Walker Gilmer, pastor, born July 25, 1834, died April 5, 1869. I know that my Redeemer liveth."

† Historical sketch of Fredericksburg, 1883, by Robert B. Berrey.

And as the sweet, solemn notes fell upon the ears of the curious crowd the jeering ceased, and before the hymn was concluded many persons were melted to tears.

The Baptist church of Fredericksburg was organized by Rev. Andrew Broaddus, Sr., the great orator of King and Queen county and later of Caroline county, in the year 1804, who for several years was its pastor. In 1810 Rev. Robert Baylor Semple, in preparing his "History of Virginia Baptists," says of the Fredericksburg church: "They have no resident pastor, but are supplied by Mr. A. Broaddus, who attends them monthly. If there is any objection to Mr. Broaddus's ministry in this city it is that he is too popular with the irreligious. It may be said of him as was said of Ezekiel: 'Lo! thou art unto them as a very lovely song of one that hath a pleasant voice, and can play well on an instrument; for they hear thy words, but they do them not.' This remark by no means applies to the church, for, although they hear with much pleasure, they practise with more. It is a young and rising church."

The first house of worship erected in town by the Baptists was a small, frame structure built on the ground now occupied by the Richmond, Fredericksburg and Potomac Railroad Company as a depot, but before many years had passed the congregation had so increased in size the small building was found to be inadequate and a large, brick building was erected on Water street, where Shiloh, church, old site, now stands, and for thirty years or more the church worshipped in that building.

Under the preaching of able and faithful pastors the membership rapidly increased and the congregations became larger, and by the middle of the century the house on Water street was found to be too small to accommodate the increasing attendance. In the year 1854 the present large and commodious brick building was erected on Princess Ann street, mainly through the efforts of Rev. Wm. F. Broaddus,* the pastor, J. B. Benwick, Jr., architect, notwithstand-

---

* A memorial slab in the church is thus inscribed: "In memory of Rev. Wm. F. Broaddus, D. D., born April 30, 1801, died Sept. 8, 1876. The beloved and faithful pastor of this church 1853 to 1862, through whose labors and liberality this house was built. 'He was a good man and full of the Holy Ghost and faith, and much people was added to the Lord.'"

ing on a tablet in the front of the church that work is credited to another.

The new house, with a large addition to it about twelve years ago, has proved ample for the church and congregation to the present. Rev. Andrew Broaddus, the first pastor, was succeeded by the following ministers: Rev. Robert B. Semple, Rev. Carter Braxton, Rev. Mr. James, Rev. John Teasdale, Rev. John M. Waddey, Rev. George F. Adams, Rev. S. C. Smith, Rev. Wm. F. Broaddus, D. D., Rev. Wm. H. Williams, Rev. Thomas S. Dunaway, D. D., Rev. Jacob S. Dill, D. D., and Rev. R. Aubrey Williams, who is now serving the church. Dr. Dunaway's pastorate covered a period of thirty-two years, during which he greatly endeared himself to the church and people of the town, and was eminently successful in winning souls and building up the church. The Baptist church has a large and flourishing Sunday school connected with it that has had but four superintendents for sixty-three years. George W. Garnett* was superintendent for thirty and Prof. A. B. Bowering served nearly twenty-three years, S. J. Quinn ten, and B. P. Willis, having just been elected, has entered upon the work.

THE METHODIST CHURCH.

The Methodists, who, for a number of years, were designated as a society, held services in Fredericksburg as early as 1786. For a number of years they held meetings from house to house, and were very active workers. It is not known when the first church or society was formed, or by whom it was organized, but it is known that persons united with that denomination before the dawn of the nineteenth century, and that Father Kobler commenced his ministry here as a local preacher in the year 1789, and continued his labors as such for over half a century. Therefore it may be concluded that the first organization of that denomination in Fredericksburg held its meetings in private houses for more than thirty years.

---

* In the basement of the church is a memorial tablet inscribed as follows: "In memory of Deacon George W. Garnett, the faithful, efficient and beloved Superintendent of the Fredericksburg Baptist Sunday School for thirty consecutive years, who died July 9, 1876, aged 54 years. 'He was a faithful man, and feared God above many.' Erected by the school."

The first house of worship built by the Methodists in town, that we have any record or tradition of, was erected in 1822, on the lot in rear of Hurkamp park, fronting on George street, and occupied by Colonel E. D. Cole as a stable and lumber yard. It was then outside of the city limits and was known as Liberty Town. It was a small frame building and was occupied until 1841, when the old church on Hanover street was finished. The services were then held in the new house and the old frame church building was turned over to the colored Methodists, who occupied it for some time. It was destroyed by fire about 1852.

Some years after occupying the church building on Hanover street, the question of slavery, which had been so vigorously discussed by the denomination North and South, was the theme of discussion in the church at Fredericksburg. The feeling became strong between the parties and increased in intensity until it resulted in a split in the church. One division was known as the Northern Methodist, as its members opposed slavery, while the other division was known as the Southern Methodist, its members favoring slavery. When the difference became so marked and the feeling so bitter, that the parties could not longer worship together, the Southern Methodists withdrew, and held services in the second story of the town hall for some time. The Northern wing remained in the Hanover street house until the beginning of the Civil war.

In the year 1852 the southern division of the church erected a handsome brick building on the south corner of George and Charles streets, where Mr. P. V. D. Conway's residence now stands, in which they worshipped until the war came on, when the sessions of the church were almost suspended. Since the Civil war the two churches united and occupied the George-street church until about the year 1879, when the old building on Hanover street was torn down and a house of modern architecture erected in its place. Since that time the new church has been occupied and the George-street building was sold. About fifteen years ago an addition was built in rear of the church for the accommodation of the Sunday school. The church also has a parsonage on the same street, which was donated to it by Rev. John Kobler.

"Kenmore," Mansion of Col. Fielding Lewis, who married Betty Washington; now residence of Councilman Clarance R. Howard.
(See page 155)

"Union House," where Gen. Lafayette was entertained in 1824 by his friend, Mr. Ross.
(See page 144)

In 1843 Rev. John Kobler, widely known as Father Kobler, a citizen of the town, a venerable local preacher of the Methodist church, distinguished for his piety and ability and greatly beloved by all who knew him, died and was buried beneath the pulpit of the Hanover-street church. Prior to his death he wrote his "farewell to the world," which he requested should be read as a part of his funeral service, which was done. The farewell is almost as long as a sermon and is "the very perfume of piety and Christian assurance." 1st. He bids farewell to the ministry of the gospel and all the ordinances of the church of God. 2nd. He bids farewell to the church in her militant state. 3rd. He bids farewell to the communion of saints. 4th. He bids farewell to prayer. 5th. He bids a final and hearty adieu to temptation and to every species of the Christian warfare. 6th and lastly. He bids farewell to his Bible. This history of him is given on the first page of the pamphlet: "John Kobler was born 29th of August, 1768; joined the Methodist Episcopal church 6th of December, 1786; was converted 24th of December, 1787; commenced his itinerating ministry 3rd of October, 1789; and died with glory on his lips, July 26th, 1843."

Some ten or twelve years after the death of Father Kobler his devoted and saintly wife followed him to the glory land and she was interred by the side of her husband. When the old building was torn down and the new one erected the sacred dust of these two sleeping saints was left undisturbed, and so under the pulpit of the new church their mortal remains still repose. The present pastor of the church is Rev. W. L. Dolly, a faithful and zealous servant of the Lord.

THE CHRISTIAN CHURCH.

About the year 1832 the religious movement, in which Alexander Campbell was the leader, began in Fredericksburg. A number of citizens, adopting the views held by Mr. Campbell, were organized into a Christian or Disciples church. With commendable energy and zeal they went to work, purchased a lot and erected quite a comfortable church building on Main street, between Amelia and Lewis streets. The church prospered until the breaking out of the Civil war, when, like those of the other churches, its members were scattered and church services were suspended.

Several efforts have been made since the war to reorganize the church, but they were unsuccessful until 1897, when Rev. Mr. Rutledge preached here for some days, got the members together and the church was organized. The old building has been remodelled and modernized and is now occupied by the congregation. After the church was reorganized Rev. Cephas Shelburne was called as pastor, and by his energetic labors the membership was very much increased. Mr. Shelburne was succeeded by Rev. F. S. Forrer and he by Rev. I. L. Chestnutt. The church now has no pastor.

ST. MARY'S CATHOLIC CHURCH.

The Roman Catholics had no church organization in town until the year 1859. In 1856 Bishop McGill visited Fredericksburg and preached a sermon of great ability and spiritual power, and under his influence a nucleus was formed, out of which the church was organized three years afterwards. The newly organized church went earnestly to work at once to build a house of worship, and from amounts subscribed by the members and friends in town, and the assistance they received from abroad, a neat and comfortable brick building was erected on Princess Ann street, between Charlotte and Hanover. A frame parsonage was purchased some years afterwards just below the church building, which was destroyed by fire about the year 1875, after which the present brick parsonage was erected.

The church at different periods has been visited by Bishop Gibbons, now Cardinal, and Bishop Keene, by whom it was greatly strengthened. It has had for pastors since its organization Rev. Fathers Hagan, Donnelson, O'Farrell, Sears, Brady, Becker, Tiernan, Donahoe, Wilson, Kennefick, Demunych and Coleman. Rev. Father Perrig is pastor at this time.

THE COLORED BAPTIST CHURCHES.

In 1854, when the white Baptists occupied their new house of worship on Princess Ann street, they turned over to the colored Baptists their old house on Water street. Prior to that the white and colored members worshipped together in the same building. Separated to themselves, but under the care of the white Baptist church, the colored people had Rev. George Rowe to preach for them, which he continued to do, with success, until the Civil war came on.

After the war closed the colored people, being free to act for themselves, formed separate churches and selected pastors of their own color. The colored Baptists of the town formed a church, under the name of Shiloh, and called Rev. George L. Dixon to the pastorate. His pastoral care of the church continued for several years, when he was succeeded by Rev. L. G. Walden and he by Rev. Willis M. Robinson.

In 1887 the church building collapsed and a division of sentiment arose among the members as to where they should rebuild, which resulted in a division of the church and congregation and the erection of another church building. A majority of the members of the church wanted to rebuild on the old site, but a large minority preferred to sell the old site and build on Princess Ann street, near the railroad depot. The contention was sharp, the feeling was intense, satisfactory terms of separation could not be agreed upon, and finally the controversy was carried into the circuit court.

Judge Wm. S. Barton, who was judge of the circuit court, advised a compromise, which was accepted by the parties, and a division of the church and property was the result. But then another perplexing question arose that promised to give trouble. Both parties strenuously contended for the old name, Shiloh, and no other name it appeared would satisfy either division. The wishes of both parties, however, were happily met when some one suggested that the Water-street party should be known as Shiloh Old Site and the Princess Ann party as Shiloh New Site. This proposition was agreed to, the separation took place peaceably and both parties proceeded to build substantial and commodious brick houses, which are a credit to the colored people of the town.

Rev. Willis Robinson, who was pastor of the old church Shiloh, went with Shiloh New Site and became its pastor. Shiloh Old Site extended a call to Rev. James E. Brown to become its pastor, which he accepted, and served the church for several years. For some time after the old church building became unsafe for occupancy the colored people worshipped in the courthouse.

In the year 1879 several members withdrew from old Shiloh church and organized under the name of the Second Baptist church. They erected a small, but neat, frame church building on Winchester street, near Amelia, and asked for the ordination of Albert Ray, whom they had selected as pastor. A few months later he was duly ordained, entered upon the pastorate of the church and continued as such until disabled by rheumatism in 1902.

Rev. Albert Ray's church was sold a few years ago and went into possession of a new religious sect. The pastor is Rev. Roland Burgess and the sect is known as "The Church of God and the Saints of the Lord Jesus Christ." The church has made but little progress up to this time.

In 1903 Shiloh New Site had a split on the question of pastor, when a large number of the membership withdrew and erected a frame building on Wolfe street, called Rev. Willis M. Robinson as their pastor, which organization is known as Robinson's church.

At present Shiloh Old Site has for its pastor Rev. John A. Brown and Shiloh New Site has Rev. W. L. Ransom. Both churches are in a thriving condition, with large Sunday schools, and both pastors are educated and fully qualified to lead and instruct their race.

CHAPTER XV

Charitable and Benevolent Societies—The Mary Washington Hospital—Newspapers and Periodicals—Political Excitement—Strong Resolutions Condemning the Administration of John Adams—An Address Approving the President's Foreign Policy—The Names of Those who Signed the Address, &c.

Next in importance to the churches in a community, dedicated to the service of God, come the charitable and benevolent societies and institutions. The former show the state of religion among the people, or their relations to their Maker, while the latter is an evidence of that fraternal feeling existing from one to another which binds all the members in one common cause for humanity. And as Fredericksburg is not wanting in her church privileges and accommodations, so she is not deficient in the number of her charitable and benevolent societies. The oldest of these societies is the Masonic institution.

Fredericksburg Lodge, No. 4, Ancient, Free and Accepted Masons, was organized on the first day of September, 1752. Under what authority it was organized is not positively known, and therefore three authorities are suggested. The first source of authority claimed is that of Thomas Oxnard, Grand Master of St. John's Lodge, of Massachusetts and "Provincial Grand Master of all of North America." A second claim is made that the Masons in the community organized themselves into a lodge and continued as a self-constituted body until a charter was obtained from Scotland. This could hardly have been true. The third claim is, and it is believed by the best authorities to be the original source of authority, that a dispensation was obtained from the Grand Lodge of Scotland, and this was the authority by which the lodge was held until it was regularly chartered by said Grand Lodge. The lodge held its meetings under the authority of this dispensation for six years, and made Masons, among others, of George Washington, George Weedon, Hugh Mercer, Wm. Woodford, Thomas

Posey, Gustavus B. Wallace, all of whom became general officers and did distinguished service in the Revolutionary war.

In the year 1758 Daniel Campbell, for several years master of the lodge, visited Scotland, and, at the request of the lodge, applied for and obtained a charter for the lodge from the Grand Lodge of Scotland, which was dated July 21, 1758, and designated the organization "The Lodge at Fredericks-Burg," Virginia. Possessed with this charter the lodge concluded it had the authority to charter other lodges, and exercised that authority in chartering one at Falmouth, Va., and one at Gloucester Courthouse, Va. The latter soon obtained a charter from England and the former from the Grand Lodge of Virginia. In 1775 the Fredericksburg Lodge united with four other lodges in the State and organized the Grand Lodge of Virginia, and received a charter from that Grand Body, dated January 30, 1787, under the name and title of Fredericksburg Lodge, No. 4. The lodge is holding its authority now under the Virginia Grand Lodge charter, but still has in its possession the old Scotch charter, which is well preserved. The original dispensation has disappeared and was probably lost more than a century ago.

In the years 1798 and 1799 the town was the seat of frequent and heated political discussions, and the strong, not to say bitter, feeling was shared in by the entire population of the town. It was during this excitement, and because of the bad feeling it engendered, a number of members of No. 4 Lodge withdrew their membership and organized Fredericksburg American Lodge, for which a dispensation was granted in 1799 by Gov. Robert Brooke, the Grand Master of Masons in Virginia. In the following year the lodge was chartered and given the number 63. It continued to flourish until the breaking out of the Civil war, when it suspended its meetings and finally became extinct.

In the bombardment and subsequent sacking of Fredericksburg on the 11th, 12th, 13th, 14th and 15th of December, 1862, by straggling Federal soldiers, all of the records of the Masonic Lodge were destroyed or carried away except those from 1752 to 1771, which were taken to Danville, Va., and preserved by Wm. Ware, Esq., a member of the lodge.

When No. 4 Lodge first organized its meetings were held in the market house, or town hall, then on Main street near Market alley, but in 1756 the time for holding the meetings was changed to "the day before Spotsylvania county court," which was then held at Germanna, on the Rapidan river, and the place of meeting was fixed at Charles Julien's, who lived between Fredericksburg and Germanna. The lodge continued there for about six years, when it was moved back to the market house to "stay for all time to come," and continued there from 1762 to 1813, when the building was torn down preparatory to the erection of the present town hall and market house.

When it was decided to remove the old market house the meetings of the lodge were moved to the "Rising Sun Tavern," the old frame building still standing on Main street between Fauquier and Hawke streets. In the year 1815 the present Masonic hall was completed, which stands on the corner of Princess Ann and Hanover streets. The Fredericksburg Masonic Lodge has, at various periods, embraced in its membership eminent men, including soldiers, Statesmen, professional men and private citizens. Among the first two classes mentioned—soldiers and Statesmen—was the father of his country, George Washington, who, in this historic lodge, received the first degree in Masonry on November 4, 1752, the second degree on March 3, 1753, and the third degree on August 4, 1753, and continued his membership in the lodge to the day of his death. The Bible used in these interesting ceremonies is now in possession of the lodge in a fine state of preservation. It was printed by John Field, at Cambridge, in the year 1668. It is believed that John Paul Jones, the father of our infant navy, was also a member of this lodge.

By an order of the lodge, and by funds to the amount of five thousand dollars, raised by its exertions, a very beautiful and faithful statue of Washington, in Masonic regalia, was wrought out of white marble by the great Virginia artist, Hiram Powers, while he was in Rome, Italy. It was safely transported to Fredericksburg, but before it could be erected the war came on. For safe keeping it was sent to Richmond, and there perished in the terrible conflagration of April 3, 1865. Fredericksburg Lodge, No. 4, has furnished six grand masters to the Grand Lodge of Virginia, as follows: Judge James Mercer, in 1784; Governor Robert Brooke, in 1785; Major Benjamin Day, from 1797 to 1800; Hon. Oscar M. Crutchfield, in 1841; Judge Beverly R. Wellford, Jr., in 1877, and Capt. S. J. Quinn, in 1907. Fredericksburg American Lodge, No. 63, furnished Hon. John S. Caldwell, in 1856.

In 1873 Fredericksburg Royal Arch Chapter, No. 23, was organized. This chapter took the place of Fitzwilson Chapter, that flourished in town some years before the Civil war, although it did not take the old name or number.

In the year 1875 Fredericksburg Commandery, No. 1, of Knights Templar, was instituted, and has continued to flourish to the present. Some years ago the various bodies of the Scottish Rite branch of Masonry to the thirty-second degree, were organized in town of the Cerneau division, but as the question of legitimacy was raised as to that rite these organizations were abandoned. The three Masonic bodies, however, that are now in operation are in a flourishing condition and can confer all the degrees in ancient York Masonry.

On the 22nd of December, 1753, a "Royal Arch Lodge" was held in connection with the Fredericksburg Lodge, Simon Fraser, acting Grand Master. On that occasion the Royal Arch degree was conferred on Daniel Campbell, Robert Halkerson and Alexander Wodrow. The proceedings of this meeting were recorded in the record book of the lodge and are preserved to this day; and, strange as it may appear, the fact is well established and admitted by the Masonic historians of England that this is the oldest record, by nine years, of conferring this degree that has yet been discovered in any country. The next oldest record is found in York, England, which was made in 1762.

ODD FELLOWS LODGE.

The first lodge of Odd Fellows organized in Fredericksburg was in the year 1839, and was known as Rappahannock Lodge, No. 14. It continued a working lodge only about three years. The last report it made to the Grand Lodge showed a membership of thirty-nine. Its suspension seems to have been brought about by some unruly, if not unworthy, members who had brought strife and discord into the lodge. In the year 1847, on the petition of five members of the old lodge—Wm. Baily, Wm. Smith, George Waite, Wm. T. Lowery and A. B. Adams—a charter was granted for instituting Myrtle Lodge, No. 50, and which has continued in active operation to the present. It has a large membership, composed of our best citizens. The charter of this lodge was signed by Major J. Harrison Kelly, who then lived in Charlestown, now West Virginia, and who was Grand Master of the State. In after years he became a citizen of Fredericksburg and ended his days in this town.

The meetings of the lodge were at first held at private houses, and at one time in Haydon's Hall, on Charlotte street, in rear of Wheeler's livery stable. After the Civil war the meetings were held in the room immediately under the Masonic lodge-room, and continued there until about 1892, when the Odd Fellows, in connection with the Knights of Pythias, erected the splendid hall on Main street, where they held their meetings for some years, but, believing it to be to their interest to dispose of their stock in the new hall, they did so and moved the lodge to the third story of the Bradford Building.

In 1903 a second Odd Fellows Lodge was organized under a charter from the Grand Lodge, known as Acorn Lodge, No. 261. Although young, this lodge has grown with great rapidity and has a large membership. It was organized in the Masonic lodge-room, and afterward rented the hall under the said Masonic lodge, where it now holds its meetings. Among the membership of these Odd Fellows lodges may be found many of the most substantial and progressive citizens of the town.

THE BENEVOLENT ORDER OF ELKS.

The Order of Elks now stands as the youngest of the three prominent secret orders on this continent, and since it came into existence, in 1868, has shown one of the most phenomenal growths that has ever been recorded for a similar benevolent order. It has for its teaching Charity, Justice, Brotherly Love and Fidelity, and for its motto "The faults of our brothers we write in the sand, and their virtues upon the tablets of love and memory." Five years ago a few progressive spirits of Fredericksburg, catching the inspiration the order of Elks taught, met and organized a lodge of Elks. A lodge was organized on the 23rd of June, 1903, under the name Fredericksburg Lodge, No. 875, Mr. O. L. Harris being the first presiding officer. The lodge now has ninety members, C. Ernest Layton being the present exalted ruler.

There are also in Fredericksburg a number of other benevolent and charitable fraternities, whose origin is of a more recent date than the Masons, Odd Fellows and Elks, under the various names of Knights of Pythias, Knights of Honor, Royal Arcanum, Senior and Junior Orders of American Mechanics, Laboring Men's Union, Heptasophs, Maccabees, Sons of Sobriety—a temperance order which originated in Fredericksburg and was first organized as a moderate drinking society—Red Men, Knights of the Golden Horseshoe, Good Samaritans and others, all of which are in a flourishing condition and are doing a good work in dispensing charity, in providing cheap life insurance and endeavoring to elevate their fellowmen.

THE MARY WASHINGTON HOSPITAL.*

The need of a hospital in Fredericksburg had long been felt, and in January, 1897, a band of ladies, led by Mrs. W. Seymour White, invited the physicians and ministers of the city to meet with them and consider the feasibility of undertaking such a work. The medical fraternity pronounced it a necessity and the ministers heartily concurred.

The late Hon. W. Seymour White, at that time Mayor of the city, was deeply interested in the scheme from the beginning and drew up a charter, constitution and by-laws. The formal organization was effected in February, 1897, at a large, general meeting held in the courthouse. Mrs. W. S. White was elected president; Miss Rebecca Smith, vice-president; Miss Bertha Strasburger, secretary; Mrs. C. W. Edrington, treasurer.

---

* Mrs. V. M. F. prepared this article.

Entrance to the Confederate Cemetery at Fredericksburg.
(See page 185)

Lodge Room of Fredericksburg Lodge, No. 4, A. F. & A. M.; the Lodge that made Washington a Mason.
(See page 217)

Mrs. White served as president for three terms, when she resigned and her place was filled by Mrs. Walter C. Stearns. The present officers are Mrs. Judge John E. Mason, president; Miss Virginia Knox, vice-president; Mrs. Maurice Hirsh, treasurer, and Mrs. D. C. Bowman, secretary. There is a board of lady managers and an advisory board of seven gentlemen, of whom the Mayor of the city is always one. The membership fee is one dollar per year and there is a large number of names on the roll.

Immediately after the organization of the institution the city was thoroughly canvassed and both money and furnishings were contributed generally by our people, besides by a number of persons living at a distance. As soon as the amount justified the action, a large and suitable building lot, situated on the corner of Fauquier and Sophia streets, was purchased. This lot has a beautiful river view and is directly opposite Chatham, the old historic place, famous both in colonial and recent history.

The one inflexible rule, laid down from the beginning of the work, was that there should be no debt incurred, and the work of raising the necessary funds was a tedious undertaking. Every lady appealed to her friends, and the amount thus collected, together with that realized through holding bazaars, ice cream festivals, entertainments and lectures, was carefully deposited until the sum of fourteen hundred dollars was accumulated, which the ladies thought sufficient to erect a small building.

The plan was donated by Mr. George Washington Smith and proved acceptable. The corner-stone was laid April 14, 1899, this day being chosen to commemorate George Washington's latest visit to Fredericksburg and his dying mother. The corner-stone itself is a portion of the old Mary Washington monument, begun in 1833, and never completed, and was donated by Mr. John H. Myer. It was laid with imposing Masonic ceremonies by Fredericksburg Lodge, No. 4, A. F. and A. M., in which George Washington was made a Mason, District Deputy Grand Master James P. Corbin presiding, Rev. F. P. Ramsey, D. D., of Fredericksburg College, making an impressive address on the occasion.

The hospital was completed the summer following, and all the money in the treasury was expended. The house faces the east and is a modest structure, with a porch in front and an extension on the west end. Two rooms open upon the entrance hall, one of which is the operating room, the other the especial room for a single patient. Back of this is a hall, running north and south, beyond which is the kitchen, matron's room, bath-room and store rooms; cellar beneath for wood and such articles as can be kept there. In the extensions are respectively the two large, well-lighted and ventilated rooms for the men's and women's wards.

The capacity of the hospital is small, but there is plenty of room for any additions which the future may warrant being made. With the faith that characterized the movement from the beginning, the ladies met on September 25, 1899, elected a matron, Miss Virginia Aldridge, and appointed Wednesday, October 4th, "Donation Day." Their confidence was rewarded and donations poured in from every one, rich and poor. Among so many it would be invidious to mention names, but Mr. Spencer, of Snowden, a new comer to Fredericksburg, liberally furnished the single room with every appliance for comfort in illness, and the ladies gratefully named it, for him, the Spencer room. From the druggists came a generous donation of accessories, and everything—chairs and china, beds and other belongings—came in abundantly.

On Sunday, October 8th, the building was formally dedicated, Rev. W. D. Smith, rector of St. George's church, presiding, all the ministers having been invited to participate in the ceremonies, which were simple, but appropriate. The first patient was received in December, and since that time there has been continued service in the hospital. There is no endowment, and it is hoped that, seeing the work, some humanely-disposed individual may be moved to undertake this noble charity.

By heroic efforts there have been no debts incurred, the citizens having so far responded in every case of need; yet there is much lacking, both in furniture and appliances. Donations of every kind are urgently desired. The physicians are most liberal in their services and attentions and their work is to their great honor, for, of the several diffcult cases thus far operated upon each has been successful, and the recipient has returned home sounding the praises of the Mary Washington Hospital and its medical service. May the good work grow and prosper. Since this article was written the building has been greatly enlarged and improved, and the hospital is regarded as a permanent institution with a noble mission.

NEWSPAPERS AND PERIODICALS.

The first newspaper established in Fredericksburg was the semi-weekly "Virginia Herald and Falmouth Advertiser," in 1786, by Timothy Green. It was soon found that the name was too long and was no advantage to the paper, and in a few months the Falmouth Advertiser part of the name was dropped and the paper was continued as the Virginia Herald. Some years after its establishment Mr. Green associated with him in the conduct of the paper a Mr. Lacy and Mr. James D. Harrow, and the firm name was Green, Lacy & Harrow. This firm was succeeded by Wm. F. Gray, and he by James D. Harrow, a practical printer, who conducted the paper for many years, with Jesse White, afterwards known as "the old practical printer," as foreman.

Mr. Harrow died in 1851, and the office, fixtures and good will were purchased by Major J. Harrison Kelly, who conducted the Virginia Herald successfully as a semi-weekly until the year 1875, when failing health compelled him to discontinue its publication and it has never been resumed.

A bound volume of this paper, running through the years 1796, 1797 and 1798, is now owned by this writer, who prizes it very highly. Its columns have furnished accounts of incidents, dates and gatherings of the people in public meetings, noted in this historical sketch of the town.

In the year 1795 another paper was started in Fredericksburg, known as the "Genius of Liberty and Fredericksburg and Falmouth Advertiser." This name was even larger, longer and less euphonious than the first name of its competitor, the Virginia Herald, and, like its competitor, soon dropped most of it. This paper came into existence at a time when party spirit ran high and the political blood was at fever heat. It vigorously espoused the cause of what was then known as the "Strict Constructionists" of the Federal Constitution, while the "Virginia Herald" as vigorously supported the "Loose Constructionists."

The Genius of Liberty was conducted by Robert Mercer and George Carter as a weekly paper until 1798, when it was changed to a semi-weekly, at "twenty shillings per annum, ten shillings to be paid on subscribing and the remainder at the end of the year." In 1800 the paper was purchased by James Walker, who changed its name to "The Courier." Mr. Walker was both editor and proprietor, and under his management it was enlarged to "nearly double the size of the Virginia Herald." We have not been able to learn at what period its publication ceased.

A volume of this publication, from November, 1800, to November, 1801, substantially bound, is now in possession of Mrs. James L. Green, of this place. It is valuable and interesting because of its hoary age and because of the fact it was published in Fredericksburg.

"The Fredericksburg News," a semi-weekly paper, was published by Robert Baylor Semple for several years. At his death, in 1853, the paper was purchased by A. Alexander Little, who conducted it, except during the War Between the States, to the time of his death in 1877. When its publication was resumed after the war, when old things had passed away and many things had become new, it bore the name of "The Fredericksburg New Era," but neither the times nor the name suited the editor, so he changed the name back to the News and made the best he could of the times in which he lived.

After Mr. Little's death the publication of the News was continued for a few years by his sister, Miss Bella Little, who assisted him very much in the editorial management of the paper during his ownership of it, but finding it unremunerative its publication was finally suspended.

Several other publications of a less permanent nature have been started and conducted in Fredericksburg, but they were short lived and but little is known of their history, therefore they can be only mentioned as having existed.

"The Political Arena" was commenced in the year 1830 by Wm.

M. Blackford and lived for about fifteen years. In 1845 Mr. Blackford moved to Lynchburg and the publication of the paper was discontinued.

In 1848 Rev. James W. Hunnicutt established the "Christian Banner," which continued to exist until 1862, when Mr. Hunnicutt, being a Union man and opposed to the Civil war, went North, and it has been stated that the Banner office was destroyed by Southern soldiers. This statement, however, is thought not to be true.

"The Virginia Baptist" made its appearance in Fredericksburg about the year 1857. It was edited and conducted by Rev. W. R. Powell, Rev. John C. Willis and Rev. Joseph A. Billingsly as a temperance advocate. Its publication was suspended in 1860 and never resumed.

"The Democratic Recorder," established in 1842, was owned by James M. Campbell, but in 1850 he removed to Manchester, N. H., and the office was purchased and the publication of the Recorder was continued by Robert B. Alexander, S. Greenhow Daniel and James B. Sener, in the order named. Its publication was suspended during the Civil war, but upon the return of peace in 1865 it was resumed by James B. Sener, the name being changed to "The Fredericksburg Ledger." In 1872 Judge Sener was elected to Congress and the publication of the Ledger ceased.

The office and fixtures were sold by Judge Sener in 1873, and for twelve or fifteen years it changed hands often and several publications were started, only to cease after a struggle of a year or two. After the publication of the Ledger was discontinued the first paper sent out from the office was the "Independent," by Berry & Tierney. One year marked the life of the Independent and then came the "Bulletin," by Quinn & Tierney; "The True Standard," by a joint stock company, and "The Recorder," by the Mander Brothers. None of these publications lived more than two or three years at most.

In May, 1887, the office was purchased by Col. John W. Woltz and Wm. E. Bradley, who established the "Free Lance," which they conducted until the death of Col. Woltz in 1893, when it was soon purchased by a joint stock company and its publication continued to the present. Under its first management the "Free Lance" was issued as a semi-weekly, but as its circulation increased it was changed to a tri-weekly, and was the first and only tri-weekly publication the town ever had. Another innovation the "Free Lance" made in the newspaper history of Fredericksburg was the introduction of a power press. Prior to this all the newspapers were printed on Hoe hand presses, but the "Free Lance," under Woltz & Bradley, boasted of a power press of a capacity of twelve hundred papers an hour, which was soon exchanged for one of sixteen hundred an hour. A third innovation made by the "Free Lance" was the purchase and use of a folding machine. This was a new machine in town and was observed by those who had never before seen one with much curiosity. It can fold papers as fast as they are printed, and is quite an improvement on the old way of hand folding.

The publication of the "Virginia Star" was commenced in the year 1869 by Rufus B. Merchant as a semi-weekly, and was so conducted until 1895. During that year Mr. Merchant added another edition and sent out the "Daily Evening Star." This was something "new under the sun" in Fredericksburg, and its advent and probable success were freely discussed by the public and various opinions were expressed. The prevailing opinion, however, seemed to be that its publication was a mistake on the part of the proprietor and the scheme would end in financial loss. Others thought it would flourish for a short time and receive support because it was a home enterprise, but that it would eventually be crowded out by the big dailies of neighboring cities and would disappear. But such was not the case. It is yet making its daily evening visits, improves as the days go by, and has evidently come to stay.

In 1896 the Star office, with its entire outfit, was purchased by W. Seymour White and Alvin T. Embrey, who continued to publish both editions of the paper, and upon the death of Mr. White, in the early part of the year 1898, his interest was purchased by Mr. Embrey, who became the sole editor and proprietor of the Star. In 1900 Judge Embrey sold out to a joint stock company, and under its management both editions of the paper made their regular visits to the homes of subscribers. This paper has been purchased by the Free Lance Company, which sends out both the Free Lance and Daily Star.

On the 2nd day of January, 1837, the first issue of the "Masonic Olive Branch and Literary Portfolio" was published by James D. McCabe and John M. Ball. It was a semi-monthly publication, at two dollars per annum in advance, and was devoted principally to Masonry and Odd Fellowship. A bound volume of this publication is now in possession of Fredericksburg Masonic Lodge, and, from its typographical appearance, one would suppose it to have been printed by Jesse White, the practical printer, on his old Ramage hand press. By Mr. Ball's retirement a few months after the appearance of the paper, Mr. McCabe became the sole editor and proprietor. We have no information as to how long the Portfolio was published.

In 1868 "The Little Gleaner," a thirty-two page periodical, was published by Miss L. Fauntleroy. It was a monthly publication, devoted to general subjects, and intended especially to interest and instruct the young folks. After two years' labor, toil and sacrifice, not meeting with the success she had hoped for, the proprietress discontinued its publication.

In the year 1900 a number of the progressive business men of the town, feeling that Fredericksburg was not moving along in public improvements as rapidly as it should, and that the City Council was too slow in passing the necessary measures for such improvements, organized a joint stock company and commenced the publication of "The Fredericksburg Journal." The Journal, different from the other papers of the town, was at first a weekly issue, its subscription price being twenty-five cents per annum. It has informed the public in strong language that it has come to stay and progress is its watch word. In a short time it was sold to Mr. R. L. Biscoe, when he in turn sold it to the Fredericksburg Journal Company, who put more life and vim into it, and now its customers are served with both a semi-weekly and daily, which gives the general news from the surrounding country and stand for improvement of the town, honesty in city affairs, and justice to all with special favors to none.

POLITICAL DIVISIONS.

Elsewhere we have referred to party divisions in Fredericksburg about the close of the eighteenth century. This division showed itself, prior to the Revolutionary war, because many of the people of the town were strongly opposed to separation from the mother country, deeming the grievances complained of insufficient for such a radical movement. But even the war and its result did not allay the bitter feeling. It was still kept up after peace was declared on all public questions, and became more intense, even to boiling over at times. This ebullition arose with the question of the adoption or rejection of the Constitution of the United States, and after its adoption it continued with increasing intensity over the construction of that instrument and the authority it conferred upon the President. New fuel was added to the flame when Congress passed the act known as the Alien and Sedition law, which conferred extraordinary power on the President in times of peace.

These questions were the theme of spirited, and even angry, discussions at all gatherings of the people on court greens, market places and elsewhere, but the climax of feeling was reached when the foreign policy of President John Adams was developed, especially with reference to our attitude towards France. Mr. Monroe, a citizen of this town, who for some time had been our foreign minister to France, had been recalled by Mr. Adams and another more in accord with the administration was sent in his stead, and it appeared that war with our former friend and ally could not be averted.

Many of the leading citizens of the town endorsed the policy of the President, while a decided majority strongly opposed it. The bitter feeling continued to increase. Not only was Fredericksburg in a state of ebullition, but such was the case with the people throughout the entire country. Fredericksburg was the first to speak her views publicly, which has always been characteristic of her people when questions affecting the public good were to be considered.

A public meeting of the people was called at the courthouse by the friends of the administration to consider and adopt an address to the President, which was then the prevailing mode of communicating popular approval of the conduct of high officials. The meeting was extensively advertised and efforts were made to have it largely attended. This brought on a lively contest. The anti-administrationists of the town determined to try their strength with their opponents by attending the meeting, vote down their address and adopt resolutions setting forth their views and condemning the policy of the administration. To accomplish this the town was thoroughly canvassed by them, which had already been done by the other party, and the courthouse was filled to its utmost capacity.

The meeting was held on the 14th day of May, 1798, and the "Virginia Herald," the presidential organ of the town, gave the proceedings in full, which will show the temper of the people and their defiant condemnation of the foreign policy of President Adams. The Herald said:

"On Monday the citizens of this corporation met, agreeably to notification published in the public papers, to express their sentiments on the present important and critical situation of this country. The meeting was called by the friends of the Executive, whose object was to address the President of the United States and to express their entire approbation of his conduct with respect to our foreign relations.

"An address to this effect was prepared and presented by Thomas R. Rootes, Esq., which he supported by very lengthy arguments. He was followed by Capt. John Mercer, Col. John Minor and Col. John F. Mercer, who successfully combatted the various arguments adduced by Mr. Rootes in support of his address. And the following resolutions then, prepared by Dr. David C. Ker, were approved and adopted. A division was called for on the address and resolutions and tellers appointed to take the number of votes, who reported that two-thirds of the citizens present were in favor of the resolutions. The meeting was more numerous than any we have ever seen in this place. During the whole of the discussion the most perfect order and decorum prevailed."

The resolutions, adopted in place of the address, will be interesting reading to our people, even in this day. They are as follows:

1. *Resolved,* As the opinion of this meeting that the administration of these States received the government of a happy and united people, in peace abroad and prosperity at home; that under their guidance, we have been led, oppressed with public, heavy debts, enormous taxes, a ruined commerce and depreciated produce, into hostility with a nation who aided to secure our independence by their own blood and treasure, with a republic the most powerful and successful that has appeared on earth for eighteen centuries, armed with every weapon to injure us, but whom we can in no wise injure; with a republic united with a confederacy so extensive as to separate us from all the civilized world but Britain, and her dependencies; that they have done this, not through ignorance and folly only, for they were at all times warned of the certain consequence of their measures; not through constraint, for although opposed, they always carried their measures; but men who have proved themselves by their own works, so unfit to govern us, even with every advantage, can never without madness be trusted in times of real difficulty and extreme danger; and that it is equally absurd to found confidence in our disasters, or to pursue that line, or to support those men who have already brought us to the verge of destruction.

2nd. Resolved, That the speech of the President of the United States to the ordinary session of Congress, was, in the opinion of this meeting, calculated to rouse the resentment of the French government and destroy any reasonable hope of successful negotiations between that republic and agents appointed by him.

3rd. Resolved, That the instructions to our envoys, so contrary to the spirit of that speech and the whole conduct of our administration, authorize this conclusion:—that they were rather intended to inflame the American mind than to produce good in France, under the well grounded expectation, that the negotiations would, from those and other causes, fail.

4th. Resolved, That the late negotiations with unauthorized swindlers in Paris, are so unexampled as to afford no justifiable ground for public measures, and that their publication, so far as they tend to excite the sensibility of our citizens, is unjustifiable, as they may commit the safety of the envoys highly imprudent.

The "Charity School," started by Benj. Day and others in the latter part of the eighteenth century.
(See page 194)

The Fire Department.
(See page 144)

5th. Resolved, That the militia are the only safe and constitutional defence of these States; that they alone are adequate to this object, and that they will ever prove so, if guided by good government.

6th. Resolved, That we hold it to be our bounden duty, and we do solemnly pledge ourselves, firmly, to support our National rights and independence whenever assailed by foreign invasion or domestic usurpation.

Fontaine Maury was chairman of this large gathering of the people and signed the resolutions adopted by the meeting. They were then sent to Hon. John Dawson, representative in Congress from this district, who laid them before the extra session of Congress for the consideration of that body. These resolutions, adopted on the 14th of May, 1798, setting forth the principles upon which their authors believed the Union was founded, and upon which the government should be administered, were the basis for the famous resolutions drawn by Mr. Madison and passed by the Virginia Legislature on the 2nd of December of the same year, which have since been the theme of Virginia Statesmen of that school when they would "revert to first principles."

The address, which was presented to the meeting and voted down by such a large majority, was directed to the President of the United States, and was as follows:

We, the subscribers, inhabitants of the town and corporation of Fredericksburg, in the State of Virginia, assembled at our town house, this 14th day of May, 1798, by a public notice, for the purpose of expressing our sense of the conduct of our government, in regard to its foreign relations, do communicate to you, as the sense of the subscribers, that your several attempts to restore that harmony between the United States and the French republic, which has been so unfortunately impaired, and to reinstate that good understanding between the two nations so desirous to the lovers of peace, have been wise and prudent, and entitle you to the highest evidence of our esteem; and that whatever may be the opinion of foreign nations, with respect to divisions among ourselves, should it be the misfortune of our country to be involved in a war with any nation, you will always find us ready with our lives and fortunes to support and defend the Constitution and laws of our country.

After the address had been voted down as not reflecting the sentiments of a majority of the citizens of the town, not to be foiled in their desire to let the President know that they approved his policy, the friends of the administration determined to make three copies of the address and leave it at three places in town for the signatures of those who approved it. The three places named were Wm. Taylor's, George W. B. Spooner's and the Herald office. The following gentlemen signed the address:

George W. B. Spooner, Wm. Drummond, Elisha Hall, Wm. Jones, Anthony Buck, Richard Richards, Robert Patton, Wm. Glassell, Tho. Southcomb, Andrew Parks, Tho. Rootes, Peter Gordon, Wm. Taylor, George Murray, James Pettigrew, Timothy Green, Wm. Payne, James Carmichael, Law. Bowes, Thos. Hodge, George French, Richard Johnston, Jr., John Anderson, John Coakley, Wm. Fitzhugh, of Chatham, Charles Croughton, David Henderson, Roger Coltart, David Blair, Jeff. Wright, Charles Yates, Wm. Lovell, Alexander Duncan, Wm. Wilson, Rob. Lilly, Thos. Cochran, James Stevenson, John Brownlow, Jos. Thornton, Benj. Day, Wm. Wiatt, Zack. Mayfield, John Newton, David Simons, Philip Lipscomb, Daniel Grinnan, James Vanshell, Daniel Stark, Samuel Stevens, Godlove Heiskell, Thos. P. Basye, John Harris, Thomas Seddon, Jr., Robert Wellford, Philip Glover, John Legg, Edward McDermot, John Alcock, Jacob Grotz, John Moore, Adam Darby, Tho. Miller, James Blair, Wm. Hamilton, R. Dykes, David Williamson, Wm. Acres, Wm. Talbot, James Ross, John Bogan, Robert Walker, John Kirck, Sam. M. Douglas, Wm. Welsh, Alexander S. Roe, John Dare, James Slater, Charles Stewart, Christian Helmstetter, Wm. Smith, Benj. Sabastian, James Adams.

CHAPTER XVI

Some Distinguished Men Buried in Fredericksburg—A Remarkable Grave Stone—Three Heroic Fredericksburgers, Wellford, Herndon, Willis—The Old Liberty Bell Passes Through Town —Great Demonstrations in its Honor—What a Chinaman Thought of it.

A town is not less renowned for the noble, heroic dead who sleep within its borders than it is for its gallant soldiers, Statesmen and others who are yet on the stage of action. Indeed its renown may be more enduring because of its dead than of its living. The deeds of the dead are embalmed in our hearts and in history and cannot be tarnished, obscured or obliterated. The greatest deeds of the living may be obscured and even almost blotted from the approving mind by some adverse, evil cloud—by some act of folly or perfidy.

If Judas Iscariot had died before he betrayed his Master his good deeds would have lived forever. If a Britton's bullet had taken off Benedict Arnold before his treasonable thoughts had resolved into action he would have been written down in history as one of the heroes of America. We, therefore, with pride refer to some distinguished men who peacefully sleep within our corporate limits.

ARCHIBALD M'PHERSON.

Archibald McPherson was born in 1715 in the northern part of England. He came to this country in early manhood and settled in Spotsylvania county. He is represented as being a gentleman of education, refinement and wealth, and a friend to the poor and needy. He died in the prime of manhood, leaving to the world an unsullied name and to the poor of the town a legacy to be expended in the education of their children, which is elsewhere mentioned in these pages.

Mr. McPherson was interred in the burial ground of St. George's church and a marble slab erected over his grave, which is now secured to the wall of the Mission House, at the west end of the lot on Princess Ann street. On that slab is the following inscription:

"Here lies the body of Archibald McPherson, born in the county of Murray, in North Britain, who died August 17, 1754, aged 49 years. He was judicious, a lover of learning, open hearted, generous and sincere. Devout, without ostentation; disdaining to cringe to vice in any station. Friend to good men, an affectionate husband.

> A heap of dust alone remains of thee,
> 'Tis all thou art, and all the proud shall be.

"Elizabeth, his disconsolate widow, as a testimony of their mutual affection, erected this monument to his memory."

COL. JOHN DANDRIDGE.

In the burial ground of St. George's church, near the northeast corner of the building, lies buried the father of Martha Washington, which fact has only some years since been brought to light, or if it had been before known, it was by the citizens of the past generation of the town. The reason it was unknown to the present generation is accounted for from the fact that the slab over the grave has been covered with dirt for more than half a century, most likely from the erection of the present church building, and was discovered only a few years ago. When the grave was discovered the slab covering it was cleaned off, and the inscription on it was found to read as follows:

"Here lies the body of Col. John Dandridge, of New Kent county, who departed this life the 31st day of August, 1756, aged 56 years."

How he came to be buried in Fredericksburg is not positively known. It has been claimed by some persons that he was here on a visit to his daughter Martha, who married Gen. Washington, and the weather was so hot that his body could not be taken back to New Kent county, but that cannot be true because he was buried here more than two years before his daughter married Washington.

The most satisfactory explanation of Col. Dandridge's presence in Fredericksburg, that we have heard given, is that he was attending the celebrated races at Chatham, held by Wm. Fitzhugh, which drew to the town people from all sections of the country. But be

History of Fredericksburg, Virginia

that as it may, this Col. Dandridge is beyond doubt the father of Martha Washington, unless there were two gentlemen by that name and bearing the same appellation residing in New Kent county at that time, which is not probable. Haydon's "Virginia Families" says of Washington:

"Married at White House, New Kent county, Va., Jan. 6, 1759, Martha Dandridge, daughter of Col. John Dandridge, of New Kent county, and widow of Daniel Parke Custis."

WM. PAUL—JOHN PAUL JONES.

There also lie interred in the burial ground of St. George's church, with an unpretentious stone marking the place, the remains of William Paul, a merchant of the town and a native of Scotland, who died here in 1773. In 1770 he purchased from Thomas and Jane Blanton, "for one hundred and twenty pounds, an acre or one-half of the lot or land lying and being in the town of Fredericksburg, and designated in the plot of said town by the number or figures 258, the same being one-half, or south end of said lot, and purchased by the said Thomas Blanton of Roger Dixon, Gent, and bound on the main street, called Caroline street, and the cross street, called Prussia, together with all houses, buildings, gardens, ways, profits, hereditraments and appurtenances whatever." This lot is designated on the map of the town to-day as 258, and the house in which Wm. Paul conducted his mercantile business is the one occupied and owned at present by Matthew J. Gately.

Notwithstanding his biographers to the contrary, Wm. Paul made a will in 1772, in which he appointed his friends, Wm. Templeman and Isaac Heslop, his executors, which was witnessed by John Atkinson, Thomas Holmes and B. Johnston. The executors declined to serve and the estate remained until late in the next year without any one being legally authorized to take charge of it. In November, 1774, John Atkinson qualified, it is supposed at the instance of John Paul, who had arrived here to wind up the estate, with John Waller, Jr., as surety, who was afterwards released and Charles Yates became his surety.

This Wm. Paul was the brother of John Paul, who afterwards

became the famous John Paul Jones. It has been asserted that Wm. Paul changed his name to Jones to inherit a plantation from Wm. Jones, either in Virginia or North Carolina. But this is shown to be a mistake from the fact that Wm. Paul, in 1770, bought property here as Wm. Paul, made his will in 1772 and signed it Wm. Paul, and died in 1773 and his tomb stone now bears on it the name of Wm. Paul. It was further asserted that in the agreement by which the plantation was to become the property of Wm. Paul, if Wm. Paul died without issue, the property was to go to John Paul on the condition that he would add Jones to his name, and that William did die without issue and the estate of William went to John. This is also a mistake. William did not die intestate, but made a will and gave his entire estate to his sister, Mary Young, and her two oldest children.

One clause of the will reads as follows: "It is my will and desire that my lots and houses in this town shall be sold and converted into money for as much as they will bring, that with all my other estate being sold, and what of my outstanding debts that can be collected, I give and bequeath to my beloved sister, Mary Young, and her two oldest children in Abigland, in the parish of Kirkbean, in Stewarty of Galloway, North Briton, and their heirs forever." It is not believed that Wm. Paul owned any property out of town from the fact that the bond of his administrator was only five hundred pounds, which was generally double the amount of the estate. His estate in town consisted of his houses and lots, his merchandise and accounts due him, which must have been worth twelve or fifteen hundred dollars. Therefore the bond of $2,500 was sufficient only for his possessions in town, and no other is alluded to or mentioned in his will. It has been held that he owned property in the county of Spotsylvania, but that arises from the fact there were others by the name of Paul in the county who had property. But this William Paul is traced by the reference in his will to the parish of Kirkbean, Galloway, where his sister, Mary Young, and brother John lived.

Why John Paul changed his name to Jones was probably known only to himself. Many writers have undertaken to explain it, but without success, and the mystery is yet unsolved. In 1775 John Paul Jones's name heads a list of naval lieutenants, and, because of his meritorious services, he was soon appointed a captain, and finally rose to the rank of commodore. His daring exploits and unequal, but successful, contests soon won for him the thanks of the American Congress, as well as the gratitude of the American people, while it carried terror and dismay to the enemies of his country. He greatly humiliated England by landing his fleet on her shores during the Revolutionary war, a thing that had not been done before for centuries, if ever, since it was a nation.

At the close of the war, in which he had covered himself with glory, he was offered an important command by the Empress of Russia against the Turks in the Black sea, which he accepted with the stipulation "that he was never to renounce the title of an American citizen." He died in Paris in 1792, and was buried in that city, aged forty-five years. General Washington, then President of the United States, had just commissioned him for an important duty, but he died before the commission reached him. As the many years rolled on, rounding up a century, his body laid in an unknown grave, notwithstanding many efforts were made to locate it. In 1900 a body was found believed to be his, and there was great rejoicing in this country over the announcement, but, when carefully examined, it was found to be the remains of another and not those of the great American commodore. But this did not discourage those who had the matter in hand, and the search continued under the direction of Gen. Horace Porter, the American Ambassador to the Court of France, under great difficulties. On the 7th of April, 1905, the body was found in a cemetery known as Saint Louis, which was laid out in 1720 for a burial place for Protestants, but which had been closed more than half a century, and buildings were constructed upon it at the time of the discovery of the body. The remains were declared to be those of John Paul Jones, after every test had been applied that could be, and they were accepted by our government as those of the great naval hero. Some time was spent in preparing to remove the remains to this country, but early in 1906 they were placed upon a United States man of war, escorted by vessels from England and France, and were landed at Annapolis, where they were reinterred in the presence of thousands of people from all parts of the country, with booming of cannon and every honor a grateful people could bestow upon him.

GEN. LEWIS LITTLEPAGE.

Gen. Lewis Littlepage, who died and was buried here in the burying ground of Masonic Lodge No. 4, was born in Hanover county, Virginia, and was one of the most brilliant men the State ever produced. His career was short, but in that short life he greatly distinguished himself as a scholar, soldier and diplomat. He was the protege of John Jay at the Court of France in 1782, was wounded at the siege of Gibraltar, was a member of the cabinet of the king of Poland, and the King's chamberlain, with the rank of major-general; negotiated a treaty with the Empress of Russia, was a secret and special envoy to the Court of France to form the Grand Quadruple Alliance; was with Prince Potempkin in his march through Tartary des Negais; commanded a flotilla under Prince Nassau at his victory over the fleet of Turkey; was sent on an important mission to Madrid, in which he was successful; resisted the Russian invaders of Poland as aide-de-camp to the King; signed the Confederation of Fargowitz; envoy to St. Petersburg to prevent the division of Poland, but was stopped by the Russian government; was with Kosciusko in his attempt to free Poland; was at the storming of Prague, and was with King Stanislaus when he was captured by the Russians.

At the death of Stanislaus, Gen. Littlepage, becoming sick of European politics and broils, and, with his health shattered and gone, returned to America, settled in Fredericksburg and died before he had reached the age of forty years. His grave, in the western corner of the Masonic cemetery, is marked by a marble slab, which has on it this inscription:

"Here lies the body of Lewis Littlepage, who was born in the county of Hanover, in the State of Virginia, on the 19th day of December, 1762, and departed this life in Fredericksburg, on the

The Christian Church.
(See page 213)

The Trinity Episcopal Church.
(See page 206)

19th of July, 1802, aged 39 years and 7 months. Honored for many years with the esteem and confidence of the unfortunate Stanislaus Augustus, King of Poland, he held under that monarch, until he lost his throne, the most distinguished offices, among which was that of Ambassador to Russia. He was by him created the Knight of St. Stanislaus, chamberlain and confidential secretary in his cabinet, and acted as his special envoy in the most important occasions of talents, of military as well as civil, he served with credit as an officer of high rank in different arms. In private life he was charitable, generous and just, and in the various public offices which he filled he acted with uniform magnanimity, fidelity and honor."

CAPT. WM. LEWIS HERNDON.

Another hero, a native of Fredericksburg, whose remains found sepulture in a watery grave far out in the ocean's depths, is worthy of mention in these pages. "Wm. Lewis Herndon, an American naval officer, born October 25, 1813, drowned by the sinking of the steamer Central America, September 12, 1857. He entered the navy at the age of fifteen, served in the Mexican war, and was engaged three years with his brother-in-law, Lieutenant Maury, in the National Observatory, at Washington. In 1851-52 he explored the Amazon river under the direction of the United States government. * * * In 1857 he was the commander of the steamer Central America, which left Havana for New York on September 8th, having on board 474 passengers, a crew of 105 men and about $2,000,000 of gold. On September the 11th, during a violent gale from the northeast and a heavy sea, the vessel sprung a leak and sunk on the evening of September 12th near the outer edge of the Gulf stream, in latitude 31 degrees 44 minutes north. Only 152 of the persons on board were saved, including the women and children; the gallant commander of the steamer was seen standing upon the wheel house at the time of her sinking."* Capt. Herndon was an uncle of Dr. Herndon, who sacrificed his life at Fernandina, Florida, elsewhere mentioned.

---

* Appleton's Encyclopedia, Volume 9.

JACOB FRIEZE.

Another man of note, remarkable for his physical endurance and strength of constitution, who lived in Fredericksburg and whose remains lie buried in the City cemetery, just to the left of the old gate on Commerce street, was Jacob Frieze. He died in 1869, just after having passed the ninety-first anniversary of his birth. He was born in France, and was one of Napoleon's soldiers from the time his remarkable career commenced in Paris until it ended so disastrously at Waterloo.

Much of the soldier life of Mr. Frieze was spent as a member of Napoleon's "Old Guard," that "could die, but could never surrender," and he was never so happy as when telling of his thrilling war experiences and narrow escapes. He was in the famous retreat from Moscow and could tell the most thrilling stories of the hardships and sufferings of the French army. The weather was intensely cold, sometimes reaching twenty-six degrees below zero, and, having to fight cold, hunger and the Russians, it is not strange that Napoleon left behind him over 330,000 French or allies, dead or prisoners. This marching, fighting, suffering and dying were all fresh in the mind of Mr. Frieze, who was a participant and eye witness, and he would entertain crowds who would gather around him for hours.

Prior to the Civil war there also lived in Fredericksburg Mr. John Eubank, who was a soldier under the Duke of Wellington at the battle of Waterloo and who stood guard over Napoleon on the Island of St. Helena. Notwithstanding the many years that had passed from their parting at Waterloo to their meeting again in Fredericksburg, Mr. Frieze and Mr. Eubank had not forgotten the sword and the spear and had not forgotten to dislike each other.

It was amusing to the bystanders to see these old soldiers meet on the streets, as they would invariably shake their fists at each other and grind their teeth and pass on without uttering a word.

Many of the citizens of the town still remember the willow baskets, of variegated colors, which Mr. Frieze made and peddled about town for a livelihood, as long as he was able to appear on the streets. Mr. Eubank moved to Charlottesville, where he died and was buried in that city.

A GRAND-NIECE OF WASHINGTON AND NAPOLEON.

The defeat of Napoleon at Waterloo sent into exile, among others, his grand-nephew, Prince Charles Louis Napoleon Achille Murat, a colonel in the defeated army, son of the exiled King of Naples and Charlotte Bonaparte. He settled in Tallahassee, Florida. Soon Col. Byrd C. Willis, of Willis Hill, moved to the same city, carrying with him his wife, Mary, daughter of Col. Fielding Lewis and Bettie Washington, and also his daughter, Catherine, who married a Mr. Grey and was left a widow at sixteen. She was beautiful, accomplished, winsome and a leader in society. She attracted the attention of the young prince, who laid siege to her affections and was victorious. The marriage soon followed. By this union Catherine, who was a grand-niece of Gen. Washington, became also a grand-niece of the great soldier, Napoleon Bonaparte. She was born where the National cemetery now stands and died in Florida August 6, 1867, in the 64th year of her age.

WELLFORD—HERNDON—WILLIS.

In the City cemetery lie the remains of Doctor Francis Preston Wellford. Dr. Wellford was a native of Fredericksburg, where he was held in the highest esteem by all who knew him for his gentle and kind disposition, his upright life, his abounding charity and his deep piety. In 1871 he left his native town and settled in Jacksonville, Florida, where he commenced the practice of medicine and established a high reputation as a skillful physician. His brethren of the profession were not slow in recognizing his ability and great worth, and made him president of the Medical Association of the State. He was holding that honorable position when the yellow fever scourge visited Fernandina, in 1877, which almost depopulated the town. For weeks it raged in the doomed city, and all of the physicians were either down with the disease or had become worn out with serving day and night. A call was made for assistance and volunteer physicians. Dr. Wellford, forgetting self, not fearing his personal danger, responded to the call and went to the sick and dying of the panic-stricken Fernandina. It was while ministering to those people he was stricken down and died of the disease. Thus went down to his grave, amidst the tears of thousands of people, the noble physician and Christian gentleman, who sacrificed his life for the good of others. Dr. Wellford's remains, some years after his death, were brought to Fredericksburg for final interment, and now repose in our beautiful cemetery.

In response to the call for physicians made by the people of Fernandina, another physician, born and raised in Fredericksburg, Dr. James C. Herndon, made his way to that city, and like Dr. Wellford, was stricken down and died from the disease. It is peculiarly appropriate that his sacrifice to professional duty should be acknowledged in connection with that of his brother physician's.

To the honor of these noble men a memorial window has been placed in St. Peter's Episcopal church in Fernandina by Dr. J. H. Upham, of Boston, who felt that they had honored the profession by the sacrifices they made, and he wanted their heroism to be placed upon a lasting record. In describing the window the Fernandina Mirror says:

"The design is that of a crown in the upper section of the arch. Below this is a beautiful shield of purple illuminated glass. A cross of mother of pearl forms the center of the window, ornamented by a bunch of grapes, with the symbol of the anchor representing Hope, the holy Scriptures, illustrating Christian Faith; alpha and omega, the symbol of the Almighty Power, the beginning and the end; the cup of salvation, and the paten, the emblem of sacrifice. In the lower part of the window an illuminated tablet has the following inscription:

> Francis Preston Wellford, M. D.,
> Born in Fredericksburg, Va.,
> Sept. 12th, 1829.
> James Carmichael Herndon, M. D.,
> Born in Fredericksburg, Va.,
> Sept. 22nd, 1831.
> Died in the faithful discharge of their
> duties, at Fernandina, Florida,
> Oct. 18th, 1877.

To whose memory as a grateful record of their noble lives and heroic deaths this window is dedicated by a New England member of the profession which they so much honored and adorned.

' Greater love hath no man than this,
That he lay down his life for his friends.'

"The beautiful execution of this window, and the noble purpose to which it is dedicated by its generous donor, deserve the admiration and warm appreciation of the citizens of Fernandina, to whom the memory of Drs. Wellford and Herndon is deservedly dear, and will be regarded by our citizens as a graceful professional tribute by Dr. Upham to these noble men, as well as an indication of his kind feelings towards our city. There is a striking coincidence in the fact that these noble men should have been born in the same city, in the same month, and, having volunteered their services, reached Fernandina in the midst of the epidemic on the same day, and that their deaths should have occurred the same day. It was, therefore, peculiarly fitting that the same memorial should have been erected to those who were faithful in life, even unto death."

William Willis, whose remains are buried in the City cemetery, left Fredericksburg for Memphis, Tenn., in the summer of 1870, which city he made his home. When the yellow fever scourge struck that place in 1878, and the city was deserted of most of its inhabitants, except the helpless, the sick and the dying, it was then, in spite of the entreaty of his friends to leave the city, that Wm. Willis stepped forth and took charge, as the chief executive in managing the affairs of the city, and in distributing food, clothing and medicine, sent from all quarters of the country, to the sick, the helpless and the needy. It was while in the execution of this noble work that he too, was stricken down, and a few days' struggle with the terrible disease and William Willis was no more. In his delirium, feeling the great necessity of some one taking up the work, he had so faithfully prosecuted, where he was compelled to lay it down, he uttered these as his last words: "Send some good man to take my place," and then peacefully passed to the spirit land.

Thus went down to their graves three Fredericksburg men in the years 1877-78 of yellow fever, who sacrificed their own lives to save the lives of others.

MRS. LUCY ANN COX.

There is buried in the City cemetery Mrs. Lucy Ann Cox, with this inscription upon her head-stone. "Lucy Ann Cox, wife of James A. Cox, died December 17, 1891, aged 64 years. A sharer of the toils, dangers and privations of the 30th Va. regiment infantry, C. S. A., from 1861 to 1865, and died beloved and respected by the veterans of that command." The stone was erected by her friends. Mrs. Cox was the daughter of Jesse White, the practical printer, and married Mr. Cox just before the Civil war. She followed him all through the campaign of the entire war, cooking and washing for the soldiers of her command, and often ministering to the sick and wounded.

Molly Pitcher carried water from a spring, at Monmouth Courthouse, New Jersey, to her husband and others who had charge of a cannon during the battle, and when she saw her husband shot down and heard an officer order the gun to the rear, having no one to man it, she dropped her pail, ran to the cannon, seized the rammer and continued loading and firing the gun throughout the battle. For this heroic act Washington praised her, gave her an honorary commission as captain and Congress voted her half pay for life.

Mrs. Cox engaged in no battle, but instead of sharing the privations and dangers of her husband at one battle she followed him through the entire war of four years, and was voted the honor of a Confederate veteran after the war by the veterans themselves. It is doubtful whether in all the past a similar instance can be found.

A REMARKABLE GRAVE-STONE.

There is to be found in the burial ground of St. George's church, at the east end of the Mission House, a grave-stone that has puzzled all antiquarians who have examined it and which has never yet been satisfactorily explained, and perhaps never will be. The inscription is as follows: "Charles M. Rothrock, departed this life

Sept. 29, 1084, aged three years." The figures that make these dates are well preserved, much better than on many slabs and headstones in the same burial ground, which do not date back a century and a half, yet on this slab the figures are quite legibly cut in the sandstone, and there can be no doubt that the year is 1084. It has been considered such a mystery and of such importance that a photograph of the stone was taken and an engraving made for this publication.

THE LIBERTY BELL.

The very name—Liberty Bell—is music to our ears, and the mention of it should fill the breast of every true American with patriotic enthusiasm. That bell hung over a hall in Philadelphia in 1776, in which the Continental Congress had met to consider the momentous question that was then stirring every patriotic heart—American freedom. Virginia was represented in that Congress by George Wythe, Richard Henry Lee, Thomas Jefferson, Benjamin Harrison, Thomas Nelson, Jr., Francis Lightfoot Lee and Carter Braxton.

That body of patriots prepared, considered and adopted the Declaration of Independence, and as they finished signing their names to the instrument, on the fourth day of July, this bell rang out the thrilling news that Americans were freemen. Since that stirring event—that memorable day—that hall has been known as Independence Hall, and the bell that hung over it as the Liberty Bell.

On the 4th of October, 1895, the old Liberty Bell passed through Fredericksburg on its way from Philadelphia to Atlanta, Georgia, where it was to be exhibited at the great exhibition in that city. Prior to its coming Mayor Rowe had been notified when it would arrive and how long it would remain for inspection. The City Council was called together and steps were taken to give the old bell a grand reception and cordial welcome. A set of patriotic resolutions was adopted, extolling the events that brought the bell into such popular favor, recounting the part taken in those events by Virginians and the precious legacy left to us by our self-sacrificing forefathers, until a patriotic fervor pervaded the town.

The bell was accompanied by Hon. Charles F. Warwick, Mayor of Philadelphia; Wencel Harman, President of the Common Council, and thirteen members of that body; Charles K. Smith, Chairman of the Select Council, and thirteen members of that body; twelve officials of the city of Philadelphia, including S. A. Eisenhower, Chief of Bureau of City Property, and Custodian of the State House and Bell, with a guard of honor, consisting of four of the reserve police of Philadelphia.

A party, including a committee from the City Council—Messrs. John T. Knight, E. D. Cole and J. Stansbury Wallace—met the bell at Quantico, where Judge James B. Sener, who had accompanied the party from Washington, delivered an appropriate address of welcome on the part of the State of Virginia. The party arrived in Fredericksburg on time, and found at the depot a vast concourse of people and a procession headed by Bowering's Band and the Washington Guards, consisting of the Mayor, ex-Mayors, Common Council, Sons of Confederate Veterans, school children and citizens generally.

All the bells in town were ringing, the steam whistles were blowing and everybody was rejoicing. Such a time had scarcely, if ever, been seen before by our people. As soon as the train bearing the bell and escort halted, Mayor Rowe and others went on board the car, and, after the usual introductions and salutations, Mayor Rowe, who was somewhat indisposed, presented Mr. W. Seymour White, who made the welcome address as follows:

Mr. Mayor of Philadelphia and Gentlemen of the Escort of the Liberty Bell:

It is with a most peculiar pleasure that we greet you and welcome this sacred relic within the boundaries of the Old Dominion. It is most fitting that it should rest upon the breast of this great old State, for it was the voice of a great Virginian that sounded the tocsin of the Revolution; it was the pen of a great Virginian that drafted the Declaration of Independence that was greeted by the voice of this bell; it was the sword of a great Virginian that made that declaration an accomplished fact, and it was while tolling the

The Free Lance—Star Office.
(See page 227)

requiem for the soul of the great Virginian jurist, John Marshall, that its voice ever became silent. It is with feelings of heartfelt delight that we welcome it within the corporate limits of Fredericksburg, connected inseparably, as she is, like your own great and proud city of Philadelphia, with the events proclaimed in that glorious past by that sacred bell; for it was in Fredericksburg, on the 29th of April, 1775, that the first resolutions breathing the spirit of the Declaration of Independence were offered; it was in Fredericksburg that Hugh Mercer lived, whose ashes rest in your beloved soil, in whose defence he died; and in Fredericksburg once lived that great American President that gave to all the ages the grand doctrine that these United States would never tolerate the acquisition of an inch of American soil by any prince, potentate or power of Europe. We are glad that this bell is going about the land, in the language of your great and good president, Judge Thayer, "stirring up everywhere as it goes those memories and patriotic impulses that are so inseparably connected with its history, and which themselves can never grow mute," and we doubt not that this bell, though voiceless now, can still "proclaim liberty throughout all the land unto all the inhabitants thereof; and who can tell but that as the rolling waves of the blue Mexican Gulf thunder upon the shores of the Queen of the Antilles, the proud, triumphal progress of the Liberty Bell, they may bear to patriots, struggling to be free in that far off land, the sympathy of the great hearts of American freemen that yet beat responsive to the efforts of those whose love of liberty is stronger than death?" We are glad that our men and women may see it, and at the sacred flame that burns about its altar replenish the patriotic fire that still is trimmed and burning in the hearts of a re-united American people. We are glad that our children may see it to learn from its presence and history that the dearest heritage left them by their fathers is that liberty and independence once proclaimed by this bell. And so we bid God speed to the bell which once "rang redress to all mankind," as it goes through the land proclaiming to all the nations of the world that a "government by the people, of the people and for the people" has not perished from off the face of the earth, but "still lives the home of liberty and the birth-right of every American citizen."

Mayor Warwick responded in a patriotic and appropriate address, after which the guests were driven around town in carriages until the time for their departure, when they boarded the train and started on their trip South, delighted with their reception in Fredericksburg.

A Chinaman who witnessed the demonstration remarked that Christians charged his people with idolatry in worshipping the dead, because they honored their deceased parents, but a Chinaman never worshipped an old bell as he had seen Christian people doing on this occasion.

CHAPTER XVII

Visits of Heroes—Gala Days—The Society of the Army of the Potomac Enters Town, &c.

Fredericksburg has received the visits of many heroes and statesmen, and on various occasions has been placed on "dress parade," and proved herself equal to the demands made upon her on every occasion. Only a few of these visits are mentioned here, but these few should be placed upon perpetual record that they may inspire our noble youth and the coming generations and cause them to appreciate more highly the great blessings transmitted to them through the efforts and achievements of those heroes.

GEN. GREEN VISITS THE TOWN.

The first we mention is the visit of Major-General Nathaniel Green, on his way from Georgia to his home in New Hampshire at the close of the Revolutionary war. In 1780 the patriot cause in Georgia and North Carolina appeared to be lost, in consequence of the overwhelming numbers of the British and the ravages of the Tories, which brought disaster to our arms. In this condition of things Washington recommended that Gen. Nathaniel Green should be placed in command, but Congress sent Gen. Gates instead. Before leaving for his new field Gen. Gates had an interview with Gen. Charles Lee—who was then without a command—in Fredericksburg, when Gen. Lee charged him in parting, "Beware that your northern laurels do not change to southern willows." Gen. Gates went to his field of operation, met with disaster, and was relieved by Gen. Green; and it is worthy of note that Gen. Gates left Fredericksburg for his southern command, and Gen. Green passed through Fredericksburg when he went down to relieve him.

Gen. Green was fortunate in having to aid him in his southern department such dashing commanders as Gen. Daniel Morgan, of Winchester; Col. Wm. Washington, of Stafford, and Col. Henry Lee, of Westmoreland county—Gen. Robert E. Lee's father and known as "Light Horse Harry." With these brave men Green succeeded in driving the British before him and subduing the Tories, thus restoring peace and quiet to that panic-stricken people, and greatly endearing him to all patriots. In grateful recognition of his services the State of Georgia gave him a magnificent farm and residence, and on his return from the South to his home, in New Hampshire, he met with grand ovations all along the route. He passed through Fredericksburg on the 12th of September, 1783. A public meeting of the citizens was called, which adopted and presented an address to the war-scarred hero. The masses gathered to greet him, and the old soldiers, who had just returned home from victorious fields, went into ecstasy over him. The following is the address of the people of Fredericksburg:

To the Honorable Major-General Green, Commander-in-Chief of the Armies of the United States of America, in the Southern Department:

SIR—We, the inhabitants of the town of Fredericksburg, impressed with just sentiments of the importance of your singular services rendered our country, as Commander of the Armies of the United States in the Southern Department, cannot omit rendering you our acknowledgements as a grateful, though small, tribute, so justly due to your distinguished character as a soldier, a gentleman and friend to American liberty. We lament that the absence of the Mayor, and other officers of the corporation, deprives us of the opportunity of rendering you this token of gratitude in the style of a corporation, but we trust, sir, that your own conscious merit will give us credit, when we assure you that we now present you the united thanks of this city for your zealous, important and successful services in recovering the Southern States from our cruel enemy, and restoring peace, liberty and safety to so great a part of our country. We cannot express, sir, our great joy in seeing you once more among us, and language is too faint to paint the contrast in the cause of liberty since you passed us to take the command of the Southern Army. Permit us, therefore, to pass over the then gloomy moment and to participate in the pleasure you now enjoy in the possession of the American *Laurel,* a crown as splendid as all the honors of a Roman Triumph. We also beg leave to follow you with our best wishes into domestic life. May you long enjoy uninterrupted, under your vine, all the happiness of that Peace, Liberty and Safety, for which you and your gallant officers and soldiers have so nobly fought and greatly conquered. We have the honor to be with every sentiment of respect, your most obedient and very humble servants. Signed by order of the inhabitants.

Sept. 12, 1783.   CHARLES MORTIMER, *Chairman.*

To this address Gen. Green responded as follows:

To the Inhabitants of the City of Fredericksburg:

GENTLEMEN—Highly flattered by your address, and no less honored by your sentiments, how shall I acknowledge fully your generosity in either! From your hearty welcome to this city and your good wishes for my future welfare I feel the overflowings of a grateful mind. The noblest reward for the best services is the favorable opinion of our fellow citizens. Happy in your assurances, I shall feel myself amply rewarded, if I have but the good wishes of my country. I have the honor to be, gentlemen, your most obedient, humble servant,

Sept. 12, 1783.   NATHANIEL GREEN.

GEN. WASHINGTON VISITS HIS MOTHER.

In December, 1783, General Washington visited Fredericksburg. He had just resigned his commission of Commander-in-Chief of the American Armies, and as a private citizen had come to visit his mother and friends at his old home. He was the uncrowned King of America, and was uncrowned only because he refused to be crowned. He came with victory upon his brow, and peace and liberty for the American people. From mouth to mouth went the message—"the great and good Washington is coming." From town and country the masses gathered to give him welcome and do him honor. The military turned out, the civic societies paraded, the cannon boomed and everybody went into raptures over his coming. The City Council was called together and the following address was adopted, amid the wildest enthusiasm, and presented to the grand American:

To his Excellency, General Washington, late Commander-in-Chief of the Armies of America:

SIR—While applauding millions were offering you their warmest congratulations of the blessings of peace and your safe return from the hazards of the field, we, the Mayor and Commonalty of the corporation of Fredericksburg, were not wanting in attachment and wishes to have joined in public testimonies of our warmest gratitude and affection for your long and meritorious services in the cause of liberty; a cause, sir, in which, by your examples and exertions, with the aid of your gallant army, the virtuous citizens of this western world are secured in freedom and independence, and although you have laid aside your official character, we cannot omit this first opportunity you have given us of presenting, with unfeigned hearts, our sincere congratulations on your returning in safety from the noisy clashing of arms to the walks of domestic ease. And it affords us great joy to see you once more at a place that claims the honor of your growing infancy, the seat of your venerable and amiable parent and worthy relatives. We want language to express the happiness we feel on this occasion, which cannot be expressed but by superior acts (if possible) of the divine favor. May the great and omnipotent Ruler of all human events, who, in blessing America, has conducted you through so many dangers, continue his favor and protection through the remainder of your life in the happy society of an affectionate and grateful people. I have the honor to be, in behalf of the corporation, with every sentiment of esteem and respect, your Excellency's most humble servant, WILLIAM MCWILLIAMS, *Mayor.*

To this beautiful and appropriate address, the noble Washington responded as follows:

To the Worshipful, the Mayor and Commonalty of the Corporation of Fredericksburg:—

GENTLEMEN—With the greatest pleasure I receive in the character of a private citizen, the honor of your address. To a benevolent Providence and the fortitude of a Brave and Virtuous army, supported by the general exertion of our common country, I stand indebted for the plaudits you now bestow. The reflection, however, of having met the congratulating smiles and approbation of my fellow citizens for the part I have acted in the cause of Liberty and Independence cannot fail of adding pleasure to the other sweets of domestic life; and my sensibility of them is heightened by their coming from the respectable inhabitants of the place of my growing infancy* and the honorable mention which is made of my revered mother, by whose maternal hand (early deprived of a Father,) I was led to manhood. For the expressions of personal affection and attachment, and for your kind wishes for my future welfare, I offer grateful thanks and my sincere prayers for the happiness and prosperity of the corporate town of Fredericksburg,

G⁰ WASHINGTON.

The ceremonies of this gala day were closed with a ball at the market-house at night, which is known in history as the "peace ball." At the special request of the citizens, Mary, the mother of Washington, attended this ball and held a reception in company with her illustrious son. She "occupied a slightly elevated position, from which she could overlook the floor and see the dancers, and among them the kingly figure of the Commander-in-Chief, who led a Fredericksburg matron through a minuet."†

It will be noticed—and the fact will no doubt be treasured with pride—that Washington, in his reply to the address on this occasion, alludes to Fredericksburg as the place of his "growing infancy,"

---

* Mayor Robert Lewis, a nephew of Washington, delivered the welcome address to Lafayette when he visited Fredericksburg in 1824, in which he said: "The presence of the friend of Washington excites the tenderest emotions and associations among a people, whose town enjoys the distinguished honor of having been the residence of the Father of His Country during the days of his childhood and youth."—Pamphlet of Reception of Lafayette at Fredericksburg, page 4.

"At this place, sir, which calls to our recollection several among the most honored names of the Revolutionary war, I did, many years ago, salute the first residence of our paternal chief, received the blessing of his venerated mother, and of his dear sister, your own respected parent."—Extract of General Lafayette's reply to the above.

"The city of Fredericksburg—first residence of Washington—may she more and more attain all the prosperity which independence, republicanism and industry cannot fail to procure." Sentiment offered by Lafayette at a banquet on the above occasion.

† Manly's Southern Literature.

which shows that, history and tradition to the contrary notwithstanding, he grew up in this town, where he was educated, and where the hand of that revered mother led him to manhood, and the address of Robt. Lewis, nephew of Washington, to Gen. Lafayette makes the same claim.

GEN. LAFAYETTE'S LAST VISIT.

On the 27th day of November, 1824, Gen. Lafayette visited the town and remained two days. He was Washington's right arm in the Revolutionary war, and was visiting for the last time the early home of Washington, where he took affectionate farewell of Washington's mother, in the early part of the year 1783, as he returned to France. The General's coming was known some days beforehand and a splendid mounted guard of honor was organized in town and country, who met him just above the "Wilderness Tavern." At that place hundreds of others joined the procession, including the volunteer companies from Fredericksburg, and thus he and his party—his son George Washington and Colonel La Vasseur—were escorted to town by hundreds of mounted men and men on foot, with martial music, amid the grandest display and wildest enthusiasm on the part of the people. He received a welcome to the town no less cordial and sincere than was accorded to 'Green and Washington, because the liberty, so highly prized and gratefully enjoyed by them, was not achieved by Green and Washington without the aid of Lafayette. A public reception was held during the day, when he was welcomed by Mayor Robert Lewis, Washington's nephew, and Lafayette's intimate friend, and thousands shook him by the hand and wished him a safe voyage home to his own beloved France.

At night a ball was given in his honor over the present markethouse, where hundreds gathered to do him honor and contribute to his pleasure. The next day being Sunday he visited the Masonic Lodge, which was the mother lodge of his "bosom friend," Washington, enrolled his name as an honorary member, eulogized Washington and attended services at St. George's Episcopal church.

On the following morning, with the same mounted escort, with

Entrance to National Cemetery, erected on Willis's Hill, a portion of the Marye Heights.
(See page 190)

The Superintendent's Lodge at the National Cemetery, constructed of the stone taken from the famous "stone wall."
(See page 191)

music and the booming of cannon, he departed for the Potomac river, on his way to the city of Washington, with the best wishes and earnest prayers of all the good people of Fredericksburg.

At the reception at the town hall were Mr. Lafayette Johnston and his good wife, Mrs. Eliza Johnston. Mr. Johnston was named for Lafayette, and having a son born to them during Lafayette's visit in this country, concluded to add a further honor to the General by naming their son for him, which they did and notified the General of it. Lafayette responded with the following letter, which is now framed and in possession of Mr. H. Stuart Johnston, a great-grandson:

WASHINGTON, *January* 6, 1825.

DEAR SIR—I am much obliged to the remembrance of my brother soldier when he gave you my name, and am now to thank you for an act of kindness of the same nature conferred upon me by his son. I beg your consort and yourself to accept my acknowledgement to you, my blessing upon the boy, and my good wishes to the family. Most truly, yours,

To Fayette Johnston, Esq. LAFAYETTE.

GEN. ANDREW JACKSON'S VISIT.

The next hero to visit the town, that we mention, was the "Hero of New Orleans," Andrew Jackson, President of the United States, who, with most of his cabinet, came on the 7th of May, 1833. The occasion was the laying of the corner-stone of the Mary Washington monument, which Mr. Silas Burrows proposed to erect to her memory. The civic and military display was very imposing and the crowd was well up into the thousands.

Military companies from Washington, Alexandria, Fauquier county, and United States marines, and our own military companies, were in line, under the command of Col. John Bankhead, of White Plains, chief marshal. Col. John B. Hill was chief architect of the monument. It was a great day in Fredericksburg.

DEDICATION OF MARY WASHINGTON MONUMENT.

The next occasion was the dedication of the Mary Washington monument, erected by the Ladies' Mary Washington Monument

Associations, national and local, on the 10th of May, 1894, sixty-one years and three days after the laying of the corner-stone of the Burrows monument. A more beautiful day could not have dawned upon the city, and everything had been well planned and faithfully executed for the grand event of the day.

The streets and houses were beautifully decorated all along the route of the march, and the private residences were adorned and made gay with national and State flags. It was a general holiday for town and country, and it appeared that everybody was present and intent upon seeing the dignitaries who were to be here and hearing the addresses and ceremonies. Besides hundreds of invited guests from different parts of the United States, distinguished men and ladies, President Cleveland and nearly the entire cabinet and their wives, Vice-President Stevenson and Mrs. Stevenson, United States Senators, Representatives in Congress, Governor O'Ferrall and his staff, two members of the Supreme Court of the United States—Chief Justice Fuller and Justice Harlan—were present. The crowd was so immense that the ground seemed to tremble under their tread. It was the biggest day Fredericksburg ever had in the memory of man.

FREDERICKSBURGERS EVERYWHERE.

Fredericksburg has one peculiarity that tradition gives her, which is worthy of a place in this sketch, and that is, that in every city of any size in the civilized world a native of Fredericksburg, or some one who has lived in Fredericksburg, can be found. This is said to have been an old saying of tourists, sailors, marines and naval officers, who candidly declared that they were always able to find a Fredericksburger in every place of any size they had visited.

Capt. George Minor, who was born and raised in Fredericksburg, and who was a captain in the United States navy, and afterwards in the Confederate navy, often related this curious fact, and stated that it was positively true as to him in all his travels both by land and sea. In connection with this singular fact he related this incident: Before the Civil war he sailed into the harbor of the city of Honolulu, on the Hawaii islands, which have recently become a part of the United States. He thought of this peculiarity of his old home town, but felt confident that no Fredericksburger could be found in Honolulu, situated as it was away out in the Pacific ocean. He made his way to the city, and, after some delay, procured a guide to conduct him about the place, who could speak English.

As they progressed on their rounds from place to place, the guide pointing out places of note, giving an interesting history of the place and people, their customs, habits and peculiarities, he found himself very much interested in his guide and his narratives, and wished to know something of his history. So he asked him: "Are you a native of Honolulu!" "No, sir," was the response of the guide. "Well," continued the Captain, "where are you from?" "I am from Fredericksburg, Virginia," answered the guide. "I learned my trade of printer under Timothy Green, in the Virginia Herald office." "I am from Fredericksburg, too, and know Mr. Green well," said Capt. Minor, and the two Fredericksburgers had a real love feast. After that experience Capt. Minor said he never expected to land anywhere that he did not find a Fredericksburg man.

THE SOCIETY OF THE ARMY OF THE POTOMAC ENTERS TOWN.

The hospitality of the people of Fredericksburg is as well known probably as any other characteristic of her citizens. It has been thoroughly tested on many occasions, and has never failed to measure up to the demands and even exceeded the expectations of the recipients. It is gratifying, too, to be able to say that even our former enemies have been partakers of the hospitalities of the town, at our private residences and in our public halls, and have found language too poor to properly express their gratification of the warm welcome and the generous hospitality they received while in our midst. This was the case with the Society of the Army of the Potomac in May, 1900.

It had been suggested by some of the prominent citizens of the town that it would be a gracious thing, and would testify our kind feeling towards the members of that organization, for the City Council to invite the Society of the Army of the Potomac to hold its thirty-first annual reunion, in 1900, in the city of Fredericksburg, as guests of the town. The society had never held a reunion on southern soil, and it was deemed appropriate that its first meeting should be here, where they could meet and mingle with Confederate veterans, where so many bloody battles were fought between the two great armies of the Civil war.

It had been intimated that members of the society, and even officials of the organization, had expressed a desire to hold a session in Fredericksburg, which would give many old soldiers an opportunity to visit again the historic grounds, over which they had fought, and view the country in times of peace. The City Council caught the spirit and approved the suggestion, and on the 27th of July, 1899, unanimously passed the following resolution:

"Resolved by the Common Council of the city of Fredericksburg, Virginia, That his honor, the Mayor, be and he is hereby, authorized and instructed to extend a cordial invitation to the Society of the Army of the Potomac to hold its annual meeting for the year 1900 in this city, and to urge the acceptance of this invitation by said society, assuring its members that they will meet with a cordial and fraternal welcome by our citizens generally, and that every effort will be made on our part to make their sojourn here pleasant and agreeable to them."

While the resolution did not authorize it, it was understood that the Mayor would attend the reunion in September of that year, either in person or by a representative, and urge the society to accept the invitation of the city authorities. Mayor Rowe, being unable to attend the meeting of the body, requested Judge James B. Sener to represent him, which he did, and presented the resolution of the Council in an eloquent and patriotic address, which was well received by the society. The result was Judge Sener was elected an honorary member of the society and the invitation was unanimously accepted.

Upon the information that its invitation had been accepted, and that May 25th and 26th, 1900, were the days fixed for holding the reunion, the Council appointed a reception committee of fifteen

—five of its own body and ten from the citizens, which was increased by the committee itself to twenty—to make all the necessary arrangements and see that the members of the society, and the visitors on that occasion, were properly received and entertained. Those appointed of the Council were Col. E. D. Cole, John T. Knight, Wm. E. Bradley, H. B. Lane, George W. Wroten. Those from the citizens were Capt. S. J. Quinn, Major T. E. Morris, St. Geo. R. Fitzhugh, H. F. Crismond, John M. Griffin, Isaac Hirsh, James A. Turner, H. H. Wallace, Thos. N. Brent and James P. Corbin.

The committee met and organized, with Col. E. D. Cole, chairman, and Capt. S. J. Quinn, secretary, and the following gentlemen were associated with the committee: Capt. M. B. Rowe, A. T. Embrey, Judge John T. Goolrick, Capt. T. McCracken and George W. Shepherd. The committee was then divided up into sub-committees and assigned to necessary and appropriate duties, which were well and faithfully discharged.

To assist at the banquet and lunch on the occasion, the committee requested the services of the following ladies, who responded cheerfully and did so nobly the parts assigned them that they merited, and received, the hearty thanks of the committee and visitors: Mrs. James P. Corbin, Miss Mary Harrison Fitzhugh, Mrs. Wm. L. Brannan, Miss Mary Shepherd, Mrs. Vivian M. Fleming, Mrs. H. Hoomes Johnston, Miss Lula Braxton, Mrs. L. L. Coghill, Mrs. E. Dorsey Cole, Miss Corson, Mrs. H. F. Crismond, Miss E. May Dickinson, Mrs. Wm. F. Ficklen, Miss Goodwin, Mrs. John T. Goolrick, Miss Alice Gordon, Miss Sallie Gravatt, Mrs. John M. Griffin, Miss Louise Hamilton, Miss Roberta Hart, Mrs. David Hirsh, Mrs. Henry Kaufman, Mrs. Harry B. Lane, Mrs. H. McD. Martin, Miss Annie Myer, Miss Eleanor McCracken, Miss Carrie Belle Quinn, Mrs. Wm. H. Richards, Miss Lena Rowe, Mrs. Edward J. Smith, Mrs. R. Lee Stoffregen, Miss Bertha Strasburger, Miss Sallie Lyle Tapscott, Mrs. W. Seymour White, Miss Nannie Gordon Willis and Mrs. Mary Quinn Hicks.

The presidential party was met at Quantico by a sub-committee consisting of Hon. H. F. Crismond, Hon. A. T. Embrey, Postmaster

John M. Griffin, Major T. E. Morris, James A. Turner and S. I. Baggett, Jr., and escorted to Fredericksburg.

At half past ten o'clock on the morning of the 25th of May, most of the members of the Society of the Army of the Potomac having arrived, the procession was formed at the courthouse, the society, under command of Gen. Horatio C. King, secretary, with the reception committee, Confederate veterans and citizens generally, headed by Bowering's band, proceeded to the depot to meet the presidential train. Col. E. D. Cole, chief marshal, with his aides, Capt. Dan. M. Lee, John T. Leavell, A. P. Rowe, Jr., and W. J. Jacobs, with a cordon of mounted police, had charge of the line.

At the depot an immense crowd of people had collected, and when the train arrived there was a vociferous greeting to the President and cabinet and Fighting (General) Joe Wheeler. The presidential party consisted of President McKinley, his private secretary, Cortelyou, Secretary Hay, Secretary Root, Attorney-General Griggs, Postmaster-General Smith, Secretary Long, Secretary Hitchcock—every member of the cabinet except Secretary Wilson—Gen. Nelson A. Miles, Commander-in-Chief of the Army, his aide, Col. Michler, Lieut. Robert S. Griffin, secretary to Secretary Long, Gen. Henry E. Tremain, Gen. W. J. Sewell, Gen. J. W. Hawley and Gen. Joseph Wheeler.

Headed by the celebrated Marine band, of Washington, sixty strong, the line of march from the depot was up Main street, to George, thence to Princess Ann and thence to the courthouse. All along the march the streets were thronged with citizens and visitors, and the waving of handkerchiefs and cheering kept the President constantly bowing to the right and left.

When the courthouse was reached the presidential party filed in, followed by the Society of the Army of the Potomac, visitors and citizens. The courthouse was densely packed and hundreds were turned away, being unable to get even standing room.

CHAPTER XVIII

Society of the Army of the Potomac Enters Town, continued.

When this great crowd entered the courthouse, after making such a long march in hot weather, most of them were willing to rest awhile before the exercises commenced. Yet Gen. King is not one to rest long when business had to be attended to, so he called the large assembly to order, and announced that illness had prevented the attendance of Gen. D. McM. Gregg, president of the society, and in his absence Gen. Martin T. McMahon would preside in his stead. Dr. J. S. Dill, pastor of the Baptist church, was presented and offered a most earnest prayer. Mr. St. Geo. R. Fitzhugh, who had been selected by the committee of entertainment to extend the welcome, was then introduced and made the following address:

MR. FITZHUGH'S ADDRESS.

Mr. Chairman: It is with feelings of profound pride and unfeigned pleasure that our entire community extends a cordial and hearty welcome to the illustrious Chief Magistrate of our country, who honors us with his presence to-day. We recognize in our President the pure patriot and the stainless statesman, whose wise and courageous administration, in both war and peace, has endeared him to the hearts of his countrymen and has shed new lustre upon the exalted office which he fills.

Our people also welcome with much pride and warmth his eminent official family, and the brilliant commander of our invincible army, and all these distinguished men before me, who are guests of the Society of the Army of the Potomac and of our city.

And now, our friends of the Society of the Army of the Potomac, I find it difficult to command adequate words with which to express to you the supreme gratification and enthusiasm of our people at your prompt acceptance of their invitation to hold your annual reunion in this old town and at your presence here to-day in such numbers.

We not only welcome you with open arms and glowing hearts,

but we feel that this action on your part rises to the dignity of an impressive epoch in our national life; and we are not surprised that our illustrious President, and all these distinguished men, should desire to grace this inspiring occasion with their presence.

It is the first time that your society has held one of its annual reunions on southern soil, and, in making this new departure, it was preëminently fit that you should honor Fredericksburg with your choice.

A French philosopher has written, "Happy the people whose annals are tiresome," but the far nobler and more inspiring thought of the Anglo-Saxon race is that "character constitutes the true strength of nations and historic glory their best inheritance."

As American citizens you are proud of the grand traditions and heroic memories that crowd your country's history; and nowhere else on this continent could your feet tread on ground more hallowed by historic memories than here.

I think before you leave us you will acknowledge that if the immortal names and deeds that this locality suggests should be stricken from the annals of time, most of the present school books of our country would be valueless and our national history itself would be as the play of Hamlet, with Hamlet left out.

The school boys and girls of our whole country are familiar with the story of Capt. John Smith and Pocahontas, and history records that right here Captain John Smith battled with and repulsed the Indians. So we may fairly claim, without the exercise of poetic license, that the struggle of the Anglo-Saxon race, to establish its civilization and supremacy on this continent, commenced on this spot in 1608, just one year after Jamestown was settled.

If we should draw a circle around this ancient city, with a radius of less than fifty miles, we should find within that narrow compass the birthplace of George Washington, of Thomas Jefferson, of James Madison, of James Monroe, of Zachary Taylor, of Chief-Justice John Marshall, of the Lees of the Revolution, of Patrick Henry, of Henry Clay, of Matthew Maury and of Robert E. Lee. If we should extend the circle but a very, very little, it would also embrace the birthplace of William Henry Harrison, of John Tyler,

A Tombstone in St. George's Churchyard, remarkable for its date.
(See page 246)

Confederate Monument in Confederate Cemetery.
(See page 189)

of Winfield Scott, and likewise the birthplace of this Republic at Yorktown.

Is there any other similar segment of space on the habitable globe so resplendent with stars of the first magnitude!

Seven Presidents of the United States and three of the greatest military leaders of modern times were born within two hours' ride of this city, estimated according to the most improved modern methods of travel!

That meteoric Mars of naval warfare, John Paul Jones, lived and kept store in this town, and went from here to take command of a ship of our colonial navy. He was the first man who ever raised our flag upon a national ship, and he struck terror to the heart of the British navy by his marvellous naval exploits during the Revolution.

It was right here that Washington's boyhood and youth were spent, and that he was trained and disciplined for his transcendent career, and it was to the unpretending home of his mother, still standing here—which you will visit—that Washington and Lafayette came when the war closed, to lay their laurels at her feet; and her ashes repose here, under a beautiful monument, erected by the Daughters of the American Revolution.

But there are other memories of heroic type, suggested by this locality, which come nearer home to our hearts, whose mournful splendor time cannot pale!

Here, and within fifteen miles of this city, in Spotsylvania county, more great armies manœuvred, more great battles were fought, more men were engaged in mortal combat and more officers and privates were killed and wounded than in any similar territory in the world. More men fell in the battles of this one small county during the Civil war than Great Britain has lost in all her wars of a century; and more men were killed and wounded in four hours at the battle of Fredericksburg than Great Britain had lost in killed, wounded and prisoners in her eight months' war in South Africa.

When the fog lifted its curtain from the bleak plains about Fredericksburg on the morning of December 13, 1862, the sun flashed down on a spectacle of terrible moral sublimity!

One hundred thousand Union veterans, with two hundred and twenty cannon, were in "battle's magnificently stern array," and in motion, with nothing to obscure their serried ranks from the view of their expectant adversaries, safely entrenched on the sloping hills adjacent. The different sub-divisions of this great army were commanded that day by consummate masters of the art of war, whose names and brilliant exploits now illumine the pages of our national history, but its commander-in-chief was deficient in both strategic and tactical ability, and his most conspicuous merit seemed to be his perfect faith in the courage and invincibility of his army.

General Burnside did not overrate the magnificent courage and sublime self-sacrifice of his army, whose contempt of death that day on the open plains about Fredericksburg seemed to strike the electric chain wherewith we all are bound, and a thrill of admiration swept down the line of Lee's army for four miles whilst yet the battle raged; but General Burnside did underrate the strength of the positions which, without inspection or information, he rashly assailed, and he did underrate the valor of the men who held those positions. The appalling magnitude of his mistake was soon apparent, alike to his officers and his men, and yet column after column of that devoted army advanced, without a halting step, to the carnival of death, over a plain swept by the ceaseless and terrible fire of protected infantry and artillery—a plain of which General E. P. Alexander, in command of the Confederate artillery, posted on the heights, remarked the evening before, that "not a chicken could live there when his guns were opened."

No honors awaited the daring of these heroes that day; no despatch could give their names to the plaudits of their admiring countrymen, their advance was uncheered by the hope of emolument or fame; their death would be unnoticed, and yet they marched to their doom with unblanched cheeks and unfaltering tread.

Pause a moment and picture those serried ranks as they marched undismayed with grim precision and intrepid step to certain death, and, very many, to unknown graves, and tell me whether heroism did not have its holocaust, and patriotism and courage their grand coronation on these plains about Fredericksburg; and tell me whether a nation's gratitude and meed of honor to these unknelled, uncoffined and unknown heroes, who thus gave up their lives for their country, in obedience to orders, should be measured by the accident of victory or defeat, or by the unclouded grandeur of the sacrifice they cheerfully made. Tell me whether the majestic memorial, which that splendid old veteran, General Butterfield, proposes to erect on the plains of Fredericksburg, to perpetuate the fame of the Fifth corps, will not commemorate a higher type of heroism than any similar memorial to that corps on the heights about Gettysburg! Tell me whether there was not more courage and more manhood required to assail Marye's Heights than to hold Cemetery Hill!

The charge of Pickett's Division at Gettysburg was far grander, even with its dreadful recoil, than was the defence of the stone wall at Fredericksburg; and the heroes of the former deserve more of their country than do the latter.

Napoleon, after the battle of Austerlitz, addressing his army, said: "Soldiers, it will be enough for one of you to say, 'I was at the battle of Austerlitz,' for your countrymen to say, 'There is a brave man.'"

Impartial history will record that the Union soldiers who fought at Fredericksburg, Chancellorsville, the Wilderness and at Spotsylvania Courthouse were not only brave men, but that their valor on those immortal fields decorated the Stars and Stripes with imperishable glory. And no American army of the future, composed of those who wore the blue and the gray, or their descendants, will ever permit that glory to be tarnished!

It was the brilliant prowess of the Confederate army on the battlefields of Spotsylvania that shed such dazzling lustre on the Union arms at Gettysburg. If we should blot out the battlefields of Spotsylvania, we should rob Gettysburg of all its glory; we should filch from General Grant half his fame as a great commander, and should obscure to the future student of the art of war Grant's invincible pertinacity and his sagacious and successful policy of concentration and attrition, which alone explains and vindicates his famous march of eighty miles from Culpeper Courthouse to Petersburg, with a loss of tens of thousands of his brave troops, when he might have transferred his army by transports to the shadow of the Confederate capital without the loss of a man.

Grant knew that the destruction of Lee's army, and not the capture of Richmond, was the profoundest strategy. The Army of the Potomac, under the consummate leadership of General Grant, won infinitely more prestige at Appomattox, where eight thousand worn-out Confederates laid down their arms, than the German army, under its great field-marshal, Von Moltke, won at Sedan, where the French Emperor, Louis Napoleon, and 86,000 French soldiers, neither footsore nor hungry, surrendered, and for the plain reason that no such conflicts as those in Spotsylvania lay across the march of Von Moltke to Sedan. The march to Appomattox was over the battlefields of Spotsylvania, and Appomattox was only the culmination of the courage and carnage of those fields.

It was the conspicuous characteristic of both the Union and Confederate armies that their courage was alike invincible; defeat could not quench it; it shone with additional splendor amid the gloom of disaster, and no soldier on either side need blush to have borne a part in any one of the great battles of the Civil war, whatever fortune may have decreed as to its temporary result.

It is noteworthy, above almost any other events of history, that the two most memorable and momentous struggles in which the Anglo-Saxon race has embarked, both closed on the soil of Virginia, a century apart, by the surrender of one Anglo-Saxon army to an army of the same race, and without the loss of prestige on either side.

For our great race, when vanquished by itself, proudly rears its crest unconquered and sublime!

One of those memorable struggles closed at Yorktown, where colonial dependence perished, national independence was secured and our great republic born. The other closed at Appomattox, where the doctrine of secession and the institution of slavery perished and a more perfect union than our fathers made was established.

Secession and slavery perished on Virginia soil, and her people, though impoverished by the loss of the latter, have shed no tears over the grave of these dead issues; but they love and cherish the memory of the Southern heroes whose sacred ashes repose in her bosom, and they proudly spurn any suggestion that such moral heroism and sublime self-sacrifice as they exhibited could be born of other than conscientious conviction!

If the South was, by a wise providence, denied in that grand struggle the honor of final triumph, her people to-day share equally with the victors of that day the glorious fruits of their victory in a more perfect and indissoluble union of indestructible States, under that superlative symbol of a world-power—the glorious Stars and Stripes.

All through this splendid address Mr. Fitzhugh was vociferously applauded, the President and his cabinet heartily and enthusiastically joining in the applause, and when he closed the demonstration was kept up for several minutes.

Gov. Tyler was then introduced and welcomed the veterans to Virginia, and assured them that when their visit to Fredericksburg was ended, Richmond, the Capital of the Confederacy, awaited them with extended hands and outstretched arms. Gen. McMahon responded in a short address, full of harmony and good feeling, and introduced Gen. Daniel E. Sickles, the orator of the occasion.

At the conclusion of the able and patriotic address of Gen. Sickles, the presidential party and Gen. Sickles, lunched at Mr. Fitzhugh's and the society and visitors were provided for at the Opera House. After lunch the visitors and citizens marched to Mr. Fitzhugh's residence, where the President held a reception and where several thousand people greeted and shook him by the hand.

The procession then formed and marched to the National cemetery, to witness the laying of the corner-stone of the monument to be erected by Gen. Daniel Butterfield to the memory of the men of the Fifth Army Corps, who fell in the several battles in Fredericksburg and vicinity.

The Masonic ceremonies were in charge of Lodge No. 4, A. F. and A. M. In accepting the invitation to preside on the interesting occasion, Gen. Horatio C. King said:

I deeply appreciate the honor of being asked to preside on this most interesting occasion, and in presence of the honored Chief Magistrate and the members of his official family. I recall with pride the fact that I first saw the light of Masonry in the Blue Lodge at Winchester, in this magnificent State, in 1864, when I was a soldier in the great war, and that from that day to this I have continued in good standing in our noble order. It may not be amiss for me to add that he who honors and graces this occasion to-day by his presence, our President, was also initiated at or about the same time in the same lodge, and that he has also held fast to the tenets of the organization through his lodge at his home in Ohio.

It is most fitting that this dedication should be made by this time-honored Fredericksburg Lodge, whose history antedates the Revolution and in whose precincts the Father of his Country was enrolled.

The occasion is one to inspire every patriot, and the generosity of Gen. Butterfield, in raising this memorial to the fallen comrades whom he so gallantly commanded, will shine through ages to come on the pages of American history.

MASONIC CEREMONIES.

The ceremonies were then conducted by the Masonic Lodge, the following officers, members and visitors being present and taking part:

Alvin T. Embrey, senior warden, acting worshipful master; Right Worshipful James P. Corbin, senior warden *pro tem;* Wm. H. Hurkamp, junior warden; Edgar M. Young, Jr., treasurer; Right Worshipful Silvanus J. Quinn, secretary; Maurice Hirsh, senior deacon; Allan Randolph Howard, junior deacon; Rev. James Polk Stump, chaplain, and John S. Taliaferro, tiler; Worshipful Brothers Albert B. Botts, James T. Lowery, Thomas N. Brent, Isaac Hirsh.

Members: Joe M. Goldsmith, John Scott Berry, John R. Bernard, John C. Melville, Robert A. Johnson, O. L. Harris, James Roach, George A. Walker, A. Mason Garner, Wm. T. Dix, Wm.

Bernard, H. Hoomes Johnston, Charles L. Kalmbach, Edgar Mersereau, Adolph Loewenson, George W. Wroten, Joseph H. Davis, J. Shirver Woods, Edwin J. Cartright and Maurice B. Rowe.

Visiting Masons: Most Worshipful J. Howard Wayt, P. G. M, Staunton, Va.; Wm. D. Carter, 102, Va.; W. J. Ford, 163, Ky.; W. C. Stump, 5, D. C.; B. P. Owens, 14, Va., and Dr. J. W. Bovee, of B. B. French, D. C.

The handsome silver trowel used in laying the corner-stone, was made by order of Gen. Butterfield for that occasion and then to be presented to the Masonic Lodge performing the service. After the service of laying the corner-stone, Gen. Edward Hill, who spoke for Gen. Butterfield, in an able address, presented the monument to the Secretary of War to be kept, cared for and preserved by him and his successors in office, to which Secretary Root responded in a brief and appropriate speech, accepting the monument and promising to preserve it as requested.

CAMP FIRE AT OPERA HOUSE.

At 8 o'clock in the evening a "camp fire" was held at the Opera House, which was crowded to its utmost capacity. Short addresses were made by Gen. McMahon, Gen. Hawley, Gen. Miles, Gen. Sewell, Gen. Tremain, Gen. Geo. D. Ruggles, Capt. Patrick, Gen. Sickles, and a letter was read from Gen. Shaw, all of whom were on the Union side. The Confederate veterans were represented by Gen. Joseph Wheeler and Private John T. Goolrick.

When Gen. Wheeler was introduced, Gen. Hawley, who had already spoken, interrupted with "Just a moment. Something occurs to me. Among the extraordinary things that are happening in the world, this is especially interesting to me. I find, on looking over the records, that Moses Wheeler, more than 250 years ago, married the sister of Joseph Hawley in Connecticut. Now, General, go on."

This produced great laughter, in which Gen. Hawley joined with much zest.

JUDGE GOOLRICK'S ADDRESS.

Judge Goolrick, who was introduced as the representative of the Confederate veterans, and especially the private soldier, of whom there are so few at this time, spoke as follows:

COMRADES, LADIES AND GENTLEMEN—With sincere sentiments of good will, commingled with a sense of gratitude, I welcome you within the gates of our city, and no man has a better right to bid you come than myself—for, just after the surrender at Appomattox, I was sitting on the roadside, weary and worn, foot-sore and hungry, with an intense solicitude for a change of my bill of fare from parched corn, upon which I had luxuriated for about three days, when a kind-hearted private soldier of the Army of the Potomac, seeing my dejected and depressed appearance, came to me with words of cheer, comfort and kindness, and, putting his hand down into his not overstocked haversack, gave me all his rations of hardtack and bacon, and immediately the gloom of defeat ceased to be so oppressive, and the intense hunger, under which I had labored, also ceased. This act of good fellowship, under the conditions which confronted me, at once inspired a fraternal feeling for my enemy. So you see, Mr. Chairman, I have a real right to be glad to see here to-day the representatives of that army of which my benefactor was a member, and bid you be of good cheer while you pitch your tents once again on the old camp ground.

You are now on a spot which is consecrated in the hearts of the soldiers from the North and the South. Within the sound of my voice Meagher's Irish Brigade immortalized itself by a charge into the jaws of death, a charge in which the Irishman expressed his loyalty to the land of his adoption, and gave evidence of that inborn bravery which has made his name illustrious all over the world.

Within this county—at Chancellorsville—the soldiers of the South conquered in a battle where death pulsated the very air, which was won by unparalleled bravery and matchless strategy, though it cost the life of the southland's idolized Stonewall Jackson, the very genius of the war. Here the two master military

St. Mary's Catholic Church.
(See page 214)

Shiloh Baptist Church, Old Site (colored.)
(See page 215)

leaders met for the first time at the Wilderness, where was commenced the march by parallel columns, which culminated in the surrender of the Army of Northern Virginia, by our grand old commander, Lee, to the great and magnanimous Grant.

On these fields Americanism, in its highest and holiest sense, was illustrated and illuminated. Here a colossal column of men marched to death, testifying thereby the very highest expression of patriotism—love of country. For greater love hath no man that this, that he lay down his life for his friends. It is to this spot you have come—a place which is, and should be, the mecca of all lovers of patriotism, self-sacrifice and lofty devotion to duty. And these have not been lost, and will not be, for as the blood of the martyrs was the seed and the seal of the church, so the blood and the bravery of the soldiers of the North and the South have already cemented this Republic in a closer union.

There has been a good deal said here, sir, to-day about peace. He who fought ceased warfare when the war ended. 'Tis true it was waged with great energy by warriors. After Lee told his boys to go home, and Grant said, "Let us have peace," these warriors, after the war, were like that chaplain in Early's army, who was seen going to the rear, while the battle was raging in front. Early met him and asked him where he was going. "To the rear—to the hospital department," said he. "Why not stay in the front?" said old Jubal, "for I have heard you urging my men for the last six months to prepare to go to heaven, and now you have an opportunity to go to heaven yourself, and you are dodging to the rear." These men who want war and talk war now had the opportunity to take part, but most of them did not feel so inclined when the battle raged fast and furious.

I suppose, sir, however, I was called to talk to-night because I am rather an unique and curious living specimen of a soldier, for I was a private, and there are few now living. It is said just before the surrender a poor old soldier laid down to sleep, and he slept *a la* Rip Van Winkle, for twenty years. Awaking up he rubbed his eyes; looking around, he called a man walking on the road-side to him. "Where," said the soldier, "is old Marse Bob

Lee and his army?" "General Lee," replied the man; why, he has been dead many years; he surrendered his army and then died." "Ah!" said the private; "ah, then where are all the generals?" "They," replied the man, "have been sent to Congress." "And what has become of the colonels?" "Why, they have been elected to the Legislature." "What about the majors, captains and lieutenants?" "They have been made sheriffs and clerks and treasurers." "Where, then, tell me, where in the world have the privates gone?" "The privates!" answered the man; "why, they are all dead." And the old soldier rolled his eyes back and fell asleep again. If he were to awake again to-day his eyes would be gladdened and his heart made happy by monuments erected in Virginia's capital city, and elsewhere, to emphasize the love and reverence with which the memory of the brave private soldiers are held by a grateful people.

Sir, far be it from me to hold in slight estimation or little esteem, the illustrious commanders. I am proud of the grand and glorious leadership of my great captains, Lee and Jackson, and I willingly pay a tribute to the greatness of Grant and to the memory of Hancock, "the superb," and the splendid Meade. I would not, if I could, attempt to dim the lustre of their names or throw any shadow over the brightness of their deeds.

I was an humble private soldier in the Confederate army, and I am proud here to proclaim that I was a follower of the peerless and illustrious Lee, but I stand here to pay my loving tribute to the private soldier of both armies. His splendid achievements, grand heroism, unfaltering loyalty and unflinching bravery, have no parallel in all time. He knew that if in the forefront of the fight he were shot down that then his name would not be written on the scroll of fame, his uncoffined body would find sepulture in a nameless grave, and that he would have for an epitaph, "unknown!" Only a private shot; and thus the story of his daring and dying would be told.

But, knowing all this, he failed not nor faltered. He was inspired by the very holiest and highest, because of an absolutely unselfish sense of duty. He was moved by a purpose to serve his country and its cause. He marched, battled and bivouacked because his determination to do, dare and die, if needs be, for the flag under which he served. Whether under the sultry sun of summer or amidst the sleet and snow of winter, he stood, unmoved from his unalterable resolve. No grander, no more beautiful, no more splendid expression of the very highest type of manhood could be found than was found in the life of the private soldier of both or either army; and when the war ended, with them verily it ended, and they all joined hands in a fraternity of comradeship which was well exhibited by that private soldier of your army who ministered to my necessities and cheered me in my sadness as I sat under the very shadow of defeat and amidst the gloom of surrender at Appomattox.

And members of the Society of the Army of the Potomac, to which that private belonged, and to which we of the Army of Northern Virginia surrendered, I meet and greet you on your first reunion south of the river whose name you bear. We of the South will ever cherish, ever pay the homage of our hearts' best devotion to the memory of our great cause and its champions, we will ever keep them hallowed and sacred, but with us the war is over. We pay allegiance and bear full fealty to this great Republic of ours, and the men and the sons of the men who followed Lee and Jackson stand ready with you to defend, always and everywhere, the honor, the integrity and the interest of this fair land of ours against all foes, whether from within or without its borders.

We worship at the same shrine of liberty. There is only one flag now. It is our flag and yours. Under its shadow we stand with the men of your army. And now, to-night, at this reunion, in this presence, let me urge, as the shibboleth, the motto of both armies, to be our inspiration in peace, our rallying cry, if needs be, in war, this: "Whom God hath joined together let no party, no people and no power put asunder."

Judge Goolrick was heartily applauded during the delivery of his address, and at its close the cheering was loud and prolonged.

There was no business session of the society the next day and very many of the Union veterans visited the various battlefields.

The most of the society and visitors went to Richmond on an excursion tendered the society by Lee Camp, where they were met and entertained by the Confederate veterans of that hospitable city.

Addresses were made on that occasion by Judge D. C. Richardson, Mayor Richard M. Taylor, Gov. Chas. T. O'Ferrall and Attorney-General A. J. Montague, of Richmond, and Gen. Horatio C. King, of New York, and Gen. Geo. D. Ruggles, of Washington.

On the return of the excursionists from Richmond a reception and lunch were tendered them at the Opera House, where they were met by a large number of the ladies and gentlemen of the town, and a most enjoyable evening was spent. Gen. King, secretary of the society, in a brief address, acknowledged the cordial welcome and unbounded hospitality they had met with in our town and the homes of our citizens, extended the hearty thanks of the society to the officials and citizens and stated that the reception was even warmer and more cordial than they had ever before met with.

RESOLUTIONS OF THANKS ADOPTED.

At the business meeting of the society on the first evening the following preamble and resolution, after very complimentary remarks of the town and people, by many of the visitors, were enthusiastically adopted:

The reunion of the Society of the Army of the Potomac at Fredericksburg is of peculiar significance, and the generous sentiment which prompted the invitation, meets with a hearty response from every patriotic soldier of that great army. Every animosity engendered by the conflict is here buried with the more than one hundred and twenty thousand gallant men who shed their blood and sacrificed their lives in their heroic devotion to conviction and to duty. The work done here is an imperishable record of the unsurpassed courage and bravery of the American soldier: therefore be it—

Resolved, That we tender to the civic authorities and citizens of Fredericksburg, and especially to the efficient local executive committee and Mr. St. Geo. R. Fitzhugh, our most hearty thanks for a welcome that sustains, in the highest, the fame of Virginia hospitality. The generous and unstinted courtesies of all will render this reunion forever memorable, and the most pleasurable emotion will always arise whenever the name of Fredericksburg is mentioned.

As a fitting sequel of this distinguished gathering and the grand reception on the part of the town and citizens, a letter, written by Gen. Horatio C. King, twenty-five years secretary of the society, en route to his home, in Brooklyn, N. Y., is inserted:

Captain S. J. Quinn, Secretary Army of the Potomac Committee:

MY DEAR CAPTAIN—The generous efforts of your citizens to kill us with kindness were well nigh successful, but happily we survive to tell the tale of the most unique and unsurpassed reunion in the history of the Society of the Army of the Potomac.

Our first meeting on the soil of the South cannot fail to have a most happy effect upon the comparatively few—mainly born since the great conflict—who do not realize that the war ended in 1865.

The sentiments expressed by your orators, Mr. Fitzhugh, your honored Governor Tyler and Judge Goolrick, and by Mayor Taylor, ex-Governor O'Ferrall and Attorney-General Montague, in Richmond, should be printed in letters of gold and circulated all over the nation. Purer or more exalted patriotism has never been expressed.

To the thanks already extended I desire to add my personal obligations for the untiring energy, zeal and efficiency of your local committee, which have made my duties comparatively light and most enjoyable; and I desire to make my acknowledgments especially to you and Brother Corbin for the promptness of your correspondence and unremitting attention.

I am afraid I but feebly conveyed to the audience last evening the warm appreciation of the superabundant and delightful lunch so gracefully provided by your people and so charmingly distributed by your ladies.

Indeed, I cannot find words to express our gratitude for a reception so complete as not to have elicited a single complaint or criticism. We can never forget it or the good people who carried the reunion to unqualified success.

ASSASSINATION OF PRESIDENT M'KINLEY.

Visiting Fredericksburg in May, to attend the meeting of the Society of the Army of the Potomac, and take part in laying the corner-stone of the Butterfield monument, where he received the most marked demonstrations of the love and loyalty of his people, without regard to party politics, President McKinley returned to our beautiful capital with a grateful heart and a determination to show himself President of the entire country, dispensing justice to all alike. He was proud of his country and rejoiced in its unparalleled prosperity. In September, 1901, he visited the exposition at Buffalo, N. Y., where, while holding a reception on the 6th of September, he was assassinated in the midst of the thousands who surrounded him. The sad news was flashed by wire throughout our land and the civilized world, and was received everywhere with unaffected sorrow.

Our City Council was assembled upon the sorrowful intelligence, and the following preamble and resolutions were adopted, and telegraphed Mrs. McKinley, which were the first adopted and received by her from any quarter:

"Whereas, we have heard, with great sorrow and indignation, of an attempt to assassinate his excellency, Wm. McKinley, President of the United States, at Buffalo, N. Y., this afternoon; and, whereas, we rejoice to learn by the latest telegram that his physicians express the firm belief he will survive the wounds inflicted, therefore—

Resolved, by the Mayor and Common Council of the city of Fredericksburg, Virginia, that we condemn, in the strongest language we can command, this dastardly and wicked act, and call upon the authorities to punish the would-be assassin to the full extent of the law.

2nd, That we tender our profoundest sympathy to Mrs. McKinley in her great affliction and earnestly pray that a kind and all-wise Heavenly Father may restore her devoted husband and our much loved Chief Magistrate to perfect health, to her and this united and happy country.

3rd, That our worthy Mayor be requested to communicate by wire this action of the Council to Mrs. McKinley."

Notwithstanding the best medical skill was employed to remain with the stricken President day and night, who endeavored to locate and extract the pistol ball, and the prayers of the nation, he calmly passed away on the 14th of September, eight days after the assassin's deadly work. The monster murderer was an anarchist from Ohio, who was condemned before the courts for his wicked act and paid the extreme penalty of the law.

As the news of the President's death was sent to the world with electric speed, and announced in Fredericksburg, the City Council was immediately assembled again and the following action taken:

"The Mayor and Common Council of the city of Fredericksburg desire to unite with all the world in paying tribute to the memory of President McKinley, as a patriot American, a pure citizen, a fearless Executive and a Christian gentleman.

It is with pride and pleasure that we recall his recent visit to our city and his expressions of gratification at being with us, and this tribute to his memory is to testify and further emphasize our sincere sorrow at his death. It is therefore—

Resolved, That the public buildings of this city be draped in mourning for thirty days; that during the hour of the funeral service that the bells of the city be tolled, and that a committee of three members of the Council be appointed by the Mayor to confer with the ministers of our churches in order to arrange a memorial meeting of our citizens, and that these resolutions be spread upon the records of this council.

Resolved, That a copy of these resolutions, with our expressions of sympathy in this hour of her great bereavement, be forwarded to Mrs. McKinley, widow of our distinguished President, signed by the Mayor, and attested by the clerk, under the seal of this city.

This action of the Council was one of the few that Mrs. McKinley personally responded to. To it she promptly replied, evincing her grateful appreciation, with the tenderest expressions, for the sympathy tendered to her in her great sorrow. The memorial services were held in St. George's church, the day of the funeral, conducted by the city pastors, Dr. T. S. Dunaway, delivering the address.

CHAPTER XIX.

Dr. Walker's Exploration—Bacon's Rebellion, so-called—The Fredericksburg Declaration—The Great Orator—Resolutions of Separation from Great Britain—Virginia Bill of Rights, &c.

It has been said, probably by the facetious or perhaps by the envious—for such are to be found in all communities—that Virginians are noted for their bragging—that find them where you may, at home surrounded by friends and companions, or abroad among strangers and aliens—bragging is their distinguishing characteristic. It is not probably known whether this charge has ever been investigated and passed upon by any competent authority, but if it has been, and the charge was pronounced true—or if the truth of the charge were admitted by the parties themselves, they can plead justification, and should be readily excused upon the ground that they really have something to boast of in the patriotism, endurance, sacrifices and achievements of a glorious ancestry. If the people of other parts of the country have whereof to boast, Virginians have more, and those in that part of Virginia in which Fredericksburg is located may well take the lead.

In this and the two succeeding chapters we propose to show what has been accomplished for this great country by the sons of Virginia, who have lived in Fredericksburg and within a radius of sixty or seventy-five miles of Fredericksburg, and show that in the extension of the borders of our infantile country, in protecting the settlers from the ravages of the brutal savages, in agitating, fostering and demanding the rights of the people, in opposing and resisting the unjust laws and oppressions, usurpations and unreasonable exactions of sordid and wicked rulers, in the separation, by solemn resolutions and declarations of this country from Great Britain, in uniting and defending the colonies and in achieving the independence of the country, in forming and administering the government, in numbering it with the family of the nations of the earth, and placing it upon the high road to prosperity and national greatness, Virginians were ever in the van, and others followed their

The present Postoffice Building at Fredericksburg.
(See page 165)

Tombstone marking grave of William Paul, brother of Commodore
John Paul Jones, in St. George's burial ground.
(See page 237)

leadership and reaped the rich fruits of their splendid achievements and their glorious victories. And this we do, not in any spirit of vanity, but that there may be grouped together and brought to public attention, in permanent form, historical facts, if known to the public, long forgotten and unappreciated, that Fredericksburg may be placed, where it rightly belongs, as the most historical spot in the most historical State in this great nation, that will soon, if it does not now, dominate the nations of the earth and fully justify her sons in recounting their deeds, if it shall be termed bragging.

DR. WALKER'S EXPLORATION.

It was Dr. Thomas Walker, of Albemarle county, a Virginian, who, with five companions, in 1750, explored the wild country, which now forms the States of Tennessee and Kentucky, and named that chain of mountains and the beautiful river that flows through the valley, Cumberland, in honor of the Duke of Cumberland, and then crossed over the country to the head waters of the Kentucky river and gave it its name, which furnished a name for that great and prosperous State.

BACON RESISTS OPPRESSION.

It was Nathaniel Bacon, of Henrico county, a Virginian, who first offered resistance to the colonial authorities in defence of the lives, liberties and property of the people and put forth a declaration of principles, which were the guiding star for those who came after him until independence was achieved, with all of its blessings and glorious fruits.

In his United States History Dr. Howison says: "In the great declaration adopted by them in 1776, just one hundred years after the movements under Bacon, we find embedded not less than five principles among the most weighty and potent that justified the overthrow of the English rule, all five of which were in active movement to produce the uprising of the Virginia people in 1676. These five principles were:

1. The right to civil and religious liberty—'life, liberty and the pursuit of happiness';

2. The right to throw off a government which had 'cut off their trade from all parts of the world';

3. Which had 'imposed taxes on them without their consent';

4. Which had 'taken away their charters, abolished their most valuable laws and altered fundamentally the powers of their government';

5. Which had 'excited domestic insurrections among them and had endeavored to bring on the inhabitants of their frontiers the merciless Indian savages, whose known rule of warfare is an undistinguished destruction of all ages, sexes and conditions.' "

Mrs. An. Cotton, who wrote an account of this Bacon movement the year it occurred, and who did not fully endorse all that Bacon did, states that a large council was held on Bacon's premises in May, at which Bacon charged that the authorities were guilty of wrong in their eagerness to get rich; that some persons were rich who were guilty of unjust methods in obtaining their wealth; that the authorities were doing nothing to encourage the arts, sciences, schools of learning or manufactories; that the Governor approves the lawlessness of the Indians against the settlers, and declines to interfere because it might diminish his revenue in trading with them; that the Governor refuses to admit an Englishman's oath against an Indian, where he accepts the bare word of an Indian against an Englishman; that the Governor is monopolizing the beaver trade in violation of law; that the traders at the heads of the rivers, being the Governor's agents, buy and sell the blood of their brethren and countrymen by furnishing the Indians with powder, shot and firearms contrary to the laws of the colony; and that Col. Cowells asserted that the English were bound to protect the Indians, even if they had to shed their own blood.

At the conclusion of Bacon's address the Council agreed to three things: 1. To aid with their lives and estates General Bacon in the Indian war. 2. To oppose the Governor's designs, if he had any, against the prosecution of the war. 3. To protect the General, the army and all who agreed to the arrangement against any power that should be sent out of England, until it was granted that the country's complaint might be heard against the Governor before the King and Parliament.

The premature death of Bacon occurring, and no competent person to take the lead being found, the movement soon ceased, the troops disbanded and went home, and many of those who aided Bacon in protecting the lives and property of the settlers were put to death by Governor Berkley on the charge of treason. Thomas Matthews, said to be a son of Gov. Matthews, and who at that time represented Stafford county in the House of Burgesses, was appointed by Bacon to the command of all the forces in this part of Virginia, but he probably had not the courage or means to carry out Bacon's plans.

Bacon died from a cold contracted in camp and was buried in Gloucester county, but for fear the authorities would exhume the body and subject it to indignities, the place of his burial was kept a secret. Bacon's effort for the people was just one hundred years before the great revolution, and when we are fully informed as to his cause of action we may debate in our minds as to whether Nathaniel Bacon was our first Thomas Jefferson or whether Thomas Jefferson was our second Nathaniel Bacon.

FIRST DECLARATION OF INDEPENDENCE.

It was in a public gathering in Fredericksburg on the 29th day of April, 1775, that resolutions were passed, approaching in spirit a declaration of independence, which was twenty-one days before the resolutions of Mecklenburg, North Carolina, were adopted. The resolutions, adopted in North Carolina, found their way into print and into the histories, while those passed in Fredericksburg did not; but they were the first adopted anywhere in the country, and more than six hundred men were ready to carry them into effect by marching to Williamsburg to redress wrongs which had been committed by Gov. Dunmore in removing the gun powder from the public magazine. Some regard this act as the beginning of the great revolution in the colonies. It was to prepare the people for any breach of the law or outrage upon the people's rights, which had been threatened by the authorities at Williamsburg, and commenced in the gunpowder act, that the Fredericksburg resolutions were adopted, and the great pity is they were not handed down to succeeding generations and preserved as the first Declaration of Independence since the days of Bacon. In referring to these resolutions, Dr. Howison, in his United States History, says, they were tantamount to a declaration of independence.

HENRY LEADS FOR LIBERTY.

It was Patrick Henry, of Hanover county, a Virginian, at the time living in and representing Louisa county, who fired the country with his matchless eloquence and set in motion forces that achieved liberty and independence to this country. It was this peerless son of Virginia, in the House of Burgesses, surrounded by such giant minds as Bland, Pendleton, Lee and Wythe, that the torch of liberty was set on fire that was never to be extinguished. We quote from Dr. Howison's United States History:

"He wrote on the blank leaf of an old law-book five resolutions which he offered to the House. They were a strong protest against the course of Parliament. The third declared that taxation by the people themselves, or their representatives duly chosen, was an essential characteristic of British freedom. The last resolution was in these words:

" 'Resolved, therefore, that the General Assembly of this colony have the sole right and power to lay taxes and impositions upon the inhabitants of this colony; and that every attempt to vest such power in any person or persons whatsoever, other than the General Assembly aforesaid, has a manifest tendency to destroy British as well as American freedom.'

"A warm debate ensued. Pendleton, Bland, Wythe and Randolph all opposed the resolutions; but Henry was the master mind, and made an impression which is felt to this day. His words were pregnant with a nation's freedom. In the heat of the debate occurred a memorable scene. Patrick Henry reached a climax. 'Cæsar,' he cried, 'had his Brutus; Charles the First, his Cromwell, and George the Third'—'Treason'! burst from the lips of the president. 'Treason,' 'Treason!' resounded through the house. The orator paused; then, raising himself to his full height, with eyes of fire and a voice which thrilled every soul, he concluded his sentence, 'and George the Third may profit by their example. If this be treason make the most of it.'

"The resolutions were adopted by one vote, and that evening Patrick Henry left for his home. In March, 1775, the Virginia Convention met in St. John's church, Richmond. It was a body of the most distinguished men in Virginia, and among them was Patrick Henry. He was still far in advance of the leading men of the convention, who, although there were English fleets in the waters of Virginia and armed soldiers quartered within her towns, still hoped that the evils complained of could be remedied by compromise.

"Henry did not think so, and he was unwilling to sit down quietly until it would be too late to prepare for defense. He submitted a set of resolutions, calling attention to the presence of British armies and the dangers then threatening American freedom, and proposed that Virginia should be put in a state of defense, and that measures should at once be taken for embodying, arming and disciplining such a number of men as may be sufficient for that purpose."

The proposition was strongly opposed by such men as Bland, Nicholas, Pendleton and Harrison. Dr. Howison says: "It was now that Patrick Henry appeared in power. Rising slowly from his seat, he made an appeal which in eloquence and strength, and in its effect upon the future of the world, went far beyond any effort of oratory ever previously made. It was the demonstration that the coming war was to be a war of ideas and principles, and not a mere war of brute force." No perfect production of this speech has been preserved—perhaps none were possible; yet enough has been preserved to enable the thoughtful student to feel something of its inspiration:

"Let us not, I beseech you, sir, deceive ourselves. We have done everything that could be done to avert the storm which is now coming on. We have petitioned—we have remonstrated—we have supplicated—we have prostrated ourselves before the throne and have implored its interposition to arrest the tyrannical hands of the Ministry and Parliament. Our petitions have been slighted; our remonstrances have produced additional violence and insult; our supplications have been disregarded, and we have been spurned with contempt from the foot of the throne. In vain, after these things, may we indulge the fond hope of peace and reconciliation. There is no longer any room for hope. If we wish to be free—if we mean to preserve inviolate those inestimable privileges for which we have been so long contending—if we mean not basely to abandon the noble struggle in which we have been so long engaged, and which we have pledged ourselves never to abandon until the object of our contest shall be obtained—we must fight! I repeat it, sir, we must fight! An appeal to arms and to the God of hosts is all that is left us.

"There is a just God who presides over the destinies of nations, and who will raise up friends to fight our battles for us. The battle, sir, is not to the strong alone; it is to the vigilant, the active, the brave. Besides, sir, we have no election. If we were base enough to desire it, it is now too late to retire from the contest. There is no retreat but in submission and slavery. Our chains are forged; their clanking may be heard on the plains of Boston. The war is inevitable, and let it come. I repeat it, sir, let it come!

"Gentlemen may cry, Peace! peace! but there is no peace. The war has already begun. The next gale that sweeps from the North will bring to our ears the clash of resounding arms. Our brethren are already in the field. Why stand we here idle? What is it that gentlemen wish? What would they have? Is life so dear or peace so sweet as to be purchased at the price of chains and slavery? Forbid it, Almighty God! I know not what course others may take; but as for me, give me liberty or give me death!"

A dead silence followed this speech. The feelings it excited were too deep for applause; but there was no longer any hesitation or division of opinion. The proposal of Henry was adopted, and, in a short time, Virginia was alive with military preparation.

There are two prophesies in this eloquent speech which were fulfilled; one was that the clash of resounding arms would be heard by the next gale from the North—the battle of Lexington was fought on the 19th of April; and the other was that God would raise up friends to fight our battles for us. Our independence could hardly have been secured without the aid of the French, whom Lafayette led, and who were the friends that were raised up for us by a kind Providence.

PENDLETON'S RESOLUTIONS.

It was Edmund Pendleton, of Sparta, in Caroline county, a Virginian, who prepared, and Cary presented, resolutions defining the position of the colonies and instructing the Virginia delegation to the General Congress to vote for a declaration of separation from Great Britain. These resolutions were heartily indorsed by the troops that had assembled at Williamsburg, and even by those leading Virginians who so strongly condemned Patrick Henry's first great speech.

It was Richard Henry Lee, of Westmoreland county, a Virginian, who offered, in the Colonial Congress, the resolution that embodied the views expressed in the Pendleton resolutions, and which brought forth the Declaration of Independence. The resolution was submitted on the 7th of June, 1776, which was as follows:

"That these United Colonies are, and of right ought to be, free and independent States; that they are absolved from all allegiance to the British Crown; and that all political connection between them and the State of Great Britain is, and ought to be, totally dissolved."

The discussion of this resolution showed the temper of Congress, and while the vote was postponed at the instance of some members who still thought such a measure premature, a committee to prepare and bring forward a declaration was appointed, of which Thomas Jefferson was made chairman. Mr. Lee, a member of the committee, was called home because of the sickness of his wife, but Mr. Jefferson sent him the original copy of the draft and also the amendments for his inspection, and wrote him: "You will judge whether it is the better or worse for the critics."

GEORGE MASON'S BILL OF RIGHTS.

It was George Mason, of Gunston Hall, a native of Stafford county, a Virginian, who wrote the Virginia Bill of Rights and the Constitution of Virginia. The fact that Mason was a farmer, and not a lawyer, has been emphasized by several writers, and the fact that he prepared those important documents, when there were so many eminent lawyers associated with him in those stirring times, is a matter of surprise. But that he did write them has never been disputed or questioned, and it was an honor that linked his name with those of Jefferson and Madison, and will enshrine his memory in the hearts of his countrymen for all time to come. And the honor of preparing this important instrument is enhanced when we remember they were almost original in thought as to most of the principles declared in them. It is true that some have claimed that the Bill of Rights was based upon the English Bill of Rights of 1689, yet that bill only asserted the right of subjects to petition, the right of Parliament to freedom of debate, the right of electors to choose their representatives freely, and other minor privileges. These rights had been exercised by the Colonists, but there were other rights dear to the people which they had not enjoyed and were not permitted to enjoy, and there were grievous wrongs committed upon the people that had to cease.

These things called for a different kind of paper from the English Bill of Rights and the times necessitated different demands than were made calling forth the bill of 1689. A paper was needed setting forth the rights of freemen and providing for the government of freemen, and it is asserted that the Bill of Rights was a pattern for the Declaration of Independence, while the Constitution was the first one that was written for the government of a free and independent people in all the past history of the world.

The Bill of Rights was adopted by the Virginia Convention on the 12th of June, 1776, after it had been thoroughly discussed for several days. It was written for Virginia and did not apply to

Public School Building (colored.)
(See page 144)

The Butterfield Monument. "In honor of the Fifth Army Corps, and also to the valor of every American Soldier."
Gen. Butterfield.
(See page 269)

the other colonies, yet it is so complete in all its parts we are told that other State constitutions, in defining the rights of the citizen, largely followed the phraseology of this famous instrument. All Virginians should read it, again and again, study it and treasure it as one of the most precious legacies bequeathed to them. The following is the bill in full:

1. That all men are by nature equally free and independent and have certain inherent rights of which when they enter into a state of society, they cannot, by any compact, deprive or divest their posterity; namely, the enjoyment of life and liberty, with the means of acquiring and possessing property, and pursuing and obtaining happiness and safety.

2. That all power is vested in, and consequently derived from, the people; that magistrates are their trustees and servants, and at all times amenable to them.

3. That government is, or ought to be, instituted for the common benefit, protection and security of the people, nation or community; of all the various modes and forms of government, that is best, which is capable of producing the greatest degree of happiness and safety, and is most effectually secured against the danger of maladministration; and that, when any government shall be found inadequate or contrary to these purposes, a majority of the community hath an indubitable, unalienable and indefeasible right, to reform, alter or abolish it, in such manner as shall be judged most conducive to the public weal.

4. That no man, or set of men, are entitled to exclusive or separate emoluments or privileges from the community, but in consideration of public services; which, not being descendible, neither ought the offices of magistrate, legislator or judge be hereditary.

5. That the legislative, executive and judicial powers should be separate and distinct; and that the members thereof may be restrained from oppression, by feeling and participating in the burdens of the people, they should, at fixed periods, be reduced to a private station, return into that body from whence they were originally taken, and the vacancies be supplied by frequent, certain

and regular elections, in which all, or any part of the former members, to be again eligible, or ineligible as the laws shall direct.

6. That all elections ought to be free; and that all men having sufficient evidence of permanent common interest with, and attachment to, the community have the right of suffrage and cannot be taxed or deprived of their property for public uses, without their own consent or that of their representatives so elected, nor bound by any law to which they have not, in like manner, assented for the public good.

7. That all power of suspending laws, or the execution of laws, by any authority, without the consent of the representatives of the people, is injurious to their rights, and ought not to be exercised.

8. That in all capital or criminal prosecutions, a man hath the right to demand the cause and nature of his accusation, to be confronted with the accusers and witnesses, to call for evidence in his favor and to a speedy trial by an impartial jury of twelve men of his vicinage, without whose unanimous consent he cannot be found guilty; nor can he be compelled to give evidence against himself; that no man be deprived of his liberty, except by the law of the land or the judgment of his peers.

9. That excessive bail ought not to be required, nor excessive fines imposed, nor cruel and unusual punishments inflicted.

10. The general warrants, whereby an officer or messenger may be commanded to search suspected places without evidence of a fact committed, or to seize any person not named, or whose offence is not particularly described and supported by evidence, are grievous and oppressive, and ought not to be granted.

11. That in controversies respecting property, and in suits between man and man, the ancient trial by jury of twelve men is preferable to any other, and ought to be held sacred.

12. That the freedom of the press is one of the great bulwarks of liberty, and can never be restrained but by despotic governments.

13. That a well regulated militia, composed of the body of the people, trained to arms, is the proper, natural and safe defence of a free people; that standing armies, in times of peace, should be avoided, as dangerous to liberty; and that in all cases, the military

should be under strict subordination to, and governed by, the civil power.

14. That the people have a right to uniform government; and therefore that no government separate from, or independent of, the government of Virginia, ought to be erected or established within the limits thereof.

15. That no free government, or the blessings of liberty, can be preserved to any people, but by a firm adherence to justice, moderation, temperance, frugality and virtue, and by a frequent recurrence to fundamental principles.

16. That religion, or the duty which we owe to our Creator, and the manner of discharging it, can be directed only by reason and conviction, not by force or violence; and therefore all men are equally entitled to the free exercise of religion, according to the dictates of conscience; and that it is the mutual duty of all to practise Christian forbearance, love and charity towards each other.

CHAPTER XX

The Declaration of Separation—The Declaration of Independence —Washington Commander-in-Chief—John Paul Jones Raises the First Flag—He was First to Raise the Stars and Stripes— Fredericksburg Furnishes the Head of the Armies and Navy —The Constitution of the United States, &c.

As stated in the last chapter, we continue in this references to the great deeds of the great men of Virginia that should be grouped, as we are here endeavoring to do, in the smallest possible space, and preserved to perpetuate their memory and honor their descendants through all coming time. It was Thomas Jefferson, of Albemarle county, a Virginian, who wrote the Declaration of Independence, that struck the shackles of servitude from the people of this country, and proclaimed the United Colonies a new-born nation, free and independent.

JEFFERSON AND THE DECLARATION.

A lineal descendant of Thomas Jefferson, three generations removed, Judge John E. Mason, thus writes on these subjects, for this publication:

"Some years before the Revolutionary war, the colony of Virginia had become restless under British dominion. There had been, here and there, open expressions of discontent, and a growing resentment, if not positive hostility, against the mother country. In fact, nowhere more than in Virginia, and especially in this section, had the spirit of independence more steadily grown; and when the time came for decision and concert of action by the colonies, public opinion here was ripe to break down the old barriers, and to resist, with force, the power of England.

"Among those who had taken a most active part in moulding public sentiment was Thomas Jefferson, who, because of his extreme views in antagonizing every element of English ideas, and its government as based upon an aristocracy, has sometimes been called the 'Great Commoner.' Whether he, more than others, who were upon the stage of action at that time, is entitled to the name, those who know his history must be the judge; but certain it is, he was in advance of many of his contemporaries in developing antagonism to ancient ideas and ancient customs, which were the pride of the British people.

"On the 6th of May, 1776, the delegates from the counties and cities of the Colony of Virginia, met in convention at its capitol in Williamsburg, Edmund Pendleton presiding. During this convention certain resolutions were reported from committee by Archibald Cary, which were unanimously adopted by the one hundred and twelve members present. The first of these resolutions—said to have been proposed by Thomas Nelson, and drawn as reported by Edmund Pendleton, but no doubt the work of both—after reciting certain grievances against the mother country, declared that the 'delegates appointed to represent the colony in the General Congress, be instructed to propose to that respectable body to declare the United Colonies free and independent States, absolved from all allegiance to or dependence upon the Crown or Parliament of Great Britain.'

"In Congress, on the 7th day of June, 1776, the gifted Richard Henry Lee, from this section, in obedience to instructions, offered the same resolution, which had been adopted by the Virginia Convention—that Congress should 'declare that the United Colonies are, and of right ought to be, free and independent States.' This resolution was the precursor of the formal declaration. It was offered by a Virginian, acting under instructions given by Virginians, and its answer was the Declaration of Independence.

"The debate began on this resolution on the 8th of June, but on the 10th, it having developed that five colonies north of the Potomac were not ready to vote, the final decision was then postponed until the first day of July. In the meantime a committee had been elected to draft a Declaration of Independence. Mr. Lee, the mover of the above resolution, was unexpectedly called home by the illness of his wife, and was not on the committee. The committee was not appointed by the presiding officer, but was elected by ballot.

by Congress, and Jefferson, having received the highest number of votes cast, was its chairman. Its work was completed by the 28th of June. The Declaration of Independence was, on that date, reported to the House by Jefferson, and was then read and ordered to lie on the table. The Virginia resolution was carried in the affirmative, in the Committee of the Whole July 1st. On the 2nd day the Declaration of Independence was taken up and debated each day until the fourth, when it was adopted. It will be observed that the Declaration was completed before Congress had adopted the Virginia resolution.

"The committee, elected to draft the Declaration of Independence, consisted of Thomas Jefferson, John Adams, Benjamin Franklin, Roger Sherman and Robert R. Livingston. Mr. Jefferson drew the Declaration of Independence at the request of the other members of the committee. Had another been its author, we believe the Declaration would have been different in tone, while, of course, the leading principles would have been the same. Many members were conservative, while Jefferson was radical. They had in view chiefly independence and freedom; Jefferson had the same opinions, but even then contemplated a complete revolution in the existing conditions—for anything which, in the slightest degree, partook of the nature of the government of Great Britain, her customs or traditions, was odious to him. He wished an irrevocable change, so that the new would supersede the old beyond recall.

"When, in framing that great document, he wrote these words: 'We hold these truths to be self-evident; that all men are created equal; that they are endowed by their Creator with certain inalienable rights,' * * * it doubtless did not require a prophet to tell what his future course would be, or the principles, considered radical then, for which he would stand, or the wonderful influence, 'these truths' would have in forming constitutions and shaping legislation, State and national, provided the British were beaten on the field of battle.

"It is worthy of note that the Declaration of Independence, as it came from his hands, suffered little change, except in two instances.

He inserted in the original draft what might be called an emancipation proclamation—a clause condemning as piratical warfare against human nature itself, the enslaving of Africans—the slave trade being then sanctioned by North and South—the former being carriers and the latter principally buyers—a business which Virginia would, years before, have prohibited had she not been met, in every effort, by royal vetoes. The other change was made by striking out some animadversions upon the English people. This was done by those who yet hoped for reconciliation, or something, they knew not what, which might avert the desperate struggle.

"To those who believe in freedom of thought and action; in the sovereignty of the people; in the equality of all men before the law, based upon constitutional rights, restrictions and limitations, made by the wisdom of the greatest men this world has ever produced; in opening the door to promotion to all men whose talents, integrity and general high characters entitle them to such honors, the Declaration of Independence must forever commend itself; and it seems to the writer that upon the strict adherence to the principles, therein enunciated, rests the very life of the government of the United States.

"There are many other great things which came from the brain of Jefferson besides the Declaration of Independence, though the Declaration may have been the basis of all. The principles of the Declaration having been once established, these followed as a natural sequence. In a limited space only a few can be simply noted. After he retired from Congress, in 1776, to become a member of the Virginia Legislature, he presented, in the session of that year, a bill for the revisal of the laws of the State, which was soon passed, and Jefferson, Pendleton, Wythe, George Mason and Thomas L. Lee were appointed a committee for revision.

"This committee of distinguished men met in Fredericksburg on the 13th day of February, 1777. Here various propositions were submitted and discussed—Mason, Wythe and Jefferson almost always agreeing and voting together, and Pendleton, of all, being the most unwilling to depart from the old conditions, except, to the astonishment of the committee, he proposed a new system, that all common law and equity jurisprudence, which had received the sanction of ages, should be abrogated—a new institute, after the model of Justinian or Bracton, should be reported, thus giving us what is called, in this day, a code law, which would have been set afloat, without a precedent to guide it, and to construe which, would have taken our courts from that time to this.

"After this committee had agreed on measures and propositions, and the general outline of the system to be pursued, Mason and Lee, having given the other members the benefit of their advice, retired from further participation in its labors, because they were not lawyers, and left the work to be done by the other three members, who then divided it, and completed the arduous task in 1779.

"There were four measures proposed by Jefferson before the full committee, then sitting in Fredericksburg, which were his especial pride, and these were the repeal of the laws of entail, the abolition of primogeniture, the establishment of a system of public education, and the act for the establishment of religious freedom. These four bills, he himself afterwards said, he 'considered as forming a system by which every fibre would be eradicated of ancient, or future, aristocracy, and a foundation laid for a government truly republican.'

"To use his own language again, 'the repeal of the laws of entail would prevent the accumulation and perpetuation of wealth in select families and preserve the soil of the country from being more and more absorbed in mortmain.'

"Not only was the abolition of the laws of entail resisted by some of the best talent in Virginia, but when Jefferson proposed to abolish also the law of primogeniture—a relic of feudalism—there was strong opposition from the same sources—men who had risked fortunes and lives in the struggle for independence, but who were unwilling to join Jefferson in his attack upon institutions whose very age commanded veneration. One of the chief opponents of Jefferson was Edmund Pendleton, his friend, whose candor, great ability and benevolence in all these struggles won his admiration.

"It was Pendleton, who, when he found the old law could not prevail, suggested that the Hebrew principle be adopted, by which

The Old Planters' Hotel. The stone in front was used as a "stand" for slaves when hired or sold at public "outcry."
(See page 165)

The Opera House. It occupies the ground of the bank and other buildings burnt at the bombardment, December 11, 1862.
(See page 269)

the eldest son should inherit double the amount of real estate which would descend to the heirs of the ancestor. The reply of Jefferson was characteristic and terse—'I observed,' he says, 'that if the eldest son could eat twice as much and do double work, it might be a natural evidence of his right to a double portion; but being on a par, in his powers and wants, with his brothers and sisters, he should be on a par also in the partition of the patrimony.'

"The statute of descents in Virginia was drawn by him—a statute which has justice and 'natural right' in every line, and so clear and perspicuous is it, that in all these years only one serious question has been raised regarding it, calling for a decision of the Supreme Court of Appeals.

"Jefferson gave an impetus to public education which is felt at this time. He proposed to the General Assembly of Virginia three bills: the first, establishing elementary free schools for all children; the second, for colleges; and the third, for the highest grade of sciences. Only the first of these was passed by the Assembly, and before this was done it was so amended that it could not be operative unless the county courts so decided. Now, as the justices who presided over these courts, while among the most honorable and talented men in Virginia, were generally of a class who did not care to bear the taxes necessarily entailed upon them by the adoption of the system, no free schools were established in any county within the Commonwealth under this act, with possibly the exception of one county.

"It was a fact that our ancestors, especially when under the English system of government, did not favor education at public expense, and the royal Governors, as a rule, threw the weight of their influence against it. But after the Revolutionary war had closed, and the government of the States was made a government by the people, Virginians, like Jefferson, proceeded on the theory that to have a good government, the people—the sovereigns—must be educated, so that they would take, not only a deeper interest in the affairs of State, but would do so with intelligence—the more knowledge disseminated the better would be the government, and the less danger there would be of its falling into the hands of a favored and exclusive class.

"The principle of free education, however, so earnestly forced to the front by Jefferson, eventually bore fruit, though the ripening was slow. It was gradually adopted by the people of Virginia, until now a system, backed by a sound public sentiment, is established in every county and city in the State, and the doors of the colleges are open to those who have not been favored with fortune. It may be safely predicted that when the State shall have fully recovered from the wreck and havoc of the Civil war, that a complete and thorough system will be established, such as that which was first proposed by Jefferson, and the people of the State will rejoice to see it done.

"No more important measure was proposed to the committee which met in Fredericksburg, on the 13th of January, 1777, than that of Jefferson's for the establishment of religious freedom, just as it now appears, with slight modifications in the preamble, in the statute books to-day. The fact that this act was written in Fredericksburg, we have never heard questioned; and the people of this city have the same right to claim that this 'second declaration' had its birth here, that the people of Philadelphia have to claim that city as the birth-place of the first. It was, however, a long time before its advocates were able to secure its passage by the Legislature. Having been written in 1777, it did not become the law of the land until 1785.

"In making his fight for religious freedom, the courage, the persistence and the power of this statesman shone in all their splendor. We consider this as his most difficult task, but it is his crowning glory. He had arrayed against him the advocates of a long cherished policy, sustained by law; one around which tradition had woven a peculiar sanctity, and he who would lift his hand against it was deemed guilty of sacrilege. There, too, were the clergy, strong in resistance, backed, as they were, by a wealthy and powerful class, Jefferson himself belonging to a family whose members, though loyal in exacting faithful obedience to changes in existing conditions, loved this church and worshipped in its sacred, but State protected walls; yet, in spite of all of this, believing that freedom of conscience was one of the 'inalienable and natural rights,' with a boldness, which all must commend; with a persistence, which all must admire, he headed the forces which took the last citadels of monarchial institutions and leveled them to the ground, thus forever separating church and State and eliminating the combination of political policy and religion, so that henceforth no man could be 'compelled to frequent or support any religious worship, place or ministry, but all men shall be free to profess, and by argument maintain, their opinions in matters of religion, and the same shall in no wise diminish, enlarge or effect their civil capacity.'

"In justice to those who were adherents to the established church, it must be said that some supported Jefferson, and after the change came, none were more devoted in maintaining the statute, and all others of kindred import; many being in positions charged with their proper enforcement, gave them sound judicial interpretation in exact conformity to all theories of the newly formed government.

"This act for the establishment of religious freedom is not only a monument to him, as a liberator of men, but its elegant diction, its easy and smoothly flowing style, show his genius as a writer. It is worthy of note, its preamble contains over five hundred words, yet it is but one sentence; only finished in the body of the act itself, where the first period appears; and, although he says this preamble was somewhat mutilated by others, there is nothing doubtful or uncertain as to its meaning, purpose and scope.

"To do full justice to the subject in hand would require a volume, but we must content ourselves with what has been written to show in part the wonderful and rapid changes then made in old and settled conditions, and the powerful influence this section had in moulding a government based on 'natural rights and justice,' and in shaping its destinies."

WASHINGTON GAINS INDEPENDENCE.

It was George Washington, a native of Westmoreland county, raised in Fredericskburg, who led the American armies in the Revolutionary war and gained American independence. He was called the "Great and Good Washington." He was truly great. He was great in the eyes of Americans; he was great in the eyes of his opposing enemies; he was great in the eyes of the world. He was an uncrowned king, because he refused to be crowned. We cannot properly appreciate his greatness, because he was so great we have no one to compare him with.

It is said a famous scholar has written a long essay in which he argued that the "traditional Washington" must give place to the new Washington. Referring to this, Senator Lodge says: "This is true in one sense. A new idea of Washington comes up in the mind of each generation, as it learns the story of the father of this country; but in another sense, the idea of a new Washington is wrong. He cannot be discovered anew, because there never was but one Washington."

As to the esteem in which Washington is held all over the world, Senator Lodge says: "Even Englishmen, the most unsparing critics of us, have done homage to Washington from the time of Byron and Fox to the present day. France has always revered his name. In distant lands, people who have hardly heard of the United States know the name of Washington. Nothing could better show the regard of the world for this great giver of liberty to the people than the way in which contributions came from all nations to his monument in Washington. There are stones from Greece, fragments of the Parthenon. There are stones from Brazil, Turkey, Japan, Switzerland, Siam and India. In sending her tribute, China said: 'In devising plans, Washington was more decided than Ching Shing or Woo Kwang; in winning a country, he was braver than Tsau Tsau or Ling Po. Wielding his four-footed falchion, he extended the frontiers, and refused to accept the royal dignity. The sentiments of the three dynasties have reappeared in him. Can any man of ancient or modern times fail to pronounce Washington peerless?' These comparisons, which are so strange to our ears, and which sound stranger still when used in comparison with Washington, show that his name has reached further than we can comprehend."

Speaking of the Declaration of Independence, Maury says:

"From beginning to end it was the work of Virginia. A Virginia planter (Mason) conceived it; a Virginia lawyer (Jefferson) drafted it; and a Virginia soldier (Washington) defended it and made it a living reality."

FIRST FLAG RAISED BY JOHN PAUL JONES.

It was John Paul Jones, a Fredericksburg man, who raised the first flag over our infant navy, and the first to throw our National flag—the Stars and Stripes—to the breeze of heaven. The National Portrait Gallery, volume 1, giving a short sketch of Jones's life, says: "On the organization of the infant navy of the United States, in 1775, John Paul Jones received the appointment of first of the first lieutenants in the service, in which, in his station on the flag-ship Alfred, he claimed the honor of being the foremost on the approach of the Commander-in-Chief, Commodore Hopkins, to raise the new American flag. This was the old device of a rattle-snake coiled on a yellow ground, with the motto, *'Don't tread on me,'* which is yet partially retained in the seal of the war-office. * * * By the resolution of June 14, 1777, he was appointed to the Ranger, newly built at Portsmouth—a second instance of the kind—had the honor of hoisting for the first time the new flag of the Stars and Stripes."

HEADS OF THE ARMY AND NAVY.

It was Fredericksburg that gave to the country the head of the armies of the United States in the great war for independence, in the person of the peerless Washington, and also furnished the greatest naval commander of that war in the person of the dauntless John Paul Jones. In addition to Washington, the small town of Fredericksburg sent to the field during the great Revolution five other generals—Gen. Hugh Mercer, Gen. George Weedon, Gen. Wm. Woodford, Gen. Thomas Posey and Gen. Gustavus B. Wallace, besides many officers of the line of high rank.

MADISON THE FATHER OF THE CONSTITUTION.

It was James Madison, of Orange county, a Virginian, born a few miles below Fredericksburg, at Port Conway, in King George county, who gave that wonderful instrument, the Constitution of the United States, to the country, that has been described as the "grand palladium of our liberty, the golden chain of our union, the broad banner of freemen, a terror to tyrants and a shining light to patriots."

Hon. James D. Richardson, of Tennessee, in his great work of compiling the messages and papers of the Presidents, with short biographical sketches of each, after recounting the labors, works and achievements of Mr. Madison, says: "It was not for these things or any of them his fame is to endure. His act and policy in the framing of the marvellous instrument, the constitution of our country, his matchless advocacy of it with his voice and pen, and his adherence to its provisions at all times and in all exigencies, obtained for him the proudest title ever bestowed upon a man, the title of the 'Father of the Constitution.' It is for this 'act and policy' he will be remembered by posterity."

JUDGE WALLACE ON THE CONSTITUTION.

Hon. A. Wellington Wallace, at one time Judge of the Corporation Court of Fredericksburg, contributes for this work the following paper on the Constitution of the United States:

"No historical sketch of Fredericksburg and its locality would be complete without at least an epitome of the constitutional form of government of the United States; for within a radius of seventy-five miles from Fredericksburg were reared the leading men who inspired the Federal Constitution. There are few, if any, similar areas in magnitude that can furnish, in one epoch of time, such a splendid galaxy of names. George Washington, Richard Henry Lee, James Madison, Patrick Henry, John Blair, George Wythe, Edmund Randolph, and George Mason, the deputies appointed by Virginia to frame the Federal Constitution, were natives of this territory.

"The inspiration given to the men of the age when our constitution was framed, was a wonder to the world. No nation had ever attempted by a written paper to provide a fundamental basis for government to last for all time and to provide for every emergency which might arise. The British Constitution, which had been the maternal chart of government before the Revolution, was a collective name for the principles of public policy on which the government of the United Kingdom was based. It was not formulated in any document, but the gradual development of the political intelligence of the English people, resulting from concessions from the Crown, successive revolutions, numerous enactments of Parliament and from the established principles of the common law. But here in this new country, by young men, born in the territory around Fredericksburg, was inaugurated a departure from the traditions of our ancestors to govern by a written fundamental law, a nation, whose progress thereunder has been phenomenal and has been, and will ever be, a continuing cause of astonishment to the civilized world.

"As has been stated in this chapter, the Constitution of Virginia, of 1777, drawn by George Mason, was the first written constitution. Subsequently, the several colonies that revolted against Great Britain, entered into written articles of confederation for the common defense and for government in time of war, but when the independence of the United States had been recognized by Great Britain, these articles of confederation were found totally inadequate for the powers of government.

"The power of making war, peace and treaties, of levying money and regulating commerce and the corresponding judicial and executive authorities, were not fully and effectually vested in the Federal Union; so it became necessary that the freed colonies should either become weak, independent sovereignties, or should be bound together by stronger obligations, and, that for the general welfare, the separate sovereignties should surrender certain rights and powers to central control. With a view to this object, on the 21st day of January, 1786, a resolution passed the Legislature of Virginia for the appointment of five commissioners, any three of whom might act, to meet similar commissioners from other States of the Union; and, under this resolution, the commissioners appointed fixed the first meeting in September following as the time, and the city of Annapolis, Maryland, as the place of meeting.

"Edmund Randolph, James Madison and Saint George Tucker attended, representing Virginia, and, as a result of this conference a convention was called of all the States, to be held in Philadelphia, on the 25th day of May, 1787, and to that convention Virginia sent the deputies mentioned before in this paper, and, of these deputies, George Washington was chosen president of the assembled body. An extended account of the proceedings of that convention would be inappropriate in this brief narration. It is sufficient to state that the convention adjourned, having completed its work on the 17th day of September, following its meeting, and that while all the Virginia delegates assisted in the work of the convention, only three of the delegates, George Washington, James Madison and James Blair, signed the Constitution.

"The Constitution went into effect on the 4th day of March, 1789, although George Washington, the first President of the United States under it, was not inaugurated until the 13th day of April— eleven of the thirteen States having ratified it, the others, North Carolina and Rhode Island, not ratifying, the former until November 21, 1789, and the latter until May 29, 1790.

"The Constitution is a document comprised in seven original articles and fifteen amendments. Of the original articles the first deals with the legislative body, prescribing the mode of election to the House of Representatives and the Senate, the qualifications of members, the method by which bills shall be passed, and those subjects on which Congress shall be qualified to act. The second relates to the Executive Department, prescribing the method of election and qualifications and duties of the President. The third relates to the Judicial Department, providing for the Supreme Court and such other inferior courts as Congress may think necessary. The fourth deals with the relations of the Federal Government and the separate States, and provides for the admission of new States. The fifth relates to the power and method of amendments to the Constitution; the sixth to the National Supremacy, and the seventh to the establishment of the government upon the ratification of the Constitution by nine of the States.

"The amendments, according to one of the methods provided,

Shiloh Baptist Church, New Site (colored.)
(See page 215)

The Church of God and Disciples of the Lord Jesus Christ
(colored.)
(See page 216)

were proposed by Congress and ratified by the States. The first twelve were submitted under acts passed in 1789, 1790, 1793 and 1803, and the last three after the Civil war, under acts of 1865, 1868 and 1870. The most important of the amendments are the twelfth, which changed the method of electing the President and Vice-President to the existing method; the thirteenth, which abolishes slavery; the fourteenth, which disqualifies any one who has been engaged in rebellion against the government from holding office, unless his disqualification has been removed by Congress, and prevents the assumption and payment of any debt incurred in aid of rebellion; and the fifteenth, which prohibits the denial to any one the right to vote because of race, color or previous condition of servitude.

"This is an epitome of the Constitution of the United States, by virtue of which the government has been maintained to the present time; and the principles laid down therein were, to a very large extent, the suggestions of the men we have mentioned from the locality of Fredericksburg. The Republic based upon this Constitution was an experiment, but it has, for more than a century, withstood the most terrific shocks of the most troublous times. It has waged foreign wars successfully; wild party spirit has always been foiled in efforts to undermine it; the bloodiest internecine strife in the world's history, sustained on both sides by unsurpassed valor, has but cemented its strength and prosperity at home and its power and prestige abroad; from thirteen small, feeble colonies, it has become a great nation of nearly eighty millions of people, its domain not only spreading from ocean to ocean, but extending far over the seas, and the protecting ægis of the Constitution, and the laws passed thereunder, guarding every race from every clime.

"No more splendid apostrophe to the Constitution could be added than the tribute of Mr. Gladstone, of England, the ablest advocate of human rights the century just closed has produced, when he said, in substance, that it was the grandest and greatest compendium of principles that had ever emanated from the brain, or been written down by the pen, of man."

CHAPTER XXI

The First Proclamation for Public Thanksgiving—Pennsylvania Whiskey Rebellion—John Marshall and the Supreme Court—Religious Liberty—The Monroe Doctrine—Seven Presidents—Clarke Saves the Great Northwest—The Northwest Explored—Louisiana Purchase—Texas Acquired—Mexico Adds to Our Territory—The Oceans Measured, Sounded and Mapped—The Ladies' Memorial Association—The Mary Washington Monument, &c.

This chapter is taken up with a continuation and conclusion of the subjects of the last two chapters—that is, a brief reference to what has been accomplished for the country by the giant minds, and through the dangerous and daring exploits of the men who lived in Fredericksburg and within a radius of seventy-five miles of Fredericksburg; therefore no farther introduction to the chapter is necessary.

FIRST THANKSGIVING PROCLAMATION.

It was Richard Henry Lee, of Westmoreland county, a Virginian, styled the Cicero of America, who wrote the first proclamation for public thanksgiving in this country. Congress, with the government, had moved from Lancaster, in Pennsylvania, where it had gone for safety, to York, in the same State, then containing about 1,500 inhabitants. At that time the chief cities in the country were in the hands of the enemy, except Richmond and Savannah, and the American army—again defeated at Germantown—retreating before a victorious enemy. Congress had been in session for nine months in York in the years 1777 and 1778, and while there heard the news of the surrender of Burgoyne, adopted the Articles of Confederation, received the news from Benjamin Franklin at Paris of the decision of the French government to aid the Americans in their struggle for liberty, and issued the first national thanksgiving proclamation.

The President of Congress appointed Richard Henry Lee, of

Virginia, with Samuel Adams, of Massachusetts, and Gen. Roberdeau, of Pennsylvania, to draft the proclamation. It was written by Mr. Lee, and for its beauty and comprehensiveness, and being the first paper of the kind ever prepared and issued by authority in this country, it will, we are sure, be regarded with interest and veneration. It is as follows:

"For inasmuch as it is the indispensable duty of all men to adore the superintending providence of Almighty God, to acknowledge, with gratitude, their obligations for benefits received, and to implore such further blessings as they stand in need of; and it having pleased him, in his abundant mercy, not only to continue to us the many blessings of his common providence, but also to smile upon us in the prosecution of just and necessary war, for the defence and establishment of our rights and liberties; particularly that he has been pleased, in so great a measure, to prosper the means used for the support of our troops and to crown our arms with signal success.

"It is, therefore, recommended to the legislatures, or executives, powers of these United States, to set apart Thursday, the 18th of December next, for solemn thanksgiving and praise; that with one heart and one voice the people of this country may express their grateful reverence, and consecrate themselves to the service of their divine benefactor, and that together, with their sincere acknowledgments, they may join in a penitent confession of their manifold sins, whereby they had forfeited every favor, and their humble and earnest supplication may be that it may please God, through the merits of Jesus Christ, mercifully to forgive and blot them out of remembrance; that it may please him graciously to shower his blessings on the government of these States, respectively, and to prosper the public council of the whole United States; to inspire our commanders, both by land and sea, and all under them, with that wisdom and fortitude which may render them fit instruments, under the providence of Almighty God, to secure for these United States the greatest of all blessings—independence and peace; that it may please him to prosper the trade and manufactures of the people, and the labor of the husbandman, that our land may yield its increase; to protect schools and seminaries of learning, so necessary for cultivating the principles of true liberty, virtue and piety, under his nurturing hand, and to prosper the means of religion for the promotion and enlargement of the kingdom which consists of righteousness, peace and joy in the Holy Ghost.

"It is further recommended that all servile labor and such recreation as at other times innocent may be unbecoming the purpose of this appointment on so solemn an occasion."

This historic document was adopted by Congress on the 30th of October, 1777, and sent to the governors of the respective States on the 1st of November by the President of the Congress, Henry Lawrens, of South Carolina, who had just been elected to fill the vacancy caused by the resignation of John Hancock, of Massachusetts.

THE WHISKEY REBELLION.

It was Henry Lee, of Westmoreland county, a Virginian, known through the war for independence as "Light Horse Harry," who, in 1792, crushed out the Whiskey Rebellion in Pennsylvania and restored order to the four counties in rebellion. He was at the time Governor of Virginia, and was in command of 15,000 troops, raised by special requisition of President Washington from the States of Virginia, Pennsylvania, Maryland and New Jersey. It was this Henry Lee who delivered the funeral oration in Congress on Washington, in which he used those words which will last in history as long as the memory of Washington shall be revered, "He was first in war, first in peace and first in the hearts of his countrymen."

CHIEF JUSTICE MARSHALL AND SUPREME COURT.

It was John Marshall, of Fauquier county, a Virginian, who, by his great ability and firmness of character, brought the Supreme Court up from a tribunal of little importance and consequence to one of great dignity and to one equal in power and importance with the executive and legislative branches of the government. He did more—he established not only the fact that the Supreme Court was the proper tribunal to declare what was and what was not law, under the Constitution, but it was to set limits to the powers and prerogatives of the chief executive himself.

In an address on the Supreme Court by Justice Brown in 1896, he said: "The Constitution had been adopted by the vote of the thirteen States of the Union, but its construction was a work scarcely less important than its original creation. With a large liberty of choice, guided by no precedents, and generally unhampered by his colleagues upon the bench, the great Chief Justice (Marshall) determined what was law by what he thought it ought to be, evolved from his own experience of the defects of the Articles of Confederation and from an innate consciousness of what the country required, a theory of construction which time has vindicated and the popular sentiment of succeeding generations has approved. In the case of Marbury against Madison, which arose at his very first term, he declared the judicial power to extend to the annulment of an act of Congress in conflict with the Constitution, a doctrine peculiar to this country, but so commending itself to the common sense of justice as to have been incorporated in the jurisprudence of every State in the Union. The lack of this check upon the action of the Legislature has wrecked the constitution of many a foreign State, and it is safe to say that our own would not have long survived a contrary decision. Had Marshall rendered no other service to the country, this of itself would have been sufficient to entitle him to its gratitude." And Judge A. W. Wallace, writing of Justice Marshall, said: "By his canons of construction he fortified the foundations of the Constitution and builded thereon the jurispudence of the United States—whose opinions, nearly a century old, stand, like a great sea-wall, breasting every billow of political frenzy that has threatened to engulf the safety, permanence and perpetuity of our institutions."

RELIGIOUS LIBERTY.

It was Thomas Jefferson, of Albemarle county, a Virginian, who wrote the act of the General Assembly of Virginia, passed on the 26th day of December, 1785, establishing religious liberty in Virginia, which has been adopted, or a law of similar import, by every State in the United States, and made a part of the Constitution of the United States, by the first amendment made to that instrument.

It is one of the grandest achievements of Mr. Jefferson, and stamps him as a patriot who could and did rise superior to his environments and surroundings, and even his predilections and life-long attachments, and secure to the people, by a law which he expressed the hope would never be repealed, their rights in matters of conscience as to religion and the worship of their God. It has permeated this whole country, and its influence is felt more or less throughout Christendom, and as a little leaven will leaven the whole lump, so its influence is still at work and time only can tell what it shall accomplish.

The act was written in Fredericksburg, and, omitting the long preamble, which is written in Mr. Jefferson's best and most vigorous style, is as follows: "That no man shall be compelled to frequent or support any religious worship, place or ministry whatsoever, nor shall be inforced, restrained, molested or burthened, in his body or goods, nor shall otherwise suffer on account of his religious opinions or belief; but that all men shall be free to profess, and by argument to maintain, their opinions in matters of religion, and that the same shall in no wise diminish, enlarge or affect their civil capacities."

THE MONROE DOCTRINE.

It was James Monroe, a native of Westmoreland county, but for years a citizen of Fredericksburg, a Virginian, who announced the American principle, known as the "Monroe Doctrine" that declared that no foreign power should acquire territory on this continent, which has been the guiding principle of the United States government since its enunciation, and which has been the safeguard to all the governments of this hemisphere.

The Monroe doctrine and the causes that called it forth, are succinctly stated in volume 10 of the "Messages and Papers of the Presidents," and are as follows: "After the overthrow of Napoleon, France, Russia, Prussia and Austria formed the so-called Holy Alliance in September, 1815, for the suppression of revolutions within each other's dominions and for perpetuating peace. The Spanish colonies in America having revolted, it was rumored that this alliance contemplated their subjugation, although the United States had acknowledged their independence. George Canning, English Secretary of State, proposed that England and America unite to oppose such intervention. On consultation with Jefferson, Madison, John Quincy Adams and Calhoun, Monroe, in his annual message to Congress in 1823, embodied the conclusions of these deliberations in what has since been known as the Monroe Doctrine. Referring to the threatened intervention of the powers, the message declares: 'We owe it, therefore, to candor and to the amicable relations existing between the United States and those powers to declare that we should consider any attempt on their part to extend their system to any portion of this hemisphere as dangerous to our peace and safety. With the existing colonies or dependencies of any European power we have not interfered and shall not interfere. But with the governments who have declared their independence and maintained it, and whose independence we have, on great consideration and on just principles, acknowledged, we could not view any interposition for the purpose of oppressing them, or controlling in any other manner their destiny, by any European power in any other light than as the manifestation of an unfriendly disposition toward the United States.' "

ESTABLISHED THE YOUNG REPUBLIC.

And furthermore: Not only did Fredericksburg and vicinity furnish the leader of the American armies to victory and independence, and the leading spirit in the navy; not only did they furnish the author of the Declaration of Independence and the Father of the Constitution, but they furnished the Presidents of the United States for thirty-two years of the most trying and difficult part of the history of the Republic,—it being the formative period of an experiment,—except the four years of John Adams's administration, during which but little, if any, progress was made. Washington was the first President, serving eight years; Jefferson succeeding Adams, who served eight years; then Madison eight years, followed by James Monroe for eight years, thus making the thirty-two years. Besides these four Presidents, Virginia furnished three others, who lived or were born within the circle of seventy-five miles of Fredericksburg, namely, Wm. Henry Harrison, John Tyler and Zachary Taylor. It is rather remarkable that both Harrison and Tyler should have been born in Charles City county, Virginia, elected on the same ticket, Harrison, who had moved to Ohio, as President, and Tyler as Vice-President, the death of the former just one month after his inauguration, elevating Tyler to the Presidency. President Taylor was born in Orange county.

THE GREAT NORTHWEST RECLAIMED.

It was George Rodgers Clarke,* of Albemarle county, a Virginian and a Fredericksburg man, by the authority of Virginia's Governor, Patrick Henry, with volunteers from Virginia and Kentucky, explored and conquered the great Northwest Territory. This territory belonged to Virginia under original grant in her charter, but the British at this time held it, established strong posts there and encouraged the Indians to make war on the white settlements. The Continental Congress could spare no troops to reclaim this territory, though appealed to by Virginia to do so. For this dangerous task Geo. R. Clarke proffered his services, which were accepted by the Governor. Enlisting volunteers, he marched into that region, and by real ability, rare skill, heroic courage and patience in bearing every hardship and privation, captured Forts Kaskaskia and Vincennes and other posts, and floated the flag of Virginia over the whole of the Northwest Territory, it being designated Illinois county, Virginia.

This campaign cleared that entire country of the British, and secured to Virginia a clear title to that vast territory, out of which the States of Ohio, Illinois, Indiana, Wisconsin, Michigan and a part of Minnesota were afterwards carved, and which Virginia gave to the Union as a free-will offering, the most imperial gift that State or nation ever laid on the altar of country.†

---

* A son of Jonathan Clarke, who lived at Newmarket, in Spotsylvania county, and afterwards moved to Fredericksburg. For many years he was clerk of the county court of Spotsylvania. George Rodgers Clarke is said to have been born while his father lived at Newmarket.—A letter from a descendant.

Jones's U. S. History.

R., F. & P. Railroad Company's Iron Bridge over the Rappahannock River.
(See page 328)

Senator Daniel W. Voorhees, of Indiana, in his defence of Cook, at Charlestown, now West Virginia, in 1859, one of the John Brown raiders, said in his opening remarks:

"The very soil on which I live, in my western home, was once owned by this venerable Commonwealth, as much as the soil on which I now stand. Her laws there once prevailed, and all her institutions were there established as they are here. Not only my own State of Indiana, but also four other great States in the Northwest, stand as enduring and lofty monuments of Virginia's magnanimity and princely liberality. Her donation to the general government made them sovereign States; and since God gave the fruitful land of Canaan to Moses and Israel, such a gift of present or future empire has never been made to any people."

THE WEST EXPLORED.

It was Meriwether Lewis, of Albemarle, and Wm. Clarke,* of Fredericksburg, both Virginians, who explored that great stretch of country from the Mississippi river to the Pacific ocean, and made it less difficult for John C. Fremont, who afterwards explored the same territory and received the proud appellation of the "Great Path Finder," which appellation rightly belonged to Lewis and Clarke.

THE LOUISIANA PURCHASE.

It was Thomas Jefferson, of Albemarle county, a Virginian, who, while President of the United States, made the "Louisiana Purchase," which brought to the possession of the United States more than one million square miles of territory. This immense territory belonged to the French government. It embraced the present States of Louisiana, Arkansas, Missouri, Nebraska, Iowa, Indian Territory, North and South Dakota, Montana, and parts of Kansas, Minnesota, Wyoming and Colorado. The price paid was $11,250,000 in money and the assumption by the government of debts due our citizens by France, amounting to $3,750,000, making in all $15,000,000.

---

* Capt. Wm. Clarke was a Fredericksburg man. He was a son of Jonathan Clarke, of Fredericksburg, who was clerk of Spotsylvania county court. He was, therefore, a brother of General Geo. Rodgers Clarke, who conquered the great northwest territory.—A letter from a descendant of Wm. Clarke. See also Maury's History of Virginia, page 158.

The purchase of this vast territory was bitterly opposed,—as all acquisitions of territory by the United States have been—especially in New England, where they threatened to secede from the Union, if it was consummated, and the legislation of Massachusetts passed and sent to the President and Speaker of the House a resolution to the effect that they would consider the adding of the Louisiana territory, to the domain of the United States, just cause for exercising their right of secession.*

THE FLORIDA PURCHASE.

It was James Monroe, of Fredericksburg, a Virginian, who purchased Florida from the Spanish government for $5,000,000, a land of "Fruits and Flowers," and a favorite health resort for winter tourists from all parts of the country. Its Spanish name Pascua Florida, translated, means Flowery Easter, which indicates that in Florida the flower season is perpetual.

ACQUISITION OF TEXAS.

It was Sam Houston, of Rockbridge county, a Virginian, who wrested the great State of Texas from Mexico and afterwards ceded it to the United States, John Tyler, of Charles City county, a Virginian, signing the bills for its admission three days before his presidential term ended. By this acquisition the government added to its possessions territory sufficient, it is said, to furnish comfortable homes for the present population of the United States, which would then be less crowded than many of the States of Europe.

THE MEXICAN WAR.

It was Gen. Winfield Scott, of Dinwiddie county, a Virginian, and Gen. Zachary Taylor (Rough and Ready), of Orange county, also a Virginian, who subdued Mexico, by which there were added to the territory of the United States the great States of California, Arizona and New Mexico.

And thus it will be seen, that all of the territory acquired by the United States Government, from the union of the colonies for the

---

* Jones's U. S. History.

common defence to the purchase of Alaska, except the Gadsden purchase, was secured through Virginians, who were born and raised, and many of them at the time lived, in or near Fredericksburg.

COMMODORE F. M. MAURY.

It was Matthew Fontaine Maury, of Spotsylvania county, and later a resident of Fredericksburg, a Virginian, who marked out the tracks of speed and safety for mariners of every clime over the ocean's bosom, and showed the beds on the bottom of the seas, where the cable lines now safely lie, of whom all the officers of the maritime nations came to learn, on whom kings and emperors bestowed orders, medals and decorations, and of whom the great Humboldt said he had created a new science.*

The following paper, on this great man's life, character and achievements, to whom the world is so greatly indebted, was prepared by Rev. J. S. Dill, D. D., then a resident of this place, and pastor of the Baptist church, for this volume:

"On the 14th of January, 1806, only ten miles from the city of Fredericksburg, in the county of Spotsylvania, was born Matthew Fontaine Maury. He came of goodly stock, for there mingled in his nature, in equal parts, the sturdy religious life of the French Huguenots and the gallantry of the English Cavalier. On his mother's side he belonged to the Minor family, of Virginia, while his name testifies that his paternal ancestors were among those who, from the persecutions of France, stretched their arms to the New World.

"When Maury was five years old, his parents emigrated to Tennessee and settled near the present town of Franklin. Thus, in the primeval forests of Tennessee, far away from the ocean's tuneful chant, there grew up the lad, who was to become 'The Pathfinder of the Seas.'

"The early educational advantages of young Maury were but scant. An accident, disqualifying him for farm service, gave him his best opportunity at an academy, and this he did not fail to use.

---
* General D. H. Maury's History of Va.

Maury looked to the army for a profession, but his parents denied him. When, without their knowledge, he then secured his appointment to the navy, they again objected, and he left home without his father's blessing. In 1825, an inland lad of nineteen years, Maury was assigned to duty as a midshipman on the Brandywine. It became evident that he had resolved to master his profession, and his promotion was rapid. In 1831 he was appointed master of the sloop of war Falmouth, which was ordered to Pacific waters. Diligently he sought information as to the best track for his vessel. Finding no reliable chart for his guidance, he realized the need of such help and his mind began at once to grapple with that problem, the solution of which afterwards immortalized him.

WONDERFUL WORKS ON NAVIGATION.

"At home for a time in 1834, he was married to Miss Ann Herndon, of Fredericksburg, and from this time on we find much of his family life woven into the history of our city. On Charlotte street, between Princess Ann and Prince Edward, still stands the house* where he lived and his children were born. At this time he published his first book—a 'Treatise on Navigation'—which for many years, even after the Civil war, was made a text book in the naval academy at Annapolis. His pen now became active in newspaper articles that startled the country, and there even arose a sentiment to elevate him to the portfolio of Secretary of the Navy.

"In the fall of 1839, by the upsetting of the stage in which he was travelling, his knee was severely fractured. But this untoward accident, under the guiding hand of God, put him into the very position in which he was to perform his life-work. His lame leg being unseaworthy, he was placed in charge of the 'Depot of Charts and Instruments,' at Washington. Here he grasped his great opportunity. Here, at the capital of the nation, he wrought for twenty years, and these two decades, from 1841 to 1861, mark the high tide of his service to the world.

"At Washington Maury found the vast accumulation of the 'log books' of the United States warships, stored away as mere rub-

---

* Pointed out to the author by Mrs. Ann Maury, his widow.

bish. This he utilized as valuable data. He also set in operation plans for still more complete and accurate collections of all kinds of hydrographic and meteorologic observations. With all this before him, with pains-taking toil, he prepared his wonderful 'charts and sailing directions.' His work took ultimate form in a series of six 'charts' and eight large folio volumes of 'sailing directions,' and these comprehended all waters, in every clime, where fly the white sails of civilized commerce.

"The charts exhibit, with wonderful accuracy, the winds and currents, their force and direction, at different seasons, the temperature of the surface waters, the calm belts and trade winds, the rains and the storms. The eight volumes of 'sailing directions,' are brim full of the most valuable nautical information, and are perfect treasures to the intelligent seaman. This effected a revolution in the art of navigation. The practical result was that the most difficult of all sea voyages—that from New York to San Francisco, around Cape Horn—has been shortened by forty days; and it has been estimated, that in shortening the time and lessening the dangers of sea voyages, there has been a saving to the world's commerce of not less than $40,000,000 annually.

"In writing about these sea routes he has mapped out, Maury has this to say: 'So to shape the course on voyages as to make the most of winds and currents at sea, is the perfection of the navigator's art. How the winds blow and the currents flow along this route or that, is no longer matter of opinion or speculation. The wind and the weather, daily encountered by hundreds, who have sailed the same voyage before him, have been tabulated for the mariner; nay, his path has been literally blazed for him on the sea; mile posts have been set upon the waves, and finger-boards planted and time-tables furnished for the trackless waste.'

"The simple 'Depot of Charts and Instruments,' over which Maury was placed, soon became the 'National Observatory,' with this man of genius as its superintendent. The vast work was international and, in 1853, brought about the great Brussels conference. On his return from this conference, ladened with honors, Maury stood before the world as the founder of the twin sciences of hydrography and meteorology. No less a man than Alexander von Humboldt declared him the founder of a new science.

FOUNDER OF WEATHER BUREAU.

"The limits of this sketch forbid more than a bare mention of the many other directions in which the genius of this wonderful man blessed the world. The great Atlantic cable, that flashes the news from continent to continent, is one of the radiant sparks that flew from his anvil as he wrought. Cyrus Field declared, at its completion, 'Maury furnished the brains, England gave the money, I did the work.' He established the river gauges of the Mississippi and the daily observations that give our best knowledge of that great river. He established the great circle routes for ocean steamship travel, and the 'steam laws' now used in ocean travel are his. He applied his system of meteorology to land as well as sea, and outlined the work of the 'signal service' and 'weather bureau' of to-day.

"The 'National Observatory,' under Maury, comprehended in all essential particulars what now is divided into no less than four departments at Washington. In 1855 Maury published his popular work 'The Physical Geography of the Sea and its Meteorology.' The work has passed through twenty editions, and has found its way into the languages of Continental Europe. It is the very poetry of his great science, analyzing and tabulating millions of observations of the sea—its currents and its climates, its winds and rains and storms, its myriads of animal life, and marvellous formations of shore-lines and bottoms—he found his way to the heart of nature and laid before us, like an open book, her majestic laws. And never did scientific man touch nature in more devout spirit. In all he saw the handiwork of God. Investigations into the broad-spreading circle of phenomena, connected with the winds of heaven and the waves of the sea, never failed to lift his mind to the Creator. As he pondered these things, he heard a voice in every wave that clapped its hand, he felt a pressure in every breeze that blew, he knelt and worshipped God.

STOOD WITH THE SOUTH.

"The life of Maury fell on times when there were at work other currents than those of sea and river. Political passions blew to a gale and the nation drifted to Civil war. His supreme sense of duty, and loyalty to his own State, was the current that bore him away from Washington and stranded him in the final wreck of the Southern Confederacy. In those unhappy times no man sacrificed more than Maury. He not only resigned his high position at Washington, but turned his back upon tempting offers from Russia and France, in order to suffer affliction with his own people. In the Civil war he rendered most valuable service by introducing submarine torpedo warfare, and inventing a sure method of explosion by electricity. Much of his time was spent in England purchasing navy supplies and perfecting inventions in navy warfare.

"After the war, Maury turned to Mexico and joined his fortunes to the Emperor Maximilian; but the tragic end of this friend and patron, again left him stranded. When, in 1868, the enactment of a general amnesty removed his political disabilities, Maury accepted the Chair of Meteorology in the Virginia Military Institute, and there spent the closing years of his life. He greatly rejoiced in this return to old friends and scenes, and addressed himself with ardor to congenial pursuits. But a constitution, not the strongest, gave way to the storms of the last years. The middle of October, 1872, on his return from a fatiguing lecture tour, as he crossed his threshold he said 'I am come home to die.' For four long months he lay weak and suffering. The end came on the 1st of February, 1873. A heavenly breeze bore him to the anchorage beyond the sea, and the trusting child of nature rested with his God.

"Than Matthew Fontaine Maury no American has received higher honors from foreign countries. Orders of Knighthood were bestowed upon him by the Emperor of Russia, King of Denmark, King of Portugal, King of Belgium, and the Emperor of France; while Prussia, Austria, Sweden, Holland, Sardinia, Bremen and France, struck gold medals in his honor The Pope sent him a full set of all the medals struck during his pontificate; Maximilian decorated him with 'The Cross of Our Lady Guadaloupe;' while Germany bestowed upon him the great 'Cosmos Medal,' struck in honor of Von Humboldt. It is the only duplicate of that medal in existence. He became corresponding member of more literary and scientific circles, and received more honorary diplomas, at home and abroad, than any other man known to history.

"Our own National Government has failed to honor his memory by appropriate memorial, yet his name is so woven with his great science that it must live. The Hon. Mellin Chamberlain, late Librarian of Congress, in calm judicial tone, has declared, 'I do not suppose there is the least doubt that Maury was the greatest man America has ever produced.'

"A bill to honor Commodore Maury, with an appropriate monument, lies mouldering in the archives of Congress. It will some day see the light. During the last years of Maury's life the smoke of a great conflict gathered about him and hid his face from the National Government; but the smoke is fast lifting, and the healthy breezes of a great national fraternity will soon blow it far away. Then his nation will look upon his face and see the clear outlines of his character—then will he take his own proper place in America's galaxy of the great."

THE LADIES' MEMORIAL ASSOCIATION.

It was in Fredericksburg, and by the ladies of Fredericksburg, Virginians, that the first memorial association was organized and chartered for looking after the dead soldiers, for providing them a final resting place in some convenient cemetery laid out for the purpose, and strewing their graves with the first flowers of spring as the years pass by. This was their second care after their return to their homes at the close of the Civil war, their first being their own homes, which were almost in ruins; and since the organization of that memorial association no season of flowers has passed that these graves have not been piously remembered.

MARY WASHINGTON MONUMENT.

It was the ladies of Fredericksburg, Virginians, who inaugurated the move, and carried it on to complete success, to raise a monu-

Commodore Matthew Fontaine Maury, the "Path Finder of the Seas."
(See page 315)

ment to a woman, the tallest and most imposing of its kind that is to be found on this continent. It towers over fifty feet high, the shaft is solid granite, and it marks the grave of the greatest of American women—Mary, the mother of Washington. It is true, that after the work was commenced, the plans laid, and some money raised, the ladies were assisted by the National Mary Washington Monument Association, which did good service, but even that association, brought into being through the local association at Fredericksburg, was made more active and efficient by the energy and persistence of the pioneers in the movement. That monument is grand and beautiful, and reaches high into the heavens, and while it marks the last resting place of that sainted woman, it reflects great honor upon all the ladies who assisted in its erection.

These are some of the things in which Virginians took the lead and which were accomplished by them. There may be omissions of noble acts and brave deeds that might have been mentioned of whose existence we are in ignorance, but these we have mentioned will suffice to show that they were the leading spirits in throwing off the British yoke of oppression, in uniting the colonies for common defence, in proclaiming to the world our grievances and declaring for freedom, in waging a long and bloody war and securing independence, in forming and conducting the government from its infancy through its experimental period, in extending its territorial limits and in contributing to its national greatness. If for all this—if for what has been achieved by their ancestors in field and forum, on land and sea, an honest pride should well up in the breast of the Virginians of the living present, that should find expression in words, where is the individual that can rise up and charge them with vain boasting?

CHAPTER XXII.

Fredericksburg at Present—The Health of the City—Its Financial Solidity—Its Commercial Prosperity—Its Lines of Transportation—Its Water Power—Its Official Calendar—List of Mayors, &c.

We now come to the closing words of the history of our venerable city, and what we shall add in closing will be of Fredericksburg as it is at present, without going into tiresome details, but before proceeding with that interesting topic we must turn aside to mention some useful and honored organizations of the ladies of the town, which failed to receive attention in a former chapter, after which our subject, "Fredericksburg at Present," will be resumed.

DAUGHTERS OF THE AMERICAN REVOLUTION.*

The Betty Washington Lewis Chapter, Daughters of the American Revolution, was organized in 1899 at the Exchange Hotel. Several prominent members of the National Society were present and explained the scope and work of the association. Mrs. Wm. Key Howard, of Kenmore, was appointed regent, by Mrs. Hugh N. Page, State regent, and twelve charter members were obtained. At the end of the first year Mrs. Howard resigned, and, in February, 1900, at a meeting at Kenmore, once the home of the sister of Washington, whose name the chapter adopted, Mrs. John T. Goolrick was elected regent; Mrs. H. M. D. Martin, vice-regent; Mrs. B. C. Chancellor, registrar; Mrs. V. S. F. Doggett, treasurer; Miss Sallie N. Gravatt, secretary, and Mrs. V. M. Fleming, historian. In addition to these officers the following charter members were present: Mrs. Marion Maria Mason Daniel, Mrs. Kate Tichenor Dill, Mrs. C. R. Howard, Mrs. Florence C. Richards, Mrs. Lettie M. Spencer and Mrs. Florence F. Weir.

In the preliminary work of organization, which was undertaken by Mrs. John T. Goolrick, one of her warmest supporters was Mrs.

---
*Paper prepared by Mrs. J. T. G.

Martin. She actively interested herself in the cause, her house was always open for meetings and through her several members were added to the chapter. The work of Mrs. V. S. F. Doggett was valuable and effective, and to the time of her death her zeal and interest were unabated. Mrs Lucilla S. Bradley, a "real daughter," and Mrs. Maria Jefferson Carr Mason, a great granddaughter of Thomas Jefferson, were honorary members.

This chapter has aided many worthy causes outside and inside of the society, both local and foreign. Colonial balls and other entertainments have, at different intervals, been given, among the handsomest being a reception at Kenmore, where an address on John Paul Jones was delivered by Capt. S. J. Quinn, before a large and appreciative audience.

In 1904 the State Conference was entertained by the Fredericksburg Chapter, and the guests were unstinted in their praises of the hospitality accorded them here. The chapter is at present as vital a force as when organized, and prepared to use opportunities when found to do work along historical and helpful lines. The officers elected at a recent meeting are Mrs. John T. Goolrick, regent; Mrs. W. H. Richards, vice-regent; Mrs. B. C. Chancellor, registrar; Mrs. H. M. Eckenrode, treasurer, and Miss Sallie N. Gravatt, secretary.

DAUGHTERS OF THE CONFEDERACY.

The Daughters of the Confederacy was organized on the 28th of February, 1896, with the following officers: Mrs. Joseph Nicholas Barney, president; Mrs. J. Horace Lacy, vice-president; Mrs. Vivian M. Fleming, secretary, and Miss Sallie Nelson Gravatt, treasurer, and an executive committee of fourteen ex-Confederates. The chapter rapidly grew in numbers and at one time had upon the roll nearly two hundred names. This society has been quite active since its organization and has done much good in the way of helping destitute veterans, looking after and administering to the sick and burying the dead. It has been the channel of distributing the Confederate crosses, and if any cross has been bestowed upon the unworthy, it was because of the ability of the unworthy to obtain vouchers from genuine Confederates. This chapter has done a good work in looking after the remains of Confederate soldiers, when found upon the battle-fields or elsewhere, and having them interred in the Confederate cemetery. One of the praiseworthy acts of the society, a few years ago, was to disinter the remains of the brave Gen. Abner Perrin, killed at the "Bloody Angle" while gallantly leading his brigade, and buried on the Hicks farm near the courthouse, and Lieut. Wm. H. Richardson, of Alabama, killed at the same time, and buried by the General, and to place them side by side in the Confederate cemetery. And yet there is other work for these self-sacrificing ladies to do. By annual elections Mrs. Barney has remained at the head of the chapter and is the present presiding officer, with Miss Sallie M. Lacy as secretary, who is an active support to the president.

ASSOCIATION FOR THE PRESERVATION OF VIRGINIA ANTIQUITIES.*

The Fredericksburg Branch of the Association for the Preservation of Virginia Antiquities is a small but active band. They have acquired the Mary Washington House and "Rising Sun Tavern." The "Tavern" has been recently repaired, but retains in all respects its original style of architecture. Both buildings are furnished in "ye olden style," and are centers of great interest to visitors. The officers of this branch are Mrs. Vivian M. Fleming, directress; Miss Rebecca C. Mander, secretary, and Mrs. Charles Wallace, treasurer.

THE CITY MISSION.

The City Mission was organized on the 14th of March, 1901, mainly through the efforts of Rev. W. D. Smith, rector of St. George's church, and Mrs. J. B. Ficklen. It has been quite an active society and much good has resulted from its labors. The main object of the society is to afford relief to the destitute of the town, especially the sick, and as it is composed altogether of benevolent and kind hearted ladies, we know, from this and their splendid labors in the past, that their mission will be well performed. They do more than look after the sick. These ladies gather up second-hand clothing from those who can spare it and sell the same at a

---

*Paper prepared by Miss R. C. M.

cheap rate to those able to purchase and give to the destitute. The society is composed of ladies from all religious denominations, and the city is laid out in districts, each of which is placed in charge of three ladies, to whom applications for assistance by parties living therein are referred. By this method impositions are rare and needy persons are not overlooked. The present officers of the society are Mrs. J. B. Ficklen, president; Mrs. B. B. Montgomery and Miss Jennie Hurkamp vice-presidents; Miss Rebecca C. Mander, secretary; Miss Annie Myer, treasurer, and Mrs. Isaac Hirsh, purchasing agent.

THE FREDERICKSBURG TEACHERS' ASSOCIATION.*

The faculty of the public schools of Fredericksburg met and organized the Fredericksburg Teachers' Association in September, 1906. The officers elected at that meeting were as follows: Miss Kate James Mander, president; Miss Clarice Crittenden Davis, vice-president; Miss Jennie M. Goolrick, secretary, and Miss Maggie L. Honey, treasurer. The president of the School Board, Mr. A. B. Bowering, after the teachers were organized, was requested to outline a plan for a library, which he did, and the teachers commenced the work. After obstacles and delays, by solicitation, and dessert sales, a sufficient amount of money was raised to commence the purchase of books, and quite a nice collection of the best publications was secured. Since that additions have been made as the means of the association would justify, and now the library is an institution formed on a solid basis. It is popular with the children, and from it they derive much pleasure and instruction. The present officers are Miss Kate James Mander, president; Miss Mary Page Waller, vice-president; Miss Agnes P. Roach, secretary, and Miss Maggie L. Honey, treasurer.

FREDERICKSBURG AT PRESENT.

Fredericksburg is a healthy town—a true Virginia city—almost free from the fevers and diseases that visit other cities of the coast or even of tidewater. It is beautifully situated on the west bank

---

*Paper prepared by Miss K. J. M.

of the Rappahannock river, at the head of tidewater, where its inhabitants escape the malaria of the lowlands and the fevers peculiar to the mountains. Therefore, when we compare the death rate of Fredericksburg, which is made every month by Dr. J. N. Barney, our health officer, with that of other neighboring cities, we find it quite favorable to our town.

PURE WATER SUPPLY.

Our main source of water supply, the Rappahannock river, has no city or town of any size above us, and for that reason the water is almost free from foreign substances, and as pure as are the mountain springs from which it flows. The analysis of this water, which has often been made in the years gone by, and repeatedly in the past few years, shows ninety-eight per cent., which probably more nearly approaches absolute purity than any other stream of its size in the country. Besides this aid to health, the sanitary condition of the town is carefully looked after by the Board of Health, and everything that threatens the introduction of disease is at once removed or reduced to a healthy condition. In addition to this, as a convenience for the citizens, and an aid to health conditions, the main part of the city has been sewered within the past four years, and laterals are in course of construction to reach those portions of the town not now sewered. With these aids to health and our lynx-eyed Board of Health, who are always on the alert, we may hope for and confidently expect, as we now have, an unusually healthy city.

FINANCIAL CONDITION OF THE CITY.

The financial condition of Fredericksburg is good, and her credit is undoubted. It is true that the debt of the city is large, but for every bond issued there is something substantial standing for it, except nearly $120,000 of ante-bellum bonds, issued by our forefathers in an honest and earnest endeavor to secure for our people improvements of a permanent and profitable character. But the improvements proved worthless to the town. Those who voted for them have passed over the river of death, leaving this indebtedness as a legacy to their descendants, and we take great pleasure in providing for it. The other bonds were issued for improvements the town needed and was compelled to have. They are all in use at present, successfully operated, and are valued far in advance of the price paid for them by the city, and it is only a question of private or corporation ownership, as to whether it was a wise policy for the city to erect and operate them. The City Council thinks it acted for the best interests of the town and the people back it up in that opinion. Nearly all of the bonds issued by the city bear four per cent., were sold at or above par and purchased mostly by our own citizens. This, it would appear, is a strong indication that our financial affairs are in a satisfactory condition.

PRESENT COMMERCIAL CONDITION.

The commercial prosperity of the town is probably far in advance of what it ever was before. We have now about one hundred and fifteen wholesale and retail stores, each one doing a thriving business. In these stores the customer will be able to find any article of merchandise he may need and at as low price as he could find it in the larger cities. In the last few years there has been a spirit of improvement in business houses, and at present there are to be found store-houses that would be a credit to a city of larger pretentions. So changed is the business portion of Main street by reason of this enlargement and ornamentation that citizens of the town have often had to inquire for the places they wished to visit. In addition to this, our manufactures have increased and are still increasing, and in them hundreds of persons find employment at living wages. Among the manufacturing institutions may be mentioned two large flouring mills, one woolen mill, one pants factory, one silk mill, two sumac mills, three excelsior mills, one mattress factory, two pickle factories, one canning factory, one shoe factory, one shirt factory, one spoke factory and six repair shops. The assessed taxable value of property in town is, personal property $703,782, real estate $1,676,133, making a total of $2,379,915. Besides this, our several banks, in their periodical statements, made to the Government, show largely over a million dollars on deposit, subject to individual checks. In view of these facts truly it may be said that Fredericksburg is in a prosperous commercial condition and is rapidly adding to that prosperity.

LINES OF TRANSPORTATION.

The lines of transportation running to and from Fredericksburg are sufficient for all the requirements of the town, both as to freight and passenger travel, yet our citizens would not object to the construction of another road, starting at some deep water point on the coast, crossing the Rappahannock river at this place and connecting north of us with the great trunk lines, traversing this extensive country in all directions. But for this important improvement we must patiently wait.

The great line of travel and traffic through Fredericksburg, north and south, at present, is the Richmond, Fredericksburg and Potomac railroad. This road is probably one of the best conducted roads in the country and seldom has an accident. Not until a few years ago did it share its track with any other road, but now three or more companies are running their cars over this line and the carrying business is immense. This large increase in business necessitated a double track of the entire line—from Richmond to Washington—which was done with great rapidity. The present service on this road that passes through town is nine passenger trains north and ten south each twenty-four hours. In addition to this, the increase in freight has also increased the number of freight trains, and so we now have fifty to pass through in a day and night, and yet it is more than probable that this large number will soon be further increased. This road has a new iron bridge spanning the Rappahannock river at this point.

The Piedmont, Fredericksburg and Potomac railroad—Narrow Gauge—runs daily from Fredericksburg to Orange, a distance of forty miles. It connects Fredericksburg and intermediate points, with that great trunk line, the Southern, at that point, which is an accommodation to the travelling public along its entire line. Although a narrow gauge road, it does quite a large business and it has been rumored that it may be extended beyond the mountains some day, in which event it will become a line of greater importance than at present.

The Office of the Fredericksburg Water Power Company.
(See page 330)

"Marye Mansion," Gen. Longstreet's headquarters at Battle of Fredericksburg, December 13, 1862; now the residence of Capt. M. B. Rowe.

(See page 91)

The former citizen, who went out from us even a few years ago, on his return to his old home now, would find, among other changes, that the Weems Line of steamers from Fredericksburg to Baltimore, had transferred its business to another company, and the old familiar name of Weems, of more than a half century standing, whose line was so intimately interwoven with all the interests of Fredericksburg, was a name of the past. But he would also find a line —The Maryland, Delaware and Virginia railroad, not that their steam boats run upon railroad tracks—had taken its place, and, by its splendid steamers, so well adapted to the river trade, had brought us into rapid and easy communication with Norfolk and Baltimore, by the Rappahannock river and Chesapeake bay, and thence with the whole busy world beyond.

A SPLENDID WATER POWER.

Some one writing of our water-power some years ago said: "The water-power of the Rappahannock river at Fredericksburg, made available by the erection of a magnificent dam, has been harnessed for work to some extent, but not yet to its full capacity." That this is true is a pity, but that it will not long be true is a blessing. The old dam, which gave us only five thousand horse-power, is rapidly yielding to the touch of time, and already another is in course of construction that will be more substantial and give us more power than the present dam gives at its best. A gentleman, well informed as to the plans of the present company, says: "The dam now in process of construction will be built just below the present dam and will be of reinforced concrete. It will be about twenty-two feet above the present water level below the old dam, and will husband the entire plan of the river; or rather, will render the entire plan available for power purposes, but will not, strictly speaking, husband the entire plan, because the pond behind the dam will be rather limited in capacity owing to the closeness of the hills on either side of the river and the abrupt fall of the stream. This dam will afford about eight thousand horse-power, utilized in the city, and at a power-house of the company to be built near the silk mill, but to the east of the main Falmouth road.

Just above Taylor's quarry it is planned to build another dam seventy-six feet high, or about one hundred and thirty-eight feet above the sea, with quite a large pond or storage reservoir behind it, reaching up the river some ten miles or more. And then above this reach, and at or about the junction of the two rivers, the large dam, about eighty-four feet high, or two hundred and twenty-two feet above sea level, will complete the development so far as the Fredericksburg Power Company is concerned. This last level reaches to about Germanna. The whole contemplated scheme will yield about thirty thousand horse-power." This will be such an enormous increase of power over what we now have that we cannot realize it. But the question is, what is to be done with this immense power? Shall it be used in Fredericksburg or transmitted to neighboring cities to increase their facilities for manufactures? Capitalists and manufacturers must answer this question.

It will thus be seen that Fredericksburg, with its quiet ways and want of bustling activity, is a manufacturing center of considerable importance, and lying, as it does, on the line of travel from north to south, there is no good reason, as we have intimated, why it may not be a manufacturing center of much greater importance.

It is true that those who estimate a place solely by the number of industrial enterprises which it encourages, or the amount of traffic which comes to it, would not rank Fredericksburg as highly as some of the more busy or bustling towns of other parts of the country, but those who recognize other agencies besides water wheels and steam engines, and other earthly products, besides dry goods, groceries and general merchandise, will find much here to admire and interest them.

It is also true that with the manufacturing facilities that we possess we would gladly see them greatly enlarged and more fully developed, also new ones erected and operated, but with this accomplished we would not forget that there are better fabrics than those that are manufactured by mechanical appliances. With a climate unsurpassed, an immunity from epidemics, a situation enviable because of its surroundings, water as pure as ever came from mountain springs, with all the advantages as we have before said of tidewater, without its malaria, with all the benefits of the mountains, without the mountain fevers, together with a refined and elevated society—if these, with the additions of home virtues and home joys, be regarded as valuable in life, then Fredericksburg must rank much higher than many a place that has more outward show of prosperity.

The pursuit of gain and the exacting cares of business have not engaged altogether the thoughts and attentions of our people, to the exclusion of those things which tend to the *pleasure, comfort* and *health* of the community, and to its intellectual development. For the benefit of the first mentioned of these classes, Hurkamp Park has been located, Washington Avenue and the National Boulevard have been laid out, completed and adorned, and the Free Bridge has been constructed, while "Lovers' Lane" remains the same that it was in the century past.

For those who would derive comfort from inhaling the pure, fresh air of the morning or evening in a drive, on horse-back or on a bicycle, can find on the avenue and boulevard beautifully graded drives, and a variety of scenes which are ever pleasing to the eye, while the beautiful sun risings and settings, and the deep blue sky above rival in grandeur and sublimity those of far-off Italy.

For those who would spend the twilight hours in a pleasant walk with her who "claims his thoughts by day and dreams by night," in search of health the Free Bridge and the enchanting walks beyond are equal to the far-famed "Lovers' Lane," which in olden times was so attractive, even enchanting, as it is now, to the belles and beaux, where words were spoken and vows made that led to unions of hands and hearts that nothing earthly could weaken or sever.

For those whose tastes and inclinations lead them to intellectual enjoyment, the Library and Reading Room, located in the north wing of the Courthouse and the Wallace Library, soon to be in operation, afford excellent facilities. The Library at the Courthouse is furnished with splendid books—historical, biographical, religious and miscellaneous, and the number is added to as the funds at the command of the association will allow. It is conducted by the ladies of the town, who are always ready to give, toil and even sacrifice to benefit, elevate and make more useful the masses of the people.

All of these advantages belong to Fredericksburg, with many others that we have probably inadvertently omitted, that make it one of the most desirable residential cities in the country; and we can readily agree with Captain John Smith, the great explorer, "that Heaven and earth never agreed better to frame a place for man's habitation," than the beautiful valley of the Rappahannock, and Fredericksburg is located on the most beautiful, picturesque and healthy spot of that far-famed valley.

And yet, with all these advantages, pointing out Fredericksburg as a most desirable place for her educational, industrial, commercial and residential advantages, its prosperity is not what it should be; but with a full development of all her varied facilities which we trust will be done in the near future and which can be done if our people will work harmoniously, we may hope for more prosperous days; for

"Reason's whole pleasure—all the joys of sense—
Lie in three words—HEALTH, PEACE and COMPETENCE."

OFFICIAL CALENDAR—September 1, 1908.

HUSTINGS COURT.

Hon. John T. Goolrick, *Judge.*
Hon. Granville R. Swift, *Commonwealth's Attorney.*
A. Bacon Yates, *Clerk.*
John Scott Berry, *Deputy Clerk.*
J. Conway Chichester, *City Sergeant.*
Baylor S. Pates, *Deputy City Sergeant.*

MUNICIPAL OFFICERS.

H. Lewis Wallace, *Mayor.*
Robert T. Knox, *Treasurer.*
A. B. Bowering, *Commissioner of Revenue.*
A. P. Rowe, *City Tax Collector.*
E. H. Randall, *City Surveyor.*

MAGISTRATES.

Upper Ward—S. J. Quinn, S. E. Eastburn, R. E. Bozel.
Lower Ward—A. G. Billingsly.

CITY COUNCIL.

William E. Bradley, *President.*
A. Mason Garner, *Vice-President.*
Samuel E. Eastburn, *Clerk.*

Upper Ward—Wm. E. Bradley, Harry B. Lane, Josiah P. Rowe, Joseph M. Goldsmith, John C. Melville, Clarance R. Howard.
Lower Ward—A. Mason Garner, W. S. Embrey, Jr., Henry Warden, J. W. Masters, F. L. W. Green, Arthur Brown.

Council Committees.

On Finance—Harry B. Lane, John C. Melville, Wm. E. Bradley.

On Public Property—Wm. E. Bradley, A. Mason Garner, J. W. Masters.

On Water Works—Josiah P. Rowe, Harry B. Lane, A. Mason Garner.

On Streets—W. S. Embrey, Jr., J. M. Goldsmith, C. R. Howard.

On Light—John C. Melville, J. W. Masters, Harry B. Lane.

On Almshouse—A. Mason Garner, Wm. E. Bradley, Josiah P. Rowe.

On Public Interest—Joseph M. Goldsmith, C. R. Howard, Henry Warden.

On Ordinances—Clarance R. Howard, W. S. Embrey, Jr., F. L. W. Green.

On Auditing—Authur Brown, F. L. W. Green, John C. Melville.

On Health and Police—John W. Masters, Henry Warden, Arthur Brown.

On Schools—Henry Warden, Josiah P. Rowe, J. M. Goldsmith.

On Fire Department—F. L. W. Green, Arthur Brown, W. S. Embrey, Jr.

SUPERINTENDENTS OF DEPARTMENTS.

S. J. QUINN, *Superintendent City Water Works.*
B. F. BULLOCK, *Superintendent City Gas Works.*
WM. KEY HOWARD, *Superintendent City Electric Light.*
JOHN W. BALL, *Superintendent Almshouse.*
SAMUEL FITZHUGH, *Clerk of Market.*

POLICE DEPARTMENT.

Upper Ward—WALLACE N. TANSILL, J. A. STONE.
Lower Ward—JOHN H. ROBINSON, WM. R. HALL.
Special Police—CHARLES A. GORE.

CITY REGISTRARS.

Lower Ward—J. Fred. Brown.
Upper Ward—John J. Berrey.

PUBLIC FREE SCHOOL BOARD.

A. B. Bowering, *President.*
S. J. Quinn, *Clerk.*
B. P. Willis, *Superintendent.*

Upper District—Isaac Hirsh, W. L. Brannan, J. R. Rawlings.
Lower District—A. B. Bowering, W. H. Hurkamp, Geo. Freeman, Jr.

BOARD OF HEALTH.

Mayor H. Lewis Wallace.
Dr. J. N. Barney, *Secretary and Health Officer.*
Dr. William Jeffries Chewning.
A. Bacon Yates.

CITY CORONER.

Dr. Andrew C. Doggett.

MAYORS OF FREDERICKSBURG IN THEIR CHRONOLOGICAL ORDER.

CHARLES MORTIMER ....from March, 1782, to March, 1783
WILLIAM MCWILLIAMS ....from March, 1783, to March, 1784
JAMES SOMERVILLE ....from March, 1784, to March, 1785
GEORGE WEEDON ....from March, 1785, to March, 1786
CHARLES MORTIMER ....from March, 1786, to March, 1787
JAMES SOMERVILLE ....from March, 1787, to March, 1788
CHARLES MORTIMER ....from March, 1788, to March, 1789
GEORGE FRENCH ....from March, 1789, to March, 1790
BENJAMIN DAY ....from March, 1790, to March, 1791
WILLIAM HARVEY ....from March, 1791, to March, 1792
JAMES SOMERVILLE ....from March, 1792, to March, 1793
FONTAINE MAURY ....from March, 1793, to March, 1794
GEORGE FRENCH ....from March, 1794, to March, 1795
WILLIAM HARVEY ....from March, 1795, to March, 1796
FONTAINE MAURY ....from March, 1796, to March, 1797
WILLIAM HARVEY.......from March, 1797—died in office March 13, 1798
WM. TAYLOR..................from March 17, 1798 to March 19, 1798
FONTAINE MAURY ....from March, 1798, to March, 1799
GEORGE FRENCH ....from March, 1799, to March, 1800
DAVID C. KER ....from March, 1800, to March, 1801
WILLIAM S. STONE ....from March, 1801, to March, 1802
DAVID C. KER ....from March, 1802, to March, 1803
GEORGE FRENCH ....from March, 1803, to March, 1804
BENJAMIN DAY ....from March, 1804, to March, 1805
GEORGE FRENCH ....from March, 1805, to March, 1806
CHARLES L. CARTER.......from March, 1806—resigned August 11, 1808
WILLIAM SMOCK................from August 11, 1808, to March, 1809
RICHARD JOHNSTON ....from March, 1809, to March, 1810
GEORGE FRENCH ....from March, 1810, to March, 1811

JOSEPH WALKER ....from March, 1811, to March, 1812
GEORGE FRENCH ....from March, 1812, to March, 1813
CHARLES L. CARTER ....from March, 1813, to March, 1814
GEORGE FRENCH ....from March, 1814, to March, 1815
JOHN SCOTT ....from March, 1815, to March, 1816
GARRET MINOR ....from March, 1816, to March, 1817
ROBERT MACKAY ....from March, 1817, to March, 1818
GARRET MINOR ....from March, 1818, to March, 1819
ROBERT MACKAY ....from March, 1819, to March, 1820
DAVID BRIGGS ....from March, 1820, to March, 1821
ROBERT LEWIS..........from March, 1820—died in office Feb. 10, 1829
THOMAS GOODWIN........from Feb. 12, 1829—died in office Jan. 15, 1836
JOHN H. WALLACE............from January 20, 1836 to March 22, 1838
BENJAMIN CLARKE.............from March 22, 1838, to March 22, 1844
ROBERT BAYLOR SEMPLE..from Mar. 20, 1844—died in office Feb. 8, 1853
JOHN L. MARYE, JR..............from Feb. 12, 1853, to March 21, 1854
PETER GOOLRICK ....from March 21, 1854, to March 21, 1855
JOHN S. CALDWELL ....from March 20, 1855, to March 17, 1857
PETER GOOLRICK ....from March 17, 1857, to March 22, 1859
WILLIAM S. SCOTT............from March 22, 1859, to March 22, 1860
PETER GOOLRICK.............from March 21, 1860—resigned April 4, 1860
MONTGOMERY SLAUGHTER, from April 4, 1860, removed by military April 28, 1868.
CHARLES E. MALLAM, appointed by military April 28, 1868, removed by military July 15, 1869.
WILLIAM E. NYE, appointed by military July 15, 1869, resigned Feb. 23, 1870.
LAWRENCE B. ROSE....elected by Council Feb. 23, 1870, to June 30, 1870
WILLIAM ROY MASON, elected by the people July 1, 1870, resigned July 28, 1870.
LAWRENCE B. ROSE ....from July 28, 1870, to June 30, 1872
ROBERT BANKS BERREY ....from July 1, 1872, to June 30, 1874
LAWRENCE B. ROSE......from July 1, 1874—died in office April 10, 1877
HUGH S. DOGGETT...............from April 12, 1877, to June 30, 1880

JOSEPH WARD SENER...............from July 1, 1880, to June 30, 1884
JOSIAH HAZARD ....from July 1, 1884, to June 30, 1888
ABSALOM P. ROWE ....from July 1, 1888, to June 30, 1896
WM. SEYMOUR WHITE....from July 1, 1896—died in office Nov. 26, 1897
HENRY R. GOULDMAN..........appointed Nov. 30, 1897, to June 30, 1898
ABSALOM P. ROWE........from July 1, 1898—died in office June 1, 1900
MARION G. WILLIS............appointed June 15, 1900, to June 30, 1902
MARION G. WILLIS................elected July 1, 1902, to June 30, 1904
THOMAS P. WALLACE...........elected July 1, 1904, to August 31, 1908
H. LEWIS WALLACE..............elected Sept. 1, 1908, and now serving.

INDEX.

Accoqueck, 19.
Acorn Lodge, I. O. O. F., 221.
Acquisition of Territory—Walker's exploration, 281; the Great Northwest, 312; the Louisiana purchase, 313; the Florida purchase, 314; acquisition of Texas, 314; the territory from Mexico, 314.
Adams, Capt. Andrew B., 221.
Adams, John, 230, 294.
Adams, John Quincy, 311.
Adams, Rev. Geo. F., 211.
Adams, Samuel, patriot, 307.
A great revival of religion, 93.
Aldridge, Miss Virginia, 224.
Aler, George, 141.
Alexander, Capt. Robert H., 184.
Alexander, Gen. E. P., 91, 266.
Alexander, Philip, 134.
Alexander, Robert B., editor, 227.
Allen, John, town trustee, 42.
Allen, Wm., 140, 142.
Allison, John W., Jr., 167.
Alsop, Boswell, 168.
Ames, Michael, hostage prisoner, 77, 79.
Amoroleck, Smith's prisoner, 15, 17.
Anasheroans, Indian tribe, 19.
Anderson, Capt. John K., 184.
Anstice, Mrs. Judith, teacher, 197.
Argall. Capt., 20.
Armistead, Henry, court clerk, 130.
Arts and manufactures encouraged, 46.
Assembly's Home and School, 198.
Association for the P. V. A., 324.
Atkinson, John, 237.

Bacon, Nathaniel, 281, 283.
Baggett, Samuel I., 262.
Baggett, Wm. M., 141.
Bagnall, Anthony, historian, 13, 15.
Bailey, William, 221.
Ball, Col. Wm. B., 83.
Ball, John M., publisher, 229.
Ball, John Wesley, 174.

Bankhead, Col. John, 257.
Barber, Rev. H. H., 207.
Barbour, Gov. James, 132.
Barksdale, Gen. Wm., 81, 88, 97, 99.
Barlosius, Charles F., 167.
Barney, Dr. J. N., 326.
Barney, Mrs. Joseph Nicholas, 326.
Barton, Thomas B., hostage prisoner, 74, 77.
Barton, Judge Wm. S., 68, 183, 215.
Battle of Fredericksburg, 91, 92.
Beale, Wm. C., 138, 139, 140.
Beckwith, Frank, 174.
Benson, Wm., 171.
Benwick, J. B., Jr., architect, 141, 210.
Bernard, Wm., 46.
Berrey, John J., hostage prisoner, 79, 142.
Berrey, Robert B., mayor, 184. 209.
Beverley, Harry, town trustee, 39.
Beverley, Robert, 28, 35.
Billingsly, Rev. Joseph A., editor, 227.
Biscoe, Robert L., publisher, 229.
Blackburn, Robert, 167.
Blackford, Wm. M., editor, 227.
Blair, John, 302, 304.
Blanton, Thomas, 237.
Boardman, Stephen A., teacher, 197.
Board of Health, 335.
Bonaparte, Charlotte, 243.
Bonaparte, Emperor Napoleon, 243, 310.
Boswell, Capt. J. K., engineer, 96.
Botts, Benjamin, 172.
Bowen, Wm., 167.
Bowering, Benjamin, machinist, 169, 176.
Bowering, Prof. A. B., 169, 192, 201, 211, 325.
Bowman, Mrs. D. C., 223.
Bradley, Capt. James H., hostage prisoner, 77, 78.
Bradley, Mrs. Lucilla S., 323.
Bradley, Wm. E., 127, 147, 176, 177, 227, 261.

[339]

Bradford, Daniel, 166.
Braxton, Capt. Carter, 70 71, 72.
Braxton, Carter, signer D. I., 247.
Braxton, Rev. Carter, 211.
Brent, Thomas N., 197, 261.
Bridges—Chatham, 171; Stafford, 171; Free, 171.
Briggs, David, 64.
Broaddus, Rev. Andrew, 210, 211.
Broaddus, Rev. Wm. F., D. D., 74. 77, 78, 197, 211.
Brockenburg, Dr. John, 193.
Brooke, Judge Francis, 125.
Brooke, Gov. Robert, 130, 218, 220.
Brown, James, 172.
Brown, John, 183, 313.
Brown, Rev. James E., 216.
Brown, Rev. John A., 216.
Buckner, Cuthbert, teacher, 198.
Buckner, Robert, 38, 39, 40.
Bullock, B. F. Supt. gas, 178.
Burgess, Roland, 216.
Burrows, Silas, 157, 257.
Butterfield, Gen. Daniel, 191, 269.
Byrd, Col. Wm., 26, 43.

Caldwell, J. S., mayor, 141, 220.
Campbell, Daniel, 218, 220.
Campbell, James M., editor, 227.
Campbell, Mrs. Wm. A., teacher, 198.
Campbell, Rev. Alexander, 213.
Carter, Col. J. W., 13th Miss., 89.
Carter, George, publisher, 226.
Carter, Robert, 49.
Caruthers, Wm., teacher, 198.
Cary, Archibald, 168 293.
Cary, Col. Milton, 72.
Castle, Henry, 60.
Champ, John, 46.
Chancellor, Mrs. B. C., D. A. R., 322. 323.
Chancellor, M. S., 175.
Chancellor, Rev. Melzi, 96.
Chancellorsville campaign, 94; Gen. Hooker in command, 94; moved to Chancellorsville, 94; Gen. Sedgwick in town, 95; defeated at Salem church, 96; Hooker beaten at Chancellorsville, 95.
Chestnutt, Rev. I. L., 214.
Chew, Col. Robt. S., 72, 130, 183, 184, 192.
Chew, John James, 68, 116, 130, 138, 142.
Chew, John, 125.
Chew, John. Jr., 130.
Chew, Robert S., 130.
Chiles, Rev. James, 209.
Churches, 202; St. George's, 203; Trinity, 206; Presbyterian, 207; French Memorial Chapel, 208; Baptist, 209; Methodist, 211; Christian, 213; St. Mary's Catholic, 214; Shiloh Old Site, 215; Shiloh New Site, 215; Robinson's, 215; Church of God, 216.
Citizens, arrested as hostages, 77, 86; second arrest and names, 102.
City Council—Accepts situation, 111; condemns assassination, 112; levies taxes, 114; orders an election, 115; reverses order, 115; city officers removed, 116; addition to oath of office, 117; new council, 120; orders new courthouse, 140; passes resolution on death of Prest. McKinley, 278, 279; standing committees, 334; Supts. of departments, 334; police department, 334.
City Hall, 143.
City Mission, the, 324.
City Officers, 52, 130, 333.
Clarke, Gen. George Rodgers, 212, 313.
Clarke, Jonathan, 312, 313.
Clarke, Rev. M., 205.
Clarke, Wm., explorer. 313.
Clay, Henry, U. S. Senator. 264.
Cleveland, Prest. Grover, 160.
Clowder, Jeremiah, 39.
Coakley, John. hostage prisoner, 77, 79.
Cobb, Col. John A., 153.
Cobb, Gen. Thomas Reade Rootes, 91.
Cole, Col. E. D., 127, 146, 170. 174, 212, 248, 261, 262.
Cole, Counsellor, 168.
Coleman, Judge Richard H., teacher, 197.
Colson, Thomas, 194.
Confederate cemetery, 185, 186, 189.
Confederate Veterans, 191.

Conflagrations, 59, 64.
Contagious diseases, 65.
Conway, P. V. D., 93.
Conway, Walker P., 120.
Cooke, Dr. James, hostage prisoner, 77, 79.
Coons, Jacob, German miner, 24.
Corbin, Hon. S. Wellford, 170.
Corbin, James P., clerk, 223, 261, 277.
Cotton, Mrs. An., 282.
Coulter, Judge John, of Chatham, 171.
Courthouse, 142.
Courts—Hustings Court established, 124; District Court, 124; Circuit Court, 125; District Court of Appeals 125; Hustings Court abolished and re-established, 126; Police Court, 126.
Cox, Abraham, hostage prisoner, 77, 79, 80.
Cox, George, 64.
Cox, James A., 246.
Cox, Mrs. Lucy Ann, 246.
Craig. Rev. Lewis, 209.
Crawford, Wm. J., architect, 159.
Criminals, punishment of, 55.
Crismond, H. F., 261.
Crutchfield, Edgar M., 200.
Crutchfield, Hon. Oscar M., 220.
Cultatawoman, Indian king, 14, 19.
Cunningham, James, 167.
Cunningham. Wm. H., 111, 201.
Curtis, Thomas, 165.
Custis, Daniel Parke, 237.

Dahlgren, Capt. Ulrich, 83.
Dandridge, Col. John, 236, 237.
Daniel, Mrs. M. M. M., D. A. R., 322.
Daniel, Major John W., 160.
Daniel, S. Greenhow, 227.
Dannehl, Henry, 170.
Daughters American Revolution, 322.
Daughters of the Confederacy, 323.
Davis, Miss Clarice C., teacher, 325.
Dawson, Hon. John, 154, 233.
Day, Major Benjamin, 194, 195, 220.
Dick, Dr. Charles, 124.
Dickey. Robert, 139, 140.

Dill, Mrs. Kate Tichenor, D. A. R., 322.
Dill, Rev. Jacob S., D. D., 211, 263, 315.
Dixon, Rev. George L., 215.
Dixon, Roger, Gent., 237.
Doggett, Capt. Hugh S., 120, 184.
Doggett, Mrs. V. S. F., D. A. R., 322, 323.
Dolly, Rev. W. L., 213.
Dow, Rev. Lorenzo, 66.
Dunaway, Rev. Thomas S., D. D., 211, 279.
Dunmore, Lord, 48.

Early, Gen. Jubal A., 96, 98, 273.
Eastburn, Oliver, 170.
Eckenrode, Mrs. H. M., D. A. R., 323.
Edrington, Mrs. C. W., 222.
Eisenhower, S. A., 248.
Electric light plant, 178.
Elks, benevolent order of, 221.
Embrey, Judge A. T., 126, 146, 228, 261.
Embrey, Major W. S., 170.
Essex, Rev. Benjamin, 123.
Eubank, John, 242.
Eve, George W., 120.

Fairs, agricultural, 44, 169, 170.
Farish, Wm. F., 165.
Fauntleroy, Miss L., editress, 229.
Federal Hill, 153.
Ferneyhough, John, 162.
Ferry, first constructed, 170.
Fetherstone, Richard, Gent, 14. 19.
Fetherstone's Bay, 19.
Ficklen, Mrs. J. B., 324, 325.
Field, John, printer, 219.
Fire Department, 144, 180, 181.
Fishback, Harman, German miner, 24.
Fishback, John, German miner, 24.
Fitzhugh, St. Geo. R., 146, 147, 261, 263, 276, 277.
Fitzhugh, Wm., of Chatham, 171. 236.
Fleming, Mrs. V. M., D. A. R., 322, 323, 324.
Floyd, Gen. John B., 81.
Fontaine, Col. W. W., teacher, 197.
Fontaine, John, diary of, 26, 27.
Ford, James W., teacher, 198.

Forrer, Rev. F. S., 214.
Forsythe, Major Robert, 134.
Fort, constructed on Rappahannock, 1681, 25.
Franklin, Benjamin, 124.
Fraser, Simon, 220.
Freaner, W. T., 166.
Fredericksburg American Lodge, 218.
Fredericksburg Artillery, 72, 73, 74.
Fredericksburg College, 198.
Fredericksburg Commandery, K. T., 220.
Fredericksburg, city of, founded, 1727; streets bear royal names, 37; act House of Burgesses, 38; seat of justice, 42; re-survey, 44; wooden chimneys, 45; limits extended, 46; military ardor, 48; under the U. S., 50; chartered by Legislature, 51; rapid growth, 53; lends money to government, 54; important center, 58; important postal point, 60; limits extended, 62; great fire, 64; trade of the town, 65: epitome of the city, 67; limits extended, 68; charter amended 1852, 1858, 69; in the Confederacy, 71; surrendered to Gen. McDowell, 74; Gen. Pope enters, 76; evacuation scenes, 81; bridges destroyed, 82; Gen. Burnside on Stafford Heights, 83; authorities consult Gen. Lee, 84; Gen. Sumner demands surrender, 85; bombardment, 88 (see Chancellorsville and Wilderness campaigns); war closes, 110; under the Stars and Stripes, 110; military supreme, 113; new charter, 117; untrammelled citizens in power, 119; ante-bellum debt, 119; present debt, 121; courts, 124; its declaration, 283; furnishes head of army and navy, 301; Fredericksburg at present, 325; financial condition, 326; commercial condition, 327; official calendar, 333; council committees, 334; registrars, 335; list of mayors, 336.
Fredericksburg Lodge, No. 4, 217.

Fredericksburg R. A. Chapter, 220.
Fredericksburg Teachers' Association, 325.
Freedman's Bureau, 127.
Fremont, Gen. John C., 313.
French, Dr. George, 172.
French, Seth B., 208.
Frieze, Jacob, 242.

Garner, A. Mason, 147, 174, 176.
Garnett, Geo. W., 211.
Garnett, Hon. James M., 169.
Garrison, Hon. Geo. T., 158.
Gas Works, 176, 177.
Gately, Matthew J., 237.
Gates, Gen. Horatio, 251.
Gaullier, John F., 172.
Gibson, Rev. John S., 207.
Gill, Beverley T., hostage prisoner, 77, 111.
Gilmer, Capt. Lucien G., 185.
Gilmer, Rev. Thomas W., 209.
Gladstone, Sir Wm. E., premier, 305.
Gooch, Wm., Esq., Governor, 42.
Goodwin, Thomas, 165.
Goolrick, John, teacher, 196.
Goolrick, Hon. John T., 126, 192, 261, 271, 272, 275, 277.
Goolrick, Miss Jennie M., teacher, 325.
Goolrick, Mrs. John T., D. A. R., 160, 322, 323.
Goolrick, Peter, 138, 139. 140, 166.
Gordon, Douglas H., 85.
Gordon, Gen. John B., 98.
Gordon, Samuel, 169.
Gordon, W. F., 184.
Gore, Charles A., 60.
Gore, Jacob, 60.
Grant, Gen. U. S., 73, 99, 109.
Gravatt, George, 111, 120.
Gravatt, Miss Sallie N., D. A. R., 322, 323.
Gray, John, 167.
Gray, Rev. J. S., 207.
Gray, Wm. F., editor, 225.
Green, Gen. Nathaniel, 251, 253.
Green, John W., 64.
Green, Mrs. James L., 226.
Green, Rev. Edwin, 207.
Green, Timothy, editor, 225, 259.
Green, Wm. D., 166.
Gregg, Gen. D. McM., 263.

Griffin, John M., 261, 262.
Griffin, Lieut. Robt. S., 262.

Hackley, Mrs. Mary, teacher, 197.
Hagen, Rev. Henry, 24.
Halkerson, Robert, 220.
Hall, Dr. Elisha, 152.
Hall, Dr. Horace B., 111, 152, 205.
Hall, Dr. Marshall C., 205.
Halsey, J. J., teacher, 197.
Hanback, ——, German miner, 24.
Hancock, John, 308.
Hanson, Thomas H., teacher, 196.
Harman, Wencel, 248.
Harris, Gen. T. M., 114.
Harris, O. L., 222.
Harrison, Benjamin, President, 247.
Harrison, Col. Archibald, 72.
Harrison, Thomas, 120.
Harrison, Wm. Henry, President, 264, 312.
Harrow, James D., editor, 225.
Hassininga, Indian king, 15, 19.
Hawley, Gen. J. W., 262, 271.
Heflin, E. G., architect, 145.
Henderlite, Rev. J. H., 209.
Henry, Edward, teacher, 197.
Henry, Patrick, 44, 264, 284, 285, 287, 302.
Henry, Rev. Patrick, 23, 44.
Herndon, Capt. Wm. Lewis, 241
Herndon, Charles, 111.
Herndon, Dr. B. S., 142.
Herndon, Dr. James C., 244.
Herndon, Jacob, 167.
Herndon, John M., 126, 208.
Heslop, Isaac, 237.
Hill, Col. John B., 257.
Hirsh, Isaac, 261.
Hirsh, Mrs. Isaac, 325.
Hirsh, Mrs. Maurice, 223.
Hitt, Peter, German miner, 24.
Hitt, W. Snowden, 196.
Hodge, Rev. A. A., 209.
Hoge, Rev. Wm. J., D. D., 94.
Holliday, John, speaker, H. B., 42.
Holmes, Thomas, 227.
Holtzclaw, Jacob, German miner, 24.
Honey, Miss Maggie L., teacher, 325.
Hooton, Albert, 174.
Hotels—Tammany Hall, 165; Rappahannock House, 165; Farmers,' 165; Exchange, 166; Eagle, 166; Alhambra, 167; Indian Queen, 167; Travellers' Rest, 168; Western, 168; Liberty House, 168; Planters', 168.
Houston, Gen. Samuel, 168, 314.
Howard, Clarance R., 155.
Howard, Mrs. Clarance R., D. A. R., 322.
Howard, Mrs. Wm. Key, of Kenmore, D. A. R., 322.
Howard, Wm. Key, 155, 179.
Howison, John, 200.
Howison, Rev. Robert R., LL. D., 81.
Howison, Samuel S., 86.
Huffman, John, German miner, 24.
Huffman, Landon J., 142.
Hunnicutt, Rev. James W., editor, 77, 227.
Hunter, Charles E., 176.
Hurkamp, Charles H., 170.
Hurkamp, John G., 111.
Hurkamp, Miss Jennie, 325.
Hurkamp, Wm. H., 192.

Ironclad Oath, 116.

Jackson, Rob., city trustee, 42.
Jackson, Capt. Wm. A., 183.
Jackson, Gen. Andrew, President, 257.
Jackson, Gen. T. J., 81, 84, 95, 272.
Jacobs, W. J., 262.
James, Rev. Wm., 132, 211.
Japazaws, Chief, 20.
Jay, Judge John, 240.
Jefferson, Thomas, 167, 247, 264, 283, 292, 294, 296, 313, 323.
Jefferys, Major M. M., 191.
Jenkins, Wm., Gaoler, 130.
Johns, Rev. Arthur S., 205.
Johnson, Major James, 128.
Johnson, Capt. Volley M., teacher, 197.
Johnston, B., 237.
Johnston, H. Stuart, 257.
Johnston, Lafayette, 257.
Johnston, Mrs. Eliza, 257.
Jones, John Paul, 218, 237, 238, 239, 265, 301, 323.
Jones, W. T., 179.
Julien, John, alderman, 124.

Kelly, Maj. J. Harrison, 170, 221, 225.
Kemper, Charles E., 23.
Kemper, John, 23, 24.
Kemper, Rev. James, 23, 24.
Kenmore, 155.
Ker, Dr. David C., 46, 66, 231.
King, Gen. Horatio C., 262, 270, 276, 277.
King, Wm. I., 177.
Kirkland, Richard, 92.
Knight, John T., 120, 177, 248, 261.
Knox, Capt. Jas. S., 146, 175, 177, 184.
Knox, Miss Virginia, 223.
Knox, Thomas F., hostage prisoner, 77, 111, 142.
Kobler, Rev. John, 212, 213.

Lacy, Maj. J. Horace, 170.
Lacy, Miss Sallie M., 324.
Lacy, Mrs. J. Horace, U. D. C., 323.
Lacy, Rev. B. T., 209.
Ladies' Memorial Association, 185, 186, 188, 189, 320.
Lafayette, Gen., 256.
Lane, H. B., chairman finance, 176, 261, 334.
Larkin, Capt. Thos. M., 185.
Laughlin, Col. W. L., 166.
Lawrens, Henry, 308.
Layton, C. Ernest, 222.
Leavell, John T., 262.
Lee, Daniel M., 192, 262.
Lee, Francis Lightfoot, 247.
Lee, Gen. Charles, 251.
Lee, Gen. Henry, 251, 308.
Lee, Gen. Robert E., 73, 83, 99, 108, 109, 110, 183, 191, 264.
Lee, Gen. Wm. H. F., 83.
Lee, Richard Henry, 247, 287, 293, 302, 306.
Lee, Thomas Ludwell, 168, 295.
Legg, John, 130.
Lewis, Col. Fielding, 155, 243.
Lewis, John, 44, 45.
Lewis, Meriwether, 313.
Lewis, Robert, 255, 256.
Lexington, battle of, 48.
Liberty Bell, 247.
Little, A. Alexander, 226.
Little, Miss Bella, 226.
Little, Mrs. John P., 197.
Littlepage, Gen. Lewis, 240.

Little, Wm. A., 74, 85, 102, 111.
Livingston, Robert R., 294.
Livingston, Wm., 41.
Lomax, Judge John T., 132, 193.
Long, Michael, 167.
Longstreet, Gen. James, 83.
Lowery, James T., 146.
Lowery, Wm. T., 221.
Low, Rev. Samuel, 132.
Lucas, Albert G., 180.
Lucas, Walker, 168.
Luck, Cadmus B., 166.

Mackay, Robert, 149.
Madison, Pres. James, 264, 301, 302, 304.
Magdalen, man-of-war, 48.
Magrath, Mrs. A. L., teacher, 197.
Mahaskahod, Indian town, 15, 16, 19.
Mander, Miss Kate James, teacher, 325.
Mander, Miss Rebecca C., 324, 325.
Mannahocks, Indian tribe, 17.
Marshall, John, 249, 264, 308.
Martin, German miner, 24.
Martin, Mrs. H. M. D., D. A. R., 322.
Marye, Capt. Edward, 73.
Marye, John L., 72.
Marye, John L., Jr., 44, 74, 138, 139, 209.
Marye, Rev. James, rector, 44, 203.
Marye, Rev. James, Jr., 203.
Marye, William B., 198.
Mary Washington Hospital, 222.
Mary Washington, House, 156; Monument, 157, 159; will, 160; 257.
Mason, George, 168, 288, 302, 303.
Mason, Judge John E., 127, 292.
Mason, Mrs. M. J. C., D. A. R., 223, 323.
Mason, Rev. J. K., rector, 205.
Massauteck, 19.
Massawomeks, Indian tribe, 16.
Maury, Com. M. F., 264, 315, 316, 318, 319.
Maury, Gen. Dabney H., 191.
Maury, Rev. Magruder, 205.
Mayors, list of, 336.
McBryde, Rev. Robert, 205.
McCabe, James D., 229.
McClellan, Gen. George B., 75, 76.

McCracken, Capt. T., 170, 176, 181, 184, 261.
McCracken, Patrick, 120.
McGuire, James, hostage prisoner, 77, 78, 111, 208.
McGuire, Rev. Edward C., 204, 205, 207.
McKinley, President Wm., 278.
McKinley, Wm. and Cabinet, 262.
McLane, Wilmer, 108.
McLaws, Gen. Lafayette, 83.
McMahon, Gen. Martin T., 263, 271.
McPhail, Rev. George W., 196, 209.
McPherson, Archibald, 194, 235, 236.
McWilliams, Wm., 124, 254.
Meade, Rev. Wm., 204.
Mebane, Rev. Benj. W., D. D., 209.
Meditation Rock, 157.
Meiggs, R. J., P. M. G., 61.
Melville, John C., 148, 178.
Mercer, Capt. John, 231.
Mercer, Col. John Fenton, 231.
Mercer, Gen. Hugh, 50, 150, 162, 217, 249, 301.
Mercer, James, 46, 130, 131, 162, 220.
Mercer, Robert, 226.
Merchant, Rufus B., 228.
Metcalfe, John, 132, 141.
Miles, Gen. Nelson A., 262, 271.
Military—Fredericksburg Artillery, 72; Capt. Blackford's Co., 182; Fredericksburg Guards, 183; Mercer Rifles, 183; Washington Guards, 183; Fredericksburg Grays, 183; Coleman Guards, 184; Gordon Rifles, 184; Fredericksburg Grays (new), 184; Washington Guards reorganized, 185; Garfield Light Infantry Blues, 185.
Ministers qualify to celebrate rites of matrimony, 132.
Minor, Capt. George, 258.
Minor, John, 68, 125, 130, 140, 142, 172, 231.
Moltke, Baron Von, 268.
Monacans, Indian tribe, 16.
Moncure, John, 134.
Moncure, Mrs. Mary Knox, 154.
Moncure, Thomas, 197.
Monroe Doctrine, 310.

Monroe, James, 60, 150, 204, 264, 310, 314.
Montague, A. J., 276, 277.
Montgomery, Mrs. B. B., 325.
Moore, Austin, 28.
Moraughtacunds, Indian tribe, 17, 18.
Morgan, Gen. Daniel, 251.
Morris, Maj. T. E., 261, 262.
Morrison, Thos. F., 170.
Morrison, Wm. C., 120.
Morson, Arthur A., 134.
Mortimer, Dr. Chas., 124, 253.
Mosco, Indian guide, 13, 14, 15, 18.
Mundell, John, 64.
Murat, Catherine Willis, 243.
Murat, Prince Charles, 243.
Murdaugh, Rev. E. C., 205, 206.
Murphy, Wm. H., 167.
Myer, John H., 120, 223.
Myer, Miss Annie, 325.
Myrtle Lodge, I. O. O. F., 221.

Nandtaughtacund, Indian King, 14, 18, 19.
Napoleon Bonaparte, 310.
Napoleon, Louis, 268.
National Cemetery, 190, 191.
Nelson, Gen. Thomas., Jr., 247, 293.
Newby, James, 167.
Newspapers and Periodicals—The Virginia Herald, 225; The Genius of Liberty, 225; The Courier, 226; The Fredericksburg News, 226; The Political Arena, 226; The Christian Banner, 227; The Virginia Baptist, 227; The Democratic Recorder, 227; The Fredericksburg Ledger, 227; The Independent, 227; The Bulletin, 227; The True Standard, 227; The Recorder, 227; The Free Lance, 227; The Virginia Star, 228; The Daily Evening Star, 228; Masonic Olive Branch and Literary Portfolio, 229; The Little Gleaner, 229; The Fredericksburg Journal, 229; The Evening Journal, 229.
Normal School Building, 147.
Norton, Wm. H., hostage prisoner, 77, 79.

O'Ferrall, Gov. Charles T., 159, 276, 277.

Index

Ould, Col. Robert, 104.
Owens, Rev. Wm. B., 93, 94.

Page, Mann, Jr., 160.
Page, Mrs. Hugh N., 322.
Passasack, Indian King, 14, 18, 19.
Patrick, Gen. M. R., 75.
Paul, John, 238.
Paul, William, 237, 238.
Pendleton, Edmund, 49, 287, 293, 296.
Perrig, Rev. J. F., 214.
Perrin, Gen. Abner, 324.
Peyton, Benj., 143.
Peyton, Capt. George H., 166, 184.
Phelps, Elijah, 61.
Pierson, Charles H., 170.
Pitcher, Molly, 246.
Pocahontas, 12, 19, 20, 264.
Political divisions, 230, 231, 233, 234.
Pollock, Capt. John G., 73.
Poor Debtors' prison bounds, 134, 135.
Poor, care of, 171, 174.
Pope, Gen. John, 75, 76, 77, 81.
Porter, Gen. Horace, 239.
Porter, John S., 183.
Port Royal, 19.
Posey, Gen. Thomas, 217, 301.
Postal investigation, 60.
Postoffice burnt, 89.
Powell, D. Lee, 183.
Powell, Rev. W. R., 227.
Powell, Smith's companion, 13.
Powers, Hiram, 218.
Powhatan, Indian King, 19, 20.
Pritchard, John, 68, 142, 180, 183.
Procter, Thomas, 168.
Proctor, Thomas F., 192.
Pryor, Mrs. Roger A., 151.
Public Buildings, 137; Courthouse, 142; City Hall, 144; Fire House, 144; Union House, 144; Colored School, 144; Wallace Library, 145.
Public Free School Board, 335.
Public Schools, 199.
Pullen, Jesse, 167.

Quinn, Capt. S. J., 147, 174, 175, 176, 192, 211, 220, 261, 277, 323.
Quisenberry, Wm. P., 167.

Ramsay, Rev. F. P., 199, 223.

Ramsay, T. H., 166.
Randolph, Gov. Edmund, 124, 304.
Randolph, John, 149.
Randolph, Peyton, 49.
Randolph, Rev. A. M., 93, 205.
Ransom, Gen. Robert, 83.
Ransom, Rev. W. L., 216.
Rapahanock, Indian King, 18.
Ratliff, Lieut. Wm., 89.
Rawls, Miss Mary, 195.
Ray, Rev. Albert, 216.
Read, James G., 197.
Reaney, Rev. W. L., 207.
Reconstruction commenced, 113.
Religious liberty, 309.
Revere, John H., 184.
Rhinehart, H. W., 197.
Richards, Mrs. F. C., D. A. R., 322, 323.
Richardson, Hon. James D., 302.
Richardson, Judge D. C., 276.
Richardson, Lieut. Wm. H., 324.
Rising Sun Tavern, 148.
Roach, Miss Agnes P., 325.
Roberts, John H., hostage prisoner, 77, 79.
Robinson, John H., 181.
Robinson, John, 39.
Robinson, Rev. Willis M., 215, 21"
Roddy, Samuel, 124.
Rolfe, Capt. John, 19, 20.
Rootes, Philip, 46.
Rootes, Thomas Reade, 153, 231.
Rosebro, Rev. J. W., D. D., 146, 199, 209.
Ross, Alexander, 46.
Rothrock, Charles M., 246.
Rowe, A. P., 160, 170, 247, 248, 260.
Rowe, A. P., Jr., 146, 262.
Rowe, Capt. M. B., 170, 174, 184, 185, 261.
Rowe, Geo. H. C., hostage prisoner, 77, 78, 103, 105.
Rowe, Josiah P., 176.
Rowe, Rev. George, 215.
Royston, John, 38, 39, 40, 41.
Ruggles, Gen. Daniel, 200.
Ruggles, Gen. Geo. D., 271, 276.
Rush, Dr. Benj., 152.
Russell, saves Smith's life, 13.

Sanford, Joseph, 68, 142, 168.
Saunders, Rev. A. P., D. D., 198, 209.
Schofield, Gen. John M., 115.

School Buildings—Union House, 144; Colored School, 144; new School Building, 145.
Schooler, Miss Willie F., 194, 197.
Schools, Fredericksburg Academy, 193; Federal Hill Female College, 194; Charity School, 194; Rev. Samuel Wilson's, 195; John Goolrick's, 196; T. H. Hanson's, 196; Rev. Geo. W. McPhail's, 196; Powell and Morrison's, 197; Richard Sterling's, 197; Mrs. John P. Little's, 197; Misses Ann and Mary Drinnan's, 197; Rev. Dr. Wm. F. Broaddus's, 197; Judge Richard H. Coleman's, 197; Wm. Caruthers's, 198; Public Schools, 199; Fredericksburg College, 198, Fredericksburg Female Seminary, 198.
Scott, Capt. Benj., 185.
Scott, Charles S., 111, 171.
Scott, Dr. Wm. S., 86.
Scott, Francis S., 134.
Scott, Gen. Winfield, 265, 314.
Scott, Hugh S., 68, 142.
Scott, John F., hostage prisoner, 77, 79.
Secobeck, 19.
Seddon, Thomas, 133.
Semple, Rev. Robert B., 210, 211.
Semple, Robert B., 138, 139, 140, 226.
Sener, Capt. J. W., 111, 120, 175, 183, 184, 201.
Sener, Hon. J. B., 128, 157, 160, 227, 248, 260.
Sentry Box, 150.
Sewell, Gen. W. J., 262, 271.
Shackleford, Rev. J. Green, 207.
Shakahonea, Indian town, 15.
Shelburne, Rev. Cephas, 214.
Shepherd, George W., 59, 149, 192, 261.
Sherman, Roger, 294.
Sickles, Gen. Daniel E., 269, 271.
Slaughter, F., 142.
Slaughter, M., hostage prisoner, 74, 77, 78, 84, 86, 87, 104, 111, 112. 126.
Slaughter, Rev. Philip, D. D., 193.
Slaughter, Wm., 68, 139, 140.
Sligo, small-pox hospital, 66.
Smith, Augustin, 39.
Smith, Austin, 30.
Smith, Capt. John, 11, 12, 13, 18, 19, 20, 37, 264, 332.
Smith, Charles K., 248.
Smith, Frank W., 170.
Smith, Gen. Gustavus W., 83.
Smith, George Washington, 223.
Smith, Maj. Lawrence, 21, 37.
Smith, Miss Rebecca, 222.
Smith, Mrs. Jas. P., 158.
Smith, Rev. Jas. P., D. D., 209.
Smith, Rev. S. C., 211.
Smith, Rev. Wm. D., 205, 224, 324.
Smith, Robert, 183.
Smith, William, 22.
Smock, James, 171, 172.
Society of the Army of the Potomac, 259, 261, 271, 276.
Sockbeck, 19.
Somerville, James, 124.
Somerville, Prof. S. W., 145, 199.
Sons of Confederate Veterans, 192.
Spencer, Mrs. Lettie M., 322.
Spotswood, Governor, 22, 23, 24, 27, 32, 33, 42.
Stansbury, John L., 84.
Stearns, Frank P., 145.
Stearns, Mrs. Walter C., 223.
Stegara, Indian town, 15, 16, 19.
Sterling, Richard, 197.
Stern, Richard, 197.
Stevenson, A. E., 159, 160.
Stevenson, Carter L., 132.
Stoffregen, R. Lee, 175.
Stone, Samuel, 167.
Strasburger, Miss Bertha, 222.
Stuart, Gen. J. E. B., 86.
Sumner, Gen. E. V., 85.

Tackett, Charles E., teacher, 197, 198.
Tackett, Charles E., 166.
Taliaferro, John, 39, 42.
Tapahanock, Indian King, 19.
Tauxuntania, Indian town, 15, 16, 19.
Taylor, Col. W. W., 176.
Taylor, Mayor Richard M., 276, 277.
Taylor, Pres. Zachary, 264, 312, 314.
Taylor, William, 172.
Teasdale, Rev. John, 211.
Telephone Co., 179.

348 Index

Temple, Benj., hostage prisoner, 77, 79.
Temple, Charles W., 198.
Templeman, Wm., 237.
Thanksgiving Proclamation, 306.
Thatcher, Elisha, 171.
Thom, Reuben T., 89, 205, 208.
Thornton, Ira, 42.
Thornton, Pressley, 46.
Timberlake, James, 167.
Tobacco Inspectors, oath of office, 47.
Todkill, Smith's companion, 13.
Transportation Lines—R. F. and P. R. R., 328; P. F. and P. R. R., 328; Md., Del. and Va. R. R., 329.
Tremain, Gen. Henry E., 262, 271.
Tucker, Saint George, 304.
Turner, James A., 192, 261.
Tuttle, H. B., 166.
Tyler, Gov. Hoge, 277.
Tyler, Prest. John, 264, 312, 314.

Ultz, John, 166.
Upham, Dr. J. H., 244.
U. S. Government building, 147.
Utterback, Harman, German miner, 24.

Virginia, military district No. 1, 113.
Vorhees, Hon. Daniel W., 313.

Waddy, Rev. John M., 211.
Waite, George, 221.
Walden, Rev. L. G., 215.
Walker, Dr. Thomas 281.
Walker, George A., 184.
Walker, Joseph, 162.
Wallace. Judge A. Wellington, 126, 302, 309.
Wallace, Capt. C. Wistar, 145, 149, 184.
Wallace, Dr. J. Gordon, 74, 120.
Wallace. Gen. Gustavus B., 149, 218, 301.
Wallace, H. H., 261.
Wallace, J. Stansbury, 248.
Wallace Library, 145, 146.
Wallace, Maj. Thomas P., 146.
Wallace, Mrs. Charles, 324.
Waller, John, 39, 42.
Waller, John, Jr., 237.

Waller, Miss Mary Page, 325.
Waller, Rev. John, 209.
Waller, William, 44.
Wardwell, ——, 76.
Ware, William, 218.
Warren, William, 139, 140.
Warwick, Hon. Charles F., 248, 250.
Washington, Augustine, 42.
Washington, Bushrod, 130.
Washington, Col. Wm., 251.
Washington, George, 42, 46, 48, 49, 143, 217, 218, 253, 254, 255, 264, 299, 302, 304.
Washington, Martha, 236, 237.
Water Power, 329.
Water Works, 174, 175.
Wayman, ——, German miner, 24.
Weaver, Tillman, German miner, 24.
Weedon, Gen. George, 49, 50, 149, 150, 217, 301.
Weir, Mrs. Florence F., 322.
Wellford, Beverley R., 139, 140, 142.
Wellford, Beverley, R., Jr., 79, 220.
Wellford. C. C., hostage prisoner, 64, 77, 142, 143.
Wellford, Dr. Francis P., 243.
Wellford, W. N., 169.
Wheeler, Gen. D. D., 151.
Wheeler, Gen. Joseph, 262, 271.
White, Jesse, 225, 229, 246.
White, Mrs. W. Seymour, 222.
White, Wm. H., 138, 139, 140.
White, W. Seymour, 222, 228, 248.
Whittemore, J. M., 141, 180.
Wight, Mrs. H. Theodore, 153.
Wilderness Campaign, 99, 101, 105.
Williams, Major Charles 76, 128.
Williams, Rev. R. Aubrey, 211.
Williams, Rev. Wm. H., 211.
Willis, Catherine, 243.
Willis, Col. Byrd C., 243.
Willis, Benj. P., 146, 200, 211.
Willis, Henry, 39, 44, 45.
Willis, M. G., 177.
Willis, Rev. John C., 227.
Willis, Wm., 245.
Wilson, Rev. Samuel B., 132, 207.
Winchester, Stephen, 172.
Wodrow. Alexander, 220.
Woltz, Col. John W., 227.

Woodford, Gen. Wm., 217, 301.
Wood, Silas, 64, 143.
Wrenn, Lewis, hostage prisoner, 77, 79.
Wroten, George W., 147, 261.
Wythe, George, 168, 247, 302.

Yates, A. Bacon, 160.
Yates, Charles, 237.
Young, James, 166, 167.
Young, John James, 105, 111, 120, 201.
Young, Mary, 238.

www.ingramcontent.com/pod-product-compliance
Lightning Source LLC
Chambersburg PA
CBHW071941220426
43662CB00009B/951